AF342665

# CRIMINAL COURT
# CONSULTATION

# CRITICAL ISSUES IN AMERICAN PSYCHIATRY AND THE LAW

was edited for

## THE AMERICAN ACADEMY OF PSYCHIATRY AND THE LAW
(TRI-STATE CHAPTER)



Volume 1   Edited by Richard Rosner, M.D.

Volume 2   Edited by Richard Rosner, M.D.

Volume 3   GERIATRIC PSYCHIATRY AND THE LAW
Edited by Richard Rosner, M.D., and Harold I. Schwartz, M.D.

Volume 4   JUVENILE PSYCHIATRY AND THE LAW
Edited by Richard Rosner, M.D., and Harold I. Schwartz, M.D.

Volume 5   CRIMINAL COURT CONSULTATION
Edited by Richard Rosner, M.D., and Ronnie B. Harmon, M.A.

Volume 6   CORRECTIONAL PSYCHIATRY
Edited by Richard Rosner, M.D., and Ronnie B. Harmon, M.A.


A Continuation Order Plan is available for this series. A continuation order will bring delivey of each new volume immediately upon publication. Volumes are billed only upon actual shipment. For further information please contact the publisher.

# CRIMINAL COURT CONSULTATION

### Edited by
## RICHARD ROSNER, M.D.

*Clinical Professor, Department of Psychiatry,*
*New York University School of Medicine*
*Diplomate, American Board of Forensic Psychiatry*
*and Medical Director, Forensic Psychiatry Clinic for the New York Criminal*
*and Supreme Courts (First Judicial Department)*
*Department of Mental Health, Mental Retardation,*
*and Alcoholism Services of the City of New York*
*New York, New York*

### and
## RONNIE B. HARMON, M.A.

*Administrative Director, Forensic Psychiatry Clinic for the*
*New York Criminal and Supreme Courts (First Judicial Department)*
*Department of Mental Health, Mental Retardation,*
*and Alcoholism Services of the City of New York*
*New York, New York*

**PLENUM PRESS • NEW YORK AND LONDON**

Library of Congress Catalog Card Number 88-657025
ISBN 0-306-43061-4

To our spouses,

M. Bernice Rosner, M.S.N.

and

Michael A. Cherni

# Contributors

**Richard T. Andrias** • Supreme Court of the State of New York, New York, New York; New York County Criminal Court, New York, New York

**Niels C. Beck** • Department of Psychiatry, School of Medicine, University of Missouri—Columbia, Columbia, Missouri

**J. M. W. Bradford** • Department of Psychiatry, Faculty of Health Sciences, University of Ottawa, Ottawa, Ontario, Canada; Forensic Psychiatry and the Sexual Behaviors Clinic, Royal Ottawa Hospital, Ottawa, Ontario, Canada

**J. Richard Ciccone** • Department of Psychiatry, University of Rochester School of Medicine and Dentistry, Rochester, New York

**M. P. Duncan III** • Texas Court of Criminal Appeals, Austin, Texas

**Alan R. Felthous** • Department of Psychiatry and Behavioral Sciences, University of Texas Medical Branch—Galveston, Galveston, Texas

**Naomi Goldstein** • Department of Psychiatry, New York University School of Medicine, New York, New York

**Robert Lloyd Goldstein** • Department of Psychiatry, College of Physicians and Surgeons, Columbia University, New York, New York

**Abraham L. Halpern** • Department of Psychiatry, New York Medical College, Valhalla, New York; Department of Psychiatry, United Hospital Medical Center, Port Chester, New York

**Ronnie B. Harmon** • Forensic Psychiatry Clinic for the Criminal and Supreme Courts, New York City Department of Mental Health, Mental Retardation and Alcoholism Services, New York, New York

**Bruce Harry** • Department of Psychiatry, School of Medicine, University of Missouri—Columbia, Columbia, Missouri

**Ingo Keilitz** • Institute on Mental Disability and the Law, National Center for State Courts, Williamsburg, Virginia

**Howard Owens** • Forensic Psychiatry Clinic for the Criminal and Supreme Courts, New York, New York; Department of Psychiatry, New York University School of Medicine, New York, New York

**Michael L. Perlin** • Director, Federal Litigation Clinic, New York Law School, New York, New York

**Irwin N. Perr** • Department of Psychiatry, Robert Wood Johnson Medical School, University of Medicine and Dentistry of New Jersey, Piscataway, New Jersey; Rutgers Law School—Newark, Newark, New Jersey

**Robert L. Sadoff** • Department of Psychiatry; Center for Studies in Social-Legal Psychiatry, University of Pennsylvania, Jenkintown, Pennsylvania

**Richard Schuster** • Comprehensive Rehabilitation Consultants, 310 Madison Avenue, New York, New York; Department of Psychology, Derner Institute, Adelphi University, New York, New York

**Sheldon Travin** • Department of Psychiatry, Bronx-Lebanon Hospital Center, Bronx, New York; Albert Einstein College of Medicine, Bronx, New York

**Alan J. Tuckman** • Department of Psychiatry, New York University School of Medicine, and private practice, Pomona, New York

# Foreword

During the 1980s, those of us who were involved in forensic psychiatry have seen an increase in the interest in our subspecialty. This increased interest has been from psychiatrists, lawyers, judges, and correctional officials as well. As a part of this demand for our services, there has also been an increase in the demand for detailed quality in our reports and testimony. Whether this is the result of the educational efforts of the American Academy of Psychiatry and the Law, the establishment of the American Board of Forensic Psychiatry, the stimulation of thought by the publication of this series, *Critical Issues in American Psychiatry and the Law*, or Supreme Court decisions such as *Ake v Oklahoma* is anybody's guess. My experience as an observer of the development of the patient's rights movement was that there was a coalescence of numerous forces, such as the new human rights movement, the active mental health bar, and the development of neuroleptics. I therefore suspect that there are a multitude of factors contributing to the new interest in forensic psychiatry and the elevation of the standards of forensic experts. Regardless of the causes, those who are practicing forensic psychiatry today are expected to conduct more thorough evaluations and to report findings more completely. No longer will simple conclusory statements be acceptable. The forensic psychiatrist is expected to present data in a clear, understandable, detailed, reliable, and competent fashion whether testifying or in a report.

At present, the criminal justice system is attempting to evaluate its functioning in order to streamline its operations and coordinate its efforts. Ingo Keilitz, who is director of the Institute on Mental Disability and the Law of the National Center for State Courts, has made a good start in the mental health area. His chapter, "Mental Health Services to the Courts: A System Isolated from Judicial Administration," represents a new and somewhat unique view of the system, although I might be prejudiced because of the excellent history of the development of the Medical Office of the Circuit Court for Baltimore City (previously the Supreme Bench of Baltimore). I do, however, have some concerns about Keilitz's recommendations for integration of the courts' mental health services with the judicial system. My concerns are related to the questions raised by Howard Owens in his chapter, "Judges and Psychiatrists: The Question of a Collaborative Relationship." The integration of these systems could lead to issues of control and interference. Freedom is necessary for good clinical judgments by psychiatrists. It is difficult enough to avoid becoming burned-out by repeated exposure to serious criminal behavior and to lose that therapeutic edge that is such a necessary and expected part of the clinician. To add to this task the possibility of pressure and coercion from the judicial system, which has its own political, social, and professional needs, could be too much. A vital balance, encouraged by independence and freedom, is essential for a well-functioning court clinic. Keilitz's chapter is not an outline for reform but only a first look at these two systems, which work independently in the same place—the courthouse. When you read these two chapters by Owens and Keilitz, see what you think.

Some of us may not appreciate the impact that psychiatric disorders have on the case flow of the criminal justice system. When we stop to consider the number of pretrial forensic cases in our public mental hospitals, it should come as no surprise that the criminal justice system has to stop and wait for a large number of defendants to return from the hospital. Judge Richard T. Andrias's discussion not only looks at these issues but also presents a concise legal review of the pretrial issues.

On the same pretrial subject of competency, an always competent and cogent J. Richard Ciccone presents the history and clinical determination of and the legal issues surrounding competence to stand trial. In a later chapter, another aspect of this issue is examined by Naomi Goldstein in her comprehensive and detailed discussion, "Malingering and the Evaluation of Competency to Stand Trial."

The intriguing case of *Colorado v Connelly* raises issues that should be of concern to the forensic evaluator. Michael L. Perlin deals with these in his usual sharp and perceptive fashion.

Robert L. Sadoff defends the insanity defense with his usual vigor, whereas Abraham L. Halpern attacks it in the same fashion. Wherever you stand on this issue, these two chapters present just about all of the arguments.

Many forensic psychiatrists are unaware of some of the special pleas that may be available in a single state. It is interesting that although

California eliminated the concept of "diminished capacity," New York continues with its affirmative defense of "extreme emotional disturbance" as the criterion for mitigation in prosecutions for murder. Robert Lloyd Goldstein explains this unusual plea in a clear fashion, citing cases that exemplify the difficult clinical problems created by this plea.

Until the passage of the Insanity Defense Reform Act of 1984, there was no federal statutory insanity plea. That act has made several important changes in an insanity plea trial in federal courts. Justice M. P. Duncan III discusses one of these issues, the burden of proof, and explains this often misunderstood area of the law in a way that every forensic psychiatrist needs to understand.

With regard to giving testimony, Alan J. Tuckman obviously has been there many times before. Even the experienced expert witness can learn something from his chapter. Tuckman clarifies the issue of advocating your position versus being an advocate. Although I have always taught that you should leave the courtroom as soon as you are finished testifying, Tuckman suggests some good reasons for staying around. You be the judge.

J. M. W. Bradford writes, as only one can who is truly knowledgeable and experienced, on the special considerations of alleged sex offenders. He speaks about the various treatments available and their risks.

When the trial is over, the presentence evaluation is necessary. If the death penalty is a possibility, anxiety may be aroused in the forensic evaluator. Alan R. Felthous discusses many of the issues that must be dealt with if the presentence evaluation is to be fair to the defendant and useful to the court.

Most parole boards have psychiatric consultants. At times, in my career, I have not been too clear about what the board wished from its consultant. It appears that Bruce Harry and Niels C. Beck's experience was similar. Nevertheless, they have collected and interpreted some helpful data.

We who do forensic evaluations do not really see the defendants at their worst. Often, the police are the first-time consultants and care givers. Sheldon Travin discusses the difficult job of the police with the mentally disturbed.

Irwin N. Perr investigates our interaction with the media. When you do forensic work, the public has a right to be relieved of their anxiety. The press is always there. Perr has some timely advice.

Other chapters in this comprehensive volume deal with neuropsychological testing, a very useful assessment technique in many types of cases. I had not thought of such a battery as practical in custody cases. But Richard Schuster's clinical case examples revealed how such testing can help determine one's parenting abilities.

These are only some of the many issues that are brought into focus in this excellent collection of essays. Richard Rosner and Ronnie B. Harmon have edited a serious contribution to the forensic psychiatric literature.

There are, of course, many other areas in the criminal court that touch on our work and that are not dealt with here. Pretrial screening, report writing, and the like all need discussing. There is plenty more for future volumes. I am sure they will all be as good as this one.

JONAS R. RAPPEPORT, M.D.

# Introduction

*Criminal Court Consultation* has been a work in progress ever since 1974 and 1978, when the two editors assumed responsibility for, respectively, the medical and the administrative aspects of the Forensic Psychiatry Clinic for the New York Criminal and Supreme Courts (First Judicial Department). That agency, originally part of the New York State court system, is presently part of the New York City Department of Mental Health, Mental Retardation and Alcoholism Services. At those earlier times, such a book would have been of great practical assistance to the editors. It is in the hope of presenting the readers of this volume with the sort of book that they would have wished to have had for themselves that the editors offer this volume.

Forensic psychiatric consultation for criminal court matters is premised on the same system of analysis that was set forth in the very first book in this series, published, in 1982, by Charles C Thomas Company, Springfield, Illinois. All psychiatric-legal matters are considered in a four-step process:

1. What is the psychiatric-legal issue?
2. What are the legal criteria that define the issue?
3. What are the relevant clinical data?
4. What is the reasoning process by means of which the expert opinion has been formed?

The very same defendant may present with several issues attached. At the time of the commission of the alleged offense, was the defendant criminally responsible for his acts? Subsequently, when questioned by the police, was the defendant competent to confess? At the present instance, is the defendant competent to stand trial? Is the defendant likely to be a danger to himself or to others? In the future, will the defendant be able to understand and abide by the terms of probation? There is no such thing as a general forensic psychiatric criminal court consultation; there is only a series of specific consultations directed to a series of specific psychiatric-legal issues.

The first question to be clarified on being advised of a request for a forensic psychiatric criminal court consultation is: what is the specific issue regarding which a psychiatric-legal opinion is being sought? If the referring party is not immediately able to state such a specific issue, it may be appropriate for the consultant to explain the scope and limitations of the types of examinations that are available, so the referring party may choose from the consultation smorgasbord. Depending on the issue to be considered, the consultant will want to know the legal criteria that determine the issue; these may be found in statutes, in case law, or in administrative codes. In some instances, the consultant will be familiar with the applicable legal criteria; in others, it may be necessary to obtain them from the referring attorney or from the court. Perhaps the best-known example is that of the legal criteria for criminal nonresponsibility, which vary from state to state. However, the specific case law interpretations of such other matters as incompetence to stand trial, incompetence to confess, and diminished responsibility also differ depending on the court having legal jurisdiction over the case at hand. The data that are relevant are dependent on the legal criteria that determine the issue. For instance, present mental condition is relevant to competence to stand trial, whereas past mental condition is relevant to an insanity defense. The most crucial factor is the reasoning process by means of which the consultant connects the data to the criteria so as to support his opinion regarding the specific issue. It hardly matters that the opinion is sound if the reasoning supporting it is inadequate.

There are some professional frustrations that clinical psychiatrists with therapeutic goals encounter in criminal court consultation work. In many instances, the ends of law are contrary to the ends of clinical psychiatry. The courts are not therapeutically oriented. The task of the court system is to resolve legal disputes, not to effect therapeutic dispositions. There are some psychiatrists who have the fantasy that the courts can be used essentially to coerce unwilling potential patients into accepting treatment. Leaving aside the fundamental right of citizens to privacy and the right of competent patients to refuse treatment, this kind of therapeutic zeal reflects clinical grandiosity and naïve ignorance of the law and the legal system.

It is to avoid axiological conflicts that forensic psychiatry, directed toward legal ends, has been differentiated from clinical psychiatry, directed toward therapeutic ends. The forensic psychiatrist understands that the person being examined is not a patient, but is a defendant who does not have a doctor–patient relationship with the examining psychiatrist. Insofar as the forensic psychiatrist has any client, it is the judge, the referring attorney, or the probation officer assigned to the defendant's case. To avoid potential confusion, the person being examined must be advised, repeatedly if it seems necessary, that the examiner is *not* the defendant's doctor, notwithstanding the fact that the examiner is a physician.

The administrator of the court consultation service must deal with a variety of practical problems. The service is dependent on its interactions with other members of the local criminal justice and mental hygiene systems. From the time a referral is made, there may be obstacles to the provision of the consultation. The volume of work is generally determined by the courts and other clients, and provisions must be made for fluctuations in case load over which the manager may have little control. Outside parties, such as attorneys, family members, and probation officers, must often be relied on to provide information about the defendant to enable appropriate psychiatric evaluation. Defendants may withhold cooperation, either willfully or as a result of their mental disability, making it difficult to complete an interview. Delays may be experienced in obtaining access to defendants, due either to missed appointments by the unincarcerated or to the need to depend on an often unreliable correctional system to transport detainees. The administrator must learn to adapt in such an environment.

As with all the volumes in *Critical Issues in American Psychiatry and the Law,* this book can be read as an independent work; the reader need not be familiar with the prior volumes to appreciate this one. However, to have read the entire series would provide the reader with a broad baseline of forensic psychiatric information that would enhance appreciation of the topics addressed in this book. In a similar manner, although the present work was designed to be read from cover to cover, in the sequence in which the chapters are presented, nonetheless, each of the chapters can be read as an independent essay. Some topics are addressed in more than one chapter, although from a somewhat different perspective on each separate occasion. The planned redundancy is meant to emphasize important topics by re-presenting them.

Although the contributors have been asked to take a position on the issues, the educational purpose of this book will be served best if it is viewed not as a compendium of answers but as a stimulus to independent thought.

Richard Rosner<br>Ronnie B. Harmon

# Contents

## SECTION II.   TESTIMONY



## SECTION III.   REDUCED RESPONSIBILITY



## SECTION IV.   DISPOSITIONS

# I

*Systemic Perspectives*

1

# The Impact of Defendants' Psychiatric Disorders on Case Flow in the Criminal Justice System

RICHARD T. ANDRIAS

## INTRODUCTION

No criminal cases cause more confusion and controversy than those involving defendants with psychiatric disorders. The controversy arises in part from confusion among the public, health professionals, lawyers, and even judges over the terms *insanity defense* and *competence to stand trial*. Both concepts involve to a greater or lesser extent a mental disease or defect; however, the former term focuses on the defendant's mental state at the time of the alleged incident, and the latter on the defendant's present ability to participate in criminal proceedings.

The insanity defense simply put is an affirmative *defense* against criminal charges. By claiming lack of responsibility at the time of the alleged offense, defendants seek to be found not guilty of the charges. Thus, although defendants may be totally free of mental disease or defect at the time of trial, and may in fact admit the very acts they are accused of, they are said to lack culpability or blameworthiness because

**RICHARD T. ANDRIAS** • Supreme Court of the State of New York, New York, NY 10013; New York County Criminal Court, New York, NY 10013.

they were suffering from a mental disorder when they committed those acts.

Competency to stand trial or to proceed in the criminal action, however, does not turn on the defendant's mental state at the time of the criminal event but rather is related solely to the defendant's present ability to participate meaningfully in the criminal proceedings. This doctrine has no bearing on the trial function of determining guilt but is grounded in the doctrine of procedural fairness. If a person is unable to understand the nature of the proceedings or to assist in his or her own defense, then procedural fairness requires that the criminal action be stayed until the defendant is found fit to proceed.

Defendants with psychiatric disorders present particularly troublesome issues from a case-flow or case-management perspective. Although cases involving the insanity defense often achieve notoriety and generate calls for reform, they have little individual or cumulative impact on case-flow or caseload management. Insanity defense cases are essentially no different from other matters involving complex issues or defenses and, though the actual trial may involve expert testimony and take longer than an average trial, its pretrial course is not unusual. Furthermore, in terms of numbers, insanity defense cases are so rare that they are statistically insignificant.[1]

On the other hand, cases involving the issue of competency to stand trial have a significant effect on case-flow management goals. Individually, the mere *raising of the issue* of competency may delay the case from a few days to weeks or months. A *finding of incompetency* may delay a case for months or even years in some instances. Also, because the issue of competency is raised in a substantial number of matters,[2] these cases may have a significant overall impact on caseload or case-backlog management.

## Obstacles to Objective Studies

Studying the delay effect of cases involving defendants with psychiatric disorders is complicated by a number of factors. First, there is no universally accepted definition of the concept of competency itself, which involves the interplay of legal and medical considerations. Furthermore, there are different federal and state rules as well as differences among the federal circuits and within the local jurisdictions. Second, because a number of important procedural and substantive rights are involved, determining competency (or, more accurately, finding incompetency) is a time-consuming and complex procedure. Third, the competency issue can arise (and reappear) at any stage of a criminal proceeding, from arraignment through appeal. Finally, because a large number of participants are involved—defendants, defense counsel, prosecutors, judges, juries (in some jurisdictions) and medical professionals—tactical considerations not directly involved in the strict determination of competency often play a crucial role in the process.

Thus, although the legal and the medical literature contains a number of impressive studies and commentaries on the issue of competency in the criminal process[3] (many of which will be relied on in this chapter), because of the complicated and unpredictable aspects of the subject, it is understandable that there appears to be no comprehensive quantitative study focusing solely on case delay and psychiatric disorders. Thus, this chapter cannot possibly fill that void but should provide a comprehensive framework for future research and acquaint the reader with the myriad of procedural difficulties from the judicial management point of view. Also this chapter will concentrate on New York State and federal practice, with other jurisdictions referred to whenever appropriate.

## The Concept of Delay

Before we explore the impact of defendants' psychiatric disorders on case flow, a word about the concept of delay in the judicial process. The federal and various state constitutions guarantee defendants the right to a speedy trial.[4] Federal and state courts enforce that right either absolutely, by requiring the commencement of a trial within a certain time period, or relatively, by means of a readiness rule, whereby the prosecutor must be ready to proceed to trial within a specified period. However, if a defendant is the source of the delay, the time is usually excluded from the computation period. Thus, under the federal Speedy Trial Act,[5] the period of delay caused by defendant incompetence is excluded in computing the time within which the trial must commence. In New York "a reasonable period of delay resulting from . . . proceedings for the determination of competency and the period during which defendant is incompetent to stand trial" must be excluded in computing the time within which the People must be ready for trial.[6]

Because the time periods taken up by evaluation, hearings, and commitment are often excluded from the statutory speedy trial requirements, most jurisdictions have formally mandated times for the completion of examination and the length of time a defendant can be committed without judicial review. These restrictions will be discussed at length below.

Even with these formal constraints, however, there are numerous delays inherent in cases involving competency issues. Thus, the application of sound calendar-control principles is particularly important in these matters. The goals of sound calendar management, brief case adjournments, and productive court appearances[7] are particularly important because the time involved in competency proceedings is being excluded from speedy trial calculations. The traditional causes of delay—attorney conflicts, unavailable evidence or witnesses, attorney unpreparedness, change of counsel, vacation or illness of one of the participants, defendant's failure to appear or the failure to produce an incarcerated defendant, and adjournments by the judge in excess of that requested or appropriate—need special monitoring. Because these tactical considerations play such an important part in the delay aspect of these cases and are so related to the issue of judicial management, they will be discussed throughout the chapter rather than as a separate topic.

## THE CONCEPT OF COMPETENCY TO STAND TRIAL

### Evolution of the Concept

The doctrine that a defendant should not have to stand trial on criminal charges while in a state of "madness" has its origins in the common law of mid-17th-century England. The common law rules preventing trial of incompetent defendants were "transposed virtually intact into early nineteenth-century United States jurisprudence."[8] In *Youtsey v United States,* 97 F. 937 (6th Cir. 1899), the concept of procedural due process was first articulated: "[I]t is not due process of law to subject an insane person to trial upon an indictment involving liberty or life" (at 942).

From its common-law origins the concept of incompetency to stand trial has evolved into one of constitutional dimensions. In *Pate v Robinson* 383 U.S. 375 (1966), the Supreme Court found that the trial and conviction of a mentally incompetent defendant and the failure to provide adequate procedures to determine competence violate due process by depriving the defendant of the constitutional right to a fair trial. Because an incompetent defendant's ability to consult adequately with his attorney and to understand the proceedings is impaired, a deprivation of defendant's Sixth-Amendment right to effective assistance of counsel is also involved. (See *United States v Swanson,* 572 F.2d 523, 526 [5th Cir. 1978], *cert. denied,* 439 U.S. 849 [1978].) Both *Pate v Robinson* and *Drope v Missouri,* 420 U.S. 162 (1975), which reiterated the *Robinson* due process standard, applied the federal due process standard to the states. *Drope* further expanded the scope of the due process guarantee by placing on the trial judge an affirmative obligation to be alert to possible signs of mental incompetency.

## Present Formulation of the Concept

In the landmark case of *Dusky v United States*, 362 U.S. 402 (1960), the Supreme Court dealt first with the issue of competency to stand trial:

> [T]he test must be whether [a defendant] has sufficient present ability to consult with his lawyer with a reasonable degree of rational understanding—and whether he has a rational as well as factual understanding of the proceedings against him. (at 402)

Although the *Dusky* standard does not specifically require that the lack of competency be the result of a *mental disease* or *defect,* it has been followed in fourteen states. The *Dusky* test with the added requirement of a finding of *mental disease* or *defect* is utilized in the federal courts, in the American Bar Association (ABA) Standard, in New York, and in 37 other states.[9] In federal courts:

> At any time after the commencement of a prosecution for an offense and prior to the sentencing of the defendant, the defendant or the attorney for the Government may file a motion for a hearing to determine the mental competency of the defendant. The court shall grant the motion, or shall order such a hearing on its own motion, if there is reasonable cause to believe that the defendant may presently be suffering from a mental disease or defect rendering him mentally incompetent to the extent that he is unable to understand the nature and consequences of the proceedings against him or to assist properly in his defense. (18 U.S.C. §4241)

In New York, at any time after a defendant is arraigned, the court where the criminal action is pending *must* issue an order of examination when it is of the opinion that the defendant *may* be an "incapacitated person" (CPL §730.30). An incapacitated person is defined as "a defendant who as a result of mental disease or defect lacks capacity to understand the proceedings against him or to assist in his own defense" (CPL §730.10[1]). The ABA's Criminal Justice Mental Health Standards set forth a test taken virtually verbatim from *Dusky* and *Drope:*

> (a) No defendant shall be tried while mentally incompetent to stand trial.
> (b) The test for determining mental competence to stand trial should be whether the defendant has sufficient present ability to consult with defendant's lawyer with a reasonable degree of rational understanding and otherwise to assist in the defense, and whether the defendant has a rational as well as factual understanding of the proceedings.
> (c) The terms competence and incompetence as used within Part IV of this chapter refer to mental competence or mental incompetence. A finding of mental incompetence to stand trial may arise from mental illness, physical illness, or disability; mental retardation or other developmental disability; or other etiology so long as it results in a defendant's inability to consult with defense counsel or to understand the proceedings. (§7-4.1.[a][b][c])

Even where the standard is clearly defined, however, the problem remains in trying to *apply the test* to individual defendants. Mental health professionals are faced with the problem of taking a legally oriented concept of competence and integrating it into their clinical approach. The courts, of course, have the opposite problem of taking clinically oriented findings and utilizing them in an adversarial setting in order to arrive at the ultimate legal determination of whether to allow the defendant to proceed.

Both the courts and researchers have made extensive efforts to further refine the criteria to guide the health professional evaluators. Although many of these reformers have been criticized for allegedly injecting their political and philosophical beliefs into what they proposed as devices to attain objective assessments,[10] they have developed a trend of focusing on functional criteria that assist in evaluating a defendant's skills or abilities relevant to participating at the trial.[11]

## THE COMPETENCY DETERMINATION

### Burdens of Proof and Tactics

In most jurisdictions determination of competency is made by the court. This is the federal rule[12] and is the procedure in New York and in all but eleven states; three states require a jury to decide competency and eight others make it optional.[13] The position in ABA Standard §7-4.7(c) is that a jury determination is not constitutionally required even though a deprivation of liberty may be involved except in states where involuntary hospitalization for treatment is a jury issue. In those instances, to avoid equal protection violations, the ABA recommends a jury determination of competency.

The burden of proof and the issue of what is to be proven vary from jurisdiction to jurisdiction. Some statutes place the burden on the state to prove the defendant's competence once the issue has been raised, others place the burden on the defendant. The position in ABA Standard §7-4.8(c) is that "the party raising the issue of incompetence should have the burden of going forward with the evidence to show incompetence" but the court must find the defendant competent by the "greater weight of the evidence" before it can proceed. A federal hearing requires a finding that the defendant is suffering from a mental disease or defect by a "preponderance of the evidence."[14] New York requires proof by the People of defendant's competence by a "fair preponderance of the evidence." *People v Wright,* 105 A.D.2d 1088, 482 N.Y.S.2d 591 (4th Dept. 1984). One commentator has suggested that, because commitment often follows a finding of incompetence, the 1979 Supreme Court decision in *Addington v Texas,* 441 U.S. 418 (1979), mandating at least a clear and convincing standard for civil commitments, should also apply to competency hearings.[15]

The competency determination process usually involves three distinct phases: a motion for an examination, an examination by a health professional, and a hearing or proceeding to determine the issue of the defendant's fitness to proceed. Each step involves complicated legal issues and time-consuming delays. Because the object in any criminal proceeding, however, is to arrive at a just and appropriate disposition (whether that be dismissal, conviction, or acquittal), if carefully monitored, the steps are usually essential in reaching an appropriate result.

A number of consequences flow from the initiation of the competency determination process. Not only must counsel weigh the decision carefully but given the time and expense involved, the courts must be confident that a bona fide issue is present. For the defendant, although there is a trend away from strict remand during competency proceedings, denial of bail or inordinately high bail is still the common practice. Not only is the defendant's liberty (or chances of obtaining pretrial release) at stake, but various privileged information is normally disclosed during competency examinations. Although many jurisdictions allow counsel or the defendant's psychiatrist to observe the examination,[16] the defendant will invariably make otherwise incriminating statements and disclosures during any effective evaluation. Thus, even though counsel has an obligation not to proceed with an incompetent client and often many advantages may flow from even an eventual finding of competence (e.g., sympathy from the prosecutor or judge, additional time to prepare or evaluate a case), the decision to go forward has far-reaching consequences and involves weighing all of the above considerations.

From a judicial point of view the decision to order an examination should come as early in the criminal process as possible. However, because of the effect on bail and the probability of adverse disclosures, the defense counsel understandably does not usually make requests for examinations early in the pretrial stage of a case. Furthermore, given the possibility that the prosecutor might not have a viable case, not only should counsel be reluctant to consent to an immediate examination, but also the court should never order such an examination without a significant screening of the charges. To do otherwise might result in the hospitalization of a criminal defendant where there is no basis for the underlying criminal charges. In *Gerstein v Pugh*, 420 U.S. 103 (1975), the Supreme Court mandated a probable cause determination at the earliest possible time. The New York Court of Appeals now mandates a strict jurisdictional review of the charges at arraignment,[17] and requires by statute a misdemeanor information or felony indictment within five or

six days or the incarcerated defendant must be released.[18] The ABA
Standard takes a similar position in the strongest possible terms:

> If the court finds that the requisite probable cause for criminal prosecution
> does not exist, there should be no further inquiry into the defendant's com-
> petence to stand trial. (§7-4.4[a][1])

The Supreme Court in *Drope* imposed an affirmative obligation on
the trial court to be alert to the signs of mental incompetency. Most
jursidictions follow the federal rule of allowing the prosecution to move
for a hearing in addition to the court and the defense. The ABA Standard proposes that the prosecutor *should* move for an evaluation where it
has a "good faith doubt as to the defendant's competence" (§7-4.2[b]),
although the introduction to the ABA Mental Health Standards recites
the often heard criticism that:

> Prosecutors, who are legally empowered to inject the issue of procedural
> incompetence, have viewed the process as a mechanism to remove from
> society defendants against whom they might have a weak case or "as a means
> of curbing anticipated violent behavior; as a form of 'preventive detention' or
> legal strategy; and, finally, as a way of dealing with individuals when there
> seems to be no other legal recourse." (§7.163–7.164)

Clearly it is not only prosecutors who misuse the process of determining
competency. From the perspective of a decade of practice and a half-
decade of judicial service, I have concluded that Roesch and Golding's
North Carolina findings[19] of the abuses by defense counsel, prosecutors,
and judges are the norm in New York and are probably universal.

## Requiring a Showing before a Hearing Is Ordered

It is axiomatic that a defendant be given counsel before an examination is ordered, given the Supreme Court's holding in *Coleman v Alabama*, 399 U.S. 1 (1970) that counsel is required at any "critical stage" of
a criminal proceeding where important rights may be affected. It is
often the practice to stabilize severely agitated defendants even prior to
arraignment; however, no competency evaluation should be part of this
stabilizing treatment, and all such defendants must be immediately returned to court or an arraignment must be held at the psychiatric
facility.

As has been indicated, in most jurisdictions either the judge, defense attorney, or prosecutor can move for an examination of the defendant. Although important constitutional rights are involved, the courts
are concerned with any delay occasioned by frivolous or bad faith applications for competency examinations. Thus, certain threshold show-
ings must be made. The ABA Standard recommends that the judge

order an examination if a "good faith doubt" is raised as to the defendant's competence to stand trial (§ 7-4.4[a]). The New York rule requires "reasonable grounds" for ordering an examination, *People v Moye*, 105 A.D.2d 853 (2d Dept. 1984). The federal rule (18 U.S.C. §4241) requires the court to order a psychiatric examination whenever there exists "reasonable cause" to believe that the defendant may be suffering from a mental defect which prevents him or her from understanding the proceedings or assisting in his or her defense. The federal circuit courts disagree, however, as to the degree of discretion accorded the trial judge in determining whether to grant a motion for a psychiatric examination. The minority view is exemplified by the Ninth Circuit, which requires an examination if a facial review of the submissions reveals reasonable cause and good faith.[20] Other circuits give the trial judge discretion to explore the factual basis of movant's reasonable cause.[21] The Seventh Circuit recently tried to balance the need to insure prompt resolution of the issue and the defendant's right to a competency hearing, if reasonable doubt exists, by authorizing a hearing, including the taking of extensive evidence, on the narrow issue of whether reasonable grounds exist.[22]

## The Examination Period

Once the examination is ordered, most jurisdictions now have strict time limits for its completion. The federal rule has a 30-day requirement, although the facility director may apply for a 15-day extension.[23] The New York practice has a similar 30-day examination period, although a 30-day extension is allowed.[24] The ABA Standard urges strict time limits:

> Each jurisdiction should establish time periods by which the evaluation should be concluded and a report returned to the court. Such periods normally should not exceed [seven] days in the case of a defendant in custody nor [fourteen] days in the case of a defendant at liberty. For good cause, the time periods might be extended but should never exceed [thirty] days. (§7-4.4[c])

To insure a speedy return to court, mental health professionals must respect the limited mandate of the examination (i.e., to determine competency) and not extend the commitment in an attempt to restore the defendant to mental health.

## The Ultimate Determination

Ultimately the determination of competency is a matter for the court (or jury, in a minority of states). Often the hearing is dispensed with if all parties concur on the contents of the report. Because the defendant is entitled to full adversarial rights, including the opportunity to present expert testimony, medical evidence is often conflicting. However, the Court is not bound by the medical evidence, even when it is unanimous. (See *People v Bolling,* 114 A.D.2d 416 [2d Dept. 1985].)

The litigious nature of the competency determination process breeds judicial delay, so hearings should be held immediately upon the receipt of the reports. The ABA recommends a hearing, when necessary, within seven days of the receipt of a report on a detained defendant and within thirty days if the defendant is at liberty (§7-4.7[a]).

## The Consequences of a Finding of Incompetence

In the past, a finding of incompetence often meant an indefinite stay of the criminal proceeding while the defendant, in theory at least, was restored to competence in an institutional setting. The 1972 Supreme Court decision of *Jackson v Indiana,* 406 US 715 (1972), which held that a person charged with a criminal offense could not be committed due to incapacity more than a reasonable period necessary to determine whether he will attain competency in the foreseeable future (at 738), provided the impetus for many jurisdictions to revise their laws to limit the time defendants could be confined while incompetent. In addition, 20 states have enacted statutory provisions allowing for the resolution of certain procedural issues relevant to the trial notwithstanding the defendant's incompetency.[25]

Often a finding of incompetency can lead to a quick resolution of the criminal proceedings instead of a lengthy commitment. In New York, for example, if the charge is a misdemeanor and the defendant is found unfit, a final order of observation is issued (in effect, a civil commitment) and the criminal charges are dismissed.[26] Thus, though there is an initial delay in case processing, the ultimate result is speedy and just.

*Jackson* suggested that there were other procedures, short of dismissal, that should take place despite the defendant's incompetency (at 740–741). A number of states have adopted various procedures that allow litigation on various issues when the defendant's presence (or participation) is not crucial. In addition to probable cause hearings mentioned above, some states have gone so far as to permit trials in which only a not guilty finding would be allowed.[27] Given the problems of lost witnesses, fading memories, and other difficulties as delay before trial increases, any procedures that can preserve an incompetent defendant's Sixth-Amendment speedy trial rights are salutary.

# THE ISSUE OF COMPETENCY AT ANY STATE OF A CRIMINAL PROCEEDING

Although the issue of competency is traditionally referred to in terms of competency to stand trial, the issue can arise at "any time after the commencement of a prosecution . . . and prior to the sentencing of a defendant" (18 U.S.C. §4241). The proper question is whether the defendant is competent to proceed in a criminal action or has the capacity to proceed in the action.

## Competency at the Plea Stage

Because the vast majority of criminal convictions in the American criminal justice system are not obtained following the trial but are the result of pleas of guilty,[28] the question arises as to whether the same competency standard should be applied to each situation. The federal circuit courts are in conflict as to whether there should be a different standard. The First, Fourth, Fifth, Sixth, Seventh, and Tenth Circuits have found that the two standards are essentially parallel and that the *Dusky* standard is flexible enough to encompass the considerations involved in pleading guilty.[29] A number of state jurisdictions are in accord with this view. (See *People v Heral,* 62 Ill. 2d 329, 342 N.E. 2d 34 [1976] and *Commonwealth v Leate,* 367 Mass. 689, 327 N.E. 2d 866 [1975].) The Second and Ninth Circuits, however, have reasoned that, because a guilty plea involves the *waiver* of constitutional rights, the court should exercise greater caution if the defendant is pleading guilty.[30] In *Chavez v United States,* 656 F.2d 512 (9th Cir. 1981), the Ninth Circuit, while advancing the dual standard approach, noted that it resulted in a defendant's being found competent to stand trial but not competent to plead guilty. This anomalous situation undoubtedly explains why the majority of courts employ the same standard.[31]

## Review on Appeal

To complicate the matter further, not only can the competency issue arise throughout the pretrial and trial phase of a criminal proceeding, but the question of whether the defendant was competent at the trial phases can be raised retrospectively on appeal. Although the People generally have the burden of proving the defendant's competency when the issue is raised before or during trial, in postconviction proceedings the burden shifts to the defendant. For purposes of appellate review, the trial court's determination can be set aside only if it is clearly erroneous[32] or an abuse of discretion.[33] If there was a jury and not a judge determining the competency issue at the trial level, the appellate courts will use a "reasonable" jury standard on review.[34]

If the appellate court finds an improper denial of a competency hearing or other mistakes in the competency determining procedures, a retrial may be ordered or the case may be remanded for a retrospective hearing to determine the defendant's competence at the time of trial. Although the Supreme Court has questioned the use of retrospective hearings (see *Drope* at 182–183, *Pate v Robinson* at 387, and *Dusky* at 403) they have not forbidden them (*Drope* at 182–183). The Fifth Circuit in *Bolius v Wainwright*, 597 F.2d 986 (5th Cir. 1979) has recognized the value of such hearings if there is sufficient information in the trial record. (*Accord, United States v Johns*, 728 F.2d 953 [7th Cir. 1984].) However, if a retrospective hearing is not possible, the defendant must be retried when competent or released. (See *United States v Johns,* at 957.)

## The Issue Is Often Not Settled

Even if a judge has been attentive in seeing that an incompetent defendant when fit is returned to court promptly and has moved the matter expeditiously toward trial or disposition, he or she is often faced with the prospect of the competency issue arising again. With the advent of psychotropic medication, the competency issue can arise several times in the course of the same criminal proceeding. Even if the defendants are continued on medication, they often regress when removed from the hospital setting to the jail environment or courtroom forum. Because the competency concept concerns a defendant's present capacity to proceed, the court and the attorneys must be alert to signs of disability at every phase of the proceeding.

Psychotropic medication's ability to create a chemically competent defendant initially generated substantial controversy as to whether the defendant was truly competent to stand trial. Today, however, it is commonly accepted that a defendant's capacity to participate and understand the proceedings may be contingent on medication. Because the Courts have focused on the issue of the defendant's ability to participate, and not the source of the defendant's competence, the typical side effects of the medication may affect the defendant's appearance and ability to concentrate or articulate. Thus, the ABA Standard provides that

> [i]f the defendant proceeds to trial with the aid of treatment or habilitation which may affect demeanor, either party should have the right to introduce evidence regarding the treatment or habilitation and its effects and the jury should be instructed accordingly. (§7–4.14[b])

Although there may be inherent prejudice to this approach, it is undoubtedly preferable to a continued stay in the proceedings.


## CONCLUSION

The traditional causes of case delay are complicated by a number of factors in which competency proceedings are involved. There are procedural and substantive rights to be safeguarded, as well as the often conflicting tactical concerns of a large number of participants (defendants, defense counsel, prosecutors, witnesses, medical professionals, and judges) that must be considered. Also, the issue of competency can arise (and reappear) at any stage of the criminal proceeding from arraignment through appeal. Finally, because the period of delay caused by competency proceedings or the defendant's commitment is usually excluded from speedy trial computations, the court must be particularly sensitive to these delays.


## REFERENCES


1. In 1986, in New York State, there were only 61 defendants found not guilty by reason of insanity in felony cases out of a total of 56,356 Supreme Court felony filings. *See also* Erickson, Overton, Bennett: Competence to stand trial. 2 *ABA Standards for Criminal Justice* 7.157, 7.160 (1987) [hereinafter cited as Erickson], indicating a 1 to 100 ratio of verdicts of not guilty by reason of insanity as compared to findings of incompetency.
2. The New York County Psychiatric Clinic received 378 referrals from the New York County Criminal Court in 1986, out of a total of 88,681 filings. Of that number, 123 (33%) defendants were found incompetent.
3. *See, e.g.*, Brakel S, Parry J, and Weiner B: *The Mentally Disabled and the Law*, 3rd ed. Chicago, Ill., American Bar Foundation, [hereinafter cited as Weiner], 1985 and Roesch R and S. Golding: *Competency to Stand Trial*. Chicago, University of Illinois Press, 1980.
4. *See, e.g.*, U.S. Const. amend. VI.
5. 18 U.S.C. §§3161–3174 (1982).
6. N.Y. Crim. Proc. Law §30.30(4) (McKinney 1987).
7. Jacobs N and Chayet E: *Bang the Gavel Slowly*. New York, Criminal Justice Center, John Jay College of Criminal Justice, 1986.
8. Erickson, *supra* note 1, at 7.161.
9. Weiner, *supra* note 3, at 695.
10. Erickson, *supra* note 1, at 7.173.
11. *Id.* at 7.173–7.175.
12. 18 U.S.C. §4241(1982 & Supp. IV 1986); 18 U.S.C. §4241(1982 & Supp. IV 1986); 18 U.S.C. §4247(d)(1982 & Supp. IV 1986).
13. Weiner, *supra* note 3, at 703.

14. 18 U.S.C. §4241(d)(1982 & Supp. IV 1986).

15. Weiner, *supra* note 3, at 703.

16. *See* N.Y. Crim. Proc. Law §730.20(1) (McKinney 1987), which allows the defendant's psychiatrist to be present at the court ordered examination.

17. *People v Dumas*, 68 N.Y. 2d 729 (1986).

18. N.Y. Crim. Proc. Law §§170.70 and §180.80 (McKinney 1987).

19. Roesch and Golding, *supra* note 3, at 192–193.

20. *See Meador v United States*, 332 F.2d 935 (9th Cir. 1964). *Accord, Wear v United States*, 218 F.2d 24 (D.C. Cir. 1954).

21. *United States v Oliver*, 626 F.2d 254 (2nd Cir. 1980) and *United States v Nichelson*, 550 F.2d 502 (8th Cir. 1977).

22. *United States v Metcalfe*, 698 F.2d 877 (7th Cir. 1983), *cert. denied* 461 U.S. 910 (1983).

23. 18 U.S.C. §4247(1982 & Supp. IV 1986).

24. N.Y. Crim. Proc. Law §730.20(4) (McKinney 1987).

25. *See* Weiner, *supra* note 3, at 744–754 for a comprehensive table regarding incompetency to stand trial as handled by each of the 50 states.

26. N.Y. Crim. Proc. Law §730.40(1) (McKinney 1987).

27. Weiner, *supra* note 3, at 704–705.

28. McDonald W and Cramer J: *Plea Bargaining.* Boston, D.C. Heath and Co., 1980.

29. *Allard v Helgemore*, 572 F.2d 1 (1st Cir. 1978); *Roach v Martin*, 757 F.2d 1463 (4th Cir. 1985); *Bolius v Wainwright*, 597 F.2d 986 (5th Cir. 1979); *Williams v Bordenkircher*, 696 F.2d 464 (6th Cir. 1983, *cert. denied*, 461 U.S. 916 (1983); *United States ex rel. Heral v Franzen*, 667 F.2d 633 (7th Cir. 1981); *Wolf v United States*, 430 F.2d 443 (10th Cir. 1970).

30. *Matusiak v Kelly*, 786 F.2d 536, (2nd Cir. 1986) and *Chavez v United States*, 656 F.2d 512 (9th Cir. 1981).

31. The fifteenth annual review of criminal procedure United States Supreme Court and Courts of Appeals 1984–1985. 74 *Geo. L.J.* 499, 712 n.603 (1986).

32. *Bolius v Wainwright*, 597 F.2d 986, 989 (5th Cir. 1979); *United States v Baca*, 687 F.2d 1356 (10th Cir. 1982).

33. *United States v Oliver*, 626 F.2d 254, 258–259 (2nd Cir. 1980).

34. *White v Estelle*, 669 F.2d 973, 978 (5th Cir. 1982), *cert. denied*, 459 U.S. 1118 (1983).

**2**

# Judges and Psychiatrists

## The Question of a Collaborative Relationship

**HOWARD OWENS**

> *I have ever hated all nations, professions, and communities, and
> all my love is toward individuals: for instance, I hate the tribe of
> lawyers, but I love Counsellor Such-a-one, and Judge Such-a-
> one: so with physicians—I will not speak of my own trade—
> soldiers, English, Scotch, French, and the rest. But principally I
> hate and detest that animal called man, although I heartily love
> John, Peter, Thomas, and so forth.*
>
> Jonathan Swift, in a letter to Alexander Pope, 1725[1]

> *The more they hate us the more they need us.*
>
> Alan A. Stone, 1984[2]

In his typically satirical fashion, Jonathan Swift understood the familiar
process by which stereotypes, which modern physicians might attribute to
anxiety, projection, and paranoid fantasies, can be broken down by
actual, concrete experience with the hated and feared object—and yet the
stereotype may still live on, coexisting on a different plane of the mind
with day-to-day cordiality and cooperation. In recent years, the history of
the apparently very troubled relationship between psychiatrists and the

---

**HOWARD OWENS** • Forensic Psychiatry Clinic for the Criminal and Supreme Courts,
New York, NY 10013; Department of Psychiatry, New York University School of Medicine, New York, NY 10016.

**17**

courts has fallen into a similar pattern: many psychiatrists have approached any involvement with the courts with great trepidation, disgust, or abhorrence and have even avoided doing psychiatric-legal work if at all possible. At the same time, specialists in forensic psychiatry have found that immersing themselves in the daily problems dealt with by the courts and working as consultants to judges and attorneys can actually be fascinating, intellectually stimulating, and rewarding.

The reasons why psychiatrists have tended to hate and fear the courts, lawyers, and judges are not difficult to discover and are summarized under four major headings:

***The General Expectation of an Adversary Relationship.*** For the past two decades or more, psychiatrists have had to deal with the consequences of increasing regulation of psychiatric practice and of court involvement in what were formerly considered matters of medical decision-making. Psychiatrists have found their own practices directly affected by policy changes about civil commitment and the patient's right to refuse treatment and often feel that clinical care has suffered. At the same time, they have read reports about the increasing frequency of malpractice suits against psychiatrists for a widening number of different types of possible malpractice; even if they have never been sued themselves, the possibility of a suit makes them anxious. If they have occasionally ventured into the world of the courtroom to testify as an expert witness, they have found that their expertise can be questioned, attacked, or even ridiculed. They may have heard of (or perhaps even read) Ziskin's two-volume monograph, which exhaustively belabors the inadequacies of psychiatric diagnosis and opinion and seeks to demonstrate the psychiatrist's complete unreliability as an expert.[3] The psychiatrist's pride and self-respect may then have been damaged, as Rosner[4] has described:

> Here we touch on the issue of vanity. For many reasons, psychiatrists are often reluctant to admit, especially on a witness stand, that they do not know the answer to a question. Perhaps some psychiatrists do not know that they do not know. More often, there is something coercive and accusatory about the questions that are posed to the psychiatrist, as though implying that there may be something wrong or inadequate about him if he admits to innocence or ignorance. "What kind of an expert can *you* be, doctor, if you don't know the answer to a simple question like that?" says the hostile attorney, with his eyes wide in mock dismay. In such a setting, many a physician is conned and set up to claim a degree of knowledge that no physician can realistically possess.
>
> In fact, one of the major problems of the forensic psychiatrist . . . is that he is often asked to respond to questions he cannot possibly answer or cannot know definitely. (p 161)

***Different Conceptual Schemes.*** A considerable part of the on-going conflict between psychiatry and the law has also been traced to differences in purpose, in language, and in ideology between the two professions. On the most fundamental level, there are differences between the goals of scientific truth-seeking and of treatment on the one hand, and of legal fact-finding and dispute resolution on the other. The law tends to require value judgments that physicians habitually seek to eschew. Psychiatry and the law have even been described as having "fundamentally different conceptions of the nature of man and the human mind."[5] In addition, the language of "insanity" and "fitness" used by the courts cannot be translated directly into the evolving terminology of the *Diagnostic and Statistical Manual of Mental Disorders* (DSM III-R) (or IV).

***Actual Conflict in Particular Cases.*** It is unnecessary to belabor the obvious effect of the legal system on the psychiatrist who is actually sued for malpractice[6] or on the psychiatrist whose public expert testimony is subject to both scholarly and popular dissection (e.g., those who testified in the *Hinckley* case).[7] Even the psychiatrist who is appointed by the court to serve as its own impartial witness may come into conflict with the court. For example, a judge who orders a competency examination in a criminal case may offer subtle hints that it would be preferable to have the defendant found incompetent for the purpose of diverting the case out of the criminal justice system and into the hospital. The psychiatrist, while agreeing that the defendant needs treatment, may still find that the defendant does understand quite clearly what is going on and is therefore not incompetent, The psychiatrist may feel trepidation about offering an opinion that will be seen as obstructing the disposition of cases and might even incur the wrath of the judge. In a different context, Federal Judge Marvin Frankel has testified to the potential danger of the sadism of individual judges:

> Conditioned in the direction of authoritarianism by his daily life in court, long habituated as a lawyer to the stance of the aggressive contestant, and exercising sentencing powers frequently without practical limits, the trial judge is not discouraged from venting any tendencies toward righteous arrogance. The books and the reliable folklore are filled with the resulting horror stories. . . . The horrible cases may result from moral or intellectual or physical deficiencies—or from all together. But we can be sure there will be some substantial number of such cases.[8] (p 17)

Judge Jerome Frank has also written about the "tabu" against acknowledging that judges are, after all, human, and that their particular personalities inevitably affect their conduct and decisions:

> Now the trial judge is a man, with a susceptibility to such unconscious prejudiced "identifications" originating in his infant experiences. . . . His impressions, colored by his unconscious biases with respect to the witnesses, as to what they said, and with what truthfulness and accuracy they said it, will determine what he believes to be the "facts of the case." His innumerable hidden traits and predispositions often get in their work in shaping his decision in the very process by which he becomes convinced what those facts are.[9] (p 152)

The psychiatrist, in turn, who is well acquainted with the effects of unconscious biases, is not likely to be reassured by this kind of realization that judges are human.

***Transference Expectations of the Adversary Relationship.*** Recognition of the unconscious processes in operation in the judge leads into the problem arising in the transference of the psychiatrist to the judge (and vice versa). Both parties to this relationship may experience each other as threatening authorities who are in possession of occult and potentially dangerous knowledge and powers—judges may fear that psychiatrists can see through them or read their minds, just as psychiatrists may fear unconsciously that judges can throw them into jail or execute them. (Interestingly, Jerome Frank, writing in 1949[9], criticized judges for considering themselves "wizards," long before David Bazelon warned psychiatrists not to think that *they* possessed wizardry.) The potential for the projection of aggressive impulses onto parentlike figures by both parties in this relationship can readily be imagined.


## PSYCHIATRY AND THE COURTS: RECENT HISTORY

A review of the literature in forensic psychiatry amply documents the intensity of conflict, the climate of hostility, and the breakdowns in communication between the courts and psychiatrists. From all sides, there emerges a picture of a very complex and troubled relationship.

In 1974, the *American Journal of Psychiatry* published Judge David Bazelon's "The Perils of Wizardry," in which the judge took psychiatrists to task for the arrogance (as he saw it) of their assumptions about their diagnostic and therapeutic powers.[10] In dramatic terms, comparing the powers of psychiatrists with those of physicists' "unlocking of the secrets of the atom" in the 1940s, Bazelon warned of the dangers of increasingly invasive psychiatric therapies and of the dangers of diagnostic labeling and stigmatizing. He emphasized the potential powers of psychiatrists to do evil. On a more mundane level, he criticized psychiatrists for misunderstanding the adversary process and for failing to respond to the invitation in his *Durham* decision to share their expert knowledge with the courts and to tell what they knew (and what they did not know). He complained that psychiatrists continued to present only "a welter of confusing terms" in testimony and would not acknowledge the limits of their expertise. With perhaps unintended irony (in view of the seriousness of his criticisms), he also complained that psychiatrists maintained a "siege mentality" when it came to participating in the legal process. In the end, he compared the psychiatric expert to the Wizard of Oz, who had to acknowledge that he was a fake who had no magic.

In the same year that Bazelon's article was published, the Group for the Advancement of Psychiatry (GAP) report raised serious questions about the use and abuse of psychiatric examination for competency in the criminal justice system.[11] Throughout the sixties and seventies, in fact, there were a series of reports in the literature that documented the failures of psychiatrists and the courts to work together in an efficient and collaborative way: these articles described how the courts failed to inform psychiatrists adequately about what specific questions they wanted answered in psychiatric reports[12,13,14]; and also how the psychiatrists failed to respond to the questions posed even when the courts were specific.[12,15] In addition, courts were found to be using the psychiatric examination for competence to advance other, extraneous strategies, to produce a delay, to provide a humanitarian alternative to severe punishment, to lay the groundwork for an insanity defense, or to divert cases without having to go through with a civil commitment.[16,17] The general trend of failing cooperation might be summarized by Robey's noting in 1965 a "consistent failure by the courts to inform the examining psychiatrist what questions it wished answered"[12] and by Geller and Lister's finding in 1978 of "little relationship between the questions posed by the court and the replies made by psychiatrists."[15]

In the context of this general failure of communication, some psychiatrists, most prominently among them Alan Stone, raised questions about whether psychiatrists even belong in the courtroom as expert witnesses or would do better to withdraw. In his book *Mental Health and the Law,* Stone emphasized that the technical expertise of the mental health professional had been greatly exaggerated and oversold to the public and the courts, and that unrealistic expectations and subsequent disappointment in psychiatric expertise had resulted.[18] Summarizing his reservations in a 1984 paper "The Ethical Boundaries of Forensic Psychiatry: A View from the Ivory Tower,"[2] Stone questioned whether or not psychiatrists had anything true to say that the courts should listen to. Quoting Immanuel Kant and Sigmund Freud, he suggested that psychiatrists meddle in alien territory in involving themselves in moral and social issues. He pointed out that the psychiatrist is considered a "bad joke" in the courtroom in criminal trials, and used as an example the *Hinckley* case. His most pointed criticism was reserved for the hubris of psychiatrists who claim to know more than they possibly could: Stone argued that if psychiatrists stuck to a standard of scientific truthfulness, their lips would be sealed in the courtroom, and they could not participate at all.

In 1984, Appelbaum also presented an overview of United States Supreme Court decisions relating to psychiatry over the preceding decade.[19] Appelbaum's analysis was decidedly pessimistic, for, although he noted some decisions that were favorable in their effects on psychiatry, he attributed these decisions to a separate agenda of the Court's and not to any particular respect for psychiatric expertise. Throughout its decisions, Appelbaum found the Court to be generally skeptical of psychiatry. Citing the *O'Conner* and *Addington* decisions he noted a lack of respect for psychiatric diagnosis, a process considered by the Court to be at best "uncertain." "At its most skeptical," Appelbaum wrote, "the Court appears to question whether psychiatric diagnosis is deserving of any respect from the bench at all." In these two decisions the Court seemed to be unconvinced of the reality of severe psychiatric disorders. In *Parham v J.R.* by contrast, the justices presented a strikingly different approach to psychiatric diagnosis, apparently viewing the expertise of the examining psychiatrist as a safeguard to protect the rights of the young patient. Appelbaum explained this discrepancy by pointing out that the Court in all of these cases had been primarily motivated to find a way of limiting its intrusion into the governmental processes of the states—in a way that is only coincidentally favorable to psychiatry.

Others have testified even more recently about the disturbing hostility toward psychiatrists shown by some judges in their written opinions. Goldstein quotes one judge who criticized psychiatry in general as being relatively useless in the courtroom:

> It is difficult to think of a more inexact science than that of psychiatry. As has been said, tongue in cheek I assume, "a neurotic is a man who builds a castle in the air. A psychotic is the man who lives in it. And a psychiatrist is the man who collects the rent." . . . The opinions of psychiatrists are based almost exclusively on their subjective findings which they gather from talking to the patient and bottomed on what the patient tells them with very few, if any, objective basis. They tend to "bootstrap" one another, one psychiatrist's opinion being based, at least in part, on what he has read other psychiatrists think.[20]

Noting that this "diatribe is not one isolated example of judicial spleen," Goldstein goes on to cite other opinions, in which psychiatric testimony is referred to as "conflicting, equivocating, and highly technical," causing confusion in the jury and ultimately being of "minimal" value; and in which psychiatry is characterized as a "fog-enshrouded sea."

The weight of all the above "expert testimony" might well lead one to conclude that the relationship of judge and psychiatrist can only be one marked by conflict, misunderstanding, and hostility. There are those, however, such as Goldstein himself, who would take a more optimistic viewpoint. A recent debate, carried on in the pages of the *Bulletin of the American Academy of Psychiatry and the Law* serves to frame the issue most concisely. In this interchange between Goldstein and Stone, Goldstein first presented an argument for the usefulness of psychiatric expertise in the examination of apparently incompetent jurors (i.e., in those rare instances in which some indication is presented that a juror might be incompetent). Goldstein argued that forensic psychiatry has become an

> inextricable cog in the machinery of the law and that the system is far better off availing itself of psychiatric expertise, when the alternative is leaving the judge and jury to their own devices and the pitfalls of uninformed ignorance and commonsense myths and misconceptions.[21]

Stone's rejoinder expressed regret for the "losses on our side" in the "great war between law and psychiatry" and counseled psychiatrists not to expand even farther the reach of their involvement, lest they suffer more injuries. Stone suggested that Goldstein overlooks

> a decade of legal opinion and scholarship hostile to expert psychiatric testimony; hostility grounded on the claim that expert psychiatric testimony offends due process and fairness.[22]

## THE REAL WORLD OF THE TRIAL COURT

To reach a conclusion about the current state of cooperation between psychiatrists and the courts, based only on this collection of legal and psychiatric opinion and higher court pronouncements, would in fact result in a highly distorted picture. Recent empirical evidence suggests that in the everyday world of trial courts, the opposite situation obtains, that is, that the trial courts are quite positively disposed toward psychiatric expertise, find it useful and important as an aid to fact-finding, and indeed welcome and demand increasing psychiatric participation in the legal process. This discrepancy may be an example of what Frank has described as the "upper court myth," that is, that trial courts are presumed to be unimportant and that upper courts will inevitably control their activities.[9] From the point of view of psychiatry, and given the pessimistic analysis of Appelbaum on the Supreme Court's thinking, it is fortunate that the situation in trial courts does appear to be so much at variance with the "decade of legal opinion and scholarship" cited by Stone. Although the empirical data about lower court judges' attitudes cannot solve all the ethical questions that Stone raises—whether psychiatrists *should* be involved in courtroom work—it clearly indicates that psychiatrists are not demeaned and devalued by the average judge in anything like the manner that many commentators suggest.

In the first place, there is evidence that lower courts are usually very reluctant to set aside expert psychiatric opinion. In actual practice, courtroom testimony in notorious insanity defense cases constitutes a miniscule part of forensic-psychiatric work. Much of the forensic psychiatrist's work is done as a consultant to attorneys or judges in the many cases that will ultimately be decided without a trial. In a 1986 study done at the Yale–New Haven Psychiatric Court Clinic, Reich and Tookey found an extremely low rate of disagreement between the clinic psychiatrists' findings with regard to competence to stand trial and the final rulings of the judges.[23] Out of 390 consecutive cases, only 6 cases (1.7%) were found to show a clear disagreement, where the court rejected the psychiatric opinion. This very high degree of acceptance of psychiatric opinion is in itself a concrete indication of respect for the psychiatrist's expertise and is consistent with the hypothesis that the lower court judge feels a need for psychiatric opinion and finds it helpful in the everyday disposition of cases.

When judges have been asked directly about their views on the role of psychiatry in the courtroom, they have tended to give positive responses and even to request more psychiatric involvement than they are used to having. In a major study by Melton, Weithorn, and Slobogin, questionnaires were given to 53 judges from 24 different states who were attending a judicial workshop at the University of Virginia in 1981.[24] The judges did tend to regard mental health involvement as more useful in some types of cases than in others (e.g., they generally found it much more useful in deciding the issue of competency to stand trial than in deciding child custody). With the majority of legal-psychiatric issues, however, the usefulness of such involvement was rated very high: with regard to competence to stand trial, 68% of the judges considered psychiatric involvement "essential" and 88% considered it at least "useful most of the time;" only 2% stated that it was "never useful." In a similar fashion, 82% considered mental health involvement "useful most of the time" with regard to the insanity defense, and 77% gave the same response for the issue of civil commitment. (The comparable figure for child custody was only 38%.) The authors also found that there was a rough parallel between the degree to which the judges found mental health testimony useful and the relative frequency of actual presentation of such testimony in their own experience. This finding is of course consistent with the hypothesis that the judges derived benefit and also felt that they benefited from instances in which they had this expertise available. Perhaps most interesting of all (especially in view of Judge Bazelon's concerns about conclusory testimony in the *Durham* decision), when the authors presented programmatic recommendations to a group of lawyers and judges, they met considerable resistance to the suggestion that psychiatrists not give testimony about the ultimate issues. The lawyers and judges appeared to appreciate a straightforward statement, for example, that a defendant is not competent, and some did not even want a lengthy report to document the reasons for the opinion.

The authors concluded that their group of judges lacked expertise in behavioral science and as a result were believers in the usefulness of having experts to advise them. The authors noted that the judges beliefs may not be entirely realistic: 76% of the judges, for example, believed that clinician's opinions about dangerousness were useful most of the time. The point to note is that, contrary to the impression one gets from reading Supreme Court opinions, these lower court judges, even when misinformed or unrealistic, tended to err in the direction of being *too positively* disposed toward the mental health professional!

Further confirmation of these positive attitudes of lower court judges toward psychiatry can be found in two recent surveys done at The Forensic Psychiatry Clinic for the Criminal and Supreme Courts in New York.[25,26] These surveys were designed to determine what the judges in these two courts actually wanted to find out in ordering an examination for competence to stand trial and what they thought of the psychiatric reports that they normally received. The original hypothesis to be investigated (which was in line with the findings of Melton *et al.*) was that most of the judges would probably be very interested in a conclusion about competence and less interested in an extensive and detailed report. A total of 38 judges from the two courts filled out brief questionnaires, and follow-up interviews were held with 27 judges. Contrary to expectation, the majority of the judges expressed an interest in having even more information in the psychiatric report than they were used to receiving. A total of 26 out of the 38 judges surveyed (68%) indicated that they considered all parts of the psychiatric report, including the detailed narrative history, to be useful. At the same time, the judges appeared to be disposed to accept conclusory opinions: when asked the question, "Do you frequently adopt the psychiatrist's conclusion as to the defendant's fitness regardless of the information contained in the narrative part of the psychiatric report?," 25 out of 38 judges (66%) answered yes.

The majority of the judges also appeared to be satisfied with the results of the psychiatric examinations done for them. When asked how often they found the psychiatrist's conclusions about competence incongruous with their own observations of the defendant in court, only 6 out of 38 judges (16%) responded "fairly often." Although a minority (38%) of the Supreme Court judges expressed an opinion that the clinic found too many defendants competent, who should have been considered incompetent, not a single one of the Criminal Court judges agreed with this criticism.

In the interviews, the judges tended to emphasize more strongly their interest in obtaining more extensive psychiatric data. Very few showed any hostility toward psychiatry or psychiatrists, and many were completely sympathetic to the difficulties involved in doing examinations for competency. Most of the judges appeared to regard the clinic psychiatrists as fellow professionals who were laboring under many of the same constraints and overwhelming problems as the judges themselves. One judge remarked that judges and psychiatrists have the same problem: having to make difficult decisions and then being vilified in the media when a decision is wrong. Judges who did have complaints (such as the clinic finding too many defendants competent) also often tempered their complaints by saying that they could understand why the psychiatrist, under the circumstances, had to arrive at the conclusion that he did. One judge described how he would take it upon himself to explain to the defense attorney why the psychiatrist reached the reported conclusion.

The majority of the judges who were interviewed appeared to take a very pragmatic attitude toward their own function and toward the role of the psychiatrist. Even while expressing satisfaction with the reports they received, they tended to have relatively modest expectations of what they expected from psychiatric experts, having placed psychiatric problems in perspective as one category among many in a wide panoply of social pathology. These judges put an emphasis on efficiency and the need to maintain control over their calendars. They appeared to be able to live with the manifest flaws of the criminal justice system and to have a realistic sense of what could or would be the prognosis for the defendants before them and for what psychiatry could offer. These judges were generally receptive, cordial, and in no way antagonistic to psychiatric input. Indeed, they were disinclined to find fault with the psychiatric reports that they received, apparently because they needed psychiatric input to keep the system operating as smoothly as possible.

The degree to which these judges were receptive to psychiatric opinion can be highlighted by contrast with the small number of judges who were exceptional in their attitudes. One judge, for instance, although respectful and cordial in being interviewed, did offer the opinion that he saw little if any need for psychiatric expertise. He felt that most instances of disruptive behavior in his courtroom could be dealt with effectively by citing the defendant for contempt. No other judge went nearly so far in ruling out the usefulness of psychiatry.

One judge raised the question that it might be unethical for him to confer by telephone with a psychiatrist about a defendant's case, because the call would not be recorded and the attorneys would not know what was said. None of the other judges appeared to be concerned about this kind of problem; they welcomed almost unanimously the offer by the clinic to call the examining psychiatrist if they had any question or problems with a specific case.

Only one judge appeared in the interview to be openly angry at psychiatrists and to have difficulty maintaining composure in the discussion. This judge's major complaint, however, was that psychiatrists seemed to be able to do so little to intervene in many of the very difficult cases of mentally impaired defendants.

In general, these empirical studies suggest that trial judges are by and large unmoved by such technical arguments as Ziskin's about the validity of psychiatric opinion. They also appear to be untroubled by the concerns of Stone about the ethics of psychiatric participation in the courtroom. And they are especially unimpressed by the skepticism in Supreme Court decisions about the usefulness of psychiatric expertise. If psychiatrists were to respond to the suggestions that they should withdraw from the forensic arena, the evidence suggests that trial court judges would be among the first to protest vociferously.

## CONCLUSION

A growing number of forensic psychiatrists, many of whom now have specialty training and certification by the American Board of Forensic Psychiatry, are offering their expertise to the courts. Trial court judges are in turn generally eager and receptive to using this expertise in the everyday course of the judicial process. The evidence indicates that the more judges are exposed to effective and usable psychiatric input, the more they appreciate it and even come to demand it. The courtroom does not, in fact, have to be an inevitably hostile environment for the psychiatrist. As Goldstein has argued, the most effective approach to improving the communication and cooperation between psychiatry and the courts lies in improving the quality of training and expertise in forensic psychiatry, so that psychiatrists do respond to Judge Bazelon's plea to tell the courts what they know and what they cannot know. Although there is already a reservoir of good will toward psychiatrists among trial judges, the task remains a large one. To quote Goldstein again:

> When forensic psychiatrists can substantiate their conclusions with the available data in such a way that their own decision making processes can be clearly appreciated by the fact finder, then we will have solved the communication problem. Psychiatrists are not expected to always agree with each other; nor is psychiatry supposed to have all the answers to the questions that may arise. But in court, the bases of disagreement and the limits of knowledge must be made as clear as possible. When we have satisfied this requirement, we have done our job well.[21]

## REFERENCES

1. Swift J: *Gulliver's Travels and Other Writings.* Cambridge, Riverside Press, 1960, pp 493–494.

2. Stone A: The ethical boundaries of forensic psychiatry: A view from the ivory tower. *Bull Am Acad Psychiatry Law* 1984; 12:209–218.

3. Ziskin J: *Coping with Psychiatric and Psychological Testimony*. Venice, Calif, Law and Psychology Press, 1981.

4. Rosner R: Misguided loyalty, therapeutic grandiosity, and scientific ignorance: Limitations on psychiatric contributions to family law and juvenile justice, in Rosner R (ed): *Critical Issues in American Psychiatry and the Law*. Springfield, Ill, Charles C Thomas Publisher, 1982.

5. Rosner R: The roots of the controversy between psychiatry and the law: An essay in speculative ideological archeology, in Rosner R (ed): *Critical Issues in American Psychiatry and the Law*. Springfield, Ill, Charles C Thomas Publisher, 1982, p 231.

6. Charles S, Kennedy E: *Defendant: A Psychiatrist on Trial for Medical Malpractice*. New York, Vintage Books, 1986.

7. Low P, Jeffries J, Bonnie R: *The Trial of John W. Hinckley, Jr.: A Case Study in the Insanity Defense*. Mineola, Foundation Press, 1986.

8. Frankel M: *Criminal Sentences: Law without Order*. New York, Hill & Wang, 1973.

9. Frank J: *Courts on Trial: Myth and Reality in American Justice*. Princeton, Princeton University Press, 1973.

10. Bazelon D: The perils of wizardry. *Am J Psychiatry* 1974; 131:1317–1322.

11. Group for the Advancement of Psychiatry: *Misuse of Psychiatry in the Criminal Courts: Competency to Stand Trial*. Report 8, Part 2: 1974; pp 859–919.

12. Robey A: Criteria for competency to stand trial: A checklist for psychiatrists. *Am J Psychiatry* 1965; 122:616–623.

13. Balcanoff EJ, McGarry AL: Amicus curiae: The role of the psychiatrist in pretrial examinations. *Am J Psychiatry* 1969; 126:342–347.

14. Petrila J, Selle J, Rouse PC, *et al.*: The pretrial examination process in Missouri: A descriptive study. *Bull Am Acad Psychiatry Law* 1981; 9:60–85.

15. Geller JL, Lister ED: The process of criminal commitment for pretrial psychiatric examination: An evaluation. *Am J Psychiatry* 1978; 135:53–60.

16. Cooke G, Johnston M, Pogany, E: Factors affecting referral to determine competency to stand trial. *Am J Psychiatry* 1973; 130:870–875.

17. Hess JH, Thomas HE: Incompetency to stand trial: Procedures, results, and problems. *Am J Psychiatry* 1963; 119:713–720.

18. Stone A: *Mental Health and the Law: A System in Transition*. New York, Jason Aronson, 1976.

19. Appelbaum P: The supreme court looks at psychiatry. *Am J Psychiatry* 1984; 141:827–835.

20. Goldstein R: Castles in the air: The credibility of forensic psychiatrists. *AAPL Newsletter* 1986; 11:35–37.

21. Goldstein R: Sanctum Sanctorum: The psychiatrist's role in posttrial competency examination of jurors. *Bull Am Acad Psychiatry Law* 1985; 13:191–196.

22. Stone A: Comment on Goldstein's posttrial competency examination of jurors. *Bull Am Acad Psychiatry Law* 1985; 13:197–199.

23. Reich JH, Tookey L: Disagreements between court and psychiatrist on competency to stand trial. *J Clin Psychiatry* 1986; 47:29–30.

24. Melton G, Weithorn L, Slobogin C: *Community Mental Health Centers and the Courts*. Lincoln, University of Nebraska, 1985.

25. Owens H, Rosner R, Harmon R: The judge's view of competency evaluations. *Bull Am Acad Psychiatry Law* 1985; 13:389–397.

26. Owens H, Rosner R, Harmon R: *The Judge's View of Competency Evaluations II. Bull Am Acad Psychiatry Law* 1987; 15:381–390.

# 3

# Mental Health Services to the Courts

## A System Isolated from Judicial Administration

**INGO KEILITZ**

## INTRODUCTION

In 1917, John Rathbone Oliver was a young psychiatrist at the Henry Phipps Psychiatric clinic of Baltimore's Johns Hopkins Hospital.[1] A few blocks away was a small police court. Occasionally, the magistrate of the court would drop by the clinic to discuss cases that he referred to the clinic for diagnoses. Striking up a friendship with the magistrate, Oliver began visiting the court, frequently sitting beside the magistrate on the bench as cases were being heard by the court.

Soon Oliver was spending free afternoons in the police court and in the stationhouse, helping to identify defendants who showed signs of mental disorder. As the word of what he was doing in the police court spread, Oliver was invited to visit other magistrate courts in Baltimore. The next year, Oliver left Johns Hopkins Hospital and began his own private practice, though his interest in delinquency and "legal medicine"

This chapter is an adaptation of an address delivered at the conference, "Caring for the Mentally Disordered Offender: Systems in Isolation," held in celebration of the Tenth Anniversary of the Metropolitan Toronto Forensics Services (METFORS) in Toronto, Canada, September 21, 1987.

**INGO KEILITZ** • Institute on Mental Disability and the Law, National Center for State Courts, Williamsburg, VA 23185.

29

did not wane. An associate judge of the Supreme Bench of Baltimore City, a former classmate of Oliver's at Harvard, introduced him to the superior (felony) courts, and Oliver was soon helping the courts without compensation as he had done earlier for the magistrate courts. After two years, Oliver was appointed a bailiff—a court officer who has authority, care, or jurisdiction over some aspect of nonjudicial court operation, typically keeping order in the court, custody of the jury, or prisoner security—of the Supreme Bench of Baltimore City. He thus became one of the first psychiatrists to become an official of a court.

For several years, Oliver drew a bailiff's modest salary while he served as a consulting psychiatrist to the court. He had no office, no secretary, and no funds for purchasing equipment and materials. However, after some time and with the help of Oliver's friend, the associate judge who by this time had become chief judge and had visions of creating in Baltimore the type of mental health clinics then attached to the juvenile court in Boston and the criminal court in Chicago,[2–4] the Maryland state legislature passed a bill creating the Medical Service of the Supreme Bench of Baltimore City. This new service of the court was headed by Oliver.

Unlike the courts in Boston and Chicago, which were devoted to providing only mental examinations of cases referred to them by the courts, the Medical Service served the Supreme Bench in the whole area of forensic medicine, performing physical examinations, blood analysis, and examinations of footprints and other physical evidence. Oliver's mission for Baltimore's Medical Service foreshadowed the constitutional right of indigent criminal defendants to free mental health expert assistance articulated by the U.S. Supreme Court almost 70 years later in the case of *Ake v Oklahoma,* 470 U.S. 68 (1985):

> [O]ur ideal, was in a sense, a social one. Our service was to give the destitute offender as well as the delinquent of moderate means the same opportunities before the court that had hitherto been the privileges of the rich. The accused who has money can pay a physician to examine him and to come into court to testify to his mental or physical condition. The poor man cannot afford this, and so his real condition often remains unknown to the court. We intended that in Baltimore, so far as in us lay, the poor offender should have the same chance as the rich to make his physical or mental handicaps known to his judges.[1] (p 18)

Oliver served as the chief medical officer of the Supreme Bench until 1930 and achieved prominence as a forensic psychiatrist, prolific author, lecturer, and criminologist. He was succeeded by Manfred Guttmacher, a psychiatrist who headed the Baltimore court clinic (today known as the Medical Service of the Circuit Court for Baltimore City) from 1930 to 1966, and who expanded its operation from mental deficiency and "bastardy" to issues of criminal responsibility and competency.[5] Guttmacher achieved international eminence as a forensic psychiatrist.[6–8] After Guttmacher's death in 1966, this tradition of leadership by the head of the Baltimore Court Clinic in the field of forensic psychiatry continued with psychiatrist Jonas R. Rappeport, who has held the position from 1967 to the present.[5]

The structure and organization of mental health clinics serving the courts throughout the United States are by no means uniform.[2–8] Their variety is typified by the unique origins and idiosyncratic development of the Medical Services of the Supreme Bench of Baltimore City. Unfortunately, though quite a bit is known about *what* court clinics do (e.g., determination of criminal responsibility, assessment of competency to stand trial, and assistance to sentencing judges) and *how* they do it (i.e., the delineation, acquisition, and provision of mental health information to the courts),[2–10] what is known about how the services of court clinics are structured and organized as part of the overall administration of justice is very limited.

The purpose of this chapter is to draw attention to the structure, organization, and administration of mental health expert assistance provided to the courts, especially their integration with court management and the overall administration of justice that exist to enable the courts to resolve disputes brought to them in a just, expeditious, and economical manner.[11] The chapter is based in large part on the work of my colleagues and me at the National Center for State Courts' Institute on Mental Disability and the Law.[5,9,10]

After a brief discussion of court clinics—the most prominent, though certainly not the only structural arrangement for providing mental health expert consultation to the courts—I outline the main premise of this chapter that court clinics are isolated from both the mental health system and the judicial administration. To end this isolation and to enable courts to dispose of the disputes involving claims of mental disorder brought to them for resolution justly, expeditiously, and economically, I suggest that the structure, organization, and administration of mental health expert services for the courts become integrated with the judicial administration of the courts. After a discussion of a recent U.S. Supreme Court decision supportive of this suggestion, several proposals are made to achieve this integration. Although the focus of the chapter is on court clinics, the issues raised pertain in varying degrees to other arrangements for the provision of mental health expert assistance to the courts, including centralized state institutions (security hospitals), community and regional forensic mental health programs, state and regional correctional institutions, community corrections programs,[3,5] as well as private practitioners working for the courts on a fee-for-service basis.

## COURT CLINICS TODAY

Unfortunately, only rough estimates of the number of court clinics in the United States exist. A few commentators, however, have attempted to estimate the frequency of mental health evaluations or consultations performed on behalf of the judicial system. In 1968, Pollack estimated that the total number of "psychiatric-legal consultations" in the United States exceeds one million.[12] More recently, Shah and McGarry estimated that the annual number of forensic mental health evaluations of all types approaches or even exceeds two million.[3] Assuming that these estimates are credible approximations, that is, that as many as two million mental health evaluations and consultations are performed each year for the nation's 18,000 courts of general, limited, and special jurisdiction,[13] it is indeed surprising that so little has been written about how these "peripheral" court services are structured, organized, and administered within the courts.

In 1981, I described forensic mental health programs in five types of facilities: (1) court clinics, (2) centralized state institutions, (3) community and regional forensic mental health programs, (4) state and local correctional institutions, and (5) community corrections programs.[5] Although each provides, in varying degrees, direct or indirect mental health expert assistance to the courts (the Department of Correctional Health Services in Phoenix, Arizona, for example, conducts mental health screening of defendants who raise the issue of competency to stand trial in the Maricopa County Superior Court[14]), court clinics represent the most prevalent mechanism by which courts avail themselves of the assistance of mental health professionals. Generally speaking, court clinics are outpatient mental health clinics located in or near courthouses that are designed exclusively to serve the courts and other components of the justice system (e.g., probation departments, public defender offices, and such pretrial programs as bail release services). They may be aligned with one or more of the divisions of general or limited jurisdiction courts—civil, criminal, probate, family, or appellate. Court clinics can be differentiated on the basis of the size and nature of their caseloads, the sources of referrals (e.g., the various divisions of courts, probation departments, and law enforcement agencies), the stages in the court proceedings when referrals are made to them (e.g., pretrial, sentencing, or after conviction), staff, budget, type of reporting mechanism (i.e., written reports or testimony), treatment provisions, data collection methods, and many other factors.[5]

Typically, the staff of a court clinic consists of a group of mental health professionals (mostly psychiatrists, psychologists, and social workers), administrators, support personnel, and any number of part-time

consultants. Some clinics have large, full-time staff who are well coordinated as a team, while others rely heavily on consultants who function
relatively independently.[5] Some court clinics provide a relatively wide
range of services to the courts, including screenings, evaluations, and
consultations related to criminal matters (e.g., competency to stand trial,
bail release, insanity, and sentencing considerations), civil matters (e.g.,
involuntary commitment, guardianship, and competency to refuse medical treatment), juvenile proceedings (e.g., delinquency status), and family disputes (e.g., child custody, neglect, and divorce actions), as well as
treatment and training services. Other clinics are designed to provide
only advisory opinions on specific mental health questions for judges
and other court personnel.

A serious difficulty in determining the number of court clinics stems
from the variety of structures in which they operate. Many court clinics
in larger cities are physically located in courthouses and are admin-
istratively associated with felony courts. Others operate under the aegis
of the state mental health system or, alternatively, public or private
community mental health programs; they may be located in a centralized or regional hospital or a community mental health center.[5]
Some court clinics are funded totally by the court system they serve.
Others may be "annexed" by the courts or operated under a contractual
agreement with the court. Still other clinics are allied with the courts but
receive only a portion of their funds (e.g., for capital expenditures but
not staff) from the courts. Most court clinics are specialized according to
the requirements of a particular division of a general or limited jurisdiction court (e.g., competency to stand trial evaluations for a felony court)
and units of the legal system (e.g., assessments of amenability to treatment for a probation department). To make matters more complicated
and potentially more confusing for those wishing to identify and classify
court clinics, some court-related services operating under the rubric of
"court clinic," such as mediation services in divorce or child custody
matters, do not deal with mental health issues directly.

How many court clinics provide mental health expert assistance to
the approximately 18,000 courts in the United States? In 1966, Guttmacher identified 30 psychiatric clinics of varying descriptions serving
adult criminal courts throughout the country.[6] The responses to a 1970
survey identified 53 court clinics in 10 states and the District of Columbia.[15] As of July, 1983, 31 court clinics were offering a full range of
services in Massachusetts alone, with an additional 28 more offering
limited or partial services.[3] Ohio has close to 20 court clinics, though
they are not named as such.[5] Shah and McGarry recently estimated that
the number of court clinics most probably exceeds 100 today.[3] Although
no recent survey of court clinics exists to confirm or refute these esti-

mates, it seems reasonable to suggest that the number of organizational entities that function as court clinics is probably higher than 100 and closer to 250—the approximate number of major metropolitan areas in the United States.

The establishment of a reliable estimate of the number of court clinics may give impetus to answering important questions about the structure, organization, and administration of mental health expert assistance and other "peripheral services" of the courts (e.g., forensic investigations) not *directly* involved with the courts' fundamental dispute resolution functions. For example, are court clinics (should they be) structured and organized as an integral part or as an annexation of the judicial system, as part of state, regional, or community mental health systems, correctional system, the private sector, or some combination of these? How do such organizational structures relate to the various components and units of the judicial systems (e.g., criminal courts, civil courts, family courts, municipal courts, probation departments, public defenders offices, prosecutors offices, pretrial services, and so forth)? How does the organizational structure of court clinics relate to the legal issues and questions that clinics are asked to address by the courts? To what ends are the various structural arrangements applied? By what standards should their overall accomplishments be evaluated. Meaningful answers to such questions will depend, to a large extent, on whether court clinics and other peripheral services of the courts are viewed as integral to or outside of the purview of judicial administration.


### *AKE VERSUS OKLAHOMA*


As noted earlier, John Rathbone Oliver intended that the court clinic he founded in Baltimore in 1918 serve indigent defendants so that, in Oliver's words, the "poor offender should have the same chance as the rich to make his physical or mental handicaps known to his judges."[1] (p 18) He was expressing a fundamental concern for equality and fundamental fairness by suggesting that legal resources, in particular mental health expert assistance, should not be dependent on a defendant's ability to pay for those resources. The court should manifest a like concern for poor and wealthy litigants.[16] This same concern was voiced by the U.S. Supreme Court in 1985 in the form of a constitutional entitlement in the case of *Ake v Oklahoma*, 470 US 68 (1985). The Court ruled that an indigent criminal defendant is entitled to state-funded psychiatric assistance to help in the evaluation, preparation, and presentation of a defense if a defendant's sanity is likely to be a significant issue at trial.

The events that gave rise to the decision in *Ake* began in October of 1979, when Glen Burton Ake and an accomplice broke into the home of an Oklahoma couple, killing them both and wounding their two children. After a month of criminal activity, Ake and his accomplice were apprehended in Colorado. Ake was extradited to Oklahoma and tried in the District Court of Canadian County, Oklahoma, in November of 1979. At his arraignment, the Oklahoma trial judge found Ake's behavior to be so disruptive and "bizarre" that he ordered a psychiatric examination of Ake to determine his competency to stand trial. The psychiatrist who examined Ake found him to be delusional and diagnosed his condition as paranoid schizophrenia. He recommended that Ake undergo observation and evaluation in a mental hospital. Based on psychiatric testimony during the ensuing hearing on his competency to stand trial, Ake was determined to be unfit to stand trial and committed to a state mental hospital to regain his competency. Six weeks later, Ake was found legally competent to stand trial, provided that he continue to take antipsychotic medication three times a day to help him keep stable.

At a pretrial hearing, Ake's court-appointed attorney made known to the court his client's intention to rely on an insanity defense. He requested a psychiatric examination of Ake's sanity at state expense because Ake could not afford to pay for such assistance. The court denied the request, and the case proceeded without the benefit of a mental examination of Ake's sanity. Since Ake was therefore unable to present expert testimony in support of his insanity defense, his sole defense at trial was that he was legally insane at the time of the offense. Although testimony was presented by a court-appointed psychiatrist that Ake was dangerous to society, no mental health testimony was presented regarding his sanity at the time of the offense. A jury found Ake guilty on all counts. At a capital sentencing hearing held before the same jury, the prosecutor asked that Ake be given the death penalty. Ake presented no mitigating evidence or testimony to rebut the psychiatrist who testified about his dangerousness. The jury imposed the death sentence. Ake appealed to the Oklahoma Court of Criminal Appeals. The court rejected Ake's claims that he had been denied access to psychiatric assistance in violation of the Fourteenth Amendment to the Constitution and affirmed the guilty verdict and the death sentence. Ake sought review of the decision by the U.S. Supreme Court.

The Supreme Court reversed and remanded the case. Justice Thurgood Marshall's majority opinion held that without the assistance of an independent psychiatrist Ake would not have had a fair opportunity to present his insanity defense and thus he was denied his constitutional right to due process. When sanity is a significant factor in a criminal defense, he wrote, the state must provide a criminal defendant with a "competent psychiatrist who will conduct an appropriate examination and assist in *evaluation, preparation,* and *presentation* of the defense." The appointed psychiatrist must be independent of both the prosecution and the court, must be available for pretrial consultation as well as for trial assistance, and should be dedicated to the defendant's cause. Even though the court limited a criminal defendant's right to free mental health expert assistance by stating that a defendant does not have a constitutional right to choose a psychiatrist of his or her "personal liking" or to receive funds to hire his or her own, the Court's definition of competent expert assistance would seem to encompass almost any activity under the general rubric of "evaluation, preparation, and presentation of the defense" that an attorney would consider necessary (or desirable) for an insanity defense.[17-19]

Narrowly conceived, the *Ake* decision did no more than give constitutional dimensions to assistance that most states were already providing to indigent criminal defendants before *Ake*.[17] Viewed in broad organizational terms, however, the decision did much more than give voice to the constitutional right of indigent criminal defendants to mental health expert assistance. Its lasting significance may lie in the attention it draws to the need to link mental health expert services organizationally with some component of the justice system. It sent a clear signal to the courts that mental health expert assistance is part of the "raw materials integral to building of an effective defense" thereby linking the structure, organization, and administration of mental health expert services provided to indigent criminal defendants with indigent defense systems.

The private bar has a long tradition of assisting the nation's courts on a *pro bono publico* basis or for minimal compensation. Private lawyers provide legal representation to indigent criminal defendants and serve in judicial or quasi-judicial capacities. The assistance they give to the courts has been structured and regularized throughout the country.[17] No such tradition of public assistance exists for mental health professionals recruited to help the courts in cases involving mental health law issues. Although no one would argue that the amounts of help provided indigent defendants by lawyers and mental health professionals are comparable, the nature of the issues are quite similar. How should the help be given? By whom? How and by whom should the expert services be structured and controlled? Who should bear the costs? Should the assignment of mental health experts be ad hoc, coordinated by the courts, or administered through public defender systems? On what basis should the results of the mental health expert assistance be evaluated? By linking the provision of mental health expert assistance to the indigent criminal defense system in its decision in *Ake v Oklahoma,* the Supreme Court may have forced the integration of mental health services provided to the courts—including those provided by court *clinics*—with judicial administration.

## INTEGRATING COURT CLINICS WITH JUDICIAL ADMINISTRATION

The premise that forensic mental health programs in the courts, such as court clinics, are detached and isolated from the systems that serve mentally disordered defendants raises an important question: What systems are these programs detached and isolated from or, more importantly, what systems or components of the justice, mental health, public safety, and social service systems should these programs be integrated with? As already suggested earlier, it is my belief that these programs are much too detached from, and need to be integrated with, judicial administration and the management of the courts.

Organizational theory tells us that good managers must organize and manage the whole organizational environment, not just a unit or subset of an organization. The environment of court clinics and the work that they do is the environment or the domain of judicial administration. In August, 1969, soon after he became Chief Justice of the United States, Warren E. Burger observed:

> The courts of this country need management, which busy and overworked judges, with drastically increased caseloads, cannot give. We need a corps of trained administrators to manage and direct the machinery so that judges can concentrate on their primary duty of judging. Such managers do not exist, except for a handful who are almost entirely confined to state court systems. We must literally create a corps of court administrators or managers and do it at once.[20] (p 1)

As a result of former Chief Justice Burger's efforts and those of the National Center for State Courts, among other individuals and groups, court managers have become an increasingly important part of the courts. Today, court managers serve in most of the 18,000 court systems in the United States, and court administration has become a growth industry. To repeat the major premise and proposal of this chapter, I contend that it is court administration from which those of us who work within the forensic mental health systems—especially court clinics—have been isolated, and it is with court administration that the system needs to be integrated.

Beginning in the 1980s, an approach, consistent with this premise and proposal, referred to as "social science in the law" appeared to be gaining momentum.[21] This approach diverged with the law and society

tradition in taking an "insiders" perspective of the judge, the court manager, and the legal practitioner, rather than the "outsider" perspective
of the social scientist. The approach is applied in nature and asks what
mental health professionals and social scientists can contribute to the
functioning of the justice system. It is in sharp contrast to the approach
that uses such mental health issues as insanity, competency, or civil commitment as the research context or merely the "cover story" for advancement of social science theory (e.g., attribution theory) or as a means for
advancing disciplinary concerns (e.g., professional parity between psychologists and psychiatrists).

Assuming that the isolation of the forensic mental health system
represented by court clinics is real and that the call for its integration
with judicial administration and the management of the courts has merit, what precisely should be done to achieve this integration and put an
end to the isolation? Five proposals are offered: (1) increased attention
paid by mental health law professionals and researchers to the structure,
organization, and administration of mental health assistance provided to
the courts; (2) evaluations of court clinics and other related forensic
mental health programs in terms of established goals and standards of
*court* performance; (3) specific programs of research of forensic mental
health issues particularly germane to judicial administration; (4) demon-
strations of innovative organizational structures for delivery of forensic
mental health services to the courts; and (5) the professionalization of
the forensic mental health "practitioner–manager" working within the
courts. Arguably, some of these proposals have merit regardless of
whether forensic mental health programs are integrated with judicial
administration.

## Increased Attention to Structure, Organization, and Administration

A logical first step toward an integration of forensic mental health
programs with judicial administration is to focus greater professional
and scholarly attention on the structures, organizations, and administration of mental health programs providing services to the courts. As
suggested earlier, such attention is likely to stimulate research in an area
where little research exists today with results that are likely to be of great
interest to the field of judicial administration. Relatively simple descriptive studies, for example, could establish reliable estimates of the
number of mental health forensic units as well as their location within
the judicial system. It is highly doubtful that each of the 18,000 courts in
the United States has its own forensic mental health program, but the
total number of courts stands as the outside estimate of the number of
such programs. Other descriptive studies could ascertain the structures,

organizations, and various administrative mechanisms of the forensic mental health programs and from this information develop a tentative typology. Further, experimental research could link this typology to outcomes. Does one typology, for example, lead to better justice, swifter justice, or more satisfaction among participants in judicial proceedings?

## Court Performance Evaluation

It is axiomatic that court clinics and other mental health programs serving the courts are valued by court managers to the extent that they contribute to a court's performance according to established standards. Such standards are being developed by the National Center for State Courts[22] in six performance areas: (1) access to justice (courts shall be accessible to all those who need to, or are required to, participate in their proceedings); (2) expedition and timeliness (courts should meet their responsibilities to all individuals, groups, and entities affected by its actions and activities without delay); (3) equality and fairness (courts should provide due process and equal protection to those who have business before them and be fair in the decisions they reach and in the actions they take); (4) legality, fidelity, and reliability (courts' actions and decisions, their legal and factual antecedents, and their consequences should be well integrated); (5) institutional integrity (if courts are to fulfill their role within our constitutional form of government, they must assert their distinctiveness and independence from other components of government); and, finally, (6) public trust and confidence (the justice delivered by the courts must be seen and appreciated to be done). Assessment of the structure, organization, and administration of mental health services in the courts on the basis of *court* performance standards and measures in these areas is likely to bring such services into the mainstream of judicial administration.[17]

## Research in Judicial Administration

Research of mental health services to the courts applied to specific problems in judicial administration may help bring these services into the mainstream of judicial administration by creating new knowledge that is of interest and utility for court managers. For example, a nagging problem in judicial administration is court delay. Caseflow management (i.e., analyzing and evaluating pending caseloads and implementing effective court calendar management) is a basic function of court managers. A promising piece of applied research—one that court managers likely will find very useful—would investigate the effects of requests for mental health assistance on case-processing times. In some courts, cases in which insanity defenses are asserted—in which a defendant's competency is questioned, or in which mental health information is sought by a trial judge to assist in sentencing—and other cases involving claims of mental disorder are often not considered among those the court can adequately manage. One court administrator, who took considerable pride in his court's successful program of case delay reduction, recently remarked to me that he had repeatedly failed to control the pace of litigation of cases in his court involving claims of mental disorder. Research of delay in processing cases involving claims of mental disorder would create information useful for court managers and, thereby, help to integrate mental health services with judicial administration.

## Demonstrations of Innovations

Experimentation with and demonstration of innovative organizational structures of forensic mental health delivery systems may also have some healthy returns for moving court mental health services programs into the mainstream of judicial administration. One such innovative organizational structure may be a comprehensive, unified court clinic that is consistent with a unified court system. A unified court system is one in which a multilevel fragmented system of general, limited, and special jurisdiction courts is replaced with a unified administrative structure responsible for systemwide planning, budgeting, accounting, research, and personnel administration. In a unified court system, it is the individual judges within a general jurisdiction court, rather than the courts, who specialize. That is, the various types of cases brought before the courts—civil, criminal, probate, juvenile, and domestic relations—are heard by individual judges (perhaps organized into court divisions or departments) within a single court rather than by separate courts.

In a similar way, a unified, comprehensive court clinic would merge all functions performed by mental health and social service professionals on behalf of the courts under one organizational structure and one roof rather than keep each function matched with its own separate organizational entity (e.g., a juvenile court clinic performing services for juvenile cases exclusively). The functions of such a unified court clinic would include, but not be limited to, the following: (1) in criminal proceedings, assessments of competency to stand trial, determinations of criminal responsibility, pretrial release suitability, and assessments before and after sentencing; (2) in civil proceedings, examinations to determine a person's suitability for involuntary civil commitment, guardianship, or protective placement; and, determinations of a person's capacity to make decisions regarding treatment and financial matters; (3) in juvenile proceedings, interviews and psychological testing to assist in adjudication and disposition of delinquency cases; and (4) in family matters (e.g., divorce and custody), mental health assessments of parents and children to inform decisions about the nature and focus of mental health care or treatment and related social services.

In addition to these functions, a unified clinic may provide a certain amount of consultation and treatment. In Massachusetts, the court clinics, for example, provide a limited treatment to individuals referred by judges and probation officers. The clinics work collaboratively with probation officers on court-referred cases. Clients are accepted for short-term or long-term treatment including psychotherapy, family therapy, group therapy, and chemotherapy.[12]

Traditionally, the functions envisioned for a comprehensive, unified court clinic are performed by separate and fragmented units. In one borough of New York, for example, the criminal court clinic and the family court clinic function totally separately with no overlap in organization, staff, or operation despite the fact that these two clinics occupy two floors of the same building. Although some of the court clinics in Massachusetts come close, the concept of a unified, comprehensive court clinic has not been tried.

## Professionalization

One final proposal, if implemented, may end the isolation of forensic mental health programs aligned with the courts in a more *direct* way. It calls for the professionalization of the forensic mental health clinician–administrator through the creation of a professional organization—perhaps named the National Association of Court Clinic Managers—devoted to the improvement of the structure, organization, and administration of "peripheral" services provided to the courts. Such an organization could seek affiliation with existing professional organizations, such as the National Association for Court Management, established in 1984 by consolidation of the National Association of Trial Court Administrators and the National Association for Court Administration.[10,23] Much like the National Association for Court Management, which represents court managers, a professional organization of clinicians–administrators could become the voice of effective, well-informed professional managers of court clinics.

The staff members of court clinics often have one foot in the mental health system and the other in the justice system. Reminiscent of John Rathbone Oliver's expedient appointment as a bailiff of the Supreme Bench of Baltimore City, court clinic staff may feel themselves isolated—even alienated—from the mainstream of the court's work as well as from their primary professional group or discipline (psychiatry, psychology, or social work). Court clinic workers may be viewed as misfits by judges and other court personnel, because the peripheral services they perform for the courts may not be considered part of the mainstream of court administration, despite the widespread recognition that the services they provide are a requirement in judicial proceedings.

Within their own professions, court clinic professionals may also view themselves as misfits. Although each of the professions of psychiatry, psychology, and social work has one or more organizations concerned with mental health law issues,[3] the organizations' programs are dominated by scholarly questions (e.g., whether the insanity defense ought to be abolished), technical matters (e.g., appropriate measures of malingering by criminal defendants and plaintiffs in personal injury cases), and relatively narrow and parochial disciplinary issues (e.g., whether only psychiatrists and clinical psychologists ought to be qualified to assess competency to stand trial).

Court management appears to be the professional area where the various disciplines represented by court clinic staff converge. Virtually every writer in the field of judicial administration has stressed the need for good management of the courts by trained professionals to organize and administer nonjudicial matters under the general guidance of judges, just as city managers, school superintendents, and hospital administrators direct, organize, and manage other institutions. The time may be right to bring the peripheral services provided by court clinics into the mainstream of court management. A professional organization of clinician–managers of court clinics may achieve this goal.

## CONCLUSION

In this chapter, I urge those who provide mental health and related social services to the judicial system to become more concerned with the management and improvement of the courts and thereby end their virtual isolation from the system they serve. I recommend that they pay more attention to and refocus their inquiry on the structures, organizations, and administration of forensic mental health programs serving the courts. I also feel that they should apply performance standards established for courts to the work that they do for the courts and do more applied research directly relevant to the concerns of judicial administration (e.g., studies of the effects of mental health examinations on court delay). I urge them to experiment with different organizational structures of forensic mental health services delivery that are consistent with modern court reform (e.g., a unified, comprehensive court clinic). And, finally, I propose that they establish a national organization of clinician–managers aligned with professional court administration.

# REFERENCES


1. Oliver JR: *Foursquare: The Story of a Fourfold Life.* New York, Macmillan, 1930.
2. Slovenko R: *Psychiatry and Law.* Boston, Little Brown & Co, 1973, p 127.
3. Shah SA, McGarry AL: Psychiatry and psychology: Review of programs, training, and qualifications, in Curran WJ, McGarry AL, Shah SA (eds): *Forensic Psychiatry and Psychology.* Philadelphia, F.A. Davis, 1986.
4. Levine M, Ewing PC, Hager R: Juvenile and family mental health law in sociohistorical context. *Int J Law Psychiatry* 1987; 10:91–109.
5. Keilitz I: *Mental Health Examinations in Criminal Justice Settings: Organization, Administration, and Program Evaluation.* Williamsburg, Va, National Center for State Courts, 1981.
6. Guttmacher MS: Adult psychiatric court clinics, in Slovenko R: *Crime, Law, and Corrections.* Springfield, Ill, Charles C Thomas Publisher, 1966, pp 479–493.
7. Bromberg W: *The Uses of Psychiatry in the Law.* Westport, Conn, Quorum, 1979, pp 124–141.
8. Guttmacher MS, Weihofen H: *Psychiatry and the Law.* New York, Norton, 1952.
9. Keilitz I, Holmstrup ME: Perspectives on mental health screening and evaluation. *State Court J* 1984; 5(1):13–18.
10. Keilitz I: A model process for forensic mental health screening and evaluation. *Law Hum Behav* 1984; 8:355–368.
11. Wheeler R, Whitcomb H: *Judicial Administration: Text and Readings.* Englewood Cliffs, NJ, Prentice-Hall, 1977.
12. Pollack S: Psychiatric consultation for the courts, in Mendel WM, Solomon P (eds): *The Psychiatric Consultation.* New York, Grune & Stratton, 1968, p 132.
13. National Center for State Courts: *State Court Caseload Statistics: Annual Report 1985.* Williamsburg, Va, National Center for State Courts, 1987.
14. Keilitz I, Casey P: Evaluation of mental health expert assistance, in *Grant Progress Report,* January 26, 1988. Williamsburg, Va, National Center for State Courts. Unclassified document.
15. McGarry AL: Operational aspects, training, and qualifications in forensic psychiatry, in Curran WJ, McGarry AL, Petty CS (eds): *Modern Legal Medicine, Psychiatry, and Forensic Science.* Philadelphia, F.A. Davis, 1980, pp 643–653.
16. Forer LG: *Money and Justice: Who Owns the Courts?* New York, Norton, 1984.
17. Keilitz I, Conti SD: *Mental Health Expert Services Provided to Indigent Criminal Defendants in the Second Department, New York Supreme Court Appellate Division.* Williamsburg, Va, National Center for State Courts, 1987.
18. Perlin ML: The supreme court, the mentally disabled criminal defendant, and symbolic values: Random decisions, hidden rationales, or "doctrinal abyss?" *Ariz Law Rev* 1987; 29:1–98.
19. Perlin ML: The supreme court, the mentally disabled defendant, psychiatric testimony in death penalty cases, and the power of symbolism: Dulling the *Ake* in Barefoot's achilles heel. *New York Law School Human Rights Annual* 1985; 3:91–169.
20. *The Court Manager: A Manual.* Williamsburg, Va, National Association for Court Management.

21. Melton G: Bringing psychology to the legal system: Opportunities, obstacles, and efficacy. *Am Psychol* 1987; 42:438–495.
22. Trial Court Performance Standards Project: *Trial Court Performance Standards—First Tentative Draft (Briefing Paper Number Three).* Williamsburg, Va, National Center for State Courts, 1988.
23. Bylaws of the National Association of Court Management. *Court Manager* 1988, 3(1):23–27.

**4**

# Administration and Management of an Urban Forensic Psychiatry Clinic

## RONNIE B. HARMON

In the criminal justice system, the small provider of technical services is often at a political disadvantage in relating to court and correctional agencies, which have their own needs and agendas. Their survival may depend on the maintenance of a sufficient base of power and influence. The small forensic facility must relate to the larger actors in the system in much the same way that a private company relates to its consumers: advertising its services, creating its own market niche, keeping track of market sensitivity through research, and striving to deliver a consistently competent service. Using the example of the Forensic Psychiatry Clinic for the Criminal and Supreme Courts of New York, this chapter will illustrate several administrative and managerial methods for accomplishing these strategies. These methods include assessing the needs of the client base, establishing well-defined limits, developing effective interdepartmental liaisons, and maintaining high standards of technical competence and professional skills.

---

**RONNIE B. HARMON** • Forensic Psychiatry Clinic for the Criminal and Supreme Courts, New York City Department of Mental Health, Mental Retardation and Alcoholism Services, New York, NY 10013.

45

## THE MENTALLY DISABLED IN THE
## CRIMINAL JUSTICE SYSTEM

The Forensic Psychiatry Clinic should be viewed in the context of the larger criminal justice system of the City of New York. During 1986, the New York County Criminal Court, the court of first jurisdiction in Manhattan, processed approximately 117,000 arraignments. The Manhattan division of the Department of Probation had 13,500 active cases on its rolls as of December, 1986, with an average caseload per probation officer of 200 persons. By the middle of 1987, the census of the New York City Department of Correction had reached crisis proportions: over 16,000 inmates pushed the institutions to greater than 100% of capacity throughout the summer months, representing a census increase of more than 50% since 1984.

The tremendous increase in the census of the jail population in New York City over the past few years has had a major impact on the court and prison mental health service system. If the proportion of mentally ill inmates to the general population remained stable, the numbers of inmates in need of psychiatric care would have doubled. Although resources have been increased in the system,[1] there are still insufficient beds and staff to comfortably accommodate this type of increase. Professionals working in the prison mental health system report anecdotally that from their perspective the increase in numbers of mentally ill is more than proportionate to the overall census rise. They also believe that the degree of mental illness among the population is much higher than it has ever been. There are more seriously mentally disturbed individuals, more people in need of higher levels of care, than ever before. Comparisons are made with the back wards of the old (i.e., prior to deinstitutionalization) state hospitals. Another complicating factor for custodial personnel has been the impact of recent New York State Court decisions[2] regarding the rights of the mentally ill to refuse treatment. Jail-based psychiatric services will not force medications on any inmate who refuses to take them voluntarily. Finally, in addition to the greater numbers of chronically mentally ill in the system, a large part of the increase of the census of local jails stems from the increased incidence of cocaine abuse and the city's determination to arrest dealers and users of crack, the potent cocaine derivative. All of the above are compounded by the psychological impact of overcrowding and the NIMBY (Not In My Back Yard[3]) syndrome, which has been restricting the city's ability to expand both jail and local mental health treatment facilities.

## THE FORENSIC PSYCHIATRY CLINIC

The Forensic Psychiatry Clinic for the Criminal and Supreme Courts is the designated facility[4] in New York County to conduct (1) examinations of a defendant's competence to stand trial, and (2) mental evaluations for the Department of Probation. A staff of approximately 10 full and part-time clinicians evaluates an average annual caseload of 1,500 individuals, referred by the Courts and the Department of Probation. The Clinic is an operating arm of the New York City Department of Mental Health, Mental Retardation and Alcoholism Services. As a small part of a large system that is surrounded by the competing demands and needs of the courts and agencies, such as Probation, Correction, the prison mental health system, and the Department of Mental Health itself, the Clinic uses a combination of assertive and defensive strategies to maintain its autonomy and position.

## ASSESSING CLIENT NEEDS

One of the first priorities of a manager, in either the public or private sector, is to identify the client base. In the field of mental health services to the courts and corrections, the client will vary, depending on where in the system services are located.

In a court-consultation setting, the problem requires a reconceptualization of the way in which psychiatric professionals view their work. The psychiatrist will ordinarily consider the client to be the person whom they are interviewing and evaluating; this is the person they are trying to help. Therapist–client confidentiality is the rule. In a forensic psychiatry clinic, the physician is trying to help the court to make a decision about a legal matter. Thus, it is the court, not the particular defendant being interviewed, who is the primary client. In this instance, it is essential to advise the defendant, in advance, that the material will be shared with the court. The entire approach to the work becomes different, with the report oriented toward legal rather than clinical ends.

In correctional settings, mental health professionals, who provide treatment to detainees, often find themselves confronted with the difficulty of maintaining patient confidentiality in a custodial system where the correctional staff has a legitimate need of knowing about potential security problems. If a defendant confesses to the psychiatrist that he plans to assault another inmate, does it violate his confidentiality to advise correctional personnel of his intention? What about the protection of the intended victim, who might not be in jeopardy at all, if he were not in custody? It is the obligation of the Department of Correction to safeguard anyone in custody from harm, and it could be argued that any homicidal, suicidal, or otherwise assaultive intent should be called to its attention. In inpatient forensic settings where treatment and evaluation may be conducted, the problem lies in determining which information, obtained during the course of treatment, should be transmitted to judicial personnel in an evaluation report. Not all information revealed by the patient is pertinent for the purpose of either a competency or a presentence evaluation. Because these reports are not confidential, the clinician must be careful about what is included in the report to the court.

Once the client has been identified, the manager should proceed to orient services toward the needs of that client. To that end, it is helpful to attempt to assess those needs systematically. One method is to survey the clients individually, refining your understanding of their needs in relation to your services. In the Forensic Psychiatry Clinic, simple survey forms were distributed to the judges of the Criminal and Supreme Court, asking them for an evaluation of the Clinic's services. As a follow-up, the judges were invited to discuss their feelings over lunch with the senior staff of the Clinic.[5,6] This type of face-to-face contact was important in the establishment of good working relationships with a number of judges. It also furthered the additional goals of good public relations, consultation and/or education, and improved visibility.

Every effort should be made to cultivate an atmosphere of accessibility. Proximity to the court, if at all possible, insures that staff are generally available to consult, to answer inquiries, and, on a limited basis, to respond to emergency requests. In the case of the Forensic Psychiatry Clinic, judges and attorneys are encouraged to use the staff of the Clinic as a resource on issues of psychiatry and law, and inquiries range from case-specific procedural questions to broad philosophical issues like dangerousness or criminal responsibility.

There are times when the client may seek either a level or a type of service which it is not possible to provide. At that point, it is important to recognize that the line between the kind of good public relations that means being responsive to the client at all times and the kind of good management that does not stretch resources too thin may be a fine one.

## CLEARLY DEFINING LIMITATIONS

In a situation in which resources are limited and demand is high, it is important for the small service agency to clarify its limitations for its clients. Without that understanding, the service agency is always in the position of having to apologize for not being able to fulfill a request that is considered outside of its scope. The established service goal of the Forensic Psychiatry Clinic is an efficient turnover of a particular set of cases within court-mandated time limits. The Clinic interprets its mandate and its role in the court system narrowly, concentrating resources on those areas in which it has played a traditional part in the judicial process: evaluations for competency to stand trial, presentence investigations, prepleading mental status reports, and postsentence updates. One way in which the Forensic Psychiatry Clinic clarifies its role for its clients is in orientation sessions that are given periodically to new judges, attorneys, and probation officers. The limitations of the Clinic facilities and services are explained, and assistance is offered in obtaining outside professional consultants who could fill the gap when the Clinic is unable to accommodate the court's needs.

The following three examples illustrate ways in which the range of services can be restricted to a manageable scope:

1. *Limiting the focus of interviews to the present mental state of the defendant.*

Requests for evaluation frequently solicit descriptions of either the past or the future mental status of the inmate. Such a request, particularly for the prediction of dangerousness, is considered unfeasible by many members of the psychiatric community[7] and is not attempted by the Clinic staff. The evaluation of past mental status (with regard to criminal responsibility) is based on data that are collected from outside sources on such issues as past psychiatric history, school record, employment record, and family background. Because Clinic evaluations are done within a very limited time frame, and must frequently rely on unverified statements from the defendant for background information, judges requesting information on these types of questions are referred to privately practicing psychiatrists who may be able to respond more appropriately.

2. *Appropriately referring requests for treatment.*

The Forensic Psychiatry Clinic is not a treatment facility. As noted above, since the person being interviewed is not the client, and reports are specifically prepared for the assistance of the court, all information obtained during the interview process is nonconfidential. No doctor–patient relationship can be developed under these circumstances. The separation of the treatment function from the forensic psychiatric evaluation process is a well-established principle in the New York area, and even those inpatient units that are called on to perform both tasks endeavor to have one staff member treat a patient and another staff member prepare the diagnostic reports on that patient. Because the Clinic does not provide treatment, it refers clinical problems to other facilities in the criminal justice system. In those instances in which it is felt that medical attention would be called for, recommendations are made on simple forms that do not reveal evaluation results but advise the treating clinician, at the correctional institution, that a problem may need attention.

3. *Limit evaluations to the premises of the Forensic Psychiatry Clinic, located within the Manhattan Criminal Court building.*

Judicial personnel occasionally request that doctors report to courtrooms, holding pens, hospitals, or jails in order to conduct emergency interviews. Given the limited staff hours, any off-premises work would severely affect the Clinic's ability to complete scheduled evaluations. Judges are advised, therefore, that such requests would effectively prevent the completion of other work that may have been requested by either themselves or their colleagues. With occasional exceptions, they can be convinced to make arrangements for defendants to be produced at the Clinic. Travel and waiting time for defendants is less costly and more efficient than travel and waiting time for psychiatrists.

It has been the experience of the staff of the Forensic Psychiatry Clinic that it is better to restrict functions to what you can accomplish effectively, than to take on too many additional responsibilities and fail at them. In other words, be clear on what you can and will do, and do it well.

## INTERDEPARTMENTAL COORDINATION

The need for clear and effective communication with the client of services is a part of a larger picture of which the technical service agency must always be cognizant. In any system with multiple, independent participants, it is important for each unit to be clear about its role in the total system, and to be able to work cooperatively with the other actors in the system.

It has been suggested that the forensic psychiatry service should be an integral part of the criminal justice agency within which it operates.[8] Although there are some undeniable advantages to such a system, there are also many arguments against it, and many ways in which effective interagency coordination can provide similar advantages.

The administration of a psychiatric service, even one operating within the confines of the criminal justice system, can be handled appropriately by a supervisory structure that is accustomed to monitoring and reviewing issues, such as quality of care, patients' rights, and professional standards. Local court administrative personnel may have a limited understanding of clinical needs with regard to professional staffing, space, and equipment. In New York State, the trend in psychiatric care for the incarcerated has been to make such treatment the responsibility of the state and the local mental hygiene systems rather than of the Department of Correction. The Mid-Hudson Psychiatric Center is a New York State Office of Mental Health facility for convicted prisoners, persons incompetent to stand trial, and insanity defense acquittals, which several years ago replaced the old Matteawan Hospital (operated by the Department of Correction). The Department of Mental Hygiene has also established the Kirby Forensic Center, on the grounds of the Manhattan Psychiatric Center at Ward's Island, for inmates with shorter anticipated stays. The New York City Prison Mental Health Services, which are operated in Correction Department facilities through the New York City Departments of Health and Mental Health, and the Montefiore Hospital Prison Mental Health Service are also examples of forensic treatment services provided under the auspices of a mental hygiene administration.

Being a part of the local mental hygiene system provides the forensic psychiatry clinic with certain advantages. As outside consultants, it is possible to retain a degree of independence from the demands of the court. The competing demands of several different clients can be prioritized without prejudice. Pressure from the defense, the prosecution, a judge, or a probation officer to reach a conclusion, which might be favorable and/or useful to their needs, can be subordinated to professional standards. The forensic service can maintain a solid reputation of unbiased evaluation of the facts of each case. Timeliness, efficiency, and client satisfaction are vitally important. As a consultant, it is always necessary to compete with other diagnosticians to provide psychiatric and psychological evaluations to the court. The cost per hour of a publicly administered psychiatric staff can be considerably less than what a privately retained doctor would charge. Permanently employed staff can be available for consultations before and after the examination, and a location on court premises can facilitate the evaluation process. Ongoing monitoring of both the cost per interview and the turn-around time for cases is advised in order to keep the process in perspective.

Another advantage of being within the mental hygiene system is that it facilitates interaction with other service providers, such as the hospital-based services, the jail-based treatment units, other forensic diagnostic clinics, and community service agencies. For the small facility, this type of coordination can provide valuable assistance on long-range planning and short-term crisis management.

The term *crisis management* is being used here to refer to the manner in which a manager handles all of the day-to-day disruptions that wreak havoc on a schedule. The "emergency" case that must take priority, the lost or missing documents, the unanticipated project, and the uncontrollable delays in delivery of critical materials can all impact on service delivery. Good working relationships with local correctional personnel, with hospital-based and prison-based forensic psychiatry services, and with judges and attorneys can help to overcome and/or solve some of these emergencies as they arise.

Long-range planning is the means by which the manager attempts to keep the need for crisis management to a minimum, and here, too, cooperation with other agencies working in the system is extremely important. In a system in which individual actors are dependent on one another, a certain amount of long-range planning should be done jointly. In New York City, the Prison Mental Health Task Force functions as a work group focused on mental health services in local correctional facilities.[9] This group has been meeting for several years, and is a forum for local service providers to discuss issues and problems, such as the impact of AIDS on the correctional system, the shortage of beds for mentally ill inmates, the services available to the developmentally disabled and the alcoholic prisoner, and alternatives to incarceration. In addition to enabling long-range planning to take place, the group has allowed individual managers to get together on a regular basis. This type of interaction, in a nonconfrontational setting, establishes the sort of rapport that facilitates the crisis management discussed above.


## RECRUITING AND MAINTAINING EXCELLENCE

Low public-service salaries can make it difficult to attract and retain highly competent professional staff. In-house education can make available positions more attractive. Opportunities for staff training and education function as an incentive and morale builder in a civil service system in which monetary rewards are not easily provided. In the Forensic Psychiatry Clinic, staff are encouraged to learn about forensic psychiatry and to take the general and the specialty Board Examinations. (General Board Certification is a requirement in the recruitment of new medical staff members.) Study groups and journal clubs provide intellectual stimulation and support.

In discretionary time, staff can explore research projects, write and present papers, and become involved in professional organizations, such as the American Academy of Psychiatry and the Law and the American Academy of Forensic Sciences. Regularly scheduled case presentations can allow staff to share particularly interesting or difficult problems with colleagues. An in-house library is an educational and research resource, and staff can recommend the purchase of books or journals for that library.

In the course of creating a comprehensive staff-development program, a forensic mental health service can become a local educational center. Training programs that are sponsored and coordinated by the service can attract instructors and students from the area. One program of the Forensic Psychiatry Clinic is a continuing education course in Psychiatry and the Law, sponsored by the Tri-State (New York, New Jersey, and Connecticut) Chapter of the American Academy of Psychiatry and Law. The course meets weekly at the Clinic, facilitating easy access for the staff. It provides 9 months of training and 45 hours of continuing medical education credit that is free of charge to Clinic psychiatrists and to members of the local mental health and legal communities. The course has been attended by attorneys, probation officers, social workers, medical students, and administrators from around the region since its beginning in 1976. Clinic staff participate as organizers and lecturers, and the positive impact on staff morale is an important side effect of the program.

A forensic mental health service can participate in a postgraduate fellowship training program in Forensic Psychiatry.[10,11,12] The program with which the Forensic Psychiatry Clinic cooperates is sponsored by the New York University Medical Center, and provides clinical rotations and instruction in forensic psychiatry for four physicians each year. Each fellowship appointee serves a 3-month rotation at the Clinic, learning how to provide psychiatric services under the supervision of the Clinic staff. Other training rotations are at affiliated forensic services in the New York City and New York State systems. Because qualified, competent fellows may be invited to join the staff at the end of the year, the program also functions as a recruitment tool. Furthermore, staff members are intellectually stimulated through teaching younger professional colleagues.

Although it may be possible to improve the overall quality of staff through good recruitment and training, agencies in a civil service system often find themselves limited by existing, tenured personnel. Maintaining a high level of quality in the work product is an ongoing process, requiring the use of a variety of basic management tools. Periodic reviews of the productivity of staff in terms of quantity (numbers of forensic interviews held) and quality (content of forensic reports) can be conducted by supervisory staff. When the findings of these surveys are reported to personnel, self-correction can take place. Senior professional personnel should be available, as much as is possible, to discuss difficult cases. Annually scheduled individual employee evaluations, which are based on agreed upon performance standards and goals, summarize the year's activity, review objectives, and advise the staff members either of a job well done or of needed improvements.

A service that is respected for its professional standards and competence has an advantage in its dealings with its clients and with its competitors.

## CONCLUSION

Because of its position in the larger criminal justice system of the City of New York, the Forensic Psychiatry Clinic, like many other professional services, is frequently put into the position of having to prove its value. The need to demonstrate the services' worth, in the face of competition, makes excellence of service a necessary prerequisite for survival. By embracing the private sector parallels of marketing, targeting, and delivering a high-quality product, the small forensic agency can not only survive but also thrive.

## REFERENCES

1. In fiscal year 1985, the City of New York committed approximately $2.3 million to the creation of a new program for prison mental health services. In fiscal 1988, the total budget for prison mental health services was over $10.5 million dollars. Most of this funding has gone to provide enhanced staffing for the direct programs (administered by the Department of Health) and the contract services operated by Montefiore Hospital.
2. *Rivers v Katz,* 67 N.Y.2d 485 (N.Y. Ct. App. June 10, 1986).
3. "NIMBY": Public opposition to the development of new residential facilities, whether for the prison inmate or the mentally disabled, often takes this form. Outraged citizens express sympathy and recognition of the need for such facilities, but are not willing to consider that they be located in their neighborhood. It thus becomes very difficult to establish facilities in any neighborhood at all.
4. On February 1, 1971, then Commissioner J. Herbert Fill, M.D., of the New York City Department of Mental Health and Mental Retardation Services, formally designated, pursuant to Section 659 of the Code of Criminal Procedure, "any two of the Qualified Psychiatrists of the Supreme Court and Criminal Court Psychiatric Clinic to make evaluations at the Clinic into an individual's competency as ordered by the Supreme and Criminal Courts, New York County."
5. Owens H, Rosner R, Harmon R: The judge's view of competency evaluations. *Bull Am Acad Psychiatry Law* 1985; 13:4, pp 389–397.
6. Owens H, Rosner R, Harmon R: The judge's view of competency evaluations: Part 2. *Bull Am Acad Psychiatry Law* 1987; 15.
7. Simon I: *Clinical Psychiatry and the Law.* Washington, DC, American Psychiatric Press, 1987.
8. See, in this volume, Ingo Keilitz: Mental health services to the courts: A system isolated from judicial administration, chapter 3.

9. Harmon R: Mental health and corrections: Towards a working partnership. *J Forensic Sci* 1987; 32:233–241.
10. Rosner R: Accreditation of fellowship programs in forensic psychiatry: A preliminary report. *Bull Am Acad Psychiatry Law* 1980; 8:4.
11. Rosner R: Standards for fellowship programs in forensic psychiatry. *Bull Am Acad Psychiatry Law* 1982; 10:4.
12. Rosner R: Committee on accreditation of fellowships in forensic psychiatry. *J Forensic Sci* 1983; pp 8–14.

# II

*Testimony*

**5**

# Into the Lion's Den

## Preparation for Courtroom Testimony

ALAN J. TUCKMAN

### WHY DO WE DO IT?

When we can feel so safe and secure in the comfortable, familiar surroundings of our offices, with patients who "love us" and have been seeing us for many months, why go into an arena, in someone else's world, where one side will win and one will lose, and where everything we are, every word we utter, will be scrutinized and questioned?

I guess we are a special breed of psychiatrists. We like risks and challenges. We have the idea that we are educating the public about our field. We certainly must enjoy standing toe to toe with an adversary. Maybe we have a bit of the "gladiator fantasy" within us and the need for that surge of adrenalin, which can only come from taking on a new and somewhat frightening challenge.

Whatever our individual reasons, it certainly seems that those of us who do this work regularly know that we have to be very good at it, if we are to survive, and if the courts and attorneys are to keep us on call.

The legal profession does not want psychiatric experts who present their material and, when challenged with inconsistencies or opposing views, dodge, weave, waiver, and retreat from their positions. Nor do judges, who are faced with the enormously difficult task of determining the future of a defendant's life, or whether the defendant will live at all,

**ALAN J. TUCKMAN** • Department of Psychiatry, New York University School of Medicine, and private practice, Pomona, NY 10970.

need an expert who will wander into the ozone, pleased with him or herself for expounding an esoteric theory that is a million miles from the common-sense thinking of the average citizen.

A psychiatric expert in the courtroom is a "conduit," an individual with very special skills and knowledge, who will translate complex observations and material from a complex science into a language that is understandable and digestible by people who lack that knowledge and skill. In addition, no other participant in the legal system will spend time and collate material about the defendant's personality and life history, so that he or she becomes a three-dimensional person in the courtroom, rather than a one-dimensional defendant who committed a crime.

The psychiatrist who enters the courtroom simply to give information, with no interest in winning or losing, no allegiance to his or her position, who remains aloof from the everyday struggles of people's lives, will not only contribute little to the understanding of the case but, just as importantly, will disparage the profession and promote the image of the psychiatrist as someone who practices a vague, mystical art behind closed doors, unintelligible to anyone except other psychiatrists.

To become an "expert" in the courtroom, a psychiatrist must possess the following individual qualities:

a. A solid reputation in the community;
b. An air of self-assurance with clearness of thought and a willingness to put him- or herself on the line;
c. An ability to defend his or her opinions with extensive preparation and to formulate them in simple language;
d. The capability of teaching psychiatry to laymen;
e. A willingness to take verbal assault, challenge, or confrontation without feeling that his or her self-esteem is at stake;
f. A willingness to devote the time required, often at his or her expense for researching all aspects of a case;
g. The potential to be an exhibitionist and a showperson;
h. The ability to enjoy a "good fight" and endure extremely close scrutiny of his or her opinions, lifestyle, training, and experience;
i. A personal assurance of not having to be one of the boys or girls and a comfortable facility in chatting, often very informally, with attorneys and judges in "their world";
j. A respect for the machinations of the legal system and a belief that it is the best institution we have at present and, therefore, a willingness to be part of it; and
k. The strength not to be easily hurt or insulted when "all that work" is seemingly ignored as the attorneys and judges come to a conclusion that is totally contrary to his or her recommendations

and opinion. Also the courage to meet the needs of these people, at the time, and to recognize that we live in an imperfect world in which a defense attorney's caseload may be the deciding factor in whether he or she convinces the client to take a manslaughter plea, rather than go to trial on what seems to be a solid insanity defense.

The *goal* (and, unabashedly, *wish*) of the psychiatric expert is to have the judge or attorney remark, after your testimony: "That was fine. I understood it. It made sense to me. You were clear and forceful and could not be shaken by tricks or attacks. You connected a lot of the facts of the case, which made me recognize the relationship of the personality and the emotional problems to the legal issues and questions. And I enjoyed listening to it, without ever getting bored."

(Oh, what a wonderful fantasy!)

If there is "art" in the science of psychiatry, it is the art of being a strong, entertaining teacher while under intense pressure.

To accomplish the objective of being a superior psychiatric expert, I offer the following guidance ("from the trenches," as it were) in preparing for testimony (or for a conference with an attorney or judge) in a criminal case, with the understanding that no set of guidelines (or "cookbook") can ever replace the years of experience that is required to develop the necessary skills for a courtroom appearance. The more you testify and prepare for testimony, the more polished you become. The second time will be better than the first; the twentieth, better still. As our parents taught us: practice, practice, practice.

This chapter is not a comprehensive, step-by-step outline to follow, because each of us brings to this type of work his or her unique style. It is instead information that can be added to your own developing fund of knowledge on your journey through the field of criminal (and civil) expert testimony.

## INITIAL CONTACTS

When an attorney or a judge's law clerk first contacts you, discuss the case superficially on the telephone, taking notes as you listen. Understand at that time what is being asked of you and define what you will need in time, interviews, and materials to meet the judge's or the attorney's request. Also, define your fee structure immediately. Conclude with a request for a letter from the attorney that describes the case and your arrangement as well as a listing of the documents that are being provided. Some psychiatrists prefer to write the letter (or the contract) themselves. Other psychiatrists avoid the letter, claiming that it can be used against them at trial, if it is too explicit in its description of the attorney's opinions and position.

Understand the role you as a psychiatric expert will play in the case. Will you be an evaluator of the defendant? Will you work with the attorney in reviewing documents, testimony, and the opposing psychiatrist's reports? Will you act only as a behind the scenes consultant or will you be involved at all in helping to prepare the defendant for testimony (a dubious role, rarely requested but possible, especially with a particularly provocative defendant whose attorney is concerned about the appearance and presentation of the defendant who may be called to testify)?

Some attorneys request an initial meeting to look you over, if you are unknown to them. At that meeting, it is not appropriate to give opinions about the case with only cursory information, although some attorneys will want to pick your brains immediately, in addition simply to interviewing you. Opinions as it were from the hip are rarely valuable, are frequently incorrect, and are subsequently embarrassing. At this meeting (or phone call), even if it is not requested, advise the attorney about yourself, your experience, your credentials, the cases you have worked on, so that there is no misunderstanding later on. In essence, teach the attorney how to hire a psychiatric consultant. Be very explicit about the materials you will need and the people you will want to interview. Do not accept an attorney's holding back what may be a crucial document, for the other side may have it, or it may influence the entire direction of your opinion. Some attorneys may not want you to have certain documents or to consider certain information. Once, in a death-sentence case, an attorney requested that I render my opinion with regard to the defendant's mental state and whether he should be given a life sentence or the death penalty, without providing me with an opportunity to review the whole case, including the defendant's past legal and psychiatric histories. I declined to be involved in the case.

Many attorneys do not understand how they should proceed when using an expert. They are uncertain as to what to expect from the expert that is reasonable and unreasonable. They hope that the expert will modify his or her opinion "as needed." Your function, therefore, is to educate them about these matters, without their taking offense, even though many attorneys believe that psychiatric opinion is vague and thus can be modified with pressure.

Advise the attorney that part of his or her job is to give you as much of the material that is available to enable you to become convinced of his or her opinion. Never discourage an attorney from attempting to influence your opinion, if you believe that you are strong enough and astute enough to be able to distinguish appropriate from inappropriate material and to be aware, at all times, that the attorney is much closer to the case than you are.

Make a decision whether you want to be strictly a clinician in your practice or whether you want to participate in the discussions about the tactics of the trial testimony or the case presentation. Decide also whether you are comfortable sitting in court with the attorney during the opposing side's experts' testimony, and whether you are to assist the attorney in cross-examination. Advise the attorney, *at the outset*, of your intentions regarding these procedures.

There are two approaches to fees: an hourly rate (generally similar to your customary therapy "hour" fee) or a fee that covers all work performed up to, but not including, trial (or pretrial) testimony. With some experience, the fee can reasonably be arrived at in each type of case, and thus the need to account for every minute billed will be avoided, as well as having to discuss all areas that will be billed (such as research or travel).

As documents come in, or as you begin interviewing the defendant and others, you may identify other materials that you wish to review. Generally, in a criminal case, these will include the arrest reports and the witness statements, the indictment, the minutes of the preliminary hearing (if relevant) or of the grand jury (if relevant and available), the depositions of witnesses, any school or prior psychiatric treatment records, the autopsy (if a death has occurred) or the hospital records (in an injury), and any other documents that are relevant to specific legal questions. Employment records (or contact with employers) and a driver's license (especially if a written test was taken) may be helpful in *Miranda* challenges (to determine literacy and functional level). Jail records immediately following the arrest may be helpful in sanity evaluations (if very close in time to the incident). For various issues, videotaped confessions or statements are invaluable. As a general directive to the attorney, you may request everything that bears on the defendant's mental, intellectual, and social functioning.

As you begin to review and evaluate the material, be cautious of what might be called the "star-witness fantasy," which is the belief that you, your concepts, and your testimony will make or break the case. This fantasy (which on rare occasions is quite real) is one that must be identified very early (as a component of countertransference) and dealt with by recognizing the voluminous other materials that will be entered into the court record. An effective but humbling method to quickly dispel this impression is to sit through all other aspects of a trial, or, at least, to be in the courtroom, when the attorneys present their summations or closing arguments. Then, you will truly understand that you are only a small cog in a multifaceted and complex process.


## PREPARATION

As each item of evidence comes in, label and summarize it in preparation for the huge task of collating all the material. Along the way, as you begin to shape your opinion in the case, make another list of the cogent points of each piece of evidence that supports (or refutes) your decision. This practice will be an extraordinary time-saver at the point of writing your report and/or preparing to testify.

Keep in mind that, in themselves, interviews are generally inadequate on which to base an opinion. Although you may be able to testify that you had 5, 10, or 20 interviews with the defendant, you may discover that *one* document offered by the other side's psychiatrist, which you did not bother to acquire, will undermine all your well-intentioned interviewing and the theories based on those interviews. In like fashion, most jurors are not really impressed with a large number of interviews, because the interviews only repeat or bolster the same concept or idea, if they are not supported by other hard data. Never apologize for having seen a defendant only for 1½ or 2½ hours. A skilled psychiatrist *should* be able to gather the necessary information, when it is supported and complemented by other evidence, in that short a period of time. The psychiatrist's skill is not only in interviewing but also in evaluating and collating *all* evidence into a reasonable explanation and conclusion.

As you progress through the material and the interviews, do not allow a vacuum of silence to develop between you and the attorney, the judge, or any other agent for whom you are working. Share information along the way that will keep you currently on top of the case and that will allow the attorney to know what you are doing and the direction of your discoveries. You may find that you can save yourself much work if this sharing leads to an obvious conclusion early on, which may then end the inquiry of that defense or lead to a settlement of the case.

Of course, as stated previously, premature opinions, before all the relevant data are acquired, must also be avoided:

In one particular murder case, all the evidence along the way (interviews, background material, hospital records, witness statements, autopsy) seemed clearly to be leading to the support of an insanity defense. One omission was the defendant's statement to the police immediately after the crime, which the defense attorney was having trouble acquiring. When it finally arrived, the statement undermined the insanity defense and, instead, led to a diminished-capacity defense (extreme emotional disturbance). Fortunately, no final conclusion was reached, despite the attorney's pressing for one, until that statement was received. (One cannot help but wonder whether the attorney was purposely holding it back!)

When you use secondary reference works, always make a copy of the relevant passages (such as diagnostic criteria taken from a text or handbook) for your case file. Do not try simply to remember the reference by planning to bring the book with you to trial. In addition, always review other material in the same volume to be sure that another section could not be used to refute your contention. The opposing attorney may well have the same volume and utilize it to impeach your testimony.

Make an evaluation of the attorney you are working for. Know his or her strengths and weaknesses and be prepared to provide education to minimize the weaknesses. Do not be shy about this necessary duty, because it is almost always appreciated. If it is not, think again whether you should remain in the case.

Recognize that the attorney's function is to manipulate the witnesses to tell the story that he or she wishes to get across. Be very cognizant of the attorney's *covert* agenda, which you must be able to read and avoid falling into, if it does not comport with your position.

Although most cases do not get as far as the trial stage, always assume, at the time you prepare your report, that a case *will* go to trial and that you *will* have to defend your ideas and position during a cross-examination. Some attorneys will *assure* you that a case will never reach the trial stage, or that the opposing attorney's defense is very weak, thus trying to convince you to go forward with a weak case of your own. It is more probable that such a case will surprise everyone and go to trial, or that the inept attorney will be replaced by a "Jack the Giant Killer" prior to the trial. Every report you prepare potentially exposes you to the scrutiny of your opinions.

Do not presume that the attorney who hires you understands the case. He or she is also human, often overworked, and not usually very knowledgeable about psychiatric concepts:

I once met with a prosecutor to review the confessions of two mildly retarded defendants who were accused of beating their child to death. He advised me that the "whole case is a terrible tragedy, these people won't survive in jail anyway, and aren't even responsible, because they believed their child was possessed by the devil and they were beating him to remove *it.*" A much closer scrutiny of the confessions and of the prior hospitalization records revealed their use of the phrase "the devil in him" in a general sense, but not a concrete, specific belief of demonic possession. Apparently, the child had also been beaten previously, which attack produced healed fractures that were revealed in X rays, at least a year prior to the current incident. The district attorney was very surprised to learn that he did not understand the case and that he had a solid murder charge to deal with. I am not very sure whether or not he was happy with this outcome.

As a particular psychiatric defense develops, learn as much as you can about the legal cases that have been published in which a particular psychiatric disorder and defense were utilized. It is often surprising to discover that the law applies and understands psychiatric terms very differently from the psychiatric profession. Frequently, the psychiatric expert will be asked in court whether he or she understands the legal criteria and the applications of the psychiatric defense being discussed. Similarly, you must review the psychiatric literature to determine whether a particular disorder would manifest itself in such a manner that it could explain once again a pattern of criminal behavior. Do not presume that the attorney understands the *legal* definition of a psychiatric defense, as you may need to clarify that as well.

Irrespective of how you are paid, keep a strict tally of the time you devote to a case. For a trial, distinguish between *direct* activities that are intimately involved with your understanding of the defendant (e.g., interviews, review of statements, etc.) and *indirect* activities that have much less of a bearing on the psychiatric aspects of the defendant's behavior and that can be used against you. Indirect activities, if lumped together, can be construed as "puffing" on cross-examination (such as other grand jury testimony, other police reports, psychiatric research, extensive discussions with attorneys, travel, or preparation of a report).

As you prepare your report, focus exclusively on the legal question of the particular case and do not include gratuitous suggestions or ideas. In similar fashion, when preparing for trial, focus on the issue of the case. If, for example, the case revolves around an insanity defense, do not include anything else in your report or testimony unless specifically requested. If the case is one of child abuse, focusing on the deficiencies of the "system" as a potential contributor may be interesting but inappropriate to the issue of criminal responsibility.

The use of psychological tests (most commonly the Minnesota Multiphasic Personality Inventory [MMPI], which is self-administered and computer scored and interpreted) may be very valuable for additional information about personality and pathology. The MMPI also lends credibility to interview observations and can be used to assess malingering, drug and alcohol abuse, sociopathy, and faking illness or health. It must be clearly understood, however, that you, as a psychiatrist, are not specifically trained in psychological test interpretation (assuming you are not) but that it is interpreted by someone else, who, furthermore, may be susceptible to subpoena.

You may be requested to testify at pretrial hearings, which are designed to decide specific issues prior to the actual trial (e.g., admissibility of a confession). Although these hearings occur in the absence of a jury, all the material elicited becomes part of the trial proper. Thus, the opposing attorney may act very benign and nonconfrontational, while eliciting data about your credentials, beliefs or position in the case, which he or she will use later on. It is imperative that you prepare as adequately as you can for these hearings just as you prepare for the trial proper and that you remember or refresh your memory with transcripts of your testimony. Whatever you say can and will be used against you.

It is as important that you remember what you testified to at other similar trials and that you be consistent in your belief or be able to explain the divergence of your opinion from prior testimony (e.g., in articles you may have written or lectures you may have given). An extremely zealous attorney in an important case may certainly have an investigator explore all of these possibilities for purposes of impeachment.

Throughout the trial, try to remember that you are a *psychiatrist* exclusively and not an *attorney*. You cannot possibly see the entire scope of the case or know the law or the basis for legal decisions that are being made. You certainly have no reason to be offended when an attorney accepts a plea, before trial, to manslaughter, whereas you believed the case clearly had a solid insanity defense. Such factors as the attorney's caseload, the credibility of witnesses, or even the defendant's trial testimony, were he to testify, or any other legal weaknesses may elude you but might be very much a part of the attorney's thinking. You are always seeing only one piece of a complex legal process and a multifaceted case.

Continually monitor yourself for a potential loss of your objectivity and distancing and an upsurge in "therapeutic zeal." Be forewarned that this is occurring when you hear yourself thinking about "our case," "our defendant," "the enemy," "we win or lose," or "we'll get him." Despite feeling very positively that a psychiatric expert must be an *advocate* for his or her *position,* the advocacy must always focus on your ideas and position and *not* the defendant or the prosecutor. It is never your case to win or lose. The attorney who says, "Doc (or doctor), this is your field, you lead the way, I'll follow," is abdicating his or her role to you and seducing you into more control than you deserve. The psychiatrist should never be the tactician for the legal team. This is one of the reasons why it is a bad idea to sit at the attorney's table while waiting to testify or while someone else is testifying. The image you want to project is that of an objective, independent expert, not a member of the defense or prosecution team. For that reason, it appears improper for the psychiatrist to sit, in court, with the attorney and to help with the cross-examination of the opposing expert.

When preparing to testify, go over all the material repeatedly, labelling and outlining relevant data. An effective practice, as a reminder, is to prepare a one-page outline of all the relevant data, which can be referred to (much like a cue card) during testimony.

Spend a lot of time going over each question that will be posed to you during direct examination and that might be presented during the cross-examination. Formulate each answer and assess how it will be received by the judge or the jury. Include the presentation of your credentials, emphasizing those areas that are relevant to this particular type of case and minimizing those credentials that take little effort to acquire. Be especially cognizant of not emphasizing any expertise that cannot be substantiated with professional training or experience.

Attempt to acquire transcripts of the trial testimony, as it unfolds, up to the day of your own testimony, but only if it is relevant to your understanding of the defendant's mental state.

A review of the opposing expert's report and trial testimony is always a controversial practice. It would seem untenable to have this material available and *not* review it. Yet, testifying about your opinion of it can become a very sensitive issue. It would certainly appear inappropriate to denigrate the opposing psychiatrist's opinion or report directly; but it may be appropriate to state that the opinion is "wrong," based on inadequate data or a misunderstanding of the issues, or that there are two opinions derived from the same complex data. Of course, this type of testimony may expose you to a criticism of vagueness of psychiatric procedure. Such an accusation can be countered with the statement that any complex data or science lends itself to more than one conclusion. Personally, I believe that calling the other opinion wrong and giving reasons for that opinion are certainly more definitive and helpful for the triers of facts—the judge, and the jury.

It is not inappropriate but rather helpful to utilize material acquired after your report was written and before you testify. You may be questioned about whether your opinion would have been different, if you had had that material at the time of the formulating of your opinion, as stated in your report. It is hoped, it would not be different. If it is, simply state that.

Bring to court all the materials (appropriately labelled and annotated) that you reviewed and utilized in your work to avoid having to waste time rummaging through your papers to retrieve a document you need to refer to.

## THE CHRONOLOGICAL CHART AND THE UNIFYING THEME

You, as an expert, have a critical and unique skill and function of collating and presenting to the jury or the judge a comprehensive picture of the psychological history of the defendant, including the psychiatric components of the legal issues. Anything that helps to clarify these issues will be greatly appreciated by the court.

In this vein, a unifying *theme* should develop and be defined as you work through the material. This theme becomes the *concept* that helps to explain the defendant's actions and confirms or refutes his or her contentions. The theme usually encompasses most of the diverse material available and should make sense in terms that are understandable to laymen, after they become familiar with them. This theme frequently becomes the *thread* that flows through the case:

> In a sexual harrassment case, which led to criminal charges, the complainant's diverse allegations seemed meager in contrast to the charges. Reviewing the complainant's history—a picture of a person sexually abused as a child, whose marriage broke up shortly before these allegations surfaced, whose child was sexually abused by the complainant's father when they stayed with him after the dissolution of the marriage, who was having a clandestine affair with another member of the firm unwilling to leave his wife for her, who seemed to be exaggerating the significance of the harassment—led to the development of a theme or thread of a traumatized woman, who saw the defendant as the villain in her life, displacing her hurt and rage from her father, husband, and lover onto him.

> In another case, of a police officer who murdered his estranged wife, with her parents looking on, and who then claimed a dissociative reaction with subsequent amnesia to justify his behavior, material was gathered that showed him to have acted violently in the past and to have made comments to his in-laws, during and after the murder, which indicated that he was aware of his actions. This was then tied in with a comment to his former therapist (about harming his wife, if she ever left him) and remarks of a similar nature to his first wife and another girlfriend. The theme of his behavior with women and his methods of controlling them were identified as running through most of his adult life and culminating in the murder of his wife. These facts undermine the concept that the murder was an isolated incident that was committed without conscious awareness.

In order to develop this unifying theme, the expert must work diligently to acquire and sift through a lot of background and current material. As previously stated, the interviews are rarely enough.

It is said that one picture is worth a thousand words. In a forensic case, that picture can be a *chronological chart* of the events leading to, or culminating in, the criminal act. By developing the facts and then plotting them on the chronological chart with annotations of the critical events, the jury, the judge, and, most importantly, you yourself can have a graphic picture of the case, which will often replace much unnecessary descriptive testimony. It is extremely helpful to think of a case in terms of a chronology of events surrounding (before and after) the incident in question.

## THE DIRECT EXAMINATION

While waiting to testify, you should never engage in the banter and jocularity that often occurs between attorneys, court officers, and other participants in the proceeding. First, it may demean the expert's image you should maintain as a professional and, second, it cannot help the defendant, who is observing all this "fun" while feeling very miserable about his or her predicament. In addition, irrespective of who is paying the bill, you must preserve the image of an independent professional; "buddying up" to any of the attorneys, or even the judge, can undermine this image.

Direct testimony allows for much flexibility, on the part of the expert, in describing what he or she has done to reach a conclusion. Yet the presentation must always be crisp, clear, and offered in simple language. It must be relevant to the questions and be presented concisely, without endless descriptions of unnecessary events. *Relevance* is the single most appropriate concept in choosing the material to offer. We, as psychiatrists, know that words and phrases have different meanings to different people. For example, in psychiatry, the word *diagnosis* means a label of several words defining a symptom complex. When attorneys ask, "Doctor, can you give your 'diagnosis' of this case," they are usually referring to the psychiatrist's "analysis" of the patient, which is generally a full description of the personality, pathology, and circumstances leading to the crime. It is essential that you never presume you know what the attorney is asking. When in doubt, ask.

Often, in situations in which you are appointed psychiatric expert by the court and are then called to testify by agency personnel (e.g., the assistant district attorney or the public defender), you may be expected merely to appear in court without preparation. Attempt, if at all possible, to have at least a telephone conversation with the attorney who will perform the direct examination. Know what will be covered and consult the attorney on how to proceed before the actual trial. This tactic can make for a much smoother and more understandable presentation.

Always look at the jury or the judge, making eye contact whenever possible. These are the people who are the objects of your information, not the questioning attorney.

It may be helpful, during the direct exam, to develop a *rhythm of the information that is reviewed* and the conclusions that are drawn. Thus, the process may be something like this: "I interviewed the defendant. . . . I learned the following. . . . I reviewed the records. . . . I learned the following. . . . I administered the MMPI. . . . I learned the following. . . . I met with the victim. . . . I learned the following."

Of course, each one of these sections is prompted by the appropriate question from the attorney. Then, with prompting by the attorney, of "Doctor, having learned what you did, from each of these parties or records, did you come to an opinion (with a reasonable degree of psychiatric certainty) about (the legal question)?" This answer may be broken down into its component parts or presented as one single explanation, depending on the legal issues being addressed.

Keep mental notes when you feel that relevant questions were not asked about important information, in order to try to get that material in at a later, more propitious point in your testimony, or even during the cross-examination.

Use your notes (especially the outline you prepared and, most importantly, any summaries you made of relevant documents and interviews) and refer to them whenever necessary to give an accurate answer, particularly when a direct quote is called for. Some judges and attorneys will object to the repeated use of notes, but their disapproval can generally be dealt with by explaining that it is necessary in order to refresh your memory. Do not go into court without your notes, no matter how much you pride yourself on the excellence of your memory.

During the voir dire (the presentation of your credentials) and the entire direct examination, be cautious about inflating how frequently you appear in court. Although a psychiatrist may benefit from habitual court appearances, a jury may look somewhat askance at the psychiatrist who testifies regularly. They may think that psychiatrists should be treating patients and only professional experts should appear in court all the time. In addition, it is often a good idea to have available a list of case names, and the courts that you testified in, to counter the question of whether you only testify for one side.

During the direct examination and the cross-examination, distinguish scrupulously between moral opinions (as well as opinions any layperson may have) and professional opinions based on available concrete data. This caution becomes most evident in such cases as death-penalty determination, child abuse and neglect, and any issue that stimulates emotional feelings and moral impressions. In a similar vein, opinions should always be based on data, not on personal feelings. Statements such as "I believe her," "He's trustful," "She's a good parent," or "This type of person doesn't generally abuse their child," are personal value judgments and have little place in an expert's presentation of opinions based on facts.

The same caution can be applied to the use of phrases such as "My gut feeling" or "I feel." These phrases are very unprofessional and should always be replaced by "My opinion is," "My impression was," or "My conclusion was." No one can ever explain the basis for a "gut feeling."

Always recognize that, although what you say is critically important, *how* you say it and what you *look* like are probably as significant. Jurors frequently get global feelings and impressions about witnesses, which may have as much bearing on their conclusions as the facts testified to. You should always look professional and self-confident, conforming with the standards of dress for a courtroom, and *not* what you would wear in a psychiatric conference or therapy session. The phrase "dress for success" has pervaded the business world and may be similarly applicable to forensic psychiatrists in the courtroom.

## CROSS-EXAMINATION

Before you respond to the cross-examination, take a deep breath and try to relax; unclench your fists and be alert. Do not think of the cross-examination as an attack on you personally, even when the attorney is questioning your credentials, your work or your judgment. He or she is just challenging you to support your position and looking for weaknesses in your arguments—truly a very *intellectual exercise,* if you allow yourself to see it that way!

Always attempt to avoid answering yes or no to questions, whenever you have material to offer, even if the attorney asks for a yes or no answer only. Most judges will recognize that experts should not be limited in that way and will allow you to expound (a *little*) on your answer.

When presented with a hypothetical question, understand that everything in the supposition has been entered into the court record (but not everything from the record is necessarily in the question). Thus, the question may really *not* be hypothetical after all. At the same time, be sure that you understand the entire question and always attempt to bring it back to the *specific case* before the court. It is all too easy to be led astray by a hypothetical question, which produces an overly broad or overly narrow answer, and then to be put into the uncomfortable position of having to qualify your answer subsequently on a redirected examination.

Do not claim any text or author in psychiatry as "authoritative," because this will imply that all that is in the book or all of that person's ideas must be accepted by you. You would have a difficult time disagreeing with what has been written or said, in subsequent questions posed to you. Suppose the cross-examiner throws you a string of such questions as "Doctor do you consider Freud authoritative?" (And you reply no.) "Do you consider Searles authoritative?" (No.) "Do you consider Rosner authoritative?" (No.) "Oh, Doctor, are you saying *you* are the only authority on this subject?" You can explain that no one in psychiatry should be considered authoritative, because that would require blind allegiance to all of their writings, but that certainly they should be recognized as having made major contributions to the field.

Never simply wait for the next cross-exam question. Always continue thinking about where the attorney is going next, where the weaknesses are in your presentation (and in his), and what you might offer, gratuitously, when you have the opportunity.

Do not ever allow yourself to get into an argument with the cross-examiner, no matter how provocative he or she may be. At the same time, do not appear too cool, smug, and detached during a blistering attack. You are, first and foremost, a human being and should respond with feeling—but just a little.

If you are firm and unshakeable in your answers, the cross-examiner will begin to recognize that each question is burying him or her a little more and will realize it probably is better to stop before you hurt the case too badly.

If you have not considered something posed to you, or have not reviewed a particular piece of evidence, do not hesitate to concede. You will be hurt more by appearing rigid and dogmatic rather than conceding what is usually a minor point. Even if it is hurtful to your position, it is *not* up to you to "save the day." The attorney you are testifying for is responsible for the entire case as well as for rehabilitating you on redirect, or explaining your answer during a summation. Do not try to work too hard to make amends for a concession. It is perfectly appropriate to say, "I don't know," "I don't have an opinion," or "There isn't enough data available for me to have an opinion."

Whatever you say "off the record" to an opposing attorney, whether in the hallway, on the phone, or anywhere else, may very well be used against you in court. You may have thought that your comment was idle chatter or plain old gossip. The opposing attorney (or expert) may be willing to dispense with "good taste" and use it to discredit you. Although such behavior frequently snaps back to hurt the questioner, it is much more appropriate to use caution during these "unofficial" conversations so that you do not have to explain yourself or retract the comment later. You may be very ethical in the way you treat colleagues, but the next person may live by an entirely different set of standards, especially in a courtroom under cross-examination.

The cross-examiner may request to see your notes and then, while looking at them, begin to question you. Always ask to have your notes returned to you *before* you answer. This ploy by the attorney is intended to separate you from your data, which he or she has usually seen previously. Thus, when you are answering a question under such circumstances send the message clearly that you will not fall for these tricks.

Generally, there are two types of cross-examination styles: the "shotgun approach" and the "rhythm method." The shotgun approach is characterized by the manner in which questions come from all directions, in a haphazard fashion, and is presumably designed to confuse you and break your train of thought. This approach is used by attorneys who are unsure of how to proceed, who are unprepared, or who are fishing for any piece of helpful material they can gather while throwing out a broad net. Everyone, especially the judge, eventually becomes bored with this approach, which ends abruptly, often with you sitting there scratching your head and wondering why the attorney bothered at all.

The "rhythm method" is employed by a well-prepared attorney, who has direction and logical sequence to his or her questions. This approach, which is also more helpful for the psychiatric expert because it is logical, enables you to participate in an ideal inquiry into the facts. Try to remain one or two steps ahead of the questioner, as you follow along and attempt to identify the themes.

Occasionally (but, fortunately, rarely), you will encounter an attorney who is specifically planning on (and capable of) devastating a psychiatrist's testimony, without any interest in obtaining the facts. This cross-examiner's sole purpose is to discredit *all* psychiatric testimony and not provide an opportunity for any rebuttal experts. In this instance, the best approach is to answer succinctly and candidly without defensiveness, allowing the cross-examiner to run through his or her litany of stock questions. In your response, it may be possible to attempt to bring the line of questioning back to the particular case on trial: for example, "That's not the situation in *this* case," or "That didn't occur in *this* case," or "I don't understand the relevance to this case." Eventually, someone will give up and quit; but let it not be you, first. Again, this approach is very rare, but you *will* live through it.

Regardless of how much you have reviewed, organized, labeled, and annotated the material that you have used, there will always come a time when an attorney will ask you about a part of a record that you do not remember. Do not ever attempt to respond to the question by answering, "Yes, I remember that" and hoping you can get enough from the question to answer it. Instead, concede that you do not remember the passage and ask to see it; then answer appropriately. In addition, if the attorney reads from a record you *have* reviewed, always request to see the record and read the passage (as well as the preceding and following passages) before you answer.

The same procedure holds true when the attorney reads from your prior testimony at a pretrial conference (or at a prior trial). Always ask to see the transcript to be sure that your statements are not being misquoted or taken out of context or qualified in the next paragraph. Do not assume you can remember what you have said.

Be cautious whenever a cross-examiner extends his or her line of questioning beyond the scope of the hearing or the trial, particularly, if the other attorney or the judge does not object. If the trial (and your examination) is for competency to stand trial, do not answer questions pertaining to the defendant's state of mind at the time of the crime, or treatment considerations not directly relevant to the competency question. The cross-examiner's purpose for this maneuver is either to gather information to be used later in the trial, or to confuse the judge or jury, or to utilize the answer in summations. In any event, always limit your testimony to the specific issue for which you evaluated the defendant and for which you were called to testify. If the judge directs you to testify, demur by explaining that you do not have an opinion on that subject.

A frequently asked question on cross-examination relates to whether or not you have become biased against, or in favor of, the defendant by reviewing all the documents prior to the interview of the defendant; in essence, whether you already have a predetermined opinion based on the material given to you (presumably selectively) by the defense or the prosecuting attorney. This question is usually countered by identifying the documents that were favorable to the defendant (in the prosecutor's packet) or damaging to him or her (in the defense attorney's packet) and by describing your general methods of inquiry, which are designed to weigh all the materials provided.

Many of these trick-question types have been published elsewhere and have been omitted from this chapter. Questions such as whether or not psychiatry is a science or an art, why many psychiatrists disagree with each other, or whether psychiatric diagnoses have any reliability seem very powerful and interesting when discussed in forensic psychiatry seminars or books designated to thwart psychiatric testimony. Yet most of us have realized that attorneys, judges, and jurys are eager to have experts explain criminal behavior and the functioning of the human mind. In their view, these assaults by attorneys are nothing more than entertainment or puffing, having little to do with the practical considerations of a given case. Jurors and judges do want help with their overwhelming burdens of determining a defendant's future. They generally do not look kindly on anyone attempting to disparage a seemingly benevolent, credible "helper."

## AFTER ALL IS SAID AND DONE

When all the testimony is completed, do not pack your materials and leave, because the most instructive part of the trial is yet to come. It is always helpful to listen to other experts testify, *after* you have testified in your trial, as well as at other trials. It is extraordinarily valuable to listen to the summations of the attorneys and to speak with them after the trial is over, when the jury has had the opportunity to discuss the case with the attorneys (if they so wish). At this point, you can learn a significant amount (if *you* wish) about your testimony, presentation, and demeanor, which can be invaluable in future cases. Too many psychiatrists believe that they are the "stars" until they listen to a jury of peers tear apart their "brilliant" presentation. Only then can you get a true picture of how the layman, who must make the crucial decision, views you.

Be particularly cautious about clients or attorneys in forensic cases who request to become your private patients. This practice is generally inappropriate (the mixing of forensic consultant and therapist roles); send them to someone else.

Finally, remember that the more you do, the more you will learn; the more risks you take, the more you will benefit. Although forensic psychiatry is not for the meek, in the final analysis, it is certainly the most stimulating and exciting subspecialty in psychiatry.

# III

# *Reduced Responsibility*

# 6

# Confronting the Burden of Proof under the Federal Insanity Defense

**M. P. DUNCAN III**

## INTRODUCTION

On March 5, 1843, in response to the equivalent of a motion for an instructed verdict, Lord Chief Justice Tindal of the Central Criminal Court in London declared that Daniel M'Naghten was not guilty of murdering Mr. Edward Drummond because of insanity.[1] Although the insanity defense was not new to the law of England in 1843, the Parliamentary response to Daniel M'Naghten's acquittal elevated the concept to a controversial prominence from which it has not escaped.

On June 22, 1982, the front-page headline of the *Washington Post* read: "Hinkley [*sic*] Found Not Guilty, Insane."[2] A succession of articles, editorials, and commentaries followed, most of which echoed the then nearly 140-year-old comments of the Lord Chancellor, made to the House of Lords on March 13, 1843, in response to Daniel M'Naghten's acquittal:

> My Lords . . . a gentleman in the vigour of life of most amiable character (hear, hear), incapable of giving offence or doing an injury to any individual, was murdered in the streets of this metropolis in opcn day. The assassin was secured—was commited for trial: that trial has taken place, and he has es-

---

**M. P. DUNCAN III** • Texas Court of Criminal Appeals, Austin, TX 78711.

caped with impunity. Your lordships will not be surprised that this circumstance should have created a deep feeling in the public mind, and that many persons should, on the first impression, be disposed to think that there is some great defect in the laws of the country with reference to this subject, and that there should be a full revision of those laws, in order that a repetition of such outrages may be prevented. My lords, I felt it my duty, in consequence of some suggestions of your lordships, to consider, in consultation with others, this interesting and important subject, with the view of ascertaining not only what the law is with reference to it, but for the purpose of ascertaining, if there should turn out to be a defect, what practical remedies should be applied, and what the nature of those remedies should be.[3]

From such charge, the well-known M'Naghten Rule did ascend. In 1984, almost 1½ centuries after the House of Lords, relying on the Christian-Judeo concept of free will, the jurisprudence of a post-Romantic and pre-Victorian England, and what little medical evidence was then available, expressed their consensus of what the insanity defense should be, the United States Congress rode Chapter IV of the Comprehensive Crime Control Act of 1984 as a Wellsian time machine to recapture the moment when only the inability to recognize moral good from evil would absolve one from punishment as a criminal.

One of the more interesting things about the still raging controversy over the insanity defense is the contrast between its relative jurisprudential insignificance and the substantial popular, and therefore political, interest it has generated.[4] It is doubtful that the cry for reform would have been so virulent had John Hinckley shot a bus driver. But such is the stuff from which reform springs.

Before the Insanity Defense Reform Act of 1984,[5] the insanity defense in federal prosecutions enjoyed a substantially different role. Quite simply, there was no federal statutory insanity defense. The insanity defense was nonetheless a recognized and accepted justification for what would otherwise be criminal conduct. The basis for the jurisprudential reception of the insanity defense and its associated procedures was *Davis v United States*.[6]

The United States Supreme Court's unanimous decision in *Davis v United States*[7] set the substantive and procedural stage on which the insanity defense was to play in the federal courts for nearly 60 years. Factually, the defendant, Dennis Davis, was convicted and sentenced to hang for murdering Sol Blackwell at the Creek Nation in the Indian Territory, within the western district of Arkansas on September 18, 1894.

During the trial a question as to the defendant's mental capacity arose. He was described variously, yet similarly as being "weak-minded . . . [and] half crazy"[8] "half-crazy, weak-minded, and . . . not of sound mind."[9] As a part of some rather elaborate and often redundant jury instructions, the trial court noted that an issue as to Davis's mental capacity had arisen and commented that the law "presumes every man is sane, and the burden of showing it is not true is upon the party who asserts it."[10] In his concluding instructions to the jury the trial court commented:

> When you start into a trial of a case, as I have already told you, you start in with the presumption of sanity. Then comes in the responsibility resting upon the Defendant to show his condition; to show his irresponsibility under the law. He is required to show that to your reasonable satisfaction—I say, to your reasonable satisfaction,—that it is a state of case where he is excusable for the act.[11]

Defining for the jury the term *insanity* the trial court stated:

> The term "insanity" as used in this defense, means such a perverted and deranged condition of the mental and moral faculties as to render a person incapable of distinguishing between right and wrong, or unconscious at the time of the nature of the act he is committing.[12]

In summary, the trial court further instructed the jury that there was a legal presumption that a criminal defendant is sane and therefore legally responsible for his criminal conduct. If, however, the defendant intends to claim insanity, he must raise the issue and also prove it to the reasonable satisfaction of the jury.

The principle issue in Davis's appeal, as expressed by the Supreme Court, was where the proof of the criminal act is evident:

> Can the jury properly return a verdict of guilty of the offense charged if upon the whole evidence . . . they have a reasonable doubt whether, at the time of killing, the accused was mentally competent to distinguish between right and wrong or to understand the nature of the act he was committing?[13]

Reviewing and quoting extensively from several other courts' opinions, including M'Naghten's case,[14] Justice Harlan made the following contemporarily ironical observations:

> No one, we assume, would wish either the courts or juries when trying a case of murder to disregard the humane principle, existing at common law and recognized in all the cases ending to support the charge of the court below, that "to make a complete crime cognizable by human laws, there must be both a will, and an act; and" as a vicious will without a vicious act is no cvil crime so, on the other hand, an unwarrantable act without a vicious will is no crime at all. So that to constitute a crime against human laws, there must be, first, a vicious will; and, secondly, an unlawful act consequent upon such vicious will.[15]

The Court's opinion continued by acknowledging that in some jurisdictions, consistent with the procedural aspects of the M'Naghten case, and the proposition that every man is presumed to be sane, the burden of proving one's insanity rests on the accused, presumably by a preponderance of the evidence. And, in some other jurisdictions, the defendant must prove his defense of insanity beyond a reasonable doubt.

Rejecting these procedural standards, Justice Harlan stressed that the mental capacity that usually makes one criminally responsible for one's conduct is essentially an element of an offense, just as any other substantive element of a crime. The Court conceded, however, that there is a presumption of sanity, and it is usually sufficient to prove this element. However, this presumption of sanity is "not a conclusive presumption, which the law upon grounds of public policy forbids to be overthrown or impaired by opposing proof."[16] Thus, the presumption of sanity is merely a "rebuttable presumption,"[17] that can "be absolutely and imperatively presumed to exist in every case."[18]

Syllogistically, according to Justice Harlan:

> To hold that such presumption [sanity] must absolutely control the jury until it is overthrown or impaired by evidence sufficient to establish the fact of insanity beyond all reasonable doubt or to the reasonable satisfaction of the jury [preponderance of the evidence?], is in effect to require him [the defendant] to establish his innocence, by proving that he is not guilty of the crime charged.[19]

And, because the burden of proof is never on an accused person to prove his innocence,

> [i]f the whole evidence, including that supplied by the presumption of sanity, does not include beyond reasonable doubt the hypothesis of insanity, of which some proof is adduced, the accused is entitled to an acquittal.[20]

because the evidence failed to prove satisfactorily that "his will and his acts . . . joined in perpetrating the murder charged."[21]

Concluding the opinion, Justice Harlan somewhat vaguely asserted that if evidence of a defendant's insanity is proffered, the presumption of sanity is equalized. Consequently, an element vital to the proof of criminal conduct is lacking: the defendant's mental capacity to commit the crime. As a result, a reasonable doubt as to an element of the crime therefore exists and unless contrary evidence, sufficient to prove the defendant's sanity beyond a reasonable doubt, is presented, "the rule is that the defendant is entitled to the benefit of that doubt and to an acquittal."[22]

## INSANITY DEFENSE REFORM

Section 401 of Chapter IV of the Comprehensive Crime Control Act of 1984 states: "This chapter may be cited as the 'Insanity Defense

Reform Act of 1984.'"[23] Thus, the first federal statutory recognition of the insanity defense, along with its clinical and procedural ramifications, began. The new federal legislation regarding the insanity defense substantively and procedurally revised the previous law as established in *Davis v United States*[24] in two principal areas: the definition of insanity and the burden of proof. The defense of insanity is now substantively defined as follows:

> It is an affirmative defense to a prosecution under any Federal Statute that, at the time of the commission of the acts constituting the offense, the defendant, as a result of a severe mental disease or defect, was unable to appreciate the nature and quality of the wrongfulness of his acts. Mental disease or defect does not otherwise constitute a defense.[25]

As an affirmative defense the burden of proof now rests on the shoulders of the defendant. This is similar to many states' laws regarding the insanity defense.[26] In contrast to most of those laws of insanity, however, is the extent of the defendant's responsibility in meeting that burden. Now, a defendant who raises an issue of his insanity at the time of the offense not only must prove it, he must prove it "by clear and convincing evidence."[27] And, that rather gross standard of proof is the load that will effectively hinder a successful presentation of the insanity defense, except in the most pronounced instances.

Is such a burden constitutional? Yes. Somewhat surprisingly, in 1952, Oregon had a law that required a defendant to prove his insanity beyond a reasonable doubt. The constitutionality of imposing the burden of proving such a defense beyond a reasonable doubt was questioned and found valid in *Leland v Oregon*.[28] The Supreme Court initially observed that the Oregon statute comported with the predominant opinion in 1864, when the statute was originally adopted, that because "most men are sane, a defendant must prove his insanity to avoid responsibility for his acts."[29] Furthermore, the Court said this was the prevailing rule in the United States when the Court decided *Davis v United States*.[30] The Court also noted that the decision in *Davis*[31] did not create a federal constitutional principle and commented that, although Oregon was then the only state that required proof of insanity beyond a reasonable doubt, "twenty states place the burden on the accused to establish his insanity by a preponderance of the evidence or some similar measure of persuasion."[32] Observing that more than one procedure may meet constitutional standards, the Court simply decided that it would not "interfere with Oregon's determination of its policy with respect to the burden of proof on the issue of sanity."[33]

Recently, in *United States v Amos*,[34] the Eighth Circuit Court of Appeals reviewed a Fifth Amendment due process challenge to the Insanity

Defense Reform Act[35] and similar to the foregoing comments concluded that, since requiring a defendant to prove insanity beyond a
reasonable doubt was constitutionally permissible,[36] then "[it] is axiomatic, therefore, that a lesser standard of proof, such as clear and
convincing standard, may be imposed."[37]

The Insanity Defense Reform Act of 1984[38] also survived a constitutional challenge in the Eleventh Circuit in *United States v Freeman*.[39]

The changes mandated by the Insanity Defense Reform Act of
1984[40] fundamentally altered the procedural processes established in
*Davis v United States*.[41] As is patently obvious, the insanity defense is now
an affirmative defense;[42] thus, the defendant must not only raise the
issue of his insanity, he must also assume the burden of proof and the
burden of persuasion. The conclusion in *Davis*[43] that the mental capacity
to commit a crime is but an element of the offense is surely logical, but
requiring the prosecuting agency to disprove one's claim of insanity
beyond a reasonable doubt is just as surely an impossible task at times.
Thus, the statutory role is reversed. Objectively speaking, imposing on a
defendant the responsibility of proving his insanity is not too great an
obligation. The statutory-required quantity and quality of proof necessary to accomplish that task is indeed another matter.

Most of the states in which insanity is an affirmative defense have
limited the extent of the defendant's burden of persuasion to a preponderance of the evidence.[44] Other states, however, have used less common terminology to describe the defendant's burden of persuasion. For
example, in Georgia an instruction that the defendant must prove his
insanity to the extent that it "satisfy the minds of the jury to a reasonable
certainty that the defense is true" was approved in *Bowden v State*.[45] Of
all the various standards used by the states, none, however, uses clear
and convincing.

## STANDARDS OF PROOF

The most traditional and common descriptions of proof essential to
a litigant prevailing are (1) preponderance of the evidence, (2) beyond a
reasonable doubt, and (3) clear and convincing. Familiarity with these
classic terms does not necessarily produce uniformity in interpretation.
As McCauliff commented in the Introduction to her authoritative article
on burdens of proof:

> Even with respect to these commonplace uses of burdens of proof, confusion
> exists about whether "burden of proof" refers to the objective quantum of
> evidence or to the subjective conviction of certainty in the mind of the trier of
> fact.[46]

The reason that a thorough understanding of these terms is essential is because their primary function is to guide the decision maker

through the process of weighing the evidence and thereby ultimately resolving a dispute. Without an adequate explanation, beyond the language of the terms, conscious deliberation with an appropriate focus is displaced by mere whim influenced by conjecture and speculation.

With very rare exceptions, the trial of any case, civil or criminal, is merely an exercise in recreating for the jury past events. A trial and the mental processes employed in the decision-making process is simply inductive reasoning that rests ultimately on the theory of probability. It is impossible for one to reach an unassailable conclusion as to past events—the best that can be hoped for is an opinion based on probabilities. In other words, just as "circumstantial evidence can never prove absolutely that a man is guilty"[47] and is only a persuasive tool, the trier of fact can only be persuaded by the evidence to a degree of self-generated probability. This degree of self-generated probability is the legal standard of proof that is supposed to guide the decision maker. There is, consequently, an inexorable joining of both quality and quantity of proof. Or, in other words, one is not only concerned with how reliable the evidence is, but to what degree is it probably true or not true.

The social and moral significance of certain conduct has historically established the standards of proof or the appropriate level of conviction for the trier of fact. For example, in most civil cases, the standard of proof that one must achieve to prevail is a preponderance of the evidence. Judicially approved instructions that elaborate on this terminology make it the easiest of the three to comprehend. The recent trend is for courts to interpret preponderance of the evidence based on logical deductions. In *Todd v Weilkle*,[48] for example, the Maryland court concluded that this standard of proof is achieved if the evidence, either direct or circumstantial, makes a disputed fact more likely so than not so. Similarly, in *Appeal of Tucker*,[49] preponderance of the evidence was interpreted to mean that a fact is more probably true than not true.

In civil cases in some states, such as Texas, preponderance of the evidence is defined in the court's instructions to the jury. In a manner different from those courts that view preponderance of the evidence as merely an exercise in probabilities, the Texas courts define its value by weight: the greater weight of credible evidence.

The unavoidable ambiguity present in the language that tries to classify any subjective standard is most apparent in what is perceived as the highest standard: beyond a reasonable doubt. This standard is commonly associated with the quantity and quality of evidence necessary to convict one of a criminal offense. The beyond-a-reasonable-doubt standard acquired a constitutional dimension in 1977, when the United States Supreme Court in *In Re Winship*,[50] stated:

> Lest there remain any doubt about the constitutional stature of the reasonable-doubt standard, we explicitly hold that the Due Process Clause protects

> the accused against conviction except upon proof beyond a reasonable doubt
> of every fact necessary to constitute the crime with which he is charged.[51]

The court arrived at this conclusion by weighing the interests of the accused, who could loose his freedom if convicted, the stigma attached to one being labeled a criminal, and the interest of a free society that demands a criminal justice system which insures that only the guilty be punished. This policy consideration was repeated in *Patterson v New York:*[52]

> The requirement of proof beyond a reasonable doubt in a criminal case is
> "bottomed on a fundamental value determination of our society that it is far
> worse to convict an innocent man than to let a guilty man go free."[53]

The principles that form the basis for imposing such a standard in criminal cases are honorable, but they do little, if anything, to give adequate guidance to the factfinder as to when and at what conceptual point beyond a reasonable doubt is reached. Most courts have done very little to alleviate this problem. In Texas, for example, the Court of Criminal Appeals—the state's highest appellate court for criminal cases—has for over 100 years consistently adhered to a rather unique Texas legal principle that beyond a reasonable doubt should not be defined for a jury, because "reasonable doubt needs no amplification or attempt on the part of the trial court to explain the term."[54] And, as the Texas Court of Criminal Appeals more recently held: "[I]n Texas only a nondefinitional charge on 'reasonable doubt' is normally given in a criminal case."[55]

Principally because of *Holland v United States*,[56] the policy of defining and thus, it is hoped, explaining beyond a reasonable doubt in federal courts is converse to the policy of the Texas courts. In *Holland*,[57] the Supreme Court approved the following definition of "beyond a reasonable doubt":

> the kind of doubt that would make a reasonable person hesitate to act in the
> conduct of their more serious and important personal affairs.[58]

This same instruction or one essentially similar has been approved by every circuit Court of Appeals.[59]

Perhaps it can be argued that such a definition of reasonable doubt merely exacerbates the difficulty of understanding what the standard really means and is ineffective in answering the question "How convinced must we be to convict?" It does, nevertheless, employ common language rather than subjectively inspired legal jargon to assist the factfinder's effort to reach a proper decision.

The remaining standard of proof is "clear and convincing evidence" and it is, as are "preponderance of the evidence" and "beyond a reasonable doubt," enclosed within a shield of ambiguity and vagueness, which makes the term of little value to a jury. On the whole, the acceptable variations of interpretation of the words that make up the term are the sources of the difficulty. It has been correctly observed that:

> [A] word is vague if the things *habitually* characterized by it are not sharply distinguished from those things which are *habitually* denied characterization—with the consequence that for some things falling within its range of application the use of the word is indeterminate.[60]

For instance, and abstracting a word from the term, does "clear" mean "visible, with clarity," or "unobstructed"? And what about "convincing"—the word merely begs the question. In fact, is not the answer used in the question? These are words that are indeterminate and combining them does not create anything even approaching absoluteness.

As a standard of proof, clear and convincing gained both its recent popularity and notoriety principally as a result of *Addington v Texas*.[61] The Supreme Court, contrasting the "individuals interest in not being involuntarily confined indefinitely and the state's interest in committing the emotionally disturbed,"[62] rejected preponderance of the evidence as an acceptable standard to justify an involuntarly, indefinite commitment.

On the other hand, relative to beyond a reasonable doubt being the proper standard, as *Addington* obviously argued, the Court made essentially four particularly relevant observations. First, civil commitments are not utilized by the state as a punitive exercise against its citizens. Second, beyond a reasonable doubt is a very special term, both symbolically and semantically, and is usually reserved for criminal cases. Therefore, "we should hesitate to apply it too broadly or casually in noncriminal cases."[63] Third, an individual's interest in remaining free from an erroneous involuntary commitment, and society desiring to avoid an erroneous involuntary commitment, is not as great as the similar contrasting interests in a criminal case. Fourth, because psychiatric diagnoses are replete with subjective analysis that render definite conclusions about a person extremely suspect, "there is a serious question as to whether a state could ever prove beyond a reasonable doubt that an individual is both mentally ill and likely to be dangerous."[64]

Somewhere in between is where we need to be, said the Court. So, the Court approved the standard of clear and convincing because it is a "middle level of burden of proof [standard of proof] that strikes a fair balance between the rights of the individual and the legitimate concerns of the state."[65] Other than noting that clear and convincing is by necessity quantitatively more than a preponderance of the evidence, the Court made no effort to express what clear and convincing actually means.

Most of the state courts that have reviewed this standard have themselves done little more than note the obvious—it is more than a preponderance of the evidence, but less than beyond a reasonable doubt.[66]

However, although also abundant with ambiguity that probably invites speculation, the Texas Supreme Court defined the clear-and-convincing-evidence standard as follows:

> [T]hat measure or degree of proof which will produce in the mind of the trier of fact a firm belief or conviction as to the truth of the allegations sought to be established.[67]

All the efforts to define further any standard of proof will always be plagued by limitations of connotation inherent in the English language. Therefore, attempting to prove the existence of any fact necessarily incorporates both the credibility and reliability of the evidence. Or, how likely is it? Or, is it possible? Or, is it probable? And, if probable, how probable? And, that is what must be confronted. As previously stated, the burden is now on the defendant who asserts the insanity defense to produce evidence of his insanity and persuade the factfinder that he was insane at the time of the offense. But, the question still remains: how much is clear and convincing evidence of insanity? As is obvious, words have provided little, if any, guidance. Because of the impossibility of the language to deal adequately with the problem, the use of another discipline may be appropriate.

## PSEUDOMATHEMATICAL DEVICES

Although reducing standards of proof to mathematical values, more specifically percentages, is arbitrary and maybe even capricious, it appears, at the very least, as a more objective exercise than mentally strolling through a myriad of words that possess no inherent qualities beyond their own connotation. A number of surveys were made in an effort to equate the escalating standards of proof with escalating percentages, with absolute truth being given the unobtainable value of 100%. The most well-known of these surveys was made in conjunction with the case of *United States v Fatico*.[68] In this survey, ten judges, all within the Eastern District of New York, were requested to give their opinions as to the percentage of probability that should be associated with these four standards of proof: (1) preponderance of the evidence, (2) clear and convincing evidence, (3) clear, unequivocal and convincing evidence, and (4) beyond a reasonable doubt. The third standard, clear, unequivocal and convincing, was recognized as a variation of clear and convincing by the Supreme Court in *Addington v Texas*.[69]

The result of this one survey was noteworthy for a number of reasons, but particularly because it confirmed the elusive nature of what clear and convincing evidence actually is. For example, all ten judges responded that preponderance of the evidence was numerically just slightly in excess of 50%. All but one judge viewed beyond a reasonable doubt as at lest 80%. Three judges valued it as exactly 80%, and two judges valued it as exactly 90%. One judge rated beyond a reasonable doubt as 95%.

Combining clear and convincing with clear, unequivocal and convincing caused a greater variation in numerical values to be realized. The lowest percentage attributed to clear and convincing was 60% (three judges), and one of those valued it as an indeterminate 60% to 70%. Another respondent calculated it as 65%, while another, being either convinced or facetious, equated the standard with 67%. Two other respondents gave the standard a 70+%, while one other suggested 75%. Two of the judges were quite clear in their responses: "Standard is elusive and unhelpful;"[70] "Cannot estimate numerically."[71] The values given to clear, unequivocal and convincing were not significantly different, except one of the judges thought this was a higher standard (90%) than beyond a reasonable doubt (85%). The obviously frightening aspect of this last response is that much of the public may interpret the language in a similarly erroneous fashion.

Using this survey as a preliminary format, McCauliff, in 1981, in preparation for an article on burden of proof,[72] sent a similar questionnaire to all active, senior, and retired federal judges, including those on the Supreme Court. Of those sent the questionnaire, 170 assigned the standard of clear and convincing evidence a numerical value. The great majority of those judges (112) rated the clear-and-convincing standard as 70% or 80%. Only four of these judges gave the standard less than 60% (50% and 55%). On the other hand, a same number of respondents gave it a value of over 90%, and one of those judges said "that the standard" is the equivalent of 100%.

The actual percentages given to the three primary standards of proof in either survey are really irrelevant. What is relevant and significant is the substantial difference between the values given preponderance of the evidence and clear and convincing, and conversely, the little difference between clear and convincing and beyond a reasonable doubt. Notice, in Judge Weinstein's survey the greatest percentage given preponderance of the evidence was only 51%, while most respondents gave it the nonspecific 50+%. Clear and convincing was in most instances minimally valued at least 20% higher. Whereas, the normal difference between clear and convincing and beyond a reasonable doubt in the same survey was just 10%.

The obvious import of these differences in values is most apparent when viewed in the context of the new federal insanity defense. As was previously noted, those states that designate the insanity defense as an affirmative defense establish the standard of the defendant's burden at a preponderance of the evidence. Assuming—and this is a great assumption—that the values in the survey are reflective of society's perception of the standards of proof, in all states a defendant claiming the insanity defense must present proof of his insanity to an extent just slightly beyond 50%. Engaging in this same assumption, under the new federal standard, the defendant asserting the insanity defense must prove his insanity, by an average of both surveys, to 75% of absolute. To employ a trite metaphor, just tipping the scales of justice (preponderance of the evidence) is substantially easier and more readily achievable than weighing them down (clear and convincing evidence).

The insanity defense carries with it a rather engaging paradox that recognizes a civilized society's abhorrence with brutal, unprovoked conduct: the more bizarre and less "normal" the criminal conduct, the greater the chance of one's successfully urging the insanity defense. Or, as the noted columnist George Will observed:

> The most morally indefensible crimes are becoming the most legally defendable . . . the more odious the crime—premeditated or spontaneous—the more reasonable doubt there is about the person's sanity at the time.[73]

But this is not really surprising. As the Supreme Court in *Addington v Texas*[74] correctly observed:

> At one time or another every person exhibits some abnormal behavior which might be perceived by some as symptomatic of a mental or emotional disorder.[75]

When, however, this less than what society judges as normal behavior manifests itself in legally impermissible conduct, then the extent of the disorder becomes legally and socially relevant. The insanity defense is without question as much a moral valuation as it is a legal issue. Therefore, the comparative level of the defendant's immoral conduct to his mental status is the ultimate resolution of the legal responsibility question.

What then is the practical value of the insanity defense in the federal criminal justice system? Very simply—not much. The insanity defense weathered the Congressional onslaught that followed the Hinckley verdict.[76] But, in great part, owing to the standard of proof legislatively engrafted on the law, it is substantially impaired. Objectively, requiring the government to prove a criminal defendant's sanity beyond a reasonable doubt was an awesome and often unachievable task; similarly, requiring a criminal defendant to prove his insanity by clear and convincing evidence, except in the most pronounced circumstances, will also prove to be a heavy burden that cannot be carried successfully. The cry for reforming the insanity defense did not go unanswered by Congress. Its answer was unfortunately too loud.

# REFERENCES


1. *The Times* (London), Mar. 6, 1843, at 5, col. 6.
2. *The Washington Post,* June 22, 1982, at 1, col.1.
3. *The Times* (London), Mar. 14, 1843, at 2, col. 5.
4. For example, in 1980, of the 80,000 criminal cases heard in Texas district courts, only 16 persons were found not guilty by reason of insanity. *See* Farabee and Sparley: The new insanity law in Texas: Reliable testimony and judicial review of release. 24 *So Tex Law J* 671, 672 (1983).
5. 18 U.S.C. §17.
6. 160 U.S. 469 (1895).
7. 160 U.S. 469.
8. 160 U.S. at 475.
9. 160 U.S. at 475.
10. 160 U.S. at 478.
11. 160 U.S. at 476–477.
12. 160 U.S. at 477–478.
13. 160 U.S. at 477–478.
14. 10 Clark & F. 199 (1843).
15. 160 U.S. 469 (1895).
16. 160 U.S. at 486.
17. 160 U.S. at 486.
18. 160 U.S. at 486.
19. 160 U.S. at 487.
20. 160 U.S. at 488.
21. 160 U.S. at 488.
22. 160 U.S. at 492.
23. 18 U.S.C. §17.
24. 160 U.S. 469 (1895).
25. 18 U.S.C. §17(a) (Supp. 1987).
26. Annot. 17 *A.L.R.* 3rd. 146 (1968).
27. 18 U.S.C. §17(b) (Supp. 1987).
28. 343 U.S. 790 (1952).
29. 343 U.S. at 796.
30. 160 U.S. 469 (1895).
31. 160 U.S. 469.
32. 343 U.S. at 798.
33. 343 U.S. at 799–800.
34. 803 F.2d 419 (8th Cir. 1986).
35. 18 U.S.C. §17.
36. 343 U.S. 790.
37. 803 F.2d 419.
38. 18 U.S.C. §17.
39. 804 F.2d 1574 (11th Cir. 1986).
40. 18 U.S.C. §17.
41. 160 U.S. 469.
42. 18 U.S.C. §17(a) (Supp. 1987).
43. 160 U.S. 469.
44. C. Torcia: *Wharton's Criminal Evidence,* 14th ed., §25 1985.
45. 106 S.E. 575 (Ga. 1921).
46. McCauliff MA: Burdens of proof: Degrees of belief, quanta of evidence, of constitutional guarantees? 35 *Vand Law Rev* 1293 (1982).

47. Corbett EJ: *Classical Rhetoric*. New York, Oxford University Press, 1971, p 77.
48. 376 A.2d 104 (Md. 1977).
49. 538 P.2d 626 (Okla. App. 1975).
50. 397 U.S. 358 (1970).
51. 397 U.S. at 361.
52. 432 U.S. 197 (1977).
53. 432 U.S. at 208.
54. *Whitson v State*, 495 S.W.2d 944, 946 (Tex. Crim. App. 1973).
55. *Young v State*, 648 S.W.2d (Tex. Crim. App. 1983).
56. 348 U.S. 121 (1954).
57. 348 U.S. 121.
58. 348 U.S. at 148.
59. *Hankins v State*, 646 S.W.2d 191, 212 (Tex. Crim. App. 1981) (Miller, J., concurring and dissenting).
60. Nagel E: Some reflections on the use of language in the natural sciences, in *Teleology Revisited and Other Essays in the Philosophy and History of Science*. New York, Columbia University Press, 1979, p 51.
61. 441 U.S. 418 (1972).
62. 441 U.S. at 425.
63. 441 U.S. at 428.
64. 441 U.S. at 429.
65. 441 U.S. at 431.
66. *In the Interest of C. M.*, 596 S.W.2d 846 (Tex. 1980).
67. 596 S.W.2d at 847.
68. 458 F. Supp. 388 (E.D.N.Y. 1978).
69. 441 U.S. 418.
70. 458 F. Supp. at 410.
71. 458 F. Supp. at 410.
72. *See* McCauliff, *supra* note 46.
73. "Nightline", Ted Koppel (narr.), ABC News, June 22, 1982.
74. 441 U.S. 418.
75. 441 U.S. at 427.
76. Sixteen bills filed to revise insanity defense, *Washington Times*, July 1, 1982, at 1, col. 1.

**7**

# The American Psychiatric Association Insanity Rule—A Metaphysical Subtlety

ABRAHAM L. HALPERN

> *Laws are made for men of ordinary understanding and should, therefore, be construed by the ordinary rules of common sense. Their meaning is not to be sought for in metaphysical subtleties, which may make anything mean everything or nothing at pleasure.*
>
> Thomas Jefferson[1]

## INTRODUCTION

The acquittal of John W. Hinckley, Jr., by reason of insanity in June, 1982, although it aroused a public outcry against the exculpatory insanity rule and provoked widespread criticism of the psychiatric profession, did not further the drive for abolition of the insanity defense. On the contrary, the Hinckley verdict served as a stimulus for organizations

Reprinted (with revisions) with permission from P. B. McGuigan and J. S. Pascale (Eds.), *Crime and Punishment in Modern America*. Washington, DC: The Institute for Government and Politics of the Free Congress Research and Education Foundation, 1986.

---

**ABRAHAM L. HALPERN** • Department of Psychiatry, New York Medical College, Valhalla, NY 10595; Department of Psychiatry, United Hospital Medical Center, Port Chester, NY 10573.

93

and individuals that favored retention of the defense to graft the concept onto state and federal laws more firmly than ever before.

Prior to Hinckley's attempt to assassinate the President of the United States on March 30, 1981, the movement to abolish the insanity defense, although not notably successful, was advancing with deliberate speed. A bill,[2] providing for the total elimination of the insanity plea yet permitting psychiatric testimony on the issue of criminal intent (*mens rea*), was the result of extensive study by the staff of the attorney general of Idaho.[3] The state of Montana had severely narrowed the insanity rule, virtually abolishing the plea.[4] Articles in popular magazines argued strongly for abolition.[5] Legislation had been introduced in New York State to repeal the insanity defense statute.[6] The New York State Department of Mental Hygiene had submitted a report to the Governor recommending abandonment of the insanity defense and its substitution with a comprehensive diminished capacity rule.[7] A "Great Debate" on the abolition of the insanity defense was a featured event at the Ninth Annual Meeting of the American Academy of Psychiatry and the Law in October, 1978, and a "Scientific Debate" was scheduled for the 135th Annual Meeting of the American Psychiatric Association in May, 1982. Finally, just before the assassination attempt, a bill[8], introduced in the United States Congress by Senator Orrin G. Hatch, would have severely limited the insanity defense by permitting exculpation of a mentally disordered defendant only if he lacked the state of mind required as an element of the offense charged. Like the Idaho law, in the unlikely event that a still dangerous mentally ill individual were acquitted, this legislation, because it did not provide for a federal postacquittal confinement system, would have looked to state commitment statutes to hospitalize such a person. In other words, the Hatch bill would not have created "an insanity defense industry within the Federal Government",[9] in contradistinction to all the post-Hinckley insanity bills introduced in the Congress, including the Insanity Defense Reform Act of 1984, which was signed into law by President Reagan on October 12, 1984.[10]

With the acquittal of John Hinckley, advocates of the insanity defense mounted a powerful, coordinated, and highly publicized campaign[11-14] to preserve the defense in some form. A spate of articles [15-18] appeared in the professional literature in the ensuing two years, proclaiming the moral basis to the existence of the insanity defense over the centuries, even equating abolition of the insanity defense with holding a two-year-old child criminally responsible for its misconduct.[19] Several states avoided the issue of the elimination of the insanity defense by enacting legislation,[20-24] which was patterned after laws previously passed in Michigan,[25] Illinois,[26] and Indiana,[27] adopting an additional verdict of "Guilty but mentally ill" while retaining the insanity defense, indeed, requiring, that the insanity plea be asserted before the guilty-but-mentally-ill plea could be considered. Opposition to abolition reached its zenith when the American Psychiatric Association (APA), in a personal communication[28] to every member of Congress, attacked the *mens rea* approach, which was represented by the Hatch bill mentioned above, and warned that such legislation could "result in less protection for the general public." The reasoning of the APA in this regard[29–30] is incomprehensible in view of the fact that conviction, not acquittal, is the almost inevitable outcome when the *mens rea* standard is used in cases of mentally disordered offenders charged with violent crime. It should be noted, moreover, that the *mens rea* approach, found by legal scholars[31–34] to be rooted in sound legal principles, has been endorsed by the American Medical Association[35] and, in a recent case decided by the Supreme Court of Montana,[36] declared to be in accord with constitutional requirements.

## CHANGING THE INSANITY RULE: A DISTINCTION WITHOUT A DIFFERENCE

Prior to promulgation of the "American Psychiatric Association Statement on the Insanity Defense" in December, 1982,[37] I had demonstrated in several articles[38–41] that nothing short of abolition of the insanity defense could permit a rational approach to the handling of mentally disordered offenders who come to trial. I pointed out that regardless of the legal standard to be followed, actual practice proved that the most liberal rule could be contracted (resulting in conviction) and the narrowest rule expanded (resulting in acquittal), depending on the whim or conscience of the factfinder. The use of the insanity defense in many jurisdictions over the years, no matter what the language of the insanity test might be, substantiates my view that no insanity rule is amenable to construction by the ordinary rules of common sense. At a hearing before the Committee on the Judiciary of the United States Senate on August 2, 1982, I testified[42] that there is no place to go in the quest for a new insanity formulation, no matter how narrow; that every insanity definition is irrelevant and essentially meaningless; and that abolition of the insanity defense is the only rational path. I now assert even more strongly that the exculpatory insanity concept is inapplicable to a rational administration of criminal justice. To illustrate the validity of my position, I will offer examples of how the insanity rule is employed by psychiatrists and psychologists presenting expert testimony on behalf of criminal defendants pleading insanity. First, however, let me stress that the most ardent proponents of the insanity defense will acknowledge that the wording of the test is irrelevant. Let us examine, for example, the statements of several representatives of the American Psychiatric Association who testified at a hearing before the Subcommittee on Criminal Law on June 30, 1982,[43] a few weeks before I addressed the Senate Judiciary Committee:

> DR. LOREN H. ROTH [*Chairperson, APA Commission on Judicial Action, member of the APA Insanity Defense Work Group, and principal author of the APA Statement on the Insanity Defense*]: Senator Specter, there is no difference between the various legal standards. Now, most legal scholars believe—for example, Mr Goldstein was opposed to the ALI [American Law Institute] formulation, believing that all testimony which can be introduced under ALI can also be introduced under *M'Naghten,* and that as a practical matter it does not matter. I think that this is the experience of most forensic psychiatrists.[44]

> DR. SEYMOUR HALLECK [*one of America's most distinguished forensic psychiatrists and the 1983 winner of the APA's Isaac Ray Award*]: The jury will probably come to similar conclusions, whatever the standard is.[45]

> DR. ROTH: I think one standard in practice in the great majority of cases will translate into the other standard.[46]

> DR. ALLAN BEIGEL [*Chairperson, APA Joint Commission on Government Relations and member of the Insanity Defense Work Group*]: I think it is my personal opinion that changing the standard will not change either the extent or limits of our expertise.[47]

> DR. ROTH: I believe that the idea to infinitely refine the standard, while satisfying to us as rational types who want neat categories, does not necessarily come to the final solution.[48]

At the subcommittee hearing, Dr. Alan A. Stone [*Chairperson, APA Council on Governmental Policy and Law and ex officio member of the Insanity Defense Work Group*] proposed an insanity standard that would abolish the insanity defense if factfinders were to follow it literally:

> I make this not as my perfect solution: I just bring it to you as a consideration. One could simply alter the ALI by changing two words. "A person is not responsible for criminal conduct if at the time of such conduct, as a result of severe"–I have added "severe"—"mental disease of defect, he lacks entirely the capacity either to appreciate," et cetera.
> 
> So, all I have done is put in "severe" and say "lacks entirely." Now, it seems to me that comes close to what you have been reaching for, Senator, although I think you want to move in the direction of totally different language. I think what I have done captures the sentiments you have been expressing, if not the exact words.[49]

The futility of changing the wording of the insanity rule was made clear in the following verbal exchange at the subcommittee hearing:

> SEN. ARLEN SPECTER: Well the issue that we have to decide is not what the jury is going to find, but what the judge is going to say the law is. Would it be adequate, in your judgment, if the judge said "If you find that the mother

> knew she was killing her child and intended to kill her child, then you may convict; if on the other hand, you find that the mother thought she was killing the devil, then you may acquit by reason of insanity."?
>
> DR. HALLECK: My guess is that what would happen is what happened before the American Law Institute ruling became more prevalent, and that is that people played games with the word "know." There was argument as to "know" intellectually or "know" emotionally, and good attorneys and good psychiatrists were able to convince juries that she did not really know that she was killing the child.[50]

Notwithstanding the above, the Insanity Defense Work Group recommended, and the American Psychiatric Association adopted, the following standard in the belief that it permits "relevant psychiatric testimony to be brought to bear in the great majority of cases where criminal responsibility is at issue"[51]:

> A person charged with a criminal offense should be found not guilty by reason of insanity if it is shown that as a result of mental disease or mental retardation he was unable to appreciate the wrongfulness of his conduct at the time of the offense.
>
> As used in this standard, the terms mental disease or mental retardation include only those severely abnormal mental conditions that grossly and demonstrably impair a person's perception or understanding of reality and that are not attributable primarily to the voluntary ingestion of alcohol or other psychoactive substances.

The insanity standard employed in the Hinckley trial was the ALI formulation which includes the so-called volitional rule:

> A person is not responsible for criminal conduct if at the time of such conduct as a result of mental disease or defect he lacks substantial capacity to appreciate the wrongfulness of his conduct, or to *conform his conduct* to the requirements of law.[52] (italics added)

The APA formulation purports to eliminate this prong, but, as the statement itself indicates:

> In practice there is considerable overlap between a psychotic person's defective understanding or appreciation and his ability to control his behavior. Most psychotic persons who fail a volitional test for insanity will also fail a cognitive-type test when such a test is applied to their behavior, thus rendering the volitional test superfluous in judging them.[53]

Thus, the claimed narrowing of the insanity rule is without substance. The APA standard, presumably designed to make it extremely difficult for defendants such as Hinckley to escape a guilty verdict, would neither have altered the testimony nor the result had that standard been applied at this trial. The same Washington psychiatrist would have testified that Hinckley had a serious mental illness (schizotypal personality disorder with psychosis) that drove him to shoot the President and deprived him of the ability to obey the law or to appreciate the wrongfulness of his conduct.[54] The same Harvard Medical School radiologist would have said that brain scans show Hinckley's brain is slightly shrunken and has "more folds and ventricles [*sic*] than is usual in people his age," and that this suggests organic brain disease.[55] The same Yale Medical School psychologist would have pointed out that Hinckley knew "in his head" that he was doing wrong when he shot President Reagan but was "too insane to appreciate this emotionally." He also would have testified that standard psychological tests had shown that Hinckley was plagued by extreme, longstanding depression that was part of a serious mental illness. According to this psychologist, in addition to major depressive disorder, Hinckley had borderline schizophrenia and paranoid personality disorder.[56] The same University of Maryland professor of psychiatry would have told the jury that Hinckley suffered from process schizophrenia, at least since 1976, an illness that becomes increasingly severe with age, and involved, in this case, gradual withdrawal from social contacts into an inner world dominated by delusions that had no basis in fact, eccentric or bizarre thoughts, and irrational impulses to commit violent acts.[57]

## THE PSYCHIATRIC WITNESS TESTIFIES

The psychiatrist who testifies on behalf of a patient–defendant who is charged with serious crime will invariably see the mental disorder as "severe," rendering the defendant not responsible, from a psychiatric standpoint, for his conduct. The words "know," "appreciate," "as a result of," and "at the time of" are no bar to the defense psychiatrist's seeking to explain the defendant's entitlement to exculpation. Every insanity trial, before and after Hinckley, shows this to be true. Nor will legislative changes[58] designed to prohibit an expert witness from testifying "as to whether the defendant did or did not have the mental state or condition constituting an element of the crime charged or of a defense thereto," as urged by the APA,[30,37] the National Mental Health Association,[59] and the American Bar Association,[60] significantly interfere with the psychiatrists and the psychologists who present their testimony in their customary fashion. As stated by the *New York Times*,[61] "In the last 30 years, doctors and lawyers have given juries their views about the entire personality and won't easily return to a legal straitjacket."

A striking example of testimony offered by a psychiatrist with a genuine concern for his seriously mentally ill patient-defendant is that of Dr. Robert L. Custer, a member of the DSM-III Advisory Committee on Impulse Control Disorders and this country's most highly recognized expert in the treatment of pathological gambling. The following collo-quy took place in a jury trial in which the defendant asserted an insanity plea under the *M'Naghten* rule[62]:

> Q. Doctor, is he by virtue of the condition under which he labors at the time that he drew the specific checks before you incapable or capable of dis-tinguishing right from wrong as regard that check?
>
> A. Well, here's a man who was a law enforcement officer, who knows the law well, who knows about right and wrong but a man who is in a desperate strait. He is under tremendous amount of stress at that point, does not even consid-er right and wrong. I don't think that becomes part of his thinking process. His process then is to survive. He's losing his job, his family, his children, his reputation, everything is going down. So he functions this way, in an irra-tional way to which his judgment is that impaired.
>
> Q. You say, Doctor, that he does not consider right from wrong. Can he consider the distinction between right and wrong at that juncture?
>
> A. I think he's on automatic at that point. I don't think thinking becomes a process. This man is acting only on impulse. His impulse control is totally gone. He functions. He reacts. He does not use the thinking process to enter into it so a value judgment is not placed at that point.
>
> Q. Is he capable of making a value judgment at that point?
>
> A. No.
>
> Q. Doctor, does Michael accord with the classic pattern of compulsive gam-bling as it has been defined by the Board of American Psychiatric Association in this regard?
>
> A. Yes, he does. He meets all the criteria.

In another case,[63] in a jurisdiction adhering to the American Law Institute rule, Dr. Custer testified as follows:

> Q. Dr. Custer, in your opinion, is pathological gambling a mental disease or defect?
>
> A. I would call it a disease. I don't feel it is a defect, which I consider more something within the central nervous system that isn't present or has been damaged.
>
> Q. Do you believe that a person who is a pathological gambler can be ren-dered incapable of substantially conforming their conduct to the require-ments of law?
>
> A. Since they cannot conform their conduct to standards of law.
>
> Q. At least in some cases?
>
> A. In the vast majority of them.
>
> Q. Okay.
>
> A. It depends upon the stage at which they are in. If it is in the early stage, I think they still can. Certainly in the late stage, they have lost that control.
>
> Q. All right. Do you think that persons who are pathological gamblers and incapable of conforming their conduct are equally incapable of resisting activity like embezzlement or fraud?

*A.* No, I don't feel they can resist it because they have to gamble and they have to obtain money in order to do that.

*Q.* Dr. Custer, in the DSM-III, the term mental disorder is used. Do you agree with the statement that mental disorder, as used in DSM-III, is the legal equivalent of mental disease or defect?

*A.* Yes. I feel it is equivalent to disease, not to defect.

*Q.* You have stated your opinion that some pathological gamblers are incapable of conforming their conduct substantially to the requirements of law, is that correct?

*A.* That's correct.

*Q.* Has that always been your opinion?

*A.* No, it wasn't my opinion when I first started treating them about ten years ago. I certainly didn't know what it was at that point, and I had never given it that much consideration, but it was only after I had probably treated about 25 of them that I realized I was dealing with people that actually began to think in a delusional way. Then I realized that they weren't able to control it, but it takes a while to understand this problem.

## BATTLE OF THE EXPERTS

In my view, the logical inconsistencies and the distortions that are part and parcel of every insanity rule, and the damage to the psychiatric profession, are best exemplified not by the ordinary "not guilty by reason of insanity" case, but by the 90% of insanity trials that result in a guilty verdict, by the rare case of feigned insanity, and by the increasingly common "split verdict" case.

The following cases in which the insanity plea was unsuccessful are representative of what appears from time to time in newspapers throughout the country, papers not given to sensationalistic reporting. The expert witnesses involved are in the private practice of psychiatry, some of them on medical school faculties, and are generally held in high regard in the psychiatric community.

## CASE 1

### MAN CONVICTED IN HEADLESS BARTENDER MURDER[64]

Charles Dingle, age 25, was convicted of second-degree murder, first-degree rape, second-degree kidnapping and first-degree robbery. He had been accused of shooting a bartender, raping a topless dancer and forcing a woman to cut the bartender's head off. After a month-long, non-jury trial, the judge took about 20 minutes to deliberate before rendering the verdict. Defense attorneys had presented psychiatric testimony that Dingle didn't know what he was doing when he shot Anthony Cummings, a bar owner who had asked him to leave Herbie's Bar on Jamaica Avenue in

Queens. After shooting Cummings, he handcuffed the bartender's wife, Paula, bound a barmaid and raped a topless dancer. Later, when the bar manager arrived for work, he learned that she was a licensed mortician and ordered her to remove the bullet from Cummings' head. When that failed, he ordered her to remove the head, which she did with a kitchen knife and two steak knives. Dingle later released the barmaid and dancer, called a cab and tied up the driver. He then drove into Manhattan with Mrs. Cummings, the bar manager and a box containing the bartender's head. The two women sought help after Dingle fell asleep and he was arrested a short time later inside the cab.

## CASE 2

### SUSPECT IN TEXAS NOW SAYS HE KILLED 360 PEOPLE NATIONWIDE[65]

Henry Lee Lucas was on trial for the rape and murder of an unidentified young hitchhiker whose body was found near Georgetown in Central Texas. He had pleaded guilty of one Texas slaying and was convicted of another. His lawyers insist he is not guilty by reason of insanity and also contend he was at work in Jacksonville, Florida, when the Georgetown murder occurred. With the jurors out of the courtroom, the prosecutors played a videotaped interview showing Lucas puffing on a cigarette, calmly relating that he had shot, stabbed, burned, beaten, strangled, hung and "crucified" his victims, and that some had been "fileted like fish." Mr. Lucas said he had killed an estimated 360 people in the United States, more than 60 of them in Texas

## CASE 3

### JURY REJECTS 'FUMES' DEFENSE[66]

A Massachusetts jury rendered a guilty verdict in a first-degree murder trial of a gardener who claimed he was driven insane by lawn chemicals. The defendant maintained that exposure to organophosphate pesticides had clouded his ability to tell right from wrong. He did not deny that he had become angry and choked the woman when she discovered him urinating in her yard. His insanity claim was supported by a psychiatrist's testimony, but a physician testifying for the prosecutor introduced blood tests that showed no evidence of chemical intoxication.

## CASE 4

### OHIO PHYSICIAN'S LAWYER CONCEDES 22 RAPES[67]

Dr. Edward F. Jackson, Jr. pleaded not guilty and not guilty by reason of insanity to 96 charges, including forced sex with 22 women, one of them a nun, and 38 other felonious acts. "We acknowledge to you that Dr. Jackson committed the acts for which he has been charged," the defense lawyer,

John Bowen, told prospective jurors. "Very frankly, I would describe him as a Dr. Jekyll–Mr. Hyde. I contend he is a sick man." Dr. Jackson's indictment the previous summer freed another man, a look-alike with the same last name, William Bernard Jackson, who had served five years in Ohio prisons for rapes now ascribed to the doctor.

## CASE 5

### EX-RESIDENT APPEALING KIDNAPPING CHARGES[68]

Christine Gladstone was convicted by a county jury of second-degree kidnapping, first-degree criminal use of a firearm, and third-degree criminal possession of a deadly weapon. The defense attorney is basing an appeal, in part, on the fact that the prosecution failed to counter testimony by two psychiatrists who said that the defendant was not responsible for her actions. Dr. X, a Syracuse psychiatrist, called to the witness stand by the defense, testified that Mrs. Gladstone suffered from an "atypical psychosis." He said the mental disorder would affect her capacity to understand and appreciate the nature and consequences of her actions. The prosecutor considered the testimony by the defense psychiatrist to be so absurd and outrageous that he did not bother to waste the taxpayer's money in employing his own experts, relying instead on cross-examination to controvert the defense psychiatrist's testimony. In his summation, he commented as follows: "I think the only thing they have proved is that witchcraft is alive and well in the 20th century." He asked the jury at one point, referring to the psychiatrist's testimony: "Does anybody believe this slop? You'd do a hell of a lot better to bring in some tribal warrior and have him rip open and read the entrails of a sheep."

## CASE 6

### KILLER WHO CITED VIETNAM TRAUMA CONVICTED[69]

A Vietnam veteran who contended that delayed stress from his war experience had caused him to strangle and stab his fiancée to death was convicted of first-degree murder by a New Hampshire jury. The jury heard three weeks of testimony which included defense experts who said post-traumatic stress disorder had caused the murder and a prosecution expert who said the disorder was not involved in the killing. The prosecution argued that while the defendant was troubled, he knew what he was doing when he strangled the woman by hand, then used an extension cord, and later stabbed her seven times in the heart. Defense witnesses said the smell of rice from a nearby Chinese restaurant might have reminded the defendant of being at Khe Sanh in Vietnam. Another veteran of the battle testified that the smell of rice cooking wafted into the camp just before enemy attacks. "He was so brittle and so fragile that all he needed was the stimulus of the environment, the smells," said Dr. Y, one of the defense experts. "I believe that if it was not for the post-traumatic stress disorder, this would not have happened."

## FAKED INSANITY

On occasion (all too frequently), publicity is given to a case of faked insanity, invariably making a laughingstock of the legal system and the psychiatric profession.

### CASE 8

### INSANITY PLEA UPHELD ALTHOUGH ILLNESS WAS FAKED[70,71]

A New York State appeals court ruled that a man who escaped prosecution for 16 Brooklyn robberies by faking a mental disorder can keep the rewards of his fiction because prosecutors failed to detect it until after they consented to his insanity plea. Samuel Lockett had contended that he was not criminally responsible due to his inability to appreciate the wrongfulness of his acts because of a post-traumatic stress disorder resulting from his experiences in Vietnam as a member of the United States Air Force. Based on extensive psychiatric reports which showed that he was in fact suffering from a post-traumatic stress disorder due to his service in Vietnam (at least six different psychiatrists examined him), he was adjudicated not guilty by reason of mental disease or defect. Subsequently, his military records were obtained; they showed that he had been an accounting clerk at an Air Force base in Texas during the entire time he was supposedly in combat in Indochina from 1972 to 1974. The appellate court ruled that although acceptance of Lockett's plea of "Not responsible by reason of mental disease or defect" may have been based on erroneous information given to the psychiatrists by Lockett himself, no legal authorization exists to vacate the plea and Lockett's subsequent commitment to a secure psychiatric facility. The state's highest court, however, eventually overturned the lower appeals court ruling and ordered a new trial on the grounds that he had never been subjected to the risk of conviction.[72] "An accused must first suffer jeopardy before he can suffer double jeopardy."

## SPLIT VERDICT

Legally elegant but fundamentally hypocritical, the "split verdict" concept pertains to cases in which the defendant is found guilty of a crime and not guilty by reason of insanity of another crime, the crimes' having been committed during the same period of time. The defendant receives the worst of all alternatives, for now he is pronounced both *insane and a criminal.*[73] In such cases (multiple-offense cases), the prosecution attempts to show that some of the crimes are not the result of mental disease or defect, at the same time allowing the insanity issue to stand for other crimes. The defendant, after he is released from a hospital for the criminally insane, is sent to prison to serve the sentence for the crime of which he was found guilty.

## CASE 9

### CONVICTED KILLER OF 4 FACES DEATH PENALTY[74]

The trial of Steven J. Wood in West Hartford, Connecticut, lasted over 14 weeks, after 20 weeks was spent in selecting a jury. The judge instructed the jury that the crux of its deliberations had to be determining the defendant's mental state on the day of the murders. The defendant had handcuffed and then shot his former wife and male companion, before traveling to her home and killing her daughter and mother. After 54 hours of deliberations, the six men and six women on the jury decided that the defendant was not guilty by reason of insanity for killing his former wife and guilty of murder in each of the other three deaths.

## CASE 10

The Court of Special Appeals of Maryland affirmed the split verdict in the case of Joy Ann Robey who was charged with homicide in the death of her baby.[75] The Court reasoned as follows: The psychiatrists for the prosecution diagnosed reactive depression and found the defendant to be responsible for the beatings, but the defense psychiatrist found that the defendant also suffered from an atypical impulse disorder and a dependent personality disorder. As a result of these disorders, the baby's cries triggered an intermittent explosive disorder, during which the defendant would lose control and beat the child until its cries subsided. Immediately after each beating episode, the defendant would regain her self-control and feel remorse. Consequently, she could not be held responsible for beating the baby and was acquitted of murder by reason of insanity, but could be held responsible for failing to seek medical care for the battered child after regaining self-control and was found guilty of involuntary manslaughter and child abuse. She was sentenced to a ten-year term in the custody of the Division of Correction.

## NEW FEDERAL INSANITY RULE

The Comprehensive Crime Control Act of 1984, containing the new insanity defense legislation,[10] was the result, in part, of an intense lobbying effort[76,77] by staff members of the APA's Division of Government Relations and by the Chairperson of the APA Commission on Judicial Action. The insanity standard adopted by Congress, the first such statute to be enacted for all federal jurisdictions, is patterned closely after the formulation recommended in the APA Statement on the Insanity Defense, and passage of the legislation was hailed by the APA as a "victory."[78] The new rule, replacing the more "liberal" American Law Institute standard, which, in one form or another, had been adopted over the years by the federal circuit courts, reads as follows[79]:

> It is an affirmative defense to a prosecution under any Federal statute that, at the time of the commission of the acts constituting the offense, the defendant, as a result of a severe mental disease or defect, was unable to appreciate the nature or quality or the wrongfulness of his acts. Mental disease or defect does not otherwise constitute a defense.

My argument that the various definitions of legal insanity are distinctions without a difference necessarily compels the conclusion that there will be no reduction in the number of cases in which the insanity plea is asserted. Already, under the new rule, we are seeing felony trials of defendants whose "severe" mental condition is presented as justification for acquittal by reason of insanity.

## CASE 11

### CLINIC BOMB TRIAL TOLD OF DISORDERS[80]

A defense psychiatrist testified in Federal district court in Pensacola, Florida, that three of four young defendants on trial in the bombings of three abortion clinics suffer "severe" mental disorder. The psychiatrist said that James T. Simmons, age 21; his wife, Kathren, 18; and Matthew J. Goldsby, 21, were "borderline personalities" capable of slipping into psychotic behavior. According to the psychiatrist, a fourth defendant, Kaye Wiggins, 18, suffered periodic depression but was less troubled than the others. The defense made no effort to deny that Mr. Goldsby and Mr. Simmons plotted and carried out the bombings for the stated purpose of ending what was depicted as "the murders of unborn children." Nor did they deny that Mrs. Simmons and Miss Wiggins had been enlisted to buy explosive powder for the bombs at local gun shops. The defense attempted to portray the defendants as deeply religious individuals torn by a conflicting view in American society of the human fetus as a living human being, on the one hand, and as "tissue in a minor medical procedure," on the other. At one point in the cross-examination of a prosecution witness, one of the defense attorneys described God as an "unindicted co-conspirator" in the case. Psychiatrists were called to rebut the defense's psychiatric testimony concerning the symptoms of "severe" mental disorder.[81] The two men were convicted on all counts and the women were found guilty of conspiracy.

The Insanity Defense Reform Act of 1984 contains detailed provisions relating to postacquittal confinement and release.[82] Although analysis of these provisions is beyond the scope of this chapter, I must point out that establishing, for the first time in the federal justice system, formal procedures for confining persons acquitted of violent acts by reason of insanity, and that placing on such acquittees the burden of proving by clear and convincing evidence that their release "would not create a substantial risk of bodily injury to another person or serious damage of property of another due to a present mental disease or defect," lead me to predict that there will be a considerable increase in acquittals by reason of insanity in the federal courts. This is particularly bound to occur in light of the fact that the vast majority of successful insanity cases are decided without a jury; indeed, they are resolved by acceptance of an insanity plea without a trial.

## CONCLUSION

In this chapter, I have attempted to show how the insanity defense militates against rationality in the handling of mentally disordered lawbreakers. I have elsewhere[83–88] argued that the use of the insanity plea, rather than uplifting the law's moral character, makes a mockery of the criminal justice system; that its practical application is hurtful to the population it is intended to benefit; that it undermines the processes of the law; that it tarnishes the public sense of justice; and that it results in the involuntary hospitalization, in overcrowded and chronically understaffed institutions for the criminally insane, of substantial numbers of individuals who are not mentally ill and may not have been mentally ill in the first place. Moreover, as a matter of particular concern to the psychiatric profession, the insanity defense, in every phase of its administration, fosters the extensive and systematic abuse of psychiatry. It is my view that, if it were not possible to misuse psychiatry in the period of postacquittal confinement, the insanity defense would be statutorily abolished in every jurisdiction in the United States.

Let me now outline briefly my alternative to the exculpatory insanity rule. I would include in statutes abolishing the special defense of insanity, a provision for acquittal when the defendant, as a result of mental illness, lacked the state of mind required as an element of the offense charged. The following features would be added:

1. Presentation of psychiatric and psychological testimony in the courtroom when appropriate;
2. Comprehensive presentence evaluation (including psychiatric

evaluation where indicated) of *all* persons convicted of serious crime. (This feature is already the law in a number of jurisdictions.)

3. Application of regular civil commitment laws in those few cases of acquittal in which the defendant is so severely mentally ill as not to satisfy the mental state required for conviction (yet still adjudged mentally competent to stand trial), such a person having had his own expert witnesses present convincing evidence of his serious mental illness and thus in all likelihood having demonstrated his need for mental hospitalization; and

4. Disposition of the case decided by the sentencing authority on the basis of the community's need for protection and retribution carefully balanced against the convicted person's need for treatment and rehabilitation. (Thus, a nondangerous mentally ill convicted felon might be placed on probation and required to receive in-hospital treatment if found suitable for such treatment by hospital personnel; whereas a dangerous personality-disordered individual, who may not appreciate wrongfulness as a result of his severe mental disorder, yet whose condition is not suitable for hospital treatment, or who might indeed not be treatable, would be sentenced to a correctional facility.)

In conclusion, the exculpatory insanity rule, however it is worded, is a metaphysical subtlety, a spurious attempt to soften the harshness of the criminal law. There are more humane, more ethical, and more effective alternatives. The insanity defense, in the words used 30 years ago by APA President Harry Solomon[89] in describing the large state hospitals, is antiquated, outmoded, and obsolete.


# REFERENCES


1. Jefferson T: Letter to William Johnson, June 12, 1823. *J Leg Med* 1974; 2:10.
2. Idaho Senate Bill No. 1396, signed by Governor John B. Evans on April 2, 1982.
3. Landmark legislation eliminates "insanity defense" in Idaho. *Newsletter Am Legis Exch Council* 1982; 8/5:1.
4. 1979 Montana Laws, ch. 713.
5. *See,* e.g., Gambino R: The murderous mind: insanity vs. the law. *Saturday Review,* March 18, 1978, pp 10–13.
6. Senate Bill No. 9345 and Senate Bill No. 4910 introduced on April 13, 1978, and April 2, 1979, respectively.
7. *The Insanity Defense in New York—A Report to Governor Hugh L. Carey.* Albany, NY, New York State Department of Mental Hygiene, February 11, 1978.
8. Senate Bill S.818, dated March 26, 1981.
9. Carnahan WA: In *Hearings before the Committee on the Judiciary, United States Senate, July*

*19 and 28, August 2 and 4, 1982.* (Serial No. J–97–126) Washington: U.S. Government Printing Office, 1982, p 422.

10. Public Law No. 98–473.

11. Psychiatric group urges stiffer rules for insanity plea. *The New York Times,* Jan 20, 1983, p A18.

12. Changes endorsed on insanity pleas. *The New York Times,* Feb 10, 1983, p A18.

13. APA release statement calling for reform of insanity defense. *Clin Psychiatr News,* Feb 1983, p 1.

14. APA calls for tightening of insanity defense criteria. *Psychiatr News,* Feb 4, 1983, p 1.

15. Robitscher, J, Haynes AK: In defense of the insanity defense. *Emory Law J* 1982; 31:9–60.

16. Bonnie R: The moral basis of the insanity defense. *Am Bar Assoc J* 1983; 69:194–197.

17. Hermann DHJ: Assault on the insanity defense: Limitations on the effectiveness and effect of the defense of insanity. *Rutgers Law J* 1983; 14:241–371.

18. Slovenko R: The meaning of mental illness in criminal responsibility. *J Leg Med* 1984; 5:1–61.

19. Prelinger E: Dilemmas of the expert witness: Reflections on the insanity defense. *Psychiatr Annals* 1983; 13:237–241.

20. 1982 Alaska Session Laws, ch. 143.

21. 1982 Georgia Laws 1493.

22. 1982 Ky. Rev. State. & R. Serv. ch. 113 (Baldwin).

23. N.M. Stat. Ann. §§31–9–3, 31–9–4 (1982).

24. Del. House Bill No. 567 (1982).

25. Mich. Comp. Laws Ann. §768.36 (West 1982).

26. 1981 Ill. Legis. Serv. 82–553 (West).

27. Ind. Code Ann. §§35–5–2–3, 35–5–2–6 (Burns Supp. 1980).

28. *Psychiatr News,* Aug. 17, 1984, p 5.

29. McGrath JJ: Analysis of the AMA-APA insanity defense. Presented to the American Medical Association, Dec. 6, 1983, Los Angeles, California.

30. Roth LH: Tighten but do not discard. *JAMA* 1984; 251:2949–2950.

31. Goldstein J, Katz J: Abolish the insanity defense why not? *Yale Law J* 1963; 72:853–876.

32. Morris N: Psychiatry and the dangerous criminal. *S Cal Law R* 1968; 41:514–547.

33. Morris N, Hawkins G: *The Honest Politician's Guide to Crime Control.* Chicago: University of Chicago Press, 1969.

34. Brooks A: The merits of abolishing the insanity defense. *Ann Am Acad Polit Soc Sci* 1985; 477:125–136.

35. Insanity defense in criminal trials and limitations of psychiatric testimony: Report of the AMA board of trustees. *JAMA* 1984; 251:2967–2981.

36. *State v Korell,* 690 P.2d 992 (Mont. 1984).

37. Insanity Defense Work Group: American Psychiatric Association statement on the insanity defense. *Am J Psychiatr* 1983; 140:681–688.

38. Halpern AL: The insanity defense: A juridical anachronism. *Psychiatr Ann* 1977; 7:398–409.

39. Halpern AL: The fiction of legal insanity and the misuse of psychiatry. *J Leg Med* 1980; 2:18–74.

40. Halpern AL: Uncloseting the conscience of the jury: A justly acquitted doctrine. *Psychiatr Q* 1980; 52:144–157.

41. Halpern AL, Sussman RB: The psychotic mother charged with infanticide: New dispositional developments. *NY State J Med* 1980; 80:1553–1556.

42. Halpern AL: In *Hearings Before the Committee on the Judiciary,* note 9, p 286.

43. *Hearings Before the Subcommittee on Criminal Law of the Committee on the Judiciary, United States Senate, June 24, 30 and July 14, 1982.* (Serial No. J–97–122) Washington: U.S. Government Printing Office, 1983.

44. *Id.* at 260.

45. *Id.* at 270.

46. *Id.* at 275.

47. *Id.* at 277.

48. *Id.* at 261.

49. *Id.* at 255.

50. *Id.* at 271.

51. *See* Insanity Defense, *supra* note 37, 685.

52. Model Penal Code §4.01(1) (Proposed Official Draft).

53. *See* Insanity Defense, *supra* at note 37, 685.

54. Witness says Hinckley trailed actress with gun. *The New York Times,* May 26, 1982, p A19.

55. Witness talks of Hinckley's brain scans. *Star-Gazette* (Elmira, NY), June 2, 1982, p 5A.

56. Psychologist sees split in Hinckley mind and emotions in shootings. *The New York Times,* May 22, 1982, p 16.

57. Hinckley witness pressed on stand. *The New York Times,* May 10, 1982, p A16.

58. *See, e.g., Federal Rules of Evidence,* Rule 704 (amended Oct 12, 1984).

59. *Myths & Realities: A Report of the National Commission on the Insanity Defense.* Arlington, Va, National Mental Health Association, 1983.

60. ABA Standing Committee on Association Standards for Criminal Justice: *First Tentative Draft, Criminal Justice Mental Health Standards.* Washington, American Bar Association, 1983, Standard 7–6.6.

61. Double reverse. *The New York Times,* June 4, 1985 (editorial), p A28.

62. *State of New Jersey v Michael Campanaro,* Superior Court of New Jersey, Criminal Division: Union County Indictment Nos. 632–79, 1309–79, 1317–79, 514–80, 707–80: May 5, 1981, transcript, pp 19–20.

63. *United States v Gary Lewellyn,* U.S. District Court, South District of Iowa, Central Division, Cr. No. 82–43, August 16, 1982, transcript, pp 199–200.

64. *The Daily Times* (Mamaroneck, NY), March 27, 1984, p A9.

65. *The New York Times,* April 12, 1984, p 19.

66. *American Medical News,* Feb 24, 1984, p 41.

67. *The New York Times,* Aug 23, 1983, p A12.

68. *The Daily Times* (Mamaroneck, NY), Apr 27, 1984, p A1.

69. *The New York Times,* May 24, 1984, p A14.

70. *The New York Times,* June 24, 1984, p 28.

71. *In the Matter of Samuel Lockett, Petitioner, v Michael R. Juviler et al., Respondents,* 102 App. Div.2d 869 (1984).

72. New trial ordered for a man feigning Vietnam syndrome. *The New York Times,* June 7, 1985, p B2.

73. Jeffery CR: *Criminal Responsibility and Mental Disease.* Springfield, Ill, Charles C Thomas Publisher, 1967, p 89.

74. *The Daily Times* (Mamaroneck, NY), June 29, 1984, p A7.

75. *Robey v State,* 456 A.2d 953 (Md. App. 1983).

76. *Psychiatr News,* May 18, 1984, p 4.

77. *Clin Psychiatr News,* Nov 1984, p 3.

78. *Psychiatr News,* Nov 16, 1984, p 1.

79. 18 U.S.C., ch. 1, §20.

80. *The New York Times,* Apr 21, 1985, p 32.

81. *American Medical News,* May 20, 1985, p 27.
82. 18 U.S.C., ch. 313, §4243.
83. Halpern AL: Reconsideration of the insanity defense and related issues in the aftermath of the Hinckley trial. *Psychiatr Q* 1982; 54:260–264.
84. Halpern AL: Elimination of the exculpatory insanity rule: A modern societal need. *Psychiatr Clin* 1983; 6:611–627.
85. Halpern AL: Paltering with the insanity defense: The drive to narrow the rule and to expand the legal abuse of psychiatry. Report to the Assembly of the American Psychiatric Association, Feb 5, 1984, Washington, DC.
86. Halpern AL: Further comments on the insanity defense in the aftermath of the Hinckley trial. *Psychiatr Q* 1984; 56:62–69.
87. Halpern AL: Toward rationality in the handling of the violent mentally disordered offender. *Westchester Med Bull* 1984; 52:11–12.
88. Halpern AL: The AMA report on the insanity defense in criminal trials. *Psychiatr Q* 1984; 56:236–238.
89. Solomon H: The American Psychiatric Association in relation to American psychiatry. *Am J Psychiatr* 1958; 115(7):1–9.

**8**

# In Defense of the Insanity Defense

ROBERT L. SADOFF

The insanity defense continues to be at the center of a great controversy. Most psychiatrists favor the concept of relieving a seriously mentally ill person of criminal responsibility if his mental illness significantly affects his behavior. Most attorneys also adhere to the notion that insanity is a viable defense, when significant mental illness is involved. Recently, attempts have been made to abolish the insanity defense for a number of reasons.

It is true that there have been abuses of the insanity defense by psychiatrists and by attorneys while they were defending their clients. Individuals, for example, have been found to be legally insane even though they have little or no mental illness. Sometimes a jury will find insanity because they wish to acquit the defendant and had at their disposal no other viable means. One may argue that such a procedure is an exploitation of psychiatric testimony and of the insanity defense. Others will argue that we have gone too far when we include volitional elements as part of the insanity defense. Nevertheless, there are a few seriously mentally deranged individuals whose mental illness is so severe that they cannot control the violent behavior that is directly related to their psychosis, hallucinations, and/or delusions. These individuals are extremely ill and need to be treated as mentally ill patients and not as hardened criminals. Without the insanity defense as their ally, these few

---

**ROBERT L. SADOFF** • Department of Psychiatry; Center for Studies in Social-Legal Psychiatry, University of Pennsylvania, Jenkintown, PA 19046.

**111**

deranged and psychotic individuals would be found guilty of crimes they could not avoid and that they were not even aware they were committing.

Historically, the insanity defense has been under attack for centuries. Perhaps the origin of the legal application in Anglo-American law of mental illness to criminal behavior can be attributed to Bracton, a Roman cleric and judge of the thirteenth century, who declared that a person would not be held responsible for his criminal behavior if he had "no more reason than an infant, a brute or a wild beast."[1] Later, Edward Coke and Matthew Hale noted that no felony or murder can be committed without a felonious intent or purpose:

> If a person was so deprived of reason that he resembled a beast rather than a man, he could have no felonious intent and, therefore, could not be convicted of a crime.[2]

Hale also distinguished between partial and total insanity, indicating that partial insanity is no excuse for criminal behavior.[3] Both Hale and Coke regarded insanity as a disturbance of the reason and the intellect, as well as of the will. In order to be excused for an offense, a defendant had to have a disturbance of such severity that he or she would be regarded as having less understanding than a 14-year-old person.

In 1724, in the case of *Arnold*,[4] Mr. Justice Tracey said:

> It is not every kind of frantic humor or something unaccountable in a man's actions that points him out to be such a madman as is exempted from punishment: it must be a man that is totally deprived of his understanding and memory, and doth not know what he is doing no more than an infant, than a brute or a wild beast. Such a one is never the object of punishment.[5]

Thus, until the beginning of the nineteenth century, insanity meant total deprivation of one's ability to know what one was about. In 1800, that concept changed in the case of Hadfield, in which Erskine argued that Hadfield's head injury caused Hadfield's delusions and hallucinations, as well as his offensive behavior. Erskine argued against Coke and Hale:

> If total deprivation of memory was intended by these great lawyers to be taken in the literal sense of the words: If it was meant that, to protect a man from punishment, he must be in such a state of prostrated intellect as not to know his name, nor his condition, nor his relation toward others . . . then no such madness ever existed in the world. It is idiocy alone which places a man in this helpless condition.[6]

Perhaps the one case prior to John W. Hinckley's case that raised the greatest furor in Anglo-American criminal law of insanity was the M'Naghten case of 1843.[7] In that case, the defense attorney, Mr. Cockburn, argued for M'Naghten's acquittal by reason of insanity because of the defendant's delusional beliefs that related to the crime. M'Naghten was found not guilty by reason of insanity and was sent for treatment at Bethlehem Hospital "at Queen Victoria's pleasure." Because of this acquittal, there arose a hue and cry that can only be likened to the same type of concerns that arose after Hinckley was acquitted in 1982. As a result of the concerns of the Queen and Parliament, the M'Naghten rules emerged as the first formal test of insanity that has survived to the present day in most states in the United States. Basically, the M'Naghten test is a cognitive test that assesses a defendant's ability to know the nature and quality of his acts and to determine whether he knows what he was doing was wrong. If his behavior is related to his mental illness, such that he could not pass that test, the defendant would be found legally insane.

Psychiatrists have argued that the M'Naghten test was too narrow and restrictive, and did not include all elements of the personality; therefore, the irresistible impulse test was subsequently added. This test, which was used in several states, contained a question which asked the defendant if he knew the nature and quality of his act, despite his illness, or if he knew that what he was doing was wrong but could not keep from doing the act; that is, could he adhere to the right and refrain from the wrong? The combined M'Naghten–irresistible impulse test has also survived in several states to the present time.[8]

The next major change in the insanity defense occurred in 1954, when Judge David Bazelon promulgated, in the District of Columbia, the *Durham* test,[9] which was based on the New Hampshire formulation that was influenced by Isaac Ray in the nineteenth century.[10] In *Durham* it was stated that a defendant would be found legally insane if it could be proven that his criminal behavior was a product of his mental illness. The problems in the test involved first the definition of mental illness and, subsequently, that the testimony of psychiatrists was limited to exclude the ultimate question. In 1972, the *Durham* test was replaced in the *Brawner* case[11] with the American Law Institute Model Penal Code test of criminal responsibility.[12]

The American Law Institute Model Penal Code was written by a group of lawyers, judges, and psychiatrists, and the test reflects the triple aspects of the human personality: cognitive, conative, and volitional. This test states that a defendant would not be held criminally responsible if, at the time of the committing of the crime, he was suffering from mental illness such that he lacked substantial capacity, either to appreciate the criminality of his behavior or to conform his conduct to the requirements of the law. In that test, the controversy arose over the definition of the word "substantial." There was also controversy about the volitional part of the test, which may include such illnesses of volitional character as alcohol addiction, drug addiction, and pathological gambling. For some, the test appeared to be too broad, even though it included all aspects of the personality.

It was not until after John W. Hinckley, Jr. was acquitted by reason of insanity, using the ALI Model Penal Code, that reforms of the insanity defense were demanded in Congress. Among the reforms were included the options that follow.

The first option was the abolition of the insanity defense. Three states, in essence, have abolished the insanity defense but maintained a *mens rea* (criminal intent) doctrine.[13] The *mens rea* is a guilty intent, and the doctrine includes a finding of not guilty, if it can be proven that the defendant could not form the specific intent to commit the crime, or that he did not have the *mens rea* required of the crime.

The second option was the incorporation of the guilty but mentally ill (GBMI) doctrine, which was initiated in Michigan in 1974.[14] Thirteen states have adopted the GBMI, which proclaimed that a defendant may be found guilty of the crime charged, even if he had a serious mental illness but did not meet the M'Naghten test of responsibility, or the specific test in that jurisdiction.[15] In most of these states, a lesser test is utilized for the definition of mentally ill in the label of guilty but mentally ill. In Pennsylvania, for example, the definition of mentally ill is equivalent to that of the ALI Model Penal Code, under which Hinckley was found legally insane in 1982.[16] These states provide for treatment of the defendant after the finding, and, instead of releasing him to the community (as is done in the insanity cases), he is then sent to a prison to serve out the remainder of his sentence.

The third alternative was to modify the definition of insanity in a jurisdiction. In 1984, this was done in the federal system under the Omnibus Crime Code, in which the test for insanity was modified from the ALI Model Penal Code to read that a person would not be criminally responsible for his behavior if he was suffering from mental illness at the time of the act, such that he could not appreciate the nature and quality of his act or the criminality of his behavior.[17] This new code was similar to M'Naghten but included the word "appreciate," which involves conative functions of the personality, rather than restricting the test to the cognitive aspects. This new test has removed the volitional arm, which many have supported. The vague concept of substantial capacity was also removed, and thereby a source of conflict and controversy was eliminated. By removing the words "substantial capacity" and stating that a defendant would be found to lack criminal responsibility if he "could not appreciate" indicates a more total loss of function, as noted by Hale and Coke, and not the partial insanity that had been so effectively argued by Erskine and Cockburn.

Both the American Psychiatric Association and the American Bar Association agreed that changes were needed following the Hinckley acquittal.[18] Both organizations agreed that the volitional arm should be eliminated, and both also agreed that insanity should remain a viable part of the criminal law. The American Psychiatric Association quoted from Matthew Hale's *History of the Pleas of the Crown* (which was published posthumously in 1736) that the insanity defense was rooted in the fundamental moral assumptions of the criminal law:

> Man is naturally endowed with these two great faculties, understanding and liberty of will . . . the consent of the will is that which renders human actions either commendable or culpable . . . it follows that where there is a total defect of the understanding, there is no free act of the will.[19]

Thus, the American Psychiatric Association supported the longstanding premise of the criminal law that, unless a defendant intentionally chooses to commit a crime, he is not morally blameworthy, and he should not be punished.

The American Psychiatric Association has supported the insanity defense and has urged that it be retained in some form: "Retention of the insanity defense is essential to the moral integrity of the criminal law."[20] Elsewhere, I have stated that:

> Legal history shows, therefore, that the insanity defense should be retained. Society requires an appropriate "out" in special cases that are tried. Certainly, cases of extreme mental illness or severe mental retardation in which the defendant could not even meet the M'Naghten [*sic*] test of intellectual capacity at the time of the crime should be exculpated on the grounds of insanity.[21]

Following the brief history of the insanity defense and the assertion that it is rooted in common law and statutory law as an integral part of our legal-moral fabric, I argue for its retention as a necessary means of maintaining the notion that seriously mentally ill individuals should not be punished for acts over which they have little or no knowledge or control. Perhaps a larger question for psychiatrists is not whether the insanity defense should be retained, because I believe that is a legal question beyond psychiatric expertise, but whether psychiatrists ought to have a role in the insanity defense. I assert that we should and offer the recommendations that follow.

The insanity test in all jurisdictions includes the concept of mental illness as a basis for exculpation by reason of insanity. Without mental illness, there is no legal insanity. Therefore, the determination of the mental illness is within the expertise of the psychiatrist. Perhaps the psychiatrist should stop at the level of communicating to the court the degree of mental illness, and how that illness affects the individual's thought processes and his behavior. Perhaps the psychiatrist ought to refrain from responding to the ultimate question, as he was asked to do under *Durham,* and, now, in the federal jurisdictions, under the Omnibus Crime Code of 1984. Thus, the question is not whether there ought to be an insanity defense, or whether the psychiatrist ought to be involved in the determination of insanity, but how should the psychiatrist be involved, and to what extent?

Earlier, I noted that there were cases in which individuals were found legally insane where there was no significant mental illness, or where society, through the jury, chose to acquit the defendant, utilizing insanity as the hook on which to hang the acquittal. Some of those cases involved euthanasia, or jury sympathy with the defendant, or the conviction by the jury that the case should never have been brought to court in the first place. What happens, then, to the defendant after being found not guilty by reason of insanity (NGBRI)? He will be sent to a hospital for treatment, but, if he is not significantly mentally ill, what can the hospital do for the patient? Although in all jurisdictions the court must decide whether the patient can be released after a finding of NGBRI, the hospital must retain the patient until the judge determines that he no longer has a mental illness or is no longer "dangerous" to the community if he should be released. In a recent case in Maine,[22] the judge determined that the definition of mental illness in a defendant was not similar to that which the psychiatrists diagnosed him under the criteria of the *Diagnostic and Statistical Manual of Mental Disorders* (DSM-III). The court has its own diagnostic manual and will keep check on the patient before his release.

The role of the psychiatrist, in any of these cases, is primarily that of teacher. The psychiatrist examines the defendant and presents his findings to the court. The results comprise basically medical findings that are based on a comprehensive assessment and evaluation of the defendant, including special testing (when necessary), review of school records, medical records, other hospital records, and, certainly, all the police investigation reports regarding the offense and other offenses (if available). Following a comprehensive and thorough assessment of the defendant, the psychiatrist then enters the second phase of his teaching responsibility, that is, the preparation of a report that the court may utilize in its determination of insanity or lack of criminal responsibility.

The third teaching function of the psychiatrist in these cases is that of expert witness, in which he must clearly delineate the factors of a mental illness that can affect the defendant's behavior. He must be flexible in the face of new evidence that may counter his earlier observations. He must clearly explain not only the mental illness but also the manner in which this particular mental illness affects the defendant in ways that would lead to a final determination regarding the insanity of or the absence of insanity in the defendant.

The final teaching function of the psychiatrist occurs with respect to the disposition and the facilities available for the defendant if he is found insane. As an expert witness, the psychiatrist must alert the court about the functions of the treating psychiatrists who are on staff within these institutions, and what can be expected if the defendant is hospitalized.

Finally, the psychiatric expert may return at various intervals, after reexamining the patient who has been found insane, regarding the further disposition and/or release of the patient to the community.

In summary, it is contended that the insanity defense has roots in Anglo-American law that must not be disturbed. There are sound reasons for exculpating individuals who are severely and significantly mentally ill and that decision is primarily a legal one. For the psychiatrist, the major question is not whether but how to implement the insanity defense in the most effective manner so as to aid the court in its serious determinations and deliberations regarding the confusing aspects of mental illness and that illness' effect on the behavior charged. I submit that this is a function of forensic psychiatrists, and that we can do this within our expertise, as long as we are thorough in our assessments, clear about our diagnoses, and effective in our communications to the court:

> We need the insanity defense; the law needs the insanity plea. We must all work together to improve the system, not abandon a humane alternative to retributive justice. We can find a better solution by understanding the needs of the law and applying sound psychiatric principles to the requirements of the criminal justice system.[23]

## REFERENCES


1. Bracton H, cited by Whitlock FA: *Criminal Responsibility and Mental Illness*. London, Butterworths, 1963.
2. Coke E: *Institutes, Part 3*. London, 1797.
3. Hale M: *Pleas of the Crown*. London, Shrewsbury, 1682, p 43.
4. Arnold's Case, *16 State Trials*, 695, (1724).
5. *Id.* at 702.
6. RV Hadfield, *27 State Trials*, 1281 (1800).
7. RV M'Naghten, *10 Clark and Finney*, 200 (1843).
8. Weiner BA: Mental disability and the criminal law, in Brakel SJ, Parry J, Weiner BA (eds) *The Mentally Disabled and the Law*. 3 ed, Chicago, American Bar Foundation, 1985, p 710.
9. *United States v Durham*, 214 F.2d 862 (1954).
10. *State v Pike*, 49 N.H., 399 (1869); *State v Jones*, 50 N.H., 369 (1871).
11. *United States v Brawner*, 471 F.2d 969 (1972).

12. *The American Law Institute Model Penal Code.* Philadelphia, American Law Institute, §4.01 (1962).
13. Idaho, §18–207 (1974 and Supp. 1984); Montana, §46–14–201 (1981); Utah, §76–2–305 (1978 and Supp. 1983).
14. *People v McQuillan,* 221 N.W. 2d 569 (Mich. 1974).
15. The thirteen states are Alaska, Delaware, Georgia, Illinois, Indiana, Kentucky, Michigan, Montana, New Mexico, Pennsylvania, South Dakota, Utah, and Vermont. *See* Brakel SJ, Parry J, Weiner BA (eds) *The Mentally Disabled and the Law.* 3 ed, Chicago, American Bar Foundation, 1985, p 714.
16. Senate Bill 171 of the General Assembly of Pennsylvania (amended October 27, 1981).
17. 18 U.S.C., §20 (1984).
18. Statement of the American Bar Association Policy on the Insanity Defense (February 9, 1983); Statement of the American Psychiatric Association on the Insanity Defense (December, 1982).
19. Statement of the American Psychiatric Association on the insanity defense. *Am J Psychiatr* 1983; 140:683.
20. *Id.* at 683.
21. Sadoff RL: The insanity defense: Why it should be retained. *J Leg Med* 1977; (June) 32.
22. *In Re Jonathan R. LaDew,* CV–86–469 (Ken. Cty. Feb 3, 1987).
23. Sadoff RL: Editorial comment on Halpern AL: Elimination of the exculpatory insanity rule. *Psychiatr Clin* 1983; 6(4):633.

# 9

# New York's "Extreme Emotional Disturbance" Defense

## A Hybrid Creature of the Law at the Psycho-Legal Interface

**ROBERT LLOYD GOLDSTEIN**

The diagnostic criteria for New York's "extreme emotional disturbance" defense[1] will not be found in the DSM-III-R or in any future psychiatric manual of nosology. It is important for psychiatrists to understand the statutory and case law operational criteria for this hybrid creature of the law, as well as the distinctions between extreme emotional disturbance, diminished capacity, diminished responsibility, and the insanity defense. The ability of psychiatrists to make an effective and meaningful contribution to the legal process, when they participate in cases involving this affirmative defense, will be predicated on such an understanding as well as on their clinical psychiatric expertise. As a convenient resource, brief summaries of the leading New York cases on extreme emotional disturbance, which are discussed in this chapter, are offered in the Appendix.

---

**ROBERT LLOYD GOLDSTEIN** • Department of Psychiatry, College of Physicians and Surgeons, Columbia University, New York, NY 10032.

119

## BEYOND THE HEAT OF PASSION: THE AFFIRMATIVE DEFENSE OF EXTREME EMOTIONAL DISTURBANCE

The revised New York Penal Law of 1967[2] abandoned the traditional language of "heat of passion" as the criterion for mitigation in a prosecution for murder, replacing it with a new formulation, that is, "extreme emotional disturbance for which there is a reasonable explanation or excuse." The criminal law has always recognized provocation as a formal mitigating factor in prosecutions for murder in determining whether a defendant acted in the heat of passion.[3] The heat of passion defense is qualified by objective criteria that demonstrate that the source and degree of the provocation are as significant as its subjective impact on the defendant's volitional controls. The defendant must prove that not only was he provoked by the victim's actions, but that a reasonable person would also have been so provoked. He must also demonstrate that he did not have sufficient time to "cool off" before committing the criminal act. Thus, to establish that, as a result of adequate provocation, he acted in the heat of passion when he killed the victim, the ultimate test was whether a reasonable man, confronted with the same series of events, would become impassioned to the extent that his mind was incapable of cool reflection.[4] Having satisfied the first requirement that, in a given situation, the defendant was confronted with sufficient provocation, the focus then shifted to his response, with the relevant inquiry at that point being threefold: Did he really act in the heat of passion when he killed? Did the provocation directly lead to the murder of the individual responsible for the provocation? Was there insufficient "cooling-off" time, thereby preventing a reasonable man from using his capacity to reflect before taking action?[5] An action undertaken in the heat of passion meant that the defendant had been provoked to the point that his "hot blood" prevented rational reflection about his action. If the action were not immediate, if there were time for cooling off, then there could be no heat of passion.

In enacting the extreme emotional disturbance defense, the New York legislature provided a formal mitigation formulation that differed significantly from the traditional heat of passion defense. The revision was undertaken in recognition of

> the tremendous advances made in psychology since 1881 and a willingness on the part of the courts, legislators, and the public to reduce the level of responsibility imposed on those whose capacity has been diminished by mental trauma. It is consistent with modern criminological thought to reduce the defendant's criminal liability upon proof of mitigating circumstances which render his conduct less blameworthy. (p. 582)[6]

In the landmark case, *People v Patterson*,[7] the court set forth the fundamental distinction between extreme emotional disturbance and its predecessor heat of passion defense:

> An action influenced by an extreme emotional disturbance is not one that is necessarily so spontaneously undertaken. Rather, it may be that a significant mental trauma has affected a defendant's mind for a substantial period of time, simmering in the unknowing subconscious and then inexplicably coming to the fore. (p 582)[8]

Under the present formulation, the prosecution must prove beyond a reasonable doubt the facts bearing on the defendant's intent to kill. That the defendant acted under the influence of extreme emotional disturbance does not serve to negate intent or make his act any less intentional. The purpose of the defense is to explain the defendant's intentional action, permitting him to show that his conduct was caused by a mental infirmity not rising to the level of insanity. This permits the fact finder to mitigate the punishment of certain emotionally disturbed defendants it believes to be less culpable than their "normal" counterparts, who committed the same criminal acts as a result of a calm and calculating decision.

The defense has two principal elements:

> 1) the defendant's act must be committed under the influence of extreme emotional disturbance, and
> 2) there must be a reasonable explanation or excuse, the reasonableness of which is to be determined from the viewpoint of a person in the defendant's situation under the circumstances as the defendant believed them to be. (pp 107, 109)[9]

Extreme emotional disturbance is an affirmative defense only to the crime of murder or attempted murder.[10] The defendant has the burden of proof to establish by a preponderance of the evidence that he acted under the influence of extreme emotional disturbance and, if successful, thereby automatically reduces the conviction from murder to manslaughter. (In New York State, second-degree murder carries a penalty of 15 to 25 years to life in prison; if found guilty of manslaughter, the defendant faces 8⅓ to 25 years in prison.) A successful extreme emotional disturbance defense does not exonerate the defendant or render his action guiltless. He remains guilty of an intentional homicide (i.e., manslaughter), which is punishable in a less severe manner than murder.

## EXTREME EMOTIONAL DISTURBANCE CONTRASTED WITH OTHER DOCTRINAL SUPPLEMENTS TO THE INSANITY DEFENSE

In a defense of extreme emotional disturbance, the defendant attempts to convince the fact finder that his apparent intention to cause death, if the fact finder should find there was such, was not the result of a calm and calculating decision on his part, but was influenced by extreme emotional disturbance.[11] As noted above, this defense is significantly broader in scope than the heat of passion defense it supplanted. How does it differ from other doctrinal supplements to the insanity defense?

Unlike the insanity defense, which exculpates a defendant from criminal responsibility,[12] there are a number of *partial* defenses that permit the fact finder to consider a sane defendant's mental abnormality when assessing his degree of criminal liability. These partial defenses serve to reduce the degree or nature of the crime when a sane but mentally ill defendant has committed an offense. Aside from the heat of passion and extreme emotional disturbance defenses, which have been alluded to above, there are two other partial defenses to consider: the diminished capacity and the diminished responsibility defenses.

The diminished capacity defense purports to establish that the sane defendant's mental abnormality at the time of the commission of the crime prevented him from entertaining the specific mental state required by statute as an element of the offense (e.g., that his mental incapacity was such that the was unable to form the specific intent to commit murder). Negation of the specific intent requirement of the crime charged serves to reduce the offense of murder to one with a lesser maximum penalty (i.e., manslaughter), which does not require proof of a specific intent to kill. In contrast, the defense of extreme emotional disturbance does not seek to negate intent, but to explain (and mitigate) the defendant's intentional conduct in terms of his impaired mental state at the time.[13]

Diminished responsibility refers to a defense that permits the fact finder to mitigate the punishment of a mentally disabled but sane defendant when the jury believes he is less culpable than his "normal" counterpart who commits the very same offense. Consideration of the defendant's mental abnormality by itself, without reference either to incapacity to entertain the requisite specific intent or to provocation (and the extreme emotional response thereto), permits the fact finder to mitigate the punishment to be imposed. The primary justification of the defense is that it enables the fact finder to render more precise, individualized culpability judgments.[14,15]

## ANALYSIS OF THE EXTREME EMOTIONAL DISTURBANCE DEFENSE: THE FIRST PRONG OF THE STATUTE ("UNDER THE INFLUENCE OF EXTREME EMOTIONAL DISTURBANCE")

The issue presented by this defense is invariably a close one because most intentional homicides, with the exception of those committed by cold blooded killers or during the course of a felony, are abnormal acts for the perpetrators and usually the consequence of strong emotions and stresses. The courts have attempted to analyze the proper interpretation and application of the extreme emotional disturbance formulation in a series of cases, thereby helping to resolve many of the controversies and uncertainties surrounding the nature of this hybrid creature of the law. Nonetheless, the law has not provided sufficiently precise guidelines to always aid the fact finder.

The first prong of the statute requires, as a threshold determination, that the defendant did in fact commit the criminal act while under the influence of extreme emotional disturbance. The court in *Patterson*[16] noted that the defendant's intention to cause death must not be the result of a calm and calculating decision on his part. The court also cautioned that "'extreme' [emotional disturbance] precludes mere annoyance or unhappiness or anger, but requires disturbance excessive and violent in its effect upon the defendant experiencing it" (p 576).[17] The required mental infirmity, not arising to the level of insanity, is described in the Comments to the Model Penal Code[18] (from which the present New York provisions are derived) by way of a few passing examples as "fright or terror," "great stress," or where the defendant has "just suffered a traumatic injury," or was "blind or . . . distraught with grief." No further qualitative or quantitative definitions of the term are offered. In *People v Shelton*,[19] the trial judge asked both the prosecution's psychiatric expert witness and the defense's psychiatric expert witness to state their understanding of the term:

> They agreed that this term is a creature of law and has no diagnostic classification in the glossary of the Diagnostic and Statistical Manual of the American Psychiatric Association. (p 710)[20] [At the time, DSM-II was in use.]

The prosecution's psychiatric expert witness defined extreme emotional disturbance as follows:

> It is a psychiatric classification of a transitional, situational reaction in which an individual with no apparent mental disorder, when exposed to an extreme, unusual, overwhelming stress has an extreme emotional reaction to it, which may result in a sudden impulsive, blind, irrational outburst. During this reaction, there is such a release of emotion that when it is over, the person is totally spent. It is not deliberate or intentional. (p 710)[21]

The psychiatric expert witness retained by the defense offered the following definition:

> Extreme emotional distress [*sic*] is an emotional condition where a person is directed by passion, rather than by reason. One's passions, excited beyond intellectual control, take over. Rage is then the predominant feature. The normal pattern would be to experience rage first, followed shortly thereafter by intense regret and self-criticism "for having done such a stupid thing," and after that, there would be emotional exhaustion.
>
> In general, it was agreed that a person's self-control and reason would be

overwhelmed by passion, anger and other feelings. The feelings are so intense that the usual controls fail and normal rational thinking for that individual no longer prevails at that moment. There is no time interval between the provocation and the act, and if there is time to reflect, with a cooling-off period for deliberation, this would be antithetical and diametrically opposed to extreme emotional disturbance. (p 711)[22]

The court in *Shelton* concluded that extreme emotional disturbance is the emotional state of an individual who (1) has no mental disability arising to the level of insanity as defined in the Penal Law, (2) is exposed to an extremely unusual and overwhelming stress, and (3) has an extreme emotional reaction to it, as a result of which there is a loss of self-control and reason is overborne by intense feelings, such as passion, anger, distress, grief, excessive agitation, or other similar emotions. (The court also considers whether the defendant is able to reflect dispassionately, the time interval between the provocation and the act, and, most importantly, whether the intensity of these feelings is such that his usual intellectual controls fail and normal rational thinking for him no longer prevails. The court emphasizes that *the key factor in this determination may be the loss of self-control that results*.)[23]

In *People v Moye,*[24] the court held that the defendant's

savage acts of mutilating and decapitating his victim, coupled with his statements to the police and district attorney that "something snapped" inside him when she mocked and taunted him,[25] that he went "bananas" and he needed help, were evidence of a loss of self-control associated with the defense of extreme emotional disturbance. (p 889)

so that defendant's request for the charge of extreme emotional disturbance should have been granted by the trial court. In *People v Tabarez,*[26] the court found that expert testimony to the effect that the defendant had experienced an isolated explosive episode triggered by increasing depression and immobilization, that he had been under emotional stress due to prolonged unemployment, that he suffered from a variety of diagnoses (inadequate fragile personality, residual type schizophrenia, and borderline mental retardation), and that he suffered from the residual effects of ingestion of a toxic fruit as a youngster all constituted sufficient credible evidence to warrant delivering a charge to the jury on extreme emotional disturbance.[27] In contrast, other courts have held that mere drunkenness, anger, embarrassment, or jealousy, in the absence of any credible evidence of a loss of self-control due to mental trauma or exposure to extremely unusual or overwhelming stress, are not necessarily indicative of the mental infirmity associated with extreme emotional disturbance.[28,29] The cases are in agreement that not all mental infirmities that do not arise to the level of insanity will be found to constitute extreme emotional disturbance.[30] There is no bright line to

**Table I.  Extreme Emotional Disturbance**

| | |
|---|---|
| Stage 1. | Provocation or mitigating circumstances.[a] |
| | ↓ |
| Stage 2. | Sudden, intense, extreme, uncontrollable emotion (e.g., rage, agitation, passion, anger, distress, grief, or other similar emotions) for which there is a reasonable explanation or excuse. |
| | ↓ |
| Stage 3. | Loss of usual intellectual controls; sudden breakdown of ego functioning; sudden emotion prevents rational reflection. [Depersonalization is frequently present.] |
| | ↓ |
| Stage 4. | Sudden, extreme, blind, impulsive, irrational outburst of violence. |

[a]The provocation or mitigating circumstances "may affect a defendant's mind for a substantial period of time, simmering in the unknowing subconscious and then inexplicably coming to the fore" (Patterson, at 582). Thus, a substantial period of time may elapse between Stage 1 and Stage 2.

determine which ones necessarily will. This permits the fact finder to examine the unique circumstances of each case and exercise its

> discretionary power to mitigate the penalty when presented with a situation which, under the circumstances, appears to them to have caused an understandable weakness in one of their fellows. Perhaps the chief virtue of the statute is that it allows such discretion without engaging in a detailed explanation of individual circumstances in which the statute would apply. (p 776)[31]

A stepwise schematic representation of the findings required for a determination that a defendant acted under the influence of extreme emotional disturbance is set forth in Table I.

## ANALYSIS OF THE EXTREME EMOTIONAL DISTURBANCE DEFENSE: THE SECOND PRONG OF THE STATUTE ("THERE MUST BE A REASONABLE EXPLANATION OR EXCUSE")

The first prong of the extreme emotional disturbance statute is largely *subjective* in nature, that is, it involves a determination that the particular defendant did in fact act under the influence of extreme emotional disturbance (as discussed in the preceding section). The second component is more difficult to describe and is perhaps best characterized as a combination *subjective–objective* test for determining the adequacy of the provocation. There must be a

> reasonable explanation or excuse, the reasonableness of which is to be deter-
> mined from the viewpoint of a person in the defendant's situation under the
> circumstances as the defendant believed them to be. (pp 107, 109)[32]

The Comments to the Model Penal Code, from which the New York statute was drawn, argue that at least some individual peculiarities should be taken into account "because they bear upon the inference as to the actor's character that it is fair to draw upon the basis of his act."[33] Thus, the Model Penal Code introduces a certain amount of subjectivity in its proposed test (and in some recently decided cases, the courts have demonstrated a greater willingness to consider subjective factors).[34] The draftsmen of the Model Penal Code, in this regard, indicated that they intended

> to state a middle ground between a standard which ignores all individual
> peculiarities and one which makes emotional distress decisive regardless of
> the nature of its cause.[35]

They further indicated that this ambiguity in the Code formulation provides a degree of flexibility that will permit the fact finder to consider the ultimate issue, that is, "whether the actor's loss of self-control can be understood in terms that arouse sympathy enough to call for mitigation in the sentence."[36]

In *People v Casassa,*[37] the court states:

> We conclude that the determination whether there was reasonable explana-
> tion or excuse for a particular emotional disturbance should be made by
> viewing the subjective, internal situation in which the defendant found him-
> self and the external circumstances as he perceived them at the time, however
> inaccurate that perception may have been, and assessing from that stand-
> point whether the explanation or excuse for his emotional disturbance was
> reasonable, so as to entitle him to a reduction of the crime charged from
> murder in the second degree to manslaughter in the first degree. (p 775)[38]

When making a determination of reasonableness, the critical element in the Model Penal Code formulation is the requirement that reasonableness be assessed from the viewpoint of a person in the defendant's situation.[39,40] The Model Penal Code Commentaries go on to note that

> [t]he word "situation" is designedly ambiguous . . . it is clear that personal
> handicaps and some external circumstances must be taken into account
> . . . for it would be morally obtuse to appraise a crime for mitigation of
> punishment without reference to these factors.[41,42]

Is there ever a reasonable explanation or excuse for homicide? The courts are clear on an important distinction here that must be comprehended precisely in order to appreciate the intent of the statute. As the court noted in *Casassa*[43]:

> We emphasize that this test [of reasonableness] is to be applied to determine

*whether defendant's emotional disturbance, and not the act of killing, was supported by a reasonable explanation or excuse.* [Italics added][44]

Thus, the reasonable explanation or excuse refers to and must account for the development of extreme emotional disturbance in the defendant, not for his ensuing homicidal action.

As Michael and Wechsler observed:

> Most men do not kill even on the gravest provocation; [but] the point is that the more strongly they would be moved to kill by circumstances of the sort which provoked the actor to the homicidal act, and the more difficulty they would experience in resisting the impulse to which he yielded, the less does his succumbing serve to differentiate his character from theirs. But the slighter the provocation, the more basis there is for ascribing the actor's act to an extraordinary susceptibility to intense passion, to an unusual deficiency in those other desires which counteract in most men the desires which impel them to homicidal acts.[45]

Even such a description of the defense, however, is necessarily imprecise and does not provide clearcut guidelines, thereby leaving room for the exercise of judgmental evaluation by the fact finder. The issue to be faced is whether the defendant's loss of self-control was the result of an understandable human response deserving of mercy. Professor Herbert Wechsler, chief reporter for the Model Penal Code, reflects this underlying intent of the statute's draftsmen:

> The purpose was explicitly to give full scope to what amounts to a plea in mitigation based upon a mental or emotional trauma of significant dimensions, with the jury asked to show whatever empathy it can.[46]

This interpretation of the statute is consistent with the recognized underlying purpose of any formal mitigation scheme. In *Shelton*,[47] the court in the role of the trier of fact asks itself what is meant by the defense of extreme emotional disturbance. The court is drawn to the words of Justice Benjamin Cardozo, referring to an earlier statute of a similar nature:

> What we have is merely a privilege offered to the jury to find the lesser degree when the suddenness of the intent, the vehemence of the passion, seems to call irresistibly for the exercise of mercy.[48]

In *Casassa*,[49] the defendant had killed a woman acquaintance whom he had dated casually for a brief period of time. The court determined that he had acted under the influence of extreme emotional disturbance (i.e., that he was suffering from a mental infirmity not arising to the level of insanity at the time of the crime). However, the court, in making further inquiry into the reasonableness of that disturbance, found that

the excuse offered by the defendant was so peculiar to him that it was unwor-

> thy of mitigation . . . the result of defendant's malevolence rather than an
> understandable human response deserving of mercy. (p 776)[50]

The court placed great weight on the testimony of the prosecution's psychiatric expert witness who opined that although the defendant was clearly emotionally disturbed (i. e., his mental condition satisfied the first or threshold prong of the statute), he was not acting under the influence of "extreme emotional disturbance" within the meaning of the statute, because his disturbed state was not the product of external factors, but rather was a "stress he created from within himself, dealing mostly with a fantasy, a refusal to accept the reality of the situation" (p 772).[51] In contrast, in *Moye*,[52] the court held that

> there was sufficient [credible] evidence for submission to the jury—which a
> rational jury might have accepted or rejected—of a [reasonable] explanation
> or excuse for [the] defendant's emotional state [at the time he savagely acted
> to mutilate and decapitate the victim], in his recounting of the victim's con-
> tinued ridicule and taunting about his impotence. (p 889)

## THE PSYCHIATRIC PERSPECTIVE

Psychiatrists may be called on to testify as expert witnesses when the affirmative defense of extreme emotional disturbance is raised. Although there is no express statute granting a psychiatric examination at the request of the prosecution in such a case, the court will usually issue an order directing such an examination.[53] Psychiatric expert testimony on the issue of whether a defendant acted under the influence of extreme emotional disturbance for which there was a reasonable explanation or excuse is relevant and material.[54,55] As acknowledged experts on human personality development, normal and psychopathological behavior, and the effect of psychosocial stressors, psychiatrists can often understand and explain how a particular stressor acted to trigger an acute emotional reaction characterized by a sudden breakdown of normal ego functioning and a loss of customary impulse control. The psychiatrist can explicate the central role of *depersonalization*—a state of splitting or fragmentation of the ego, an alteration of the state of consciousness—that so often develops with acute stress, causing the ego to lose control over the integrity of its functions with a resultant breakthrough of destructive (and sometimes self-destructive) impulses.[56,57] In many cases, the psychiatrist can make a diagnosis (e.g., adjustment disorder, brief reactive psychosis, and depersonalization disorder, among others) relating it specifically either (1) to the acute situation precipitated by the circumstances surrounding the victim's provocation, or (2) to preexisting psychiatric conditions (i.e., the defendant's "subjective internal situation" which contributes to his reaction). In sum, the psychiatrist may be in the best position to offer the fact finder a scientific perspective according to which it can then evaluate the ultimate issues in the case for itself. Although the determination of whether the defendant acted under the influence of extreme emotional disturbance (for which there was a reasonable explanation or excuse) remains the sole province of the fact finder, nonetheless, scientific information provided by the psychiatric expert witness will help the fact finder to reach an informed decision on the complex issues involved.

It has been nearly 20 years since Professor George Dix in his article, "Psychological Abnormality as a Factor in Grading Criminal Liability: Diminished Capacity, Diminished Responsibility, and the Like," wrote:

> Whatever the present limitation on accurately determining the psychological dynamics of particular offenders, the situation is likely to improve with practice. . . . Mental health professionals, engaged in the treatment process, seldom have the opportunity to speculate concerning the mental processes of an offender as they relate to the criminal law. If the law expects such professionals to be of more help than they have been in the past, it must provide the opportunity for them to practice their analysis. . . . From continued experimentation in this area, it is reasonable to expect the development of a more sophisticated ability to analyze particular cases as well as the development of a body of knowledge on which to build a more realistic substantive criminal law.[58]

Professor Dix's prediction has come to pass. Psychiatric expert testimony has come to play a critically important role in providing the fact finder with evidence of probative value vital to the determination of a defendant's state of mind in cases in which the defense of extreme emotional disturbance is asserted. Concomitantly, psychiatric understanding and expertise in regard to the psychopathology and psychodynamics of stress related emotional states has expanded considerably over the same period.[59]

## REFERENCES


1. The term *extreme emotional disturbance* was adopted from the Model Penal Code. Several states have enacted identical or substantially similar statutes (*see* Conn. Gen. Stat. Ann. §53a–54, subd. [a], par. [1]; Del. Code Ann. tit. 11, §641; Hawaii Penal Code, §707–702, subd. [2]; Ky. Rev. Stat. §507.020, subd. [1], par. [a]; Mont. Rev. Codes §94–5–103; N.D. Cent. Code §12.1–16–02; Or. Rev. Stat. §163.115; Utah Code Ann. §76–5–205). Historically, the justification for the defense and its predecessor was to reduce criminal liability from a capital to a noncapital offense.
2. *See,* Notes of the Staff of the State Commission on Revision of the Penal Law and Criminal Code, 1967 Gilbert, Criminal Law and Practice of New York, pp 1C–1, 1C–61, 1C–62.

3.  Comment; Manslaughter and the adequacy of provocation: The reasonableness of the reasonable man. 106 *University of Pennsylvania Law Rev* 1021 (1958).

4.  *People v Caruso,* 246 N.Y. 437 (1927).

5.  *Id.*

6.  *People v Patterson,* 39 N.Y.2d 288, 383 N.Y.S.2d 573, aff'd, 432 U.S. 1977.

7.  *Id.*

8.  *Id.* at 582.

9.  New York Penal Law §125.25, subd. 1, par. [a]; §125.27, subd. 2 par. [a] (1967).

10.  *People v Tabarez,* 113 A.D.2d 461 (1985).

11.  *People v Patterson,* 383 N.Y.S.2d 573.

12.  In New York, the test of criminal responsibility is codified in Section 40.15 of the Penal Law: A person is not criminally responsible for conduct if "at the time of such conduct, as a result of mental disease or defect, he lacks substantial capacity to know or appreciate either: (1) The nature and consequence of such conduct; or (2) That such conduct was wrong."

13.  *People v Patterson,* 383 N.Y.S.2d 573.

14.  Although some European countries have adopted diminished responsibility, no American jurisdiction has explicitly done so (e.g., Parliament adopted a diminished responsibility defense in the English Homicide Act, 1957, 5 & 6 Eliz. 2, c. 11).

15.  Arenella, P: The diminished capacity and diminished responsibility defenses: Two children of a doomed marriage. 77 *Columbia Law Rev* 827 (1977).

16.  383 N.Y.S.2d 573.

17.  *Id.* at 576.

18.  ALI Model Penal Code and Commentaries [Official Draft and Revised Comments, 1980].

19.  *People v Shelton,* 88 Misc. 2d 136, 385 N.Y.S.2d 708 (1976).

20.  *Id.* at 710.

21.  *Id.* at 710. The psychiatrists' responses to the judge's query in *Shelton* indicate an insufficient understanding of statutory and case law operational criteria for extreme emotional disturbance as well as inaccurate or idiosyncratic psychiatric interpretations of the psychopathology involved. For example, there is no requirement that the defendant have "no apparent mental disorder." Preexisting or concomitant mental disorders may be (and often are) present. The requirement is merely that the defendant's mental disorder(s) do not arise to the level of insanity. Likewise, the mental state required by the statutory defense does not make the defendant's action any less intentional, but rather explains his intentional act, thereby making it less culpable. There is no psychiatric support for the prosecution psychiatrist's conclusion that the defendant would have to be "totally spent" afterward and "would be apathetic, withdrawn, dull, exhausted and depressed about what had happened and would speak in a monotone, giving short, direct answers. . . . This reaction would last for some time until there had been a period of sleep" at p 711.

22.  *Id.* at 711. Likewise the defense psychiatrist is inaccurate on a number of issues. He confuses extreme emotional disturbance with the heat of passion defense, under prior law, when he states that a cooling-off period for deliberation would be "antithetical and diametrically opposed to extreme emotional disturbance." Likewise, there is insufficient psychiatric authority to support his contention that an affective sequence of rage, regret, self-criticism and exhaustion is required. (In a similar vein, the prosecution's psychiatrist in *People v Casassa,* 427 N.Y.S.2d 769 (1980), erroneously contended that a mental disorder not arising to the level of insanity could not be considered to be extreme emotional disturbance within the meaning of the statute.)

23.  The court in *Shelton* found that the defendant had not been exposed to an extremely

unusual or overwhelming stress, and had demonstrated no loss of control. Having found that the defendant was not acting under the influence of extreme emotional disturbance at the time of the criminal offense, the court did not reach the second element of the defense (i.e., the reasonableness of the excuse or explanation). Both psychiatrists had testified that the defendant's reaction to the situation had been unreasonable; however, they inaccurately concluded that this was properly a legal-factual rather than a psychiatric issue. (It makes "little sense, if any," to contend that out of the entire universe of individuals who might have an opinion about the rationality or irrationality, reasonableness or unreasonableness, of behavior, that psychiatrists would "know so little" about the subject that they should be totally excluded from testifying on that issue. [I am paraphrasing here the Supreme Court decision in *Barefoot v Estelle,* 103 U.S. 3383 {1983}.])

24. *People v Moye,* 66 N.Y.2d 887 (1985) at 889.

25. The defendant had been extremely insecure about his masculinity and potency and had been led to believe that the victim would be able to allay his fears that he was turning into a homosexual (a friend had advised him "that if anybody can get you an erection, it would be Gloria"). When he was impotent with her, she persisted in taunting and ridiculing him. Such provocation as well as the defendant's murderous explosive outburst constituted sufficient credible evidence to warrant a charge to the jury on extreme emotional disturbance.

26. *People v Tabarez,* 113 A.D.2d 461 (1985).

27. In *Tabarez,* the court is willing to give a substantial amount of weight to subjective factors, that is, to the defendant's preexisting psychiatric difficulties and preexisting stresses, bearing no relationship to the provocation that triggered the criminal act. Although extreme emotional disturbance is a provocation defense, the court seemingly fails to require any decisive causal nexus between the victim's provocation and the defendant's violent response. The court explicitly states that the defendant's emotional disturbance could have predated his confrontation with the victim. Does the defense apply in a situation when a defendant is provoked by A and then, days or even months or years later, kills B? Courts have consistently held that a killing under such circumstances does not qualify as manslaughter. The Model Penal Code, however, does not limit provocation to acts of the person killed (§210.3). Although paying lip service to the objective reasonable-man test requirement, the court seems to favor mitigation for an emotionally disturbed individual whose psychiatric impairment is preexisting and not directly or causally linked to provocation of the criminal act. This appears to be an example of the diminished responsibility model, permitting a fact finder to mitigate the punishment of a sane but mentally disturbed offender in any case where the fact finder believes he is less culpable than his "normal" counterpart who commits the same crime.

28. *People v Walker,* 64 N.Y.2d 741, aff'd, 100 A.D.2d 220 (1984).

29. *People v Frank,* 122 A.D.2d 620 (1986).

30. *People v Casassa,* 49 N.Y.2d 668, 427 N.Y.S.2d 769 (1980).

31. *Id.* at 776.

32. New York Penal Law, *supra* note 9, at pp. 107, 109.

33. Model Penal Code §20.3, Comment (Tent. Draft No. 9, 1959).

34. *See, e.g., People v Tabarez,* 113 A.D.2d 461.

35. Model Penal Code §201.3, Comment (Tent. Draft No. 9, 1959).

36. *Id.*

37. 427 N.Y.S.2d 769.

38. *Id.* at 775.

39. *Id.*

40. It is in this regard that the Model Penal Code suggests that the ultimate test is objective. Reasonableness is not to be determined solely and entirely on the basis of the defendant's own subjective belief that his disturbance had a reasonable explanation or excuse, but "from the viewpoint of a person in the defendant's situation under the circumstances as the defendant believed them to be [viewing the] . . . subjective, internal situation in which the defendant found himself and the external circumstances as he perceived them at the time, however inaccurate that perception may have been" (p. 775), and from such a perspective sincerely trying to understand the defendant's response in empathic human terms. (Preexisting psychiatric difficulties, intrapsychic conflicts, and distortions of reality are factors to be taken into account.)

41. ALI Model Penal Code and Commentaries §210.3 [Official Draft and Revised Comments, 1980].

42. This Commentary appears to support the diminished responsibility model as set forth in *Tabarez*. Preexisting psychiatric difficulties, personal handicaps, and peculiarities are to be taken into account as well as external circumstances when assessing the reasonableness of the explanation or excuse for the defendant's extreme emotional disturbance. *See, e.g., People v Aphaylath, New York Law Journal,* Oct. 30, 1986, at 17, col. 3 (The court may admit evidence of the psychological stress and disorientation engendered in a refugee's attempting to assimilate into the American culture, which caused a significant mental trauma resulting in extreme emotional disturbance.); *see, also, "Husband: Emotional Distress Led to Valhalla Murder-for-Hire", The Daily Times* (Mamaroneck, NY), Jan. 29, 1987, at A–13, col. 1 (describing the "Helpless Little Schmuck" syndrome).

43. 427 N.Y.S.2d 769.

44. *Id.* at 775.

45. Michael J, Wechsler H: A rationale of the law of homicide. 37 *Columbia Law Rev* 1261 (1937).

46. Wechsler H: Codification of the criminal law in the United States. 68 *Columbia Law Rev* 1425 (1968).

47. *People v Shelton,* 385 N.Y.S.2d 708.

48. Cardozo B: *Law and Literature,* pp 100–101, Harcourt, New York, 1931.

49. 427 N.Y.S.2d 769.

50. *Id.* at 776.

51. *Id.* at 772.

52. 66 N.Y.2d 887.

53. *People v Solari,* 349 N.Y.S.2d 31 (1973).

54. *People v Shelton,* 385 N.Y.S.2d 708.

55. Psychiatric testimony, however, is not controlling on the issue of extreme emotional disturbance and may be rejected by the fact finder even where the prosecution chooses to offer no psychiatric expert testimony in rebuttal. *People v Schwertfeger,* 401 N.Y.S.2d 657 (1978).

56. Stewart WA: Panel discussion of depersonalization. 12 *J Am Psychoanal Assoc* 171 (1964).

57. Waltzer H: Depersonalization and self-destruction. 125 *Am J Psychiatry* 399 (1968).

58. Dix G: Psychological abnormality as a factor in grading criminal liability: Diminished capacity, diminished responsibility, and the like. 62 *J Crim Law Criminal Police Sci* 313 (1971).

59. Terr L: Children of Chowchilla: A study of psychic trauma. 34 *Psychoanal Study Child* 552 (1979).

| Case | Extreme emotional disturbance (EED) | Reasonable explanation or excuse | Provocation or mitigating circumstances | Psychiatric disorder |
|---|---|---|---|---|
| *People v Patterson*, 39 N.Y.2d 288, 383 N.Y.S.2d 573, aff'd, 432 U.S. 197 (7) | — | ? | Defendant found wife in state of undress with boy-friend[a] | Longstanding marital problems |
| *People v Shelton*, 88 Misc. 2d 136, 385 N.Y.S.2d 708 (1976) | — | Not reached | Victim threatened to have defendant fired from job for using drugs | None stated |
| *People v Casassa*, 49 N.Y.2d 668, 427 N.Y.S.2d 769 (1980) | + | — | Defendant rejected by wom-an he had dated briefly on casual basis | Defendant "obsessed" by victim; "several personality attributes peculiar to defen-dant" |
| *People v Walker*, 64 N.Y.2d 741, aff'd 100 A.D.2d 220 (1984) | — (No credible evidence of EED; thus, court did not err in refusing to charge jury on EED) | ? | Longstanding disagreement; argument over money; victim placed his hand on defendant's plate of food | None stated |
| *People v Moye*, 66 N.Y.2d 887 (1985) | + (possibly) (Sufficient credible evidence of EED and "reasonableness"; thus court erred in refusing to charge jury on EED) | + (possibly) | Victim persisted in taunting defendant over his impo-tence | Schizophrenia, sex offender |

(continued)

**APPENDIX** (*continued*)

| Case | Extreme emotional disturbance (EED) | Reasonable explanation or excuse | Provocation or mitigating circumstances | Psychiatric disorder |
| --- | --- | --- | --- | --- |
| *People v Tabarez*, 113 A.D.2d 461 (1985) | + (possibly) | + (possibly) | Apprehended by police after committing robbery; stress of prolonged unemployment; ingestion of toxic fruit as youngster | Schizophrenia; isolated explosive disorder; borderline retardation; inadequate personality |
| *People v Frank*, 122 A.D.2d 620 (1986) | — | — | ? Jealousy (no evidence of unusual or overwhelming stress) | ? Acute intoxication |
| *People v Aphaylath, New York Law Journal*, Oct. 30, 1986, at 17, col. 3 | + (possibly) (Court's ruling excluding expert testimony was not predicated on the appropriate standard) | + (possibly) | Jealousy, stress and disorientation of refugee attempting to assimilate into the American culture. | ? Adjustment disorder |

[a]It is the law practically everywhere that homicide committed by an individual who discovers his spouse in the act of committing adultery is reasonably provoked. The criminal law generally does not recognize the existence of the so-called unwritten law, which would make this conduct a form of justifiable homicide. *See,* Roberts: The unwritten law. 10 *Kentucky Law Journal* 45 (1922); Comment: Recognition of the honor defense under the insanity plea. 43 *Yale Law Journal* 809 (1934). *But cf., Campbell v State,* 204 Ga. 399, 49 S.E.2d 867 (1948) (justifiable homicide when husband kills paramour to prevent the beginning or completion of adultery).

# IV

*Dispositions*

# 10

# The Role of the Police with the Mentally Ill

SHELDON TRAVIN

Police involvement with the mentally ill in the community has become, in recent years, a subject of increasing concern. Although the police have been recognized for some time as an important community mental health resource,[1] the increase in the number of mentally ill persons residing in the community has burdened the police with added responsibilities. This increase in the number of mentally ill persons residing in the community has been attributed to several factors: the growing emphasis on deinstitutionalization in the mental health field, the expansion of legal constraints regarding psychiatric treatment that includes stricter criteria for civil commitment and the extension of legal guidelines developed to protect the patient's right to refuse treatment, and finally the steady reduction in available funding for mental health programs.[2] These factors have resulted in a situation in which not only has the number of mentally ill persons residing in the community increased over the past decade, but also many of the poorest treatment cases (that is, patients who have had multiple psychiatric hospitalizations and have been sent from one clinic to another only to be essentially "rejected" [considered untreatable] as "bad patients"[3] or as "forfeited patients"[4]), ultimately decompensate and come to the attention of the police. If an individual becomes violent, disorderly, or violates the law, the police

---

**SHELDON TRAVIN** • Department of Psychiatry, Bronx-Lebanon Hospital Center, Bronx, NY 10456; Department of Psychiatry, Albert Einstein College of Medicine, Bronx, NY 10461.

137

officer called to the scene has to decide whether the situation should be handled as a civil case by detaining the individual for psychiatric hospitalization, as a criminal case by arresting the individual, or as a case that can be resolved in one of a variety of informal ways by utilizing available resources.[5] At times, this decision is extremely difficult to make, particularly since it depends on the officer exercising his or her own discretion about whether to invoke the criminal process,[6] to invoke the law pertaining to emergency apprehension of a mentally ill person, or not to involve the law at all.[7] Generally, the police are reluctant to invoke the law but instead try to deal informally with the situation by employing a number of available options in the community.

Because the police are, in most instances, the only social control agency in the community that is available on a 24-hour basis, they are often called for a broad range of domestic crisis situations, many of which may involve a mentally disturbed family member. Intervening in such a family crisis situation may pose particular hazards to the inexperienced officer, whose lack of experience may cause the officer inadvertently to complicate the situation and induce violent reactions.[8] Even when the police participation is a "secondary involvement" in which, for example, the police merely assist in getting the mentally ill person civilly committed by providing custody or transportation at the instigation of others, there is a risk of interagency misunderstanding, as well as a feeling on the part of some officers that this is an inappropriate police activity.[9] These considerations underscore the vital importance of adequately educating and training police officers on matters of mental illness; they also show that any such educational/training program must explain and emphasize appropriate involvement with mentally disturbed persons as authentic police work. Because of the lack of established guidelines and procedures in handling the mentally ill, the difficulties the police necessarily confront in working in an area of such inherent uncertainty are compounded. Recognizing this predicament, the Police Executive Research Forum (PERF), a national organization of chief executives of law enforcement agencies has recently published a monograph, *Special Care: Improving the Police Response to the Mentally Disabled* that provides guidelines on police response to the mentally disturbed in particular situations.[10] The PERF report is consistent with the President's Commission on Law Enforcement and Administration of Justice, which recommended the development of guidelines for situations that require the exercise of police discretion.[11] Although there is only a small risk of an officer's incurring civil liability for making an honest mistake in the line of duty,[12] the implementation and use of guidelines should be able to reduce further any apprehension about this risk. More importantly, these guidelines could serve as the basis of constructive peer review and supervision.

It should be pointed out, though, that successful police involvement with the mentally ill depends to a large extent on establishing good working relationships with other community agencies, particularly with the mental health system.[13] Unfortunately, relations between the police and the mental health system have not always been harmonious, and often, when their social control functions overlap, the result has been misunderstandings, if not outright antagonism.[14] This condition exists, for example, when the admitting psychiatrist refuses to accept the patient brought to the emergency room by the police officer. A major reason for this friction between police officers and mental health professionals probably stems from the unrealistic expectations each entertains about the other's role and functions. For this reason, a review of the social role of the police and of the legal and professional constraints that attend their work should clarify their role vis-à-vis the mentally disturbed.

## ROLES OF THE POLICE OFFICER

The modern-day police officer basically combines two historically distinct roles in his ordinary functioning. Banton[15] distinguished between *law officers,* whose role is of a punitive and inquisitory nature within a legal mandate involving offenders, and *peace officers,* whose role lies more in the line of assisting citizens "within the moral consensus of the community" than in dealing with legal offenses. Similarly, Bittner[16] noted a distinction between two relatively independent police functions: "law enforcement" and "keeping the peace." But Wilson[17] believed that the patrolman's role is more intrinsically related to his responsibility for "maintaining order" than to "his responsibility for enforcing the law." Wilson backed up his assertion by noting that the patrolman contends with many more cases of order maintenance than law enforcement, and pointed out the frequency with which the work of maintaining order exposes both the policeman and the disputants to unpredictable risks of injury and even death "when you least expect it," for example, in a family quarrel.

Modern police departments in American society are, to a great extent, derived from the early English law-enforcement models. Actually, France and other continental countries had established formal police organizations before the English finally did so in the 19th century. This delay in forming an official police force in England was occasioned by the English people's fear of the kind of oppression in which the police forces in Europe had been involved.[18] Even the word *police,* derived from the Greek *polis,* or city, which historically meant the exercise of civic authority in general, was suspect; it had already acquired connotations associated with the repressive control the French police exercised over French citizens by the time the word was introduced into England, in the early part of the 18th century.[19] Nonetheless, the increasing rate of criminal behavior in England, as well as changing social, economic, and political circumstances, made it apparent that inherited methods of police work could no longer cope with crime control and peace-keeping duties.[20] In 1829, Sir Robert Peel managed to get Parliament to pass an "Act for Improving the Police In and Near the Metropolis," which led to the creation of a new police organization. It was to be under the ultimate control of a democratically elected Parliament, and it constituted the first British Metropolitan police system.[18] The new police force also turned out to be the last of the basic components in the modern executive government to be put into place.[20] Significantly, the exact location of the police in the then existing political system was never clearly specified. Presumably, the new organization would be part of the executive branch of government, yet the nature of its duties brought it under direct control of the judiciary. But direct judicial control over police work applied only to those cases that actually culminated in the legal prosecution of offenders. As Bittner[16] pointed out:

> The judiciary has neither the authority nor the means to direct, supervise, and review those activities of the police that do not result in prosecution. (p 700)

Thus, even at the outset, the London police realized that they had a dual function as law enforcers and peace keepers; moreover, from the first, the police were responsible for a task that was all but impossible to define, for "no one can say with any clarity what it means to do a good job of keeping the peace" (p 701).[16]

Like their British predecessors, the modern American police are expected to fulfill the originally separate roles of "watchmen" and "constables." Watchmen were used to make appointed rounds and maintain order; they usually acted under vague or nonexisting laws. Constables, on the other hand, were assigned the task (for a fee) of bringing criminal offenders to the bar of justice.[17] The first unified police force in the United States, which was created in New York City, followed the London model. This model was soon adapted by many other American municipalities.

Today, the extent of police involvement with maintaining order as distinct from crime control or law-enforcement activities has been estimated to be between 80% and 90%.[21] Police are called by citizens to deal with an extraordinarily wide range of services, including severe crisis situations involving personal or interpersonal problems[22] and domestic disturbances.[23] The public expects the police to respond on a 24-hour basis to any exigency that Bittner[24] characterized as "something-that-ought-not-to-be-happening-and-about-which-someone-had-better-do-something-now" (p 30). And it is often the lowest-ranking police officers who have to handle these complicated situations and who must exercise discretion "to decide if and how the law should be applied."[25]

## POLICE EXERCISE OF DISCRETION

An often quoted definition of discretion is Davis's:

> A public officer has discretion whenever the effective limits on his power leave him free to make a choice among possible causes of action or inaction. (p 4)[26]

Police discretion in decision-making is exercised in a variety of situations and contexts and at all levels of the police hierarchy. The patrolman has to decide whether to invoke the law for disorderly conduct and other minor offenses. At the police administrative level, given the limited resources available in most jurisdictions, decisions have to be made about organizational strategies on a variety of issues, such as which of the responsibilities and aspects of police functioning should be emphasized at any one time. Discretionary decision-making throughout the police hierarchy is therefore "influenced by individual perceptions of capabilities, community attitudes, and many other factors" (p 98).[27] But, as Dow[28] pointed out, there are substantial and widely shared reasons that encourage police, at all levels of the hierarchy, to exercise discretion so as to reduce arrests, a tendency that results in only a partial enforcement of the law. There are simply not enough police, courts, or jails to handle the volume of arrests that would follow from narrow interpretations of the law. Moreover, the main issues surrounding discretionary law enforcement include the lack of visibility of these decisions and the unlikelihood of their being reviewed; the vagueness and consequent potential for broad interpretation of numerous laws, for example, disorderly conduct; the ineffective transmission of the law to the law enforcers and the intentional nonenforcement of certain law-guiding behaviors by the police; and the nonarrest of certain perpetrators necessitated by an informer system.[28]

Obviously, the power to exercise discretion in deciding whether or not to arrest someone raises serious questions about the principle of equal justice before the law.[28] Goldstein[6] criticized police discretion not to invoke the criminal process as a phenomenon of such low visibility that it rarely becomes the subject of any review, an essential requirement to the rule of law. Although total enforcement of the law is not possible because of due-process restrictions on police arrests, searches, seizures, and interorganizational activities, Goldstein[6] maintained nevertheless that the police have an obligation for the full enforcement of the law, meaning the investigation of every criminal event, the attempt to discover the perpetrators, and the presentation of the information to the prosecutor. Because "decisions not to invoke within the area of full enforcement, the police largely determine the outer limits of actual enforcement throughout the criminal process" (pp 561–562), Goldstein[6] believed that the police should not have this discretion not to invoke the criminal law. On the other hand, Breitel[29] argued that discretion in crime control is essentially desirable, although he suggested that what is needed is better "administrative means for directing discretion, preferably by shared controls, and by reviewing its exercise internally" (p 435). In his study on police nonenforcement of the law, La Fave[30] also concluded that police discretion has seldom attained legitimate status in the law because these decisions have very low visibility and because there are insufficient means of challenging specific cases of discretionary inaction. Significantly, in his exploration of some reasons why police do not readily acknowledge exercising discretion, Goldstein[31] underscored the reluctance of the police to articulate any position in public. However, Goldstein[31] observed that true professional status does not come from performing ministerial functions, but rather is earned by "making value judgments and for exercising discretion based upon professional competence" (p 148). For this reason, police should strive for a higher degree of professional acceptance by acknowledging their discretionary roles. In a later article, Goldstein[32] provided a strong argument for police participation in policy-making in the absence of adequate legislative guidelines to deal with a multitude of alternative forms of action. Their involvement in the formulation of administrative policies would enable the police to establish defensible criteria and thereby achieve more confidence in situations requiring the exercise of discretion.

## POLICE DISCRETION IN EMERGENCY SITUATIONS

Police exercise discretion when they decide on one of the three basic ways of handling mentally disturbed citizens in the community: hospitalization, arrest, or informal disposition.[33] If the decision is to hospitalize an acutely disturbed and unwilling individual, the police are generally authorized to implement emergency detention procedures to apprehend the person in order to get him or her medically evaluated for involuntary admission to a mental hospital. Matthews[34] pointed out that emergency detention of dangerously mentally ill people was authorized in common law, even before modern legislation, and cited two leading cases pertaining to such detention: the New York case of *Warner v State*[35] in 1948 and the Illinois case of *Crawford v Brown*[36] in 1926. Under the common-law rule, if subsequently sued for false arrest or malicious prosecution, the police officer had to establish that emergency circumstances existed at the time of the detention. On the other hand, under modern statutes of emergency detention, the police are legally immune if they acted "in good faith." In New York State, the Mental Hygiene Law, under Article 9.41, entitled, "Emergency Admissions for Immediate Observation, Care, and Treatment: Powers of Certain Peace Officers and Police Officers;" provides that:

> Any peace officer, when acting pursuant to his special duties, or police officer . . . may take into custody any person who appears to be mentally ill and is conducting himself in a manner which is likely to result in serious harm to himself or others . . . may direct the removal of such person or remove him to any hospital specified . . . or, pending his examination or admission to any such hospital, temporarily detain any such person in another safe and comfortable place, in which event, such officer shall immediately notify the director of community servies or, if there be none, the health officer of the city or county of such action. (p 51)[37]

Interestingly, in the 1984 case of *Gilchrist v City of Livonia*,[38] all federal claims of constitutional violation were dismissed against Michigan police who twice left the home of a mentally ill man who was creating a disturbance and beating his wife. The husband then killed himself, and his wife brought suit. The court held that no Michigan statute or city local laws required the police to detain a mentally ill person; it was left to the discretion of the police.[39]

In the first major study of police discretion in emergency psychiatric situations, Bittner[7] found that police officers were essentially disinclined to take mentally ill persons into custody. Among the reasons given for this disinclination was Bittner's finding that police attitudes about mental illness are roughly similar to those of most people in denying the existence of a problem and in doing nothing about it. The police often come into contact with different types of poorly functioning people who manage to survive without outside intervention. Moreover, they have mixed feelings about whether or not dealing with mentally ill persons is an integral part of police work. This doubt increases their tendency to be annoyed by the ordeal of taking somebody to a psychiatric hospital. Finally, they dislike getting somebody locked up over what is basically a civil matter. Nonetheless, the police do make emergency apprehensions when there is evidence of attempted suicide; when there are signs of a serious mental disorder accompanied by marked agitation, disorientation, and bizarre behavior creating a public nuisance; and when the complaint originates from someone who has an instrumental relationship (i.e., doctor, teacher, landlord) with the patient. Still, as Bittner[7] pointed out, the police handle the larger number of mentally ill persons in the community by a variety of informal means. "The policeman acts as the terminal all purpose remedial agent" (p 286); he or she provides a kind of "psychiatric first aid." They are notably proficient at locating viable support for patients, often transferring the responsibility to responsible family members or other caretakers. Although these alternative methods of handling the mentally ill cannot be explicity codified, they depend to a great extent on the ingenuity of individual officers. These methods represent aspects of the craft of "keeping the peace" police perform that "meets certain tacit expectations." In another study, Bittner[16] further indentified practical "peace keeping skills" that police employ among residents on skid-row. Interestingly, Bittner's[7] endorsement of the police peace-keeping role, a role that he regards as containing "elements of control and support in a unique combination" (p 292), is in opposition to the view of Cumming et al.[22] that the policeman's overtly supportive and overtly controlling activities are basically incompatible.

A later study by Jacobson et al.[5] comprised a comprehensive exploration of some of the issues surrounding police involvement with mentally ill persons. These researchers believe their data suggest that police become involved most frequently with the mentally ill "when the situation contains elements of both 'real police business' and 'obvious psychiatric problems'" (p 546). They found that one third of these interventions were for aggressive behavior mostly taking place at home and reported by a family member. Next in frequency was confused behavior, and the next was for shouting obscenities and/or paranoid thoughts in public. There was much evidence that different police officers respond to basically similar situations in different ways, which indicates the existence of considerable diversity in decision-making. In regard to the three major dispositions—hospitalization, arrest, or informal management of the situation—the researchers accrued some interesting data. During the general interview, 14% denied having any responsibility for decision-making; 14% claimed they always arrested a mentally ill person for a violation; 21% denied they would arrest a mentally disturbed person even if a crime had been committed; and 51% said they would "sometimes" arrest a mentally ill person for committing a crime. However, the studies of the actual decisions made by the police officers revealed considerably less inclination to arrest the mentally ill. In 46% of the cases studied, in which the officers were aware of a violation of the law, only one arrest was made; this arrest was for resisting arrest, and involved a belligerent man who swung at a California Highway Patrolman. It is interesting to note that this was the officer's first experience with a mentally ill person. The police who chose civil hospitalization, even when there was a violation of the law, did so for the following reasons: 52% of the officers felt the individual was not responsible for his or her acts; 24% felt hospitalization would be more beneficial than jail; and 24% stated they would not make an arrest for disturbing the peace without a complainant. In the cases in which an alternative to hospitalization was considered, three fourths of the officers attempted to offer some help, such as counseling or contacting a responsible caretaker. Interestingly, over half of the officers questioned acknowledged that working with the mentally ill was an undesirable part of police work.

In a major study of police management of the mentally ill, Teplin[33] collected data on the everyday activity of police officers, in a large northern city, over a 14-month period. She found that out of 1,072 police–citizen encounters involving 2,122 citizens, 85 persons involved in 70 encounters were identified as mentally disordered. In comparing the numerical distribution of the three major dispositional categories of hospitalization, arrest, and informal disposition of the nonmentally disordered and mentally disordered, Teplin[33] found that, in the hospitalized category, there were no nonmentally disordered and 11.8% of the mentally disordered; in the arrest category, there were 6.5% of the nonmentally disordered and 16.5% of the mentally disordered; and in the informal disposition category, there were 93.5% of the nonmentally disordered and 71.8% of the mentally disordered. Teplin[33] concluded that these findings confirmed Bittner's[7] observation that the police were disinclined to make emergency apprehensions of the mentally ill. In the post-deinstitutionalization era, this disinclination could be influenced by the reduced number of psychiatric admission possibilities, because community hospitals generally have strict criteria for admission. The relatively high rate of arrests among the mentally disturbed is explained by Teplin[33] as a result of the officers' recognition that the patients would be unacceptable for admission to hospitals, that the public display of disordered behavior exceeded tolerable levels, and that there was a likelihood the problems would continue. The leading disposition was that of informal means, a disposition that tended to be invoked for "neighborhood characters," "'troublesome persons,'" and "quiet unobtrusive 'mental'" cases.

## POLICE DECISION ON HOSPITALIZATION OR ARREST

In cases in which an informal disposition is untenable, for example, when the individual remains violent and seriously disturbed, the police officer called to the scene will usually have only two choices: psychiatric hospitalization or criminal arrest.

The possibility that, as a result of more stringent commitment standards, the police have been inappropriately arresting the mentally ill (a phenomenon referred to as the "criminalization of mentally disordered behavior"[40]), or that criminals have been inappropriately hospitalized (a phenomenon labelled the "psychiatrization of criminal behavior"[41]), has generated considerable discussion.[42] In a 1966 *Psychiatric News* article, Glasscote[43] observed that, at that time, it had become a common practice in much of the country to detain the dangerously mentally ill in jail for relatively long periods of time, many of the detainees without any charges. In 1968, Rock *et al.*[9] described how, at that time, the Chicago police had used the criminal process to aid in the initiation of civil commitment. For many of these officers, this was a standard operating procedure. The violent individual was arrested on a disorderly conduct complaint and detained briefly in a jail cell, which tended to "color the intervention with legal authority." Matthews,[34] in 1970, also pointed out that, because of the difficulties police encountered in getting a mentally ill person admitted to a psychiatric hospital, they often resorted to the more familiar alternative of taking the person to jail.

In an effort to compare the perceptions of mental illness and decision-making in police officers who petitioned for civil commitment versus the perceptions and decision-making in police officers who made arrests, Monahan *et al.*[42] examined 50 representative cases in each category. In 30% of the civilly committed cases, the police could have arrested the individuals but did not because they felt that the individuals either lacked criminal intent or could benefit from inpatient treatment. Also, in 30% of the cases that culminated in an arrest, the police could have petitioned for civil commitment but did not because they felt that the individuals were not sufficiently mentally ill, dangerous, or gravely disabled to have their petitions stand up at the hospitals. Monahan *et al.*[42] realized that their findings could superficially support the sociological notion that the criminal justice and mental health systems have transposable functions of social control. But they also pointed out that, in over two thirds of the cases, the police correctly perceived the cases to be inappropriate for the other system. Also, in the almost one third of the cases that could have been referred to the other system but were not, "the choice was more of a legal technicality than a perceived behavioral option" (p 517). Monahan *et al.*[42] therefore concluded that there is little evidence of the "criminalization of mentally disordered behavior" and of the "psychiatrization of criminal behavior." In fact, they believed that "the police do a suprisingly accurate job of triage along the dimensions dictated by official public policy" (p 517).

On the other hand, Steadman *et al.*[44] studied the psychiatric evaluations performed on mentally disturbed individuals, who had been taken, by the police, to the emergency room of a general hospital in New York City for examination, and obtained differing results. The proportion of police referrals was 7.1% of the total number of psychiatric consults in the emergency room, which Steadman *et al.*[44] pointed out is similar to that of another study.[45] However, Steadman *et al.*[44] found that 69.2% of their police cases were discharged outright by the emergency room staff without referral to an outpatient clinic, 23.1% were admitted to the hospital, and 7.7% were referred to an outpatient facility. These results, when compared to the results of self-referrals and referrals by family friends, Emergency Medical Services (EMS), and other sources, turned out to have the lowest rate of admissions to the hospital of any category of referrals except self-referrals (22.2%), a finding that led Steadman *et al.*[44] to conclude that police referrals were neither as violent nor as mentally disordered as has been suggested in much of the literature. This discrepancy between the perceptions of seriously disturbed patients held by police officers and the perceptions of mental health professionals could account for much of the conflict between these two groups in emergency rooms.

In an article in which she critically examined the studies conducted on the "criminalization of the mentally ill," Teplin[2] surveyed the available investigations on police decision-making in this area. One of the numerous researchers she reported on was Urmer,[46] whom she noted as finding in a 1973 California study that a number of mentally disturbed people were processed though the criminal justice system because the mental health system was reluctant to accept for admission the non-dangerous and somewhat aggressive mentally disordered person. Teplin[2] concluded that "the bulk of studies of police decision making, though somewhat mixed, provide evidence that mentally disordered persons may be processed within the criminal justice system" (p 61). In a later article in which the data on 1,382 police–citizen encounters were presented, Teplin[47] found that "for similar offenses, mentally disordered citizens had a significantly greater chance of being arrested than non-mentally disordered persons" (p 794). She believed that the reason for this finding may be in part the relative unfamiliarity of police officers with severe mental symptoms. As she pointed out, such mental symptoms as verbal abuse, disrespect, and belligerence may provoke a more severe response on the part of a psychiatrically unsophisticated police officer than the same offense might provoke when committed by a more respectful offender. Additionally, the criminal justice system may be the only alternative to those persons who cannot be (or are not) treated within the mental health system.

In this context, there seems to be only a small risk of a successful civil suit being brought against a police officer for making a false arrest or for some other common law tort. Foote[12] noted that, though the incidence of illegal arrests in general is very high, "our society permits an intolerably high proportion of illegality in police practice" (p 493). Tort remedies for police violations of individual rights have generally not succeeded. If the plaintiff is not convicted of the crime, his prior reputation can frequently be used to challenge his credibility as a witness, to mitigate damages by showing that his reputation was such as to be adversely affected by the arrest, and to mitigate damages by showing there was probable cause for the arrest. If convicted of the offense, the plaintiff would be disqualified as a witness. Once the plaintiff has been inprisoned, there is little likelihood of the legal action being continued.[12] *The American Bar Association Standards for Criminal Justice*[27] points out that the main impediment in a tort liability suit is financial considerations, with the size of the judgment likely to be small and the individual police officer judgment proof, that is, having extremely limited financial resources. In addition, the people most likely to encounter the police and be mistreated usually make poor plaintiffs (as noted above by Foote[12]).

In regard to false imprisonment as a civil rights violation, the *American Law Report* (ALR)[48] provides a synopsis of the standard of deprivation of federal rights, generally. Under Section 42, United States Code (USC) Article 1983, a police officer making an arrest is liable if, while under color of state law, he deprives someone of his or her constitutional rights. But he is not liable "if there was probable cause for the arrest or he acted under an honest misunderstanding of the law or facts." In one 1963 case cited, *Joyce v Ferrazz,*[49] the court held that police officers had not deprived the plaintiff under 42 USC 1983 of any federally secured right, privileges, or immunity. In this case, the police, investigating complaints of a disturbance, were admitted into the home by the plaintiff's wife, and found the plaintiff fighting with his son and behaving irrationally. The police took the husband to the station house. He then spent 9 or 10 days in a mental institution. The plaintiff alleged false arrest in his home and wrongful commitment to the hospital. Nonetheless, the frequency with which the police are called on to exercise their discretion in such cases highlights the need for educational training and guidelines in dealing with the mentally ill.

## EDUCATIONAL TRAINING AND GUIDELINES

The management of mentally disturbed persons is potentially one of the most risky, difficult, and explosive situations with which police officers have to contend.[50] The recent study by PERF has confirmed what has been generally surmised, which is that police departments are not adequately preparing their officers to deal with the mentally ill. According to the PERF report, the average police curriculum for training recruits devotes a mere 4.3 hours to mental health. This is certainly insufficient time to deal with such complex topics as mental disorders, recognizing and handling the mentally ill, the exercise of discretion, state and local laws, department policy, involuntary commitment procedures, rights of the mentally ill, and other issues.

Although there have been reports in the literature about mental health professionals consulting with police departments in regard to training police officers in such areas as community mental health,[51,52] human relations,[53,54] crisis intervention,[8,55] and how to distinguish mental illness,[56] there seems to be relatively less literature available on how to handle the severely mentally disturbed patient. One widely used manual, *How to Recognize and Handle Abnormal People*, dealing with the subject, was written in 1954 in a simple, clear style by two mental health professionals, Matthews and Rowland.[57] This manual was intended to aid the police officer in recognizing and managing mentally disturbed persons, as well as cases of physical illness and amnesia, drug addiction, alcoholism, and so on. In handling a disturbed or violent person, these authors stress five points for the officer to remember in such a situation:

> 1) Take time to look the situation over; 2) Do not abuse or threaten; 3) Do not let him get your goat; 4) Avoid excitement; and 5) Do not deceive.

This manual, along with Russell and Biegel's[58] *Understanding Human Behavior for Effective Police Work* and *Police Crisis Intervention* by Goldstein *et al.*,[59] contains useful information about human behavior and the treatment of the mentally ill during crisis situations.

The PERF monograph serves as a guide to police managers who are attempting to develop and implement response stategies to encounters with the mentally disturbed, and describes procedures to be used by police officers in handling the mentally ill, from the time a call for service is received until a final disposition is made. Many of these procedural recommendations consist of either typical police responses, or a synthesis of approaches previously articulated in the literature from a police perspective. For example, the chapter on "Operational Procedures" incorporates some of the recommendations found in the manual of Matthews and Roland[57] and in the book of Goldstein *et al.*[59] But in the PERF monograph, these recommendations are specified as procedures that emanate not from mental health professionals or even individual police officers, but from a national organization of chief executives of law enforcement agencies, and so should have considerably more influence.

## POLICE AND MENTAL HEALTH AGENCY INTERRELATIONSHIPS

The crucial interrelationship between police and mental health providers, which is dictated by their overlapping responsibilities for the management of the mentally disturbed in the community, makes it essential that these professions develop a better understanding of one another. As was mentioned earlier, the interrelationship between the two professional groups has often led to misunderstandings, especially in receiving hospital emergency rooms where mental health professionals and the police are most likely to come into contact and to conflict with one another. Handberg and Pilchik[60] discussed the nature of these conflicts; they concluded that a key factor in improving the situation could be the police's gain in credibility as a result of expanded training in dealing with the mentally disturbed, because the officers are frequently viewed as unreliable evaluators by mental health professionals.

Additional means of improving the working relationship of mental health professionals and the police, and of utilizing the expertise of both for the good of the community, have been developed. Treger[61] described a police–social worker team model that lasted for three years and developed viable interprofessional relationships. In this model, professional social workers and graduate students were available 24 hours a day for police referrals of crisis cases. Cesnik *et al.*[62] pointed out that police tend to lose confidence in a crisis intervention service which cannot be on the scene within a half hour in an emergency situation. By providing professional mental health workers who respond quickly on the scene to help in handling the case and who later give feedback to the officers involved, the crisis intervention service has promoted a good working relationship with the police. Everstine *et al.*[63] described a mobile emergency psychology service that serves 10 Northern California police departments. This crisis intervention service is available 24 hours a day, 7 days a week to provide evaluative, immediate therapy (up to 6 sessions) and referral for ongoing treatment if needed. Another example of a rather unique mobile crisis intervention service is described by Bengelsdorf and Alden.[64] In many respects, this service is ideal because, in addition to experienced mental health professionals, there is also a psychiatrist on the team, which is available to respond to calls on a 24-hour basis. The psychiatrist can evaluate the disturbed person for the need of emergency hospitalization. This resource relieves the police of the responsibility of having to act on their own discretion, especially in questionable cases when the individual has calmed down.

The PERF report also describes three police departments that have developed model training programs and procedures. The differences among these programs basically reflect variations in community needs and resources. Fundamentally, each one of the model programs contains certain key elements considered essential for the effective operation of a police department program for handling mentally disturbed persons. Each program

> maintains a 24-hour, on-site response capability . . . 24-hour access to the needed resources . . . trained mental health professionals (police or civilian) . . . clearly delineates the duties and responsibilities among the key actors from different agencies . . . has procedures that reduce the time officers need to spend handling mentally ill persons, and includes close and regular liaison between the participating agencies.[10]

Programs such as these seem to offer the most promising means of simultaneously improving the working relationship of these two professions and of ensuring appropriate treatment to the mentally ill in the community.

## CONCLUSION

This chapter has been an attempt to describe the role of the police in their encounters with the mentally ill in the community. In most instances, the police remain the only social control agency available to be quickly on the scene, 24 hours a day, to handle the emergency situation. During the past decade and a half, a variety of innovative mental health services, including mobile crisis intervention teams, have been established in some communities. These teams have been able to expand the scope of emergency professional services to their citizens. Nonetheless, the police are unique in being the only agency sanctioned to use force. As Bittner[24] put it, "The policeman and the policeman alone, is equipped, entitled, and required to deal with every exigency in which force may have to be used, to meet it." An especially shocking demonstration of the police use of force with a mentally disturbed person was in the Bumpurs case[65] in New York City. The particular police involved were members of the Emergency Service Unit of the New York City Police Department, who were specially trained to handle extremely dangerous situations including those involving mentally disturbed violent people. The police on the Emergency Service Unit had been trained to avoid the use of force against emotionally disturbed persons (E.D.P. in police jargon) whenever possible, but they were expected to assume the worst and have proper equipment available to handle any eventuality.[66]

In October, 1984, Police Officer Stephen Sullivan, a member of the Emergency Service Unit, fired twice from a shotgun, killing Eleanor Bumpurs, a 66-year-old black woman who had a history of emotional disturbance and violent behavior. The Housing Authority had called the police to aid in physically evicting Mrs. Bumpurs from her apartment after she fell behind in her rent payments. Indicted on a manslaughter charge, Officer Sullivan contended that he had to fire the second time because the first shot failed to stop Mrs. Bumpurs from attacking his fellow officers with a kitchen knife. At issue was whether the officer fired a "legally unjustifiable second shot." In February, 1987, he was acquitted of the charge by a State Supreme Court justice in the Bronx because the prosecution had failed to prove beyond a reasonable doubt that the officer had "grossly deviated from standards becoming a police officer" (p 1).[67] Significantly, three days after the shooting, Police Commissioner Ward revised the department guidelines in the use of force, as in the Bumpurs case, for disarming a mentally disturbed person. Henceforth, if there is no immediate threat, police are to delay action until a precint commander or captain arrives on the scene, and "taser" shock guns and other nonlethal devices are to replace shotguns or other weapons.[68]

Although the court held that no criminal laws had been violated, the Bumpurs case dramatically illustrated the potential dangers that attend police encounters with emotionally disturbed persons, dangers for both the police and the mentally disturbed individuals. Even police who have had special training in dealing with such situations consider assignments to respond to calls on the violent and emotionally disturbed person to be among the most stressful and difficult assignments.[66] Yet, in most communities, ordinary police officers are the ones who are likely to encounter the mentally ill. Whether the police are initially called in by the family, the neighbors, or an outside agency or encounter the patient in the course of patrolling their beat, the police officers' role in handling seriously mentally disturbed patients is critical. This points up the urgent need for adequate training, guidelines, supervision by experienced superior officers, and finally consultations and interactions with other agencies, and especially with the mental health system.

## REFERENCES

1. Liberman R: Police as a community mental health resource. *Community Ment Health J* 1969; 5:111–120.

  2. Teplin LA: The criminalization of the mentally ill: Speculation in search of data. *Psychol Bull* 1983; 94:54–67.
  3. Snibbe JR: The police and the mentally ill: Practices, problems, and some solutions, in Snibbe JR, Snibbe HM (eds): *The Urban Policeman in Transition.* Springfield, Ill, Charles C Thomas, Publisher, 1973.
  4. Whitmer GE: From hospitals to jails: The fate of California's deinstitutionalized mentally ill. *Am J Orthopsychiatry* 1980; 50:65–75.
  5. Jacobson D, Craven W, Kushner S: A study of police referral of allegedly mentally-ill persons to a psychiatric unit, in Snibbe JR, Snibbe HM (eds): *The Urban Policeman in Transition: A Psychological and Sociological Review.* Springfield, Ill, Charles C Thomas Publisher, 1973.
  6. Goldstein J: Police discretion not to invoke the criminal process: Law-visibility decisions in the administration of justice. *Yale Law J* 1960; 69:543–594.
  7. Bittner E: Police discretion in emergency apprehension of mentally ill persons. *Soc Probl* 1967; 14:278–292.
  8. Barocas HA: Urban policemen: Crisis mediators or crisis creators? *Am J Orthopsychiatry* 1973; 43:632–639.
  9. Rock RS, Jacobson MA, Janopaul RM: *Hospitalization and Discharge of the Mentally Ill.* Chicago, University of Chicago Press, 1968.
 10. Police Executive Research Forum (PERF): *Special Care: Improving The Police Response to the Mentally Disabled.* Washington, DC, 1986.
 11. President's Commission on Law Enforcement and Administration of Justice: *The Challenge of Crime in a Free Society.* Washington, DC, Government Printing Office, 1967.
 12. Foote C: Tort remedies for police violations of individual rights. *Minn Law Rev* 1955; 39:493–516.
 13. Group for The Advancement of Psychiatry: *Interfaces: A Communications Case Book for Mental Health Decision Makers.* San Francisco, Mental Health Materials Center, Jossey-Bass Publishers, 1981.
 14. Rosenbeck R: From conflict to collaboration: Psychiatry and the hospital police. *Psychiatry* 1985; 48:254–263.
 15. Banton M: *The Policeman in the Community.* New York, Basic Books, Inc, 1964.
 16. Bittner E: The police on skid-row: A study of peace keeping. *Am Soc Rev* 1967; 32:699–715.
 17. Wilson JQ: *Varieties of Police Behavior.* Cambridge, Mass, Harvard University Press, 1968.
 18. President's Commission on Law Enforcement and Administration of Justice: *Task Force Report: The Police.* Washington, DC, U.S. Government Printing Office, 1967.
 19. Manning PK: *Police Work: The Social Organization of Policing.* Cambridge, Mass, MIT Press, 1977.
 20. Bittner E: *The Functions of the Police in Modern Society.* Rockville, Md, DHEW Publication No. (ADM) 75–260, 1970.
 21. Bard M: The role of law enforcement in the helping system. *Community Ment Health J* 1971; 7:151–160.
 22. Cumming E, Cumming I, Edell L: Policeman as philosopher, guide and friend. *Soc Probl* 1965; 12:276–286.
 23. Parnas RI: The police response to the domestic disturbance. *Wis Law Rev* Fall 1967,:914–960.
 24. Bittner E: Florence Nightingale in pursuit of Willie Sutton: A theory of the police in Jacob H (ed): *The Potential for Reform of Criminal Justice.* Beverly Hills, Sage Publications, Inc, 1974.
 25. Niederhoffer A: *Behind the Shield: The Police in Urban Society.* New York, Doubleday & Company, Inc, 1967.

26. Davis KC: *Discretionary Justice: A Preliminary Inquiry*. Baton Rouge, La, Louisiana State University Press, 1969.

27. American Bar Association Standards For Criminal Justice: *Task Force on Urban Police Function*. Boston, Little Brown and Co, 1979.

28. Dow PE: *Discetionary Justice: A Critical Inquiry*. Cambridge, Mass, Ballinger Publishing Company, 1981.

29. Breitel CD: Controls in criminal law enforcement. *University of Chicago Law Rev* 1960; 27:427–435.

30. LaFave WR: The police and nonenforcement of the law—Part I. *Wis Law Rev* 1962; 1:104–137.

31. Goldstein H: Police discretion: The ideal versus the real. *Public Admin Rev* 1963; 23:140–148.

32. Goldstein H: Police policy formulation: A proposal for improving police performance. *Mich Law Rev* 1967; 65:1123–1146.

33. Teplin LA: Managing disorder: Police handling of the mentally ill, in Teplin LA (ed.): *Mental Health and Criminal Justice*. Beverly Hills, Sage Publications, Inc, 1984.

34. Matthews AR: Observations on police policy and procedures for emergency detention of the mentally ill. *J Crim Law Criminol Police Sci* 1970; 61:283–295.

35. *Warner v State*, 297 N.Y. 395, 79 N.E.2d 459 (1948).

36. *Crawford v Brown*, 321 Ill. 305, 151 N.E. 911 (1926).

37. *McKinney's Consolidated Laws of New York Annotated: Mental Hygiene Law, Book 34A, Cumulative Annual Pocket Part*. St. Paul, Minn, West Publishing Co, 1987.

38. *Gilchrist v City of Livonia*, 599 F. Supp. 260 (E.D. Mich. 1984).

39. *Am Law Enforcement Liability Reporter* 1985; 149:11.

40. Abrahamson M: The criminalization of mentally disordered behavior: Possible side effect of a new mantal health law. *Hosp Community Psychiatry* 1972; 23:101–105.

41. Monahan J: The psychiatrization of criminal behavior. *Hsop Community Psychiatry* 1973; 24:105–107.

42. Monahan J, Caldeira C, Friedlander HD: Police and the mentally ill: A comparison of committed and arrested persons. *Int J Law Psychiatry* 1979; 2:509–518.

43. Glassote RM: Putting the mentally ill in jail continues to be common practice in much of U.S. *Psychiatr News* 1966; 1 (May–June) p 2.

44. Steadman HJ, Morrissey JP, Braff J, Monahan J: Psychiatric evaluations of police referrals in a general hospital emergency room. *Int J Law Psychiatry* 1986; 8:39–47.

45. Bassuk GL: The impact of deinstitutionalization on the general hospital psychiatric emergency ward. *Hosp Community Psychiatry* 1980; 31:623–627.

46. Urmer A: *The Burden of the Mentally Disordered on Law Enforcement*. Sacramento, Calif, ENKI Research Institute, 1973.

47. Teplin LA: Criminalizing mental disorder: The comparative arrest rate of the mentally ill. *Am Psychol* 1984; 39:794–803.

48. *Annotation: Police Action in Connection With Arrest as Violation of Civil Rights Act*. American Law Reports, 1 ALR Fed 519, Rochester, NY and San Francisco, Cal.

49. *Joyce v Ferrazzi*, 323 F.2d 931 (1963).

50. Territo L: Assessing police procedures in handling disturbed persons. *Trial* 1983; 19:74–79, 100–101.

51. Friedman MH: Community mental health education with police. *Ment Hyg* 1965; 49:182–186.

52. Elkins AM, Papanek GO: Consultation with the police: An example of community psychiatry practice. *Am J Psychiatry* 1966; 123:531–535.

53. Sikes MP, Cleveland SE: Human relations training for police and community. *Am Psychol* 1968; 23:766–769.

54. Newman LE, Steinberg JL: Consultation with police on human relations training. *Am J Psychiatry* 1970; 125:1421–1429.
55. Bard M, Berkowitz B: Training police as specialists in family crisis intervention: A community pyschology action program. *Community Ment Health J* 1967; 3:315–317.
56. Janus SS, Bess BE, Cadden JJ, Greanwald H: Training police officers to distinguish mental illness. *Am J Psychiatry* 1980; 137:228–229.
57. Matthews RA, Rowland LW: *How to Recognize and Handle Abnormal People*, rev ed. New York, The National Association For Mental Health, Inc, 1960.
58. Russell HE, Biegel A: *Understanding Human Behavior for Effective Police Work*. New York, Basic Books, Inc, 1976.
59. Goldstein A, Monti PJ, Sardino TJ, Green DJ: *Police Crisis Intervention*. Elmsford, NY, Pergamon Press, 1977.
60. Handberg R, Pilchik S: Police handling of mental patients: Crisis intervention requirements and police behavior. *Crim Just Rev* 1980; 5:66–73.
61. Treger H, *et al: The Police-Social Work Team. A New Model for Interprofessional Cooperation: A University Demonstration Project in Manpower Training and Development.* Springfield Ill, Charles C Thomas Publisher, 1975.
62. Cesnik BI, Puls M: Law enforcement and crisis intervention services: A critical relationship. *Suicide Life Threat Behav* 1977; 7:211–215.
63. Everstine DS, Bodin AM, Everstine L: Emergency psychology: A mobile service for police crisis calls. *Fam Process* 1977; 16:281–292.
64. Bengelsdorf H, Alden DC: A mobile crisis unit in the psychiatric emergency room. *Hosp Community Psychiatry* 1987; 38:662–665.
65. *People v Sullivan* 68 N.Y. 2d 495 (1986).
66. Bodkin JE: "Psycho" call response. *Law and Order* 1980; 28(11):48, 50–53.
67. Officers acquitted in Bumpurs case. *NY Law J* 1987; 197(38) 1.
68. New York Police Union blasts D.A. over indictment of officer. *Crim Just Newsletter* 1985; 16(4):1–3.

# 11

# Criminal Confessions and the Mentally Disabled

**_Colorado v Connelly_ and the Future of Free Will**

MICHAEL L. PERLIN

## INTRODUCTION

Few sets of tea leaves are examined, analyzed, and pored over as closely as any United States Supreme Court decision involving what is generically known as a *Miranda* issue.[1] The scholarly and popular debates that have raged since a badly fractured Warren Court attempted to establish a "bright line" test for admissibility of confessions in *Miranda v Arizona*[2] have given *Miranda* a symbolic value that extends far beyond the decision's actual impact on police interrogation.[3] Although the Burger (and now the Rehnquist) Courts have expressed dissatisfaction with the constitutional and philosophical underpinnings of the doctrine, the "inescapably political overtones" of an outright reversal[4] make it likely that *Miranda* will not be overruled "at this late date."[5] Even though the doctrine—by the Court's own reckoning—remains "murky,"[6] and its empirical impact remains questionable,[7] it remains a "punch-drunk fighter, reeling on the ropes but not yet counted out."[8]

This chapter is adapted, with changes, by permission of the publisher, from Michael L. Perlin, "*Colorado v. Connelly*: Farewell to Free Will?" *Search and Seizure Law Report*, vol 14, no 5 (June 1987). Copyright 1987 by Clark Boardman Co., Ltd., 435 Hudson Street, New York, New York 10014.

---

**MICHAEL L. PERLIN** • Director, Federal Litigation Clinic, New York Law School, 57 Worth Street, New York, NY 10013.

157

## CONFESSIONS AND MENTAL DISABILITY

Although the Supreme Court's *Miranda* inroads have been (mostly) incessant, these limitations have not been uniform.[9] In a handful of cases involving mentally disabled criminal defendants, the Burger Court had appeared willing to either expand or at least to decline to contract the scope of the *Miranda* doctrine.[10] This divergence should not be too surprising, given the historic interrelationship between mental disability and the constitutional law of confessions. The first important modern case, *Blackburn v Alabama*,[11] reversed the conviction of an "indisputably insane and incompetent defendant";[12] in *Culombe v Connecticut*,[13] a case involving a severely mentally retarded defendant, the Court relied once again on the famous language from Hale's *Pleas of the Crown*: "The law will not suffer a prisoner to be made *the deluded instrument of his own conviction*" [italics added].[14] The *Miranda* case *itself* involved a putatively severely mentally disabled criminal defendant.[15]

When read together, *Blackburn, Culombe,* and *Townsend v Sain*[16] appeared to establish the firm principles that "a most basic sense of justice is affronted by the spectacle of incarcerating a human being upon the basis of a statement he made while insane,"[17] and that admissibility of a confession would be governed by a determination as to whether the defendant's "will was overborne" or whether the confession was not "the product of a rational intellect and a free will."[18] These principles, however, have been sharply called into question by *Colorado v Connelly*,[19] the Rehnquist Court's first decision involving the confession of a mentally disabled person, an opinion characterized by a leading scholar in the field as "illusion [shattering]" and as "one of the more surprising opinions I have read in the field of mental disability law."[20]

## *CONNELLY*: THE FACTUAL AND PROCEDURAL BACKGROUND

*Connelly*—in what the dissenters characterized as an "unprecedented" opinion[21]—established three sets of principles that appear to change drastically the ground rules for assessing confessions cases involving mentally disabled defendants.[22] First, in what will likely be the case's most significant legacy, the court, per Justice Rehnquist, found that coercive police activity is a necessary predicate to a finding that a confession was not voluntary within the Fourteenth Amendment's due process clause.[23] Second, a determination of "voluntariness" of a Fifth Amendment privilege waiver depends solely on the absence of police overreaching and *not* on any broad concept of "free will."[24] Third, a waiver of *Miranda* rights must be proven by the state only by the burden of preponderance of the evidence.[25] In order to understand the potential impact of these rulings—both in other *Miranda* cases and in other mental disability cases—it is necessary to examine the factual and procedural background of *Connelly* as well as the unique role of some of the interest groups that participated as amicus before the Supreme Court.

The factual underpinning of *Connelly* appears relatively clear. The defendant approached a uniformed police office in downtown Denver and stated, without any prompting, that he had murdered someone and "wanted to talk about it."[26] The policeman immediately advised the defendant of his *Miranda* rights, to which the latter replied that he understood those rights but wished to discuss a murder. In response to further questioning, the defendant denied the recent use of drugs or alcohol but stated that he had been a patient in several mental hospitals in the past, and that, although he understood he was under no obligation to speak to the officer, he wished to do so because "his conscience had been bothering him."[27]

At this point, a second officer arrived, and the defendant was again given the *Miranda* warnings; he responded that he had "come all the way from Boston" to confess to the murder of a young girl whom he had killed in Denver ten months previously.[28] After a trip to police headquarters (where it was learned that the body of an unidentified female had been found six months after the alleged murder took place), the defendant agreed to accompany two officers to the scene of the killing (which he pointed out). One of the officers subsequently testified that, throughout this episode, he "perceived no indication whatsoever that [the defendant] was suffering from any kind of mental illness."[29]

The next day, the defendant became "visibly disoriented"[30] and stated that "voices" had told him to come to Denver, and that he had "followed the directions of those voices in confessing."[31] Subsequently, he was sent to a state hospital for an evaluation; originally found incompetent to stand trial, he was eventually deemed fit to proceed.[32]

At a preliminary suppression hearing, the defendant produced Dr. Jeffrey Metzner, a state hospital psychiatrist, who testified that the defendant was a chronic schizophrenic who believed himself to be following the "voice of God," which told him to "confess to the killing or to commit suicide."[33] According to the witness, the defendant was experiencing "auditory command hallucinations" that interfered with his "volitional abilities . . . to make free and rational choices," but that did not significantly impair his cognitive abilities, thus enabling him to understand the *Miranda* rights as given by the police officers.[34]

The Colorado trial court ordered the statement suppressed, relying on *Townsend* and *Culombe,* and reasoned that the defendant's mental illness had "destroyed his volition" and "vitiated" his attempted *Miranda* waiver.[35] The Colorado Supreme Court affirmed, ruling that the absence of police coercion did not foreclose an involuntariness finding and concluding that an individual's capacity for "rational judgment and free choice may be overborne as much by certain forms of severe mental illness as by external pressure."[36] The United States Supreme Court then granted certiorari.[37]

## ROLE OF AMICUS

In addition to the parties, several amicus groups filed briefs staking out specific positions on the questions involved. Predictably, the Solicitor General and the Americans for Effective Law Enforcement (joined by the National District Attorneys Association, the International Association of Chiefs of Police, and the Legal Foundation of America) filed briefs on behalf of the state; the Coalition for the Fundamental Rights and Equality of Ex-Patients (FREE) (an umbrella group including the National Mental Health Association, the New Jersey Department of the Public Advocate, the National Mental Health Consumers Association, and other ex-patient and advocacy groups working on behalf of present and former consumers of mental health services) filed on behalf of the defendant. More startlingly, the American Psychological Association (APA) filed a brief on behalf of the state, arguing (1) that the psychiatric evidence adduced at the suppression hearing was the witness's "personal opinion, [and] not an opinion based on generally accepted and reliable scientific evidence,"[38] and (2) that the state's use of the defendant's "spontaneous precustodial confession" did not violate the due process clause.[39] This was a major change of direction of the APA,[40] which had for the past fifteen years consistently filed such amicus briefs on behalf of mentally disabled individuals in civil[41] and criminal[42] cases.

## *CONNELLY*: THE SUPREME COURT

The Supreme Court reversed.[43] Writing for himself and four others,[44] the Chief Justice stressed the absence of the "coercive governmental misconduct" that was the "catalyst" for the Court's "seminal" confession case of *Brown v Mississippi*,[45] determining that the cases decided in the subsequent half century have focused on "the crucial element of police overreaching."[46] The common ingredient in all these cases was "a substantial element of coercive police conduct . . . causally related to the confession"; without such coercive conduct, he reasoned, "there is simply no basis for concluding that a defendant's mental condition, by itself and apart from its relation to official coercion, should even dispose of the inquiry into constitutional 'voluntariness.' "[47]

The Chief Justice carefully distinguished *Blackburn* and *Townsend,* in view of the "integral element of police overreaching" in both cases;[48] whereas those cases stand for the proposition that mental condition is "surely relevant" to the defendant's *susceptibility* to police coercion, "mere examination of the defendant's state of mind can never conclude the due process inquiry."[49]

Supression of the defendant's confession would "serve absolutely no purpose in enforcing constitutional guarantees," since it could not be expected to deter future constitutional violations.[50] If the defendant were to prevail, the courts would be forced, even without the presence of a link between coercive state action and the defendant's subsequent confession, to "divine a defendant's motivation for speaking or acting," a requirement the court rejected as not constitutionally required.[51] Thus, inquiries into the defendant's state of mind should properly be guided by state evidence laws and not by constitutional standards[52]; to rule otherwise would conflict with due process principles that focus on the prevention of "fundamental unfairness in the use of evidence, whether true or false."[53]

Next, the Court considered the appropriate burden to be imposed in assessing a *Miranda* waiver question and reaffirmed its holding, in *Lego v Twomey,*[54] that a preponderance of the evidence standard was constitutionally sufficient, rejecting the suggestion that language in earlier cases, such as *Tague v Louisiana,*[55] or *North Carolina v Butler,*[56] implied that a more stringent quantum of proof was required.[57] It reasoned that, if the standard for voluntariness of a confession required only the preponderance standard (as *Lego* had held), then a waiver of the *"auxiliary protections* established in *Miranda"* should require no higher burden.[58] It thus specifically disapproved of that aspect of the Colorado Supreme Court's opinion which had ruled that the state bear its burden on this question by "clear and convincing" evidence.[59]

Further, the Court concluded that the state court had erred in its conclusion that the defendant had waived his *Miranda* rights in the case before the court, and in its methodology of assessing his ability to make a "free decision" regarding the waiver of his constitutional rights.[60] As this aspect of *Miranda* is premised on the Fifth Amendment, which is concerned only with governmental coercion,[61] the Colorado court "erred in importing into this area of constitutional law notions of 'free will' *that have no place there."*[62]

The privilege, the Court stressed, is *not* concerned with "moral and psychological pressures to confess emanating from sources other than official coercion"[63]; to adopt the defendant's "free will" rationale—and thus presumably to invalidate a waiver "whenever the defendant feels compelled to waive his rights by *any* compulsion"[64]—would "cut this Court's [*Miranda*] holding completely loose from its own explicitly stated rationale."[65] It concluded:

> *Miranda* protects defendants against government coercion leading them to surrender rights protected by the Fifth Amendment; it goes no further than that. Respondent's perception of coercion flowing from the "voice of God," however important or significant such a perception may be in other disciplines, is a matter to which the United States Constitution does not speak.[66]

## *CONNELLY*: THE OTHER OPINIONS

Justice Blackmun concurred briefly, noting that he would not have resolved the quantum of proof issue, which was neither raised nor briefed by the parties.[67] Justice Stevens concurred as to that part of the judgment that dealt with the defendant's *precustodial* statements (as they were not the product of state compulsion) but dissented on the question of the *postcustodial* utterances; once the custodial relationship was entered, the questioning became "presumptively coercive"[68] and could not continue absent a valid waiver.[69] Because the defendant was—virtually contemporaneously—found incompetent to stand trial, Justice Stevens would have found that he was not competent to waive his right to remain silent.[70] Finally, he characterized the Court's determination that a waiver could be voluntary even if not produced by the defendant's "free will" as "incomprehensible" and as conflicting with the Court's recent language in *Moran v Burbine*[71] that such a waiver must be the product of a "free and deliberate choice."[72] Although he conceded that *Moran* contrasted this freely given waiver to a situation in which a statement was obtained by "intimidation, coercion or deception,[73] this "dichotomy" was not exhaustive; "the mere absence of police misconduct does not establish that the suspect has made a free and deliberate choice when [he] is not competent to stand trial.[74]

Justice Brennan dissented, labeling the majority's opinion as "unprecedented" and "antithetical" to fundamental fairness.[75] Instead, he would have held that the absence of police wrongdoing, by itself, should not determine the voluntariness of a confession, and that the voluntariness requirement itself reflected a recognition of the importance of free will and of reliability in determining a confession's admissibility, thus demanding an inquiry into the "totality of the circumstances" surrounding the confession.[76]

The Court's decision to refuse to acknowledge the role of free will "as a value of constitutional consequence . . . ignores 200 years of constitutional jurisprudence," Justice Brennan charged.[77] The Court's focus should *not* be limited to police coercion, because the value of freedom of the will "has demanded a broader inquiry," he concluded, drawing on such cases as *Blackburn, Culombe,* and *Townsend* and noting that—though police overreaching has been an aspect of every prior confession case—in each instance, the court had made clear that "ensuring that a confession is a product of a free will is an independent concern."[78]

The issue is particularly pointed in this case, in which Justice Brennan found the majority's characterization of the record as reflecting no police wrongdoing as "clearly erroneous,"[79] reading the trial transcript to reflect police knowledge of the defendant's serious mental illness (e.g., the arresting officer first thought the defendant was a "crackpot"; the defendant informed the police of his prior institutionalizations in five different mental hospitals).[80] He concluded that the Court's holding that involuntary confessions are only those that are procured through police misconduct was "inconsistent with the Court's historical insistence that only confessions reflecting an exercise of free will be admitted into evidence."[81]

Because the court has chosen to include confessions by the mentally ill as "voluntary," the *reliability* of these confessions becomes a central concern, Brennan continued,[82] especially because no other class of evidence is as "profoundly prejudicial" as a confession.[83] The case before the court "starkly highlights" the danger of admitting a confession by a severely mentally ill individual, involving, as it does, an uncorroborated statement by an actively hallucinating, then-incompetent-to-stand-trial defendant exhibiting delusional thinking.[84] On this point, Justice Brennan concluded:

> Minimum standards of due process should require that the trial court find substantial indicia of reliability on the basis of evidence extrinsic to the confession itself, before admitting the confession of a mentally ill person into evidence.[85]

Finally, Justice Brennan dissented from the Court's holdings that waiver need be proven only by a preponderance of the evidence and that a waiver is automatically voluntary in the absence of police coercion.[86] The preponderance decision flies in the face of *Miranda*'s explicit language that waiver involves a "heavy" burden and a "high" standard of proof[87]; further, the Court's decision in *Lego* (upon which the majority relied, and in which Justice Brennan dissented),[88] a case involving a *noncustodial* defendant, was predicated on the exclusion of all involuntary confessions, a circumstance now inapplicable in light of the majority's holding in *Connelly*.[89]

In any event, even accepting the preponderance standard, Justice Brennan would have found that the prosecution failed to meet its burden of proof, given the uncontroverted testimony below that the defendant "was incapable" of making a "free decision" regarding his *Miranda* rights.[90] Finally, Justice Brennan looked at the *other* aspect of *Miranda* voluntariness: the need for a finding that the waiver was "knowing and intelligent."[91] Because the defendant was "clearly" unable to make an "intelligent" decision regarding waiver, the Colorado Supreme Court decision should thus have been affirmed.[92]

## *CONNELLY'S* PUZZLES

On many levels, *Connelly* is a puzzling decision, leaving many unanswered questions. First, the Court's crabbed readings of such cases as *Blackburn* and *Townsend*—focusing virtually exclusively on the question of "police overreaching"[93]—ignores the reality that a defendant's mental condition has historically been seen not merely as "relevant" to the inquiry of his "susceptibility to police coercion,"[94] but as *central* to that question.[95]

Second, it is puzzling that the Court chose to limit the "free will" inquiry as sharply as it did so soon after its decision in *Moran*[96] that voluntariness requires a "free and deliberate choice." Although the *Moran* Court *did* contrast that status with those of statements produced by "intimidation, coercion or deception,"[97] Justice Stevens's conclusion that "this dichotomy does not exhaust the possibilities"[98] appears to be a persuasive reading of that aspect of *Moran,* especially in light of the latter decision's subsequent admonition that "the waiver must have been made with a *full awareness* both of the nature of the right being abandoned and the consequences of the decision to abandon it."[99] Given Connelly's incontrovertible severe mental disability, it is difficult to understand how he could have exhibited this "full awareness" required by *Moran.*

This leads to the third *Connelly* puzzle. Why did the Court use this case—involving an actively hallucinating, chronic mental patient, suspected by the arresting officer of being a "crackpot"—for its draconian "free will" declaration, especially when the *sole* expert witness testified unequivocally that the defendant was "incapable" of making a "free decision" about his *Miranda* rights?[100] The use of this case is even more suprising in light of the reality of police and prosecutorial practice, which has recognized the limiting effects of mental condition on the effectiveness of *Miranda* waiver,[101] and the well-developed body of scientific studies documenting the disabling effects of such mental conditions on *Miranda* waivers.[102]

The fourth puzzle involves the Court's silent tracking of the APA's amicus brief. Although the Court does not allude to this (or to any other) amicus brief filed,[103] its holding on "free will" clearly follows the APA's arguments[104]; that this view is not a unanimous one should be self-evident.[105] Indeed, the court has recently shown a precise and explicit awareness of the competing views and interests of the disciplines of psychiatry and psychology,[106] of the predictive and diagnostic shortcomings of both disciplines,[107] and of the "pivotal role that psychiatry has come to play in criminal proceedings."[108] Given this backdrop, its cursory brushing aside of the significance of "free will" in the context of the *Connelly* case becomes even more curious.

Fifth, though the Court acknowledged that the defendant was suffering from "command hallucinations,"[109] it made no effort to explore the significance of this disability in the context of the need for a "knowing and intelligent" waiver.[110] This omission is made more stark by the severity of the command in the case before the Court—"God's voice became stronger and told [defendant] either to confess to the killing or to commit suicide"[111]—and by the generally acknowledged multiple forces that may bear on any person's "decision" to confess.[112]

Finally, it is also somewhat peculiar that the Court chose to decide the critical burden of proof issue in the context of a case in which that question was neither raised nor briefed.[113] Although the Court apparently decided the burden of proof issue to underscore that the Colorado Supreme Court's analysis was constitutionally flawed, the historic significance of burden of proof decisionmaking[114] should more appropriately have led the Court to defer disposition of this question until the issue surfaced in a subsequent case.

## UNANSWERED QUESTIONS

In addition to these case-specific "puzzles," other broader questions remain as to the ultimate future impact of *Connelly*. First, will state courts simply track the *Connelly* holding or will they choose to reject, modify, or limit it based on *state* constitutional law principles?[115]

No state court has yet invoked a parallel state constitutional provision in declining to follow *Connelly*.[116] However, several courts have chosen to factually distinguish that case in holding statements by mentally disabled defendants to be involuntary,[117] whereas at least one state Supreme Court has split sharply on the appropriate construction of *Connelly*.[118] It is yet too early to discern any meaningful trends among these decisions. On the other hand, virtually all federal cases subsequently construing *Connelly* have relied on it to find that the underlying confession was voluntarily made.[119]

Second, what are *Connelly*'s implications for the future of the *Miranda* doctrine? Does it extend the Burger Court's "prolonged and rather bloody campaign of guerilla warfare [against *Miranda,* leaving *Miranda*'s] facade . . . standing while [attacking it] from the sides and underneath,"[120] or does it truly signal the first note of the real death knell of *Miranda?* The fact that a significant *Miranda* incursion was carried out in a case involving a mentally disabled criminal defendant (representative of the one "class" of defendants that had been fairly successful in the Burger Court's *Miranda* jurisprudence) is probably more than coincidental.

Third, what will *Connelly*'s implications be for future cases involving mentally disabled criminal defendants in general? This is an area in which the Burger Court's opinions were marked by an overwhelming ambivalence, sometimes appearing almost as random decisions, defying meaningful categorization.[121] Although John Parry bravely suggests that *Connelly* "should not be taken as a reactionary shift in the way the Court will view mental disability cases generally,"[122] this conclusion may reflect one dollop too many of hope and optimism, *especially* given the new Chief Justice's "implacable" views on the interplay between mental disability and criminal procedure[123] and his "hostility" to cases brought on behalf of the mentally disabled in general.[124] Although a civil libertarian reading of *Connelly* could be suggested—that, in line with recent cases which allow certain *competent* defendants to decline to plead not guilty by reason of insanity,[125] it increases the autonomy of mentally disabled defendants to treat their confessions no different from other defendants' admissions—it does not appear that this approach reflects at all the majority's rationale.[126]

Fourth, what impact will *Connelly* have on future forensic testimony in this area? Although it is far too early to do more than speculate, Dr. Metzner (the sole witness at the suppression hearing) has recently written that, as a result of this decision and, in the aftermath of the post-*Hickley* insanity defense debate,[127] "expert witnesses should remain very cautious when testifying about issues related to free will and volitional capacity."[128]

Finally, what are the implications of *Connelly* for the Court's future disposition of *civil* mental disability cases? It has been nearly five years since the Court has read the due process clause at all expansively in a case involving the institutionalized mentally handicapped,[129] and it is not at all clear what impact, if any, *Connelly* may have on future developments in this area.[130]

# CONCLUSION

The Supreme Court has made it clear in *Connelly* that voluntariness inquiries in confessions cases are to be limited to matters involving police coercion, and that, in the absence of such coercion, "free will" is simply not a topic for constitutional consideration. Although the decision is a straightforward one, it leaves puzzles and unanswered questions in its wake. Court watchers should examine post-*Connelly* cases carefully (especially in state court settings) to see whether the case will be construed relatively narrowly, or whether the long-predicted demise of *Miranda* is, in fact, upon us.

*Acknowledgments*

The author wishes to acknowledge the helpful research assistance of Mark Dennison, Charles Gioino, and Susan Sheppard.

# REFERENCES


1. For a recent sampling, *see, e.g.*, Schulhofer: Reconsidering *Miranda*. 54 *U Chi Law Rev* 435 (1987); Bradley: Criminal procedure in the Rehnquist court: Has the Rehnquisition begun? 62 *Ind Law Rev* 273 (1987); Saltzburg: *Miranda v Arizona* revisited: Constitutional law or judicial fiat? 26 *Washburn Law J* 1 (1986); Ogletree: Are confessions really good for the soul? A proposal to Mirandize *Miranda*. 100 *Harv Law Rev* 1826 (1987). For a stark point-counterpoint debate, compare Caplan: Questioning *Miranda*. 38 *Vand Law Rev* 1417 (1985), to White: Defending *Miranda*: A reply to Professor Caplan. 39 *Vand Law Rev* 1 (1986).
2. 384 U.S. 436 (1966). As originally articulated, the *Miranda* rules stipulated:

   > [T]he prosecution may not use statements, whether exculpatory or inculpatory, stemming from the custodial interrogation of the defendant unless it demonstrates the use of procedural safeguards effective to secure the privilege against self-incrimination. By custodial interrogation, we mean questioning initiated by law enforcement officers after a person has been taken into custody or deprived of his freedom of action in any significant way. As for the procedural safeguards to be employed, unless other fully effective means are devised to inform accused persons of their right of silence and to assure a continuous opportunity to exercise it, the following measures are required. Prior to any questioning, the person must be warned that he has a right to remain silent, that any statement he does make may be used against him, and that he has a right to the presence of an attorney, either retained or appointed. The defendant may waive effectuation of these rights, provided the waiver is made voluntarily, knowingly and intelligently. If, however, he indicates in any manner and at any stage of the process that he wishes to consult with an attorney before speaking, there can be no questioning. Likewise, if the individual is alone and indicates in any manner that he does not wish to be interrogated, the police may not question him. The mere fact that he may have answered some questions or volunteered some statements on his own does not deprive him of the right to refrain from answering further inquiries until he has consulted with an attorney and thereafter consents to be questioned.

   *Id.* at 444–445 (footnote omitted).

3. *See, e.g.,* Sonenshein: *Miranda* and the Burger court: Trends and countertrends. 13 *Loy U Chi Law J* 405, 415 (1982); Israel: Criminal procedure, the Burger court, and the legacy of the Warren court. 75 *Mich Law Rev* 1319, 1374 (1977) ("Although the value of the *Miranda* ruling in effectively protecting the suspect's self-incrimination privilege is debatable, the decision has a symbolic quality that extends far beyond its practical impact upon police interrogation methods").

4. *See* Stone: The *Miranda* doctrine in the Burger Court. [1977] *Sup Ct Rev* 99, 169.

5. *Rhode Island v Innis,* 446 U.S. 291 (305) (1980) (Burger, CJ, concurring).

   On the other hand, the doctrine has been significantly reduced in a series of recent cases. *See, e.g., New York v Quarles,* 467 U.S. 649, 653–660 (1984); *Oregon v Elstad,* 470 U.S. 298, 306–314 (1985); *Connecticut v Barrett,* 107 S. Ct. 828, 831–833 (1987); *see generally,* Note: *Miranda* and the state constitution: State courts take a stand. 39 *Vand Law Rev* 1693, 1714–1717 (1986) ("Vanderbilt Note"); *but see,* Weisberg: Foreword: Criminal procedure doctrine: Some versions of the skeptical. 76 *J Crim Law Criminol* 832, 840 (1985), noting the Burger Court decisions reaffirming defendants' rights in interrogation cases—*e.g., Brewer v Williams,* 430 U.S. 387 (1977)—that we "tend to forget or deny."

6. *Elstad,* 470 U.S. at 316.

7. *See, e.g.,* LaFave, Israel: *Criminal Procedure* §6.5(c), at 483–484 "*Miranda* has had little effect upon clearance and conviction rates". St. Paul, Minn, West's, 1984.

8. Perlin ML: The supreme court, the mentally disabled criminal defendant, and symbolic values: Random decisions, hidden rationales, or "Doctrinal abyss"? 29 *Ariz Law Rev* 1,92 (1987) ("Doctrinal Abyss").

9. *Compare, e.g., North Carolina v Butler,* 441 U.S. 369 (1979) (explicit statement not necessary as predicate for *Miranda* waiver); *Quarles, supra* ("public safety" exception to *Miranda*); *Elstad, supra* (initial failure to administer *Miranda* warnings does not "taint" subsequent admissions made after warnings properly given); *Moran v Burbine,* 106 S. Ct. 1135 (1986) (*Miranda* waiver not vitiated by failure of police to inform defendant that attorney was attempting to contact him); *and Colorado v Spring,* 107 S. Ct. 851 (1987) (mere silence by law enforcement official as to subject matter of interrogation not "trickery" sufficient to invalidate *Miranda* waiver) *with e.g., Edwards v Arizona,* 451 U.S. 477 (1981) ("heavy burden" on state to prove that *Miranda* waiver—*after assertion of rights*—was voluntary, intelligent, and knowing); *and Shea v Louisiana,* 105 S. Ct. 1065 (1985) (applying *Edwards* retroactively to cases pending on direct appeal).

10. *See, e.g., Estelle v Smith,* 451 U.S. 454 (1981) (admission of psychiatrist's testimony at penalty phase of capital punishment case violated defendant's privilege against self-incrimination where defendant not advised prior to pretrial psychiatric examination of right to remain silent); *Miller v Fenton,* 106 U.S. 445 (1985) (voluntariness of confession is not issue of fact presumed to be correct in subsequent habeas corpus proceeding; interrogating officer throught defendant had "mental problem"); *Wainwright v Greenfield,* 106 S. Ct. 634 (1986) (state may not use postarrest, post-*Miranda* silence as evidence of defendant's sanity).

    For a recent attack on *Greenfield* from a prosecutor's perspective, *see* Daley, Fryklund: The insanity defense and the "testimony by proxy" problem. 21 *Valparaiso Law Rev* 497 (1987).

11. 361 U.S. 199 (1960).

12. *Id.* at 207.

13. 367 U.S. 568 (1961).

14. *Id.* at 581. *See also, e.g., Bram v United States,* 168 U.S. 532, 547 (1897) (citing Hale).

15. *See, e.g., Miranda v Arizona,* 384 U.S. 436 (1966), Brief for Petitioner, at 3 (defendant

diagnosed by court-appointed psychiatrist as schizophrenic); *see also, State v Miranda,*
401 P.2d 716, 718 (Ariz. Sup. Ct. 1965) (request for sanity determination).

16. 372 U.S. 293 (1963).

17. *Blackburn,* 361 U.S. at 207.

18. *Townsend,* 372 U.S. at 307, quoting *Reck v Pate,* 367 U.S. 433, 440 (1961), and *Blackburn,* 361 U.S. at 208.

19. 107 S. Ct. 515 (1986).

20. Parry: Involuntary confessions based on mental impairments. 11 *Ment Phys Dis Law Rptr* 2 (1987).

21. *See Connelly,* 107 S. Ct. at 525 (Brennan, J, dissenting).

22. For the classic survey article on the concept of mental illness in assessing free will in a confessions context, *see* Grano: Voluntariness, free will, and the law of confessions. 65 *Va Law Rev* 859 (1979).

23. *Connelly,* 107 S. Ct. at 519–522.

24. *Id.* at 523–524.

25. *Id.* at 523.

26. *Id.* at 518.

27. *Id.*

28. *Id.*

29. *Id.*

30. *Id.* at 518–519.

31. *Id.* at 519.

32. *Id.*

33. *Id.*

34. *Id.*

35. *Id.*

36. See *People v Connelly,* 702 P.2d 722, 728 (1985).

37. *Id.,* 106 S. Ct. 785 (1986).

38. *Colorado v Connelly,* No. 85–660, Amicus Brief of APA, at 3.

39. *Id.*

40. Neither the American Psychiatric Association nor the American Academy of Psychiatry and Law filed a brief in *Connelly.*

41. *See, e.g., Mills v Rogers,* 457 U.S. 291, 292 n.* (1982) (right to refuse treatment); *Rivers v Katz,* 504 N.Y.S. 2d 74, 76 (Ct. App. 1986) (right to refuse treatment).

42. *See, e.g., Ake v Oklahoma,* 470 U.S. 68, 70 n.* (1985) (right to psychiatric assistance in presentation of insanity defense).

43. *See Connelly,* 107 S. Ct. at 524.

44. Justice Blackmun concurred in part and in judgment; Justice Stevens concurred in part and dissented in part; Justices Brennan and Marshall dissented.

45. 297 U.S. 278 (1936).

46. *Connelly,* 107 S. Ct. at 520 and *id.* n.1, citing, *inter alia, Mincey v Arizona,* 437 U.S. 385 (1978); *Greenwald v Wisconsin,* 390 U.S. 519 (1968); *Beecher v Alabama,* 389 U.S. 35 (1967); *Culombe, supra.*

47. *Connelly,* 107 S. Ct. at 520.

48. *Id.*

49. *Id.* at 521.

50. *Id.,* citing *United States v Leon,* 468 U.S. 897, 906–913 (1984). For a recent, thoughtful analysis of the role of the *Leon* decision in the Supreme Court's new "majoritarianism" doctrine, *see* Finer: *Gates, Leon,* and the compromise of adjudicative fairness: Of aggresive majoritarianism, willful deafness, and the new exception to the exclusionary rule. (Part 2), 34 *Cleve St Law Rev* 199 (1985).

51. *Connelly,* 107 S. Ct. at 521.

52. *Id.* at 522.

53. *Id.,* quoting *Lisenba v California,* 314 U.S. 219, 236 (1941).

54. 404 U.S. 477, 488 (1972).

55. 444 U.S. 469 (1980).

56. 441 U.S. 369, 373 (1979).

57. *Connelly,* 107 S. Ct. at 522–523.

58. *Id.* at 523 (italics added).

59. *Id.* at 522.

60. *Id.* at 522–523, quoting *Connelly,* 702 P.2d at 729.

61. *Connelly,* 107 S. Ct. at 523, citing *United States v Washington,* 431 U.S. 181, (1977).

62. *Connelly,* 107 S. Ct. at 523 (italics added).

63. *Id.,* quoting *Elstad,* 470 U.S. at 305.

64. *Connelly,* 107 S. Ct. at 524 (italics added).

65. *Id.* quoting *Beckwith v United States,* 425 U.S. 341, 345 (1976).

66. *Connelly,* 107 S. Ct. at 524.

67. *Id.*

68. *Connelly,* 107 S. Ct. at 525, quoting *Miranda,* 384 U.S. at 467.

69. *Connelly,* 107 S. Ct. at 525.

70. *Id.*

71. *See Moran,* discussed *supra* note 9.

72. *Moran,* 106 S. Ct. at 1141.

73. *Id.*

74. *Connelly,* 107 S. Ct. at 525 n.5.

75. *Id.* at 525–526.

76. *Id.* at 526.

77. *Id.* at 527. Here, Justice Brennan relied, in part, on the citation to Hawkins's *Pleas of the Crown, see Bram, supra,* note 14.

78. *Connelly,* 107 S. Ct. at 527, and *see also* cases cited *id.* at 527–528 n.2.

79. *Id.* at 529 n.3.

80. *Id.*

81. *Id.* at 529.

82. *Id.*

83. *Id.* at 530.

84. *Id.*

85. *Id.* at 530–531.

86. *Id.* at 531.

87. *Id.,* quoting *Miranda,* 384 U.S. at 475.

88. *See* 404 U.S. at 490.

89. *See Connelly,* 107 S. Ct. at 531–532.

90. *Id.* at 532–533, quoting *Connelly,* 702 P.2d at 729.

91. *See Moran,* 106 S. Ct. at 1141

92. *Connelly,* 107 S. Ct. at 533.

93. *Connelly,* 107 S. Ct. at 520.

94. *Id.* at 521.

95. *See, e.g., Blackburn,* 361 U.S. at 200–204 (detailing the defendant's "lengthy siege" of mental illness); *Townsend,* 372 U.S. at 299–306 (recounting the physiological and psychological responses of the severely disabled defendant to the state-induced and -ordered injection of a truth serum drug).

96. 106 S. Ct. at 1141.

97. *Id.*

98. *Connelly,* 107 S. Ct. at 525 n.5 (Stevens, J, concurring in judgment in part and dissenting in part).

99. *Moran,* 106 S. Ct. at 1141 (italics added).

100. *See Connelly,* 107 S. Ct. at 532–533 (Brennan, J, dissenting).

101. *See e.g.,* Inbau Reid Buckley: *Criminal Interrogation and Confessions* ed 3 1986, p 57.

102. *See, e.g.,* Wulach: The assessment of competency to waive *Miranda* rights. 9 *J Psych Law* 209 (1981); *see also,* Fourth circuit review. 41 *Wash Lee Law Rev* 493, 636–654 (1984) (effect of mental disability on determining voluntariness of juvenile's confession).

103. *See* Metzner: *Colorado v Connelly*: Confessions of the mentally ill. 12 *Newsletter Am Acad Psych Law* 4, 7 (April 1987).

104. *See Connelly,* Brief of Amicus APA, at 25 ("behavioral science does not use or rely upon the concepts of 'volition' or 'free will' ").

105. *See, e.g., Connelly,* Brief of Amicus FREE, at 56–57 n.54 (citing contrary sources, including Stein *Contemporary Psychotherapies* [1961], and Frank *Persuasion and Healing* [1973]).

106. *See, e.g., McReady v Blue Shield of Virginia,* 457 U.S. 465. 478–479 (1982) (discussing alleged conspiracy by state psychiatric association and Blue Shield plan "to halt encroachment by psychologists into a market that physicians and psychiatrists sought to preserve for themselves").

107. *See, e.g., Estelle,* 451 U.S. at 472; *Addington v Texas,* 441 U.S. 418, 430 (1979); *Vitek v Jones,* 445 U.S. 480, 495 (1980); *see also, Ford v Wainwright,* 106 S. Ct. 2595 (1986).

108. *Ake,* 470 U.S. at 79.

109. *Connelly,* 107 S. Ct. at 519.

110. *See, e.g., Connelly,* Brief of Amicus FREE, at 27–32, and also sources cited *id.* at nn.21–23; *see generally,* Kolb Brodie: *Modern Clinical Psychiatry* at ed 10, 1982, at 126 ("Hallucinations conveying a command are often convincing and compelling. They may lead to direct and dangerous action. Considerations of reality are of little weight in comparison to their influence"); Kaplan Sadock (eds): *Comprehensive Textbook of Psychiatry* ed 4 1985, at 574 (hallucinating schizophrenic patients often act on their inner perceptions "as though they were more compelling that the external realities").

111. *Connelly,* 107 S. Ct. at 519.

112. *See, e.g., Michigan v Jackson,* 106 S. Ct. 1404, 1411 (1986) (Burger, CJ, concurring in judgment), quoting Reik: *The Compulsion to Confess* 1959.

113. *See Connelly,* 107 S. Ct. at 524 (Blackmun, J, concurring in part and concurring in judgment).

114. *See, e.g., In re Winship,* 397 U.S. 358, 368–372 (1970) (Harlan, J, concurring).

115. *See, e.g.,* "Vanderbilt Note," *supra* note 5, at 1730–1734; Latzer: Limits of the new federalism: State court responses, 14 *Search Seizure Law Rep* 89 (1987); *Connelly,* 107 S. Ct. at 533 (Brennan, J, dissenting) ("today's holding does not, of course, preclude a contrary resolution of this case based upon the state's separate interpretation of its own constitution").

116. *See, e.g., State v McGonigle,* 401 N.W. 2d 39, 41 (Iowa Sup. Ct. 1987); *People v Rhodes,* 729 P. 2d 982, 984–985 (Colo. Sup. Ct. 1986).

117. *See, e.g., State v Dailey,* 351 S.E. 2d 431, 434 n.2 (W. Va. Sup. Ct. App. 1986); *State v Vincik,* 398 N.W. 2d 788, 792–793 (Iowa Sup. Ct. 1987).

118. *See State v Clappes,* 401 N.W. 2d 759 (Wis. Sup. Ct. 1987); *id.* at 769 (Heffernan J, concurring); *id.* at 770 (Abrahamson, J, dissenting).

119. *See, e.g., United States v Phillips,* 812 F. 2d 1355 (11 Cir. 1987); *United States v Rohrbach,* 813 F. 2d 142 (8 Cir. 1987); *and United States ex rel. Link v Lane,* 811 F. 2d 1166 (7 Cir.

1987; *but see, Biller v Lopes,* 655 F. Supp. 292 (D. Conn. 1987) (confession involuntary due to coercion).

120. Alschuler: Failed pragmatism: Reflections on the Burger court. 100 *Harv Law Rev* 1436, 1442 (1987).

121. *Compare, e.g., Estelle; Greenfield; Ake; Ford,* all *supra, with Barefoot v Estelle,* 463 U.S. 880 (1983); *Jones v United States,* 463 U.S. 354 (1983); *Smith v Murray,* 106 S. Ct. 2678 (1986); *and Allen v Illinois,* 106 S. Ct. 2988 (1986); *see generally,* "Doctrinal Abyss," *supra* note 8.

122. Parry, *supra* note 20, at 5.

123. *See* "Doctrinal Abyss," *supra* note 8, at 281.

124. *See* Perlin ML: State constitutions and statutes as sources of rights for the mentally disabled: The last frontier? 20 *Loyola LA Law Rev* 1249, 1264–1266 n.99 (1987).

125. *See, e.g., Frendak v United States,* 408 A.2d 364 (D.C. Ct. App. 1979); *State v Kahn,* 417 A.2d 585 (N.J. App. Div. 1980).

126. The Supreme Court has recently granted certiorari in *Satterwhite v Texas,* No. 86–6284, on the question of the adequacy of warnings to be given to a criminal defendant as to the specific purposes of a psychiatric interview.

127. *See, e.g.,* Perlin ML: After *Hinckley*: Old myths, new realities and the future of the insanity defense. *Directions in Psychiatry,* 1985 vol 5, lesson 22.

128. Metzner, *supra* note 103, at 7.

129. *See, e.g., Mills,* 457 U.S. at 299 ("The parties agree that the Constitution recognizes a liberty interest in avoiding the administration of antipsychotic drugs"); *Youngberg v Romeo,* 457 U.S. 307, 324 (1982) ("Respondent thus enjoys constitutionally protected interests in conditions of reasonable care and safety, reasonably nonrestrictive confinement conditions, and such training as may be required by these interests").

130. *See, e.g.,* Perlin ML: Ten years after: Evolving mental health advocacy and judicial trends. 15 *Ford Urb Law J* 335 (1986–87); Perlin ML: Patients' rights, in 3 Cavenar, (ed): *Psychiatry* ed rev 1986 ch. 35.

**12**

# Competence to Stand Trial

## Clinical and Legal Considerations

**J. RICHARD CICCONE**

## INTRODUCTION

One of the most important and most frequent requests that courts make of psychiatrists is to give an opinion on a defendant's competence to stand trial. It is difficult to determine the number of psychiatric evaluations for competence to stand trial in a given year in the United States. One study found that 12% of the individuals referred to a court clinic setting were referred for evaluation of their competence to stand trial.[1] In fact, a larger number of referrals had been sent with a request for an evaluation of competence but, on further discussion with the referring person, it was clear that what was being requested in many cases was a psychiatric evaluation regarding need for treatment.

Although the Not Guilty by Reason of Insanity (NGRI) issue receives a great deal of media attention and concern from the public, it is the competence to stand trial evaluation that is requested much more frequently and has a greater impact on both the defendants and the legal system. Among the first to highlight the importance of the competence to stand trial evaluation were Hess and Thomas.[2] Halleck estimated that for each defendant found NGRI, more than 100 defendants are found incompetent to stand trial.[3] Scheidemandel and Kanco estimated that, in 1969, there were 15,000 psychiatric hospitalizations for



**J. RICHARD CICCONE** • Department of Psychiatry, University of Rochester School of Medicine and Dentistry, Rochester, NY 14642.



173

the evaluation of competence to stand trial in the United States and 1,450 hospitalizations as a result of NGRI verdicts.[4]

## DEVELOPMENT OF THE CONCEPT OF COMPETENCE TO STAND TRIAL

The question of competency to stand trial arose in early English courts out of a legal procedural need. Trials would come to a halt if a defendant failed to enter a plea. The defendant might remain silent as a ploy in order to avoid capital punishment or forfeiture of property. To determine if the individual was "mute by visitation of God" or "mute of malice," the court employed the *peine forte et dure* (strong and harsh punishment).[5] This alternate trial required the placing of stones of increasing weight on the defendant's chest until the defendant either made a plea or died. "Pressing the accused for an answer" was not legally abolished until 1772. Replacing *peine forte et dure* was a jury determination of a defendant's competency to proceed. Defendants found incompetent were detained until their competence was restored.

It appears that physicians entered into the issue of competency to stand trial in Great Britain in the mid-19th century when the nationwide practice of hiring physicians to work in the jails was established. The physicians working in jail settings were asked to give opinions on prisoners' competency to stand trial. Often they based their opinion on competency on the standards for civil commitment to a mental hospital. Ignored were the commonly accepted, judicially derived standards that had been developed in the late 18th century and early 19th century. These judicial standards held that the defendant must have sufficient reason to understand charges against him and to participate in his own defense at the trial.[6]

Both the British and the American legal systems have been concerned with the trial's fairness and the defendant's right to protect himself. The requirement that the person be competent to stand trial is based on the following legal tenets. First, the accused may be the only one who has exonerating factual material. Second, the defendant must be aware of the legal steps that may protect him and make relevant choices. Third, the dignity of the legal proceeding must be preserved by having a rational defendant. Fourth, if a defendant is found guilty, he must know and understand why he is being punished.[7]

It is not always easy to determine who is competent and who is not competent to stand trial. As early as 1838, Isaac Ray recommended that both the trial and the sentencing be postponed if there was a question of the defendant's state of mind. This delay would give physicians the opportunity to examine the defendant. Ray wrote that "in those cases where there are some but not perfectly satisfactory evidences of insanity, the trial or sentence should be postponed, in order that opportunity may be afforded to those who are properly qualified for observing the state of the prisoner's mind." He went on to state that in "many cases, where the issue of insanity was doubtful, at trial . . . [it could be] . . . veiled from observation, as never to be suspected even by the most intimate associate of the patient."[8]

Although there is a clear and firm tradition requiring that a defendant be competent to stand trial, the application of the criteria protecting this right is at times difficult. Most jurisdictions have retained the common-law criteria of ability to comprehend the proceedings and ability to assist in the defense. The application of these criteria, which are necessarily broad in order to allow their application in specific cases, is varied and at times confusing.

## THE LEGAL STANDARDS FOR THE DETERMINATION OF COMPETENCY TO STAND TRIAL

The criteria for competence to stand trial were defined by the United States Supreme Court in the 1960 case of *Dusky v United States*.[9] Briefly summarized, *Dusky* involved Milton Richard Dusky who was 33 years of age at the time that he and two teenage boys picked up a 15-year-old girl, an acquaintance of the two boys. They took her from Missouri to Kansas where the two boys raped the girl. Dusky attempted to rape her but was unable to complete the act. Dusky's attorney reported that he could not work with Dusky, and Dusky was sent to the federal medical center in Springfield, Missouri, for four months. Dusky was diagnosed as having a schizophrenic reaction, chronic, undifferentiated type, and he was placed on Thorazine.

At a hearing to determine Dusky's competence, the psychiatrist (an employee of the federal government) testified that, in his opinion, Dusky was able to understand the charges against him and comprehend the role of the court, but he could not work with his attorney to assist in his own defense. Nonetheless, the judge ruled Dusky competent to stand trial. Dusky was convicted and sentenced to a 45-year jail term. Dusky's attorney appealed this conviction but the appeal was denied by the Court of Appeals. An appeal was subsequently made to the Supreme Court. The Supreme Court articulated the standards for the determination of competence, reversed the conviction, and remanded the case to the District Court. The Supreme Court found that it was not sufficient that Dusky was oriented to time, place, and some events. It directed that the competency determination must be based on whether or not the defendant "has sufficient present ability to consult with his lawyer with a reasonable degree of rational understanding and—whether he has a rational as well as factual understanding of the proceedings against him." At the mandated rehearing, Dusky was once more found competent to stand trial. At the new trial, Dusky's plea of NGRI failed, and he was given a lighter sentence of 20 years with possible parole in five years.[10,11]

The standard as defined in *Dusky* has been criticized as being vague and failing to define a "reasonable degree" of rational understanding.[12] Adding to the confusion is the error, which some psychiatrists and attorneys make, of mistaking the criteria for competency to stand trial with the criteria for being found NGRI. In addition, the error of equating psychosis with incompetence continues to plague forensic reports. The wording of the legal criteria varies from state to state and from state courts to federal courts. It behooves the psychiatrist to be aware of the specific legal criteria of the jurisdiction where the competence to stand trial evaluation is requested.

## CLINICAL CRITERIA FOR AN OPINION ON COMPETENCY TO STAND TRIAL

The role of the forensic psychiatrist in the evaluation of the defendant's competence to stand trial is based on the psychiatric expertise, which the forensic psychiatrist provides. Consequently, the psychiatrist is required to conduct a thorough and thoughtful psychiatric evaluation. Ultimately, it is not the psychiatric diagnosis but the specific evaluation of the defendant's abilities and disabilities, in relation to the requirements of the law, that allow the psychiatric expert to arrive at a meaningful opinion.

The decision regarding the defendant's competency to stand trial is a legal one, and a judge, in most jurisdictions, is called on to render the decision. The role of the psychiatric expert is to provide an opinion. Robey and others have suggested that the vast majority of psychiatrists have no awareness of what legal test or criteria to apply to an evaluation of competency to stand trial.[13] In an attempt to apply the *Dusky* standard, Robey used his experience of treating patients in an 800-bed forensic hospital to devise a checklist of criteria of competency. Robey intended the checklist to provide a brief, convenient review of the areas a psychiatrist should investigate when evaluating a defendant's competence to stand trial. His checklist is divided into three major areas: comprehension of court proceedings, ability to advise counsel, and susceptibility to decompensation while awaiting or standing trial.

Robey further subdivided the three major categories of the checklist. Under the section of comprehension of court proceedings, Robey listed the following areas: surroundings, procedure, principals, charges, verdicts, penalties, and legal rights. Under ability to advise counsel, Robey highlighted facts, plea, legal strategy, maintaining relationship with lawyer, maintaining consistency of defense, waiving rights, interpreting witnesses' testimony, and testifying, if necessary. In the third and final area, Robey urged psychiatrists to consider the defendant's susceptibility to decompensation while awaiting or standing trial and to assess the defendant's potential violence, acute psychosis, suicidal depression, regression, withdrawal, and organic deterioration. Robey suggested that this checklist be used as a guide in conjunction with the psychiatrist's knowledge of the legal proceedings and of the courts' expectations, which would grow through their work with trained forensic psychiatrists. This knowledge and experience can be gained more quickly and more thoroughly through formal educational programs. An increasing number of post-residency fellowships in forensic psychiatry are increasing the number of psychiatrists who are trained to determine competency to stand trial and to provide the court with a reasoned opinion.

In 1974, McGarry and his multidisciplinary team of lawyers, psychiatrists, and psychologists published the results of an ongoing project to develop, validate, and demonstrate quantifiable clinical criteria for competency to stand trial—the Competency Assessment Instrument.[14] Each of 13 capacities was evaluated on a scale of one to five regarding degree of incapacity, with one being a total incapacity and five being no incapacity. A rating of six would mean that the item was unratable. The items are:

1. Appraisal of available legal defenses
2. Unmanageable behavior
3. Quality relating to attorney
4. Planning of legal strategy, including guilty plea to lesser charges where pertinent
5. Appraisal of role of:
   a. Defense counsel
   b. Prosecuting attorney
   c. Judge
   d. Jury

> e. Defendant
> f. Witnesses

6. Understanding of court procedure
7. Appreciation of charges
8. Appreciation of range and nature of possible penalties
9. Appraisal of likely outcome
10. Capacity to disclose to attorney available pertinent facts surrounding the offense including the defendant's movements, timing, mental state, and actions at the time of the offense
11. Capacity to challenge prosecution witnesses realistically
12. Capacity to testify relevantly
13. Self-defeating versus self-serving motivation (legal sense)

In my experience, the use of a tally sheet is inadequate for the complex and comprehensive question being asked regarding a person's competence to stand trial, but serves the clinician as a screening instrument and provides a framework for interviewing the defendant. The developers of the Fitness Interview Test, a semistructured interview, suggest that the examiner give an opinion not based on the overall score but on the "inductive and subjective weighting" of individual items.[15]

The courts are interested in understanding the specific impairment of the defendant's capacity to carry out the necessary steps of participating in a trial. It is important to keep in mind that the examination of competency calls for an evaluation of the defendant's capacity to participate in a trial, not his willingness. In addition, the presence of mental illness does not automatically exclude a defendant from being competent to stand trial. In fact, one of the most common errors made by psychiatrists in reports to the court is equating psychosis with incompetence. In my experience of reviewing reports in a variety of settings,[16] the conclusory reasoning of 19th-century physicians in Great Britain appears to be alive and well in the last quarter of the 20th century in the United States.

The overall standard of competency to stand trial is a minimum standard. It is not a high standard such as might be required in admissions to a college. It is a low or minimum standard. It allows people to defend themselves against accusations while not exposing them to undue risk arising from being unable to defend themselves in the adversarial setting. Reich and Tookey[17] found that when the court ruled that the individual was competent, in the face of the psychiatrist's opinion that the defendant was incompetent, it was usually because the psychiatrist overestimated the capacity necessary to stand trial.

A person may also be incompetent to stand trial as a result of a mental defect. As a general rule of thumb, if a person has an IQ of greater than 60, he is usually found competent to stand trial. If the defendant has an IQ of lower than 50, he is usually found not competent to stand trial. Obviously, the specific capacity of people to function will vary even when they have the same IQ score. Therefore, once again, a careful psychiatric evaluation must be completed. A more complicated circumstance occurs when the defendant has both mental retardation and a psychiatric illness. In these cases, individuals with an IQ score in the 60s or 70s are often found incompetent.[18]

The evaluation of competency to stand trial involves not only the evaluation of the defendant's mental condition but also other variables. Some of the variables to be considered include the nature of the charge and the complexity of the defense. If the defense requires that the individual testify and the defendant is unable to do so, it has been suggested that the defendant be found not competent to stand trial. On the other hand, if the defense does not involve taking the stand, a defendant's compromised ability to testify is not crucial.

An important distinction is whether a defendant's apparent incompetency is the result of a psychiatric illness or a lack of information. In the former, the defendant requires psychiatric treatment. In the latter, the defendant requires education. Likewise, if the person's intellectual ability is the major problem, it may be remedied by alerting the attorneys and the court to that fact and suggesting that they use simple, clear language and, where a more complex term must be used, that it be defined for the defendant.

In addition to interviewing the defendant and reviewing the relevant medical and legal material, the psychiatrist may gather valuable data from observing the interaction between the attorney and the client. This is especially useful in determining if the defendant's difficulties with competence are a result of mental illness or problems with the attorney. Does the attorney have a working knowledge of the legal situation and the ability to convey this information to his client? Is there a personality clash between the attorney and the defendant? Can this interpersonal difficulty be resolved? Does it require the appointment of another attorney? Other evaluations of specific competencies required when facing criminal charges include competency to confess,[19] to plead guilty, to waive an attorney,[20] to refuse an insanity plea, and to be sentenced.[21] When a competency to stand trial request is made, it is important to clarify which question is being asked. These different competency examinations have many similarities but they also have important differences. Melton, Petrila, *et al.* provide a useful discussion of these different examinations.[22]

## MISUSE OF THE REQUEST FOR A COMPETENCE TO STAND TRIAL EVALUATION

Although the individual's competence to stand trial is a critical component in protecting the individual's overall civil rights, the request for such an evaluation may be a gambit employed by any one of the principals in a trial. The judge may request a competence to stand trial evaluation as a vehicle for gaining information about a defendant prior to having to set bail or as a vehicle for committing the individual to a psychiatric institution. The defense attorney may request an evaluation in order to delay the trial. This delay may decrease the public's interest in the case, allow memories to fade, and make it more difficult to locate witnesses willing to testify. The incompetency evaluation may also provide a foundation for a defense of NGRI or for consideration of a lesser charge, in serious charges where intent is an element of the crime. Where the evidence for conviction may be thin, the district attorney may ask for an evaluation of competence to stand trial not to evaluate the defendant's competence but actually to detain him in a secure forensic hospital. Psychiatrists may view the competence to stand trial evaluation as an opportunity to provide treatment and to rescue the defendant from having to go back to court where harsh events may take place.[23]

All the people involved in the process may misuse the competence to stand trial evaluation and subvert its purpose. These abuses of the competence to stand trial evaluation, whether wittingly or unwittingly brought about, are problematic because they restrict the defendant's liberty while postponing the defendant's trial.

On the basis of knowledge, training, and experience, an expert assists the court in arriving at a decision regarding the defendant's competency by providing information to the court. This information is given in a psychiatric report that contains information regarding the individual's clinical condition. The report also reviews any incapacities caused by mental disease or defect that limit the defendant's current capacity to stand trial.

In those instances in which the forensic expert is asked to testify at a hearing regarding the person's competence to stand trial, the expert can be expected to provide information regarding the nature and duration of the examination, the information gathered, the diagnosis arrived at, and the reasoning used to arrive at a conclusion regarding the person's competence or incompetence. Some critics have held that the forensic psychiatric expert is an expert on human behavior, not legal matters, and lacks the objectivity to provide a response to the ultimate question regarding the defendant's competence to stand trial. Ciccone and Clements, in a paper on asking and answering the ultimate question, explored the role of the forensic psychiatric expert in court.[24] The psychiatrist provides the data and inferences and an opinion regarding a defendant's competence. The judge is in a position to accept or reject the psychiatrist's opinion. The expert's opinion need not intrude on the judge's role to render a legal decision.

Some would argue that psychiatrists should not participate in competency evaluations because it distorts the doctor–patient relationship. The issue of the presence or absence of confidentiality during any psychiatric evaluation is of great importance. The American Academy of Psychiatry and the Law's Ethical Guidelines for the Practice of Forensic Psychiatry states:

> Respect for the individual's right of privacy and the maintenance of confidentiality are major concerns of the psychiatrist performing forensic evaluations . . . . An evaluation for forensic purposes begins with notice to the evaluee of any limitation on confidentiality.[25]

The defendant may or may not be willing to participate and must accept the legal consequence that follows. The information derived at a competency to stand trial evaluation, in most jurisdictions, is not available for use in the criminal proceedings of the trial. Using "the fruit of the forbidden trees" doctrine, no information derived from information gathered at the competency to stand trial evaluation or hearing may be used at the trial.

Still others have suggested that the psychiatrist should not participate in competency determinations because the question deals with competence to proceed in a courtroom setting. A judge, who is knowledgeable about the courtroom setting, can assess competency more effectively. This objection to psychiatric participation in competency evaluations was dealt with by the U.S. Supreme Court in *Pate v Robinson*.[26] The Court directed that the trial judge must raise the issue of competency if there is a "bonafide doubt" of the defendant's competency, whether this doubt is raised by the court's observations or presented by either the defense attorney or the district attorney. Briefly, Robinson was convicted of murdering Flossy Mae Ward, with whom he had been living. He was sentenced to life imprisonment after an insanity defense was rejected. The attorney, who had waived a competency to stand trial hearing prior to trial, appealed the conviction in part on the basis that his client was incompetent. The Supreme Court of Illinois ruled that Robinson appeared to be "mentally alert in court." The U.S. Supreme Court held that Robinson was constitutionally entitled to a hearing on competency to stand trial, "the conviction of an accused person while he is legally incompetent violates due process." Even if waived by the defense attorney, the court has the obligation to hold a hearing "sua sponte" (of its own will) where there is substantial evidence for the court to doubt the defendant's competency to stand trial. A request for a hearing on a defendant's competency to stand trial may be made at any time—before, during or after a trial.

In *Moore v United States*,[27] the Court of Appeals underscored the fact that "substantial evidence is a term of art." When evidence appears that raises a reasonable doubt about the defendant's competency, the court must order a hearing; in the Moore case, two psychiatric reports giving evidence of severe mental disorder were filed. When a motion is made regarding a request for a hearing on the defendant's competency, the information available to the court must rise to the level of the reasonable doubt standard as called for in *Pate* before denial of a hearing leads to a denial of due process.

## THE PERMANENTLY INCOMPETENT

For many years, those defendants who were found incompetent to stand trial were committed to mental hospitals and detained there until they regained their competency. One study showed that incompetent defendants remained in a mental hospital for approximately three years.[28] Many defendants were held for longer periods of time with hospitalizations of ten years or more not being rare. McGarry *et al.*[29] found that in Massachusetts in 1970, there were 496 persons awaiting trial in the Department of Mental Health institutions on the status of indefinite commitment. On surveying the 60 courts where the commitments had originated, the researchers found that over 90% of the criminal charges against these patients/defendants had been dropped.

In the 1972 decision *Jackson v Indiana*,[30] the U.S. Supreme Court provided some guidelines for the confinement of the incompetent defendant. This case involved Theon Jackson, a 27-year-old deaf mute, who was charged with two nonviolent larcenies which he had committed in 1968 and which had netted him a total of approximately $9. He was found incompetent to stand trial and was ordered to the Indiana Department of Mental Health until his competency was restored. Jackson's attorney challenged the commitment arguing that it was unlikely that Jackson would ever be competent. Therefore, the finding of incompetency for Jackson would result in his serving what would be the equivalent of a life sentence without conviction for a minor crime. The Supreme Court reversed the lower court's decision ruling that "Indiana cannot constitutionally commit the petitioner for an indefinite period simply on account of his incompetency." For an incompetent defendant to be involuntarily hospitalized, the Supreme Court stated that the due-process and equal-protection clauses of the Constitution required that the defendant meet the state's civil commitment standards. When the defendant improved and no longer met these standards, even if he remained incompetent, he had to be released. This decision went on to cite the Sixth Amendment (speedy trial) and Fourteenth Amendment (due process) to the Constitution in a discussion of how long an incompetent person may be held to determine competency. The court further held that the continued hospitalization of the incompetent defendant must be justified by progress toward the goal of establishing his competency. The *Jackson* decision also allows for the possibility of the incompetent defendant's attorney to raise certain defenses and establish innocence without allowing a conviction.

The response to *Jackson* has varied from state to state. The length of time an incompetent defendant may be committed, as well as what treatment or progress would be seen as reasonable toward achieving the goal of regaining competency, is not clearly delineated. In some states, the defendant may be indefinitely committed, whereas other states have established a six-month limit after which the defendant may be committed only if he may be retained as a civil patient. Other states do not release the incompetent defendant until the lesser of the maximum possible sentence or five years has passed. Still other states retain the defendant for two thirds of the maximum possible sentence he could have been given if convicted.

## MEDICATION, THE RIGHT TO REFUSE TREATMENT, AND INCOMPETENCE TO STAND TRIAL

Admission to a hospital for the incompetent patient requires that the treatment focus on the restoration of competence.[31] Pharmacologic intervention is one of the most important treatment modalities used in restoring incompetent patients to competency. This effective method has been challenged on the grounds that the medication leads to "synthetic sanity," the result of a mind-altering substance which interferes with the defendant's receiving a fair trial. The phrase *synthetic sanity* is a derogatory term that shows naïveté about psychotropic agents and their effectiveness in bringing about stable, clinical remissions of psychotic illnesses and helping many incompetent defendants organize their thoughts.

In *State v Murphy*,[32] a defendant was convicted of murder. The conviction was overturned because prior to the trial he had been given a tranquilizer. As a result, he appeared "casual, cool, not at all perturbed, and showed a lackadaisical attitude," whereas without the medication he had been "extremely nervous, extremely taut . . . and unable to properly control his emotions satisfactorily." The court found that the defendant's attitude, appearance, and demeanor, as observed by the jury, raised a reasonable possibility that Murphy appeared in greater control than he actually was. This presentation of the medicated defendant appearing calm and nonpsychotic may contribute to the insanity defense seldom being successful in a jury trial. In 1976, Winick reported that 13 states automatically barred any defendant who was taking psychoactive drugs from going to a trial.[33] It has been recommended that since psychotropic medication is essential to the restoration of competence of many who are found incompetent to stand trial, the defendant be given the necessary medication. The problem of the defendant's demeanor in court can be dealt with by having a psychiatrist testify to the type and amount of medication that the defendant is taking and the medication's effect on the defendant's demeanor.[34] A videotape of the defendant's demeanor without treatment may be a more effective way of conveying the information to the jury.

Most states have not spoken on the issue of the right to refuse treatment of those defendants who are incompetent to stand trial. As opposed to the civilly committed patient, there is greater state interest in having the defendant take medication because it may be crucial in allowing the defendant to be brought to trial.[35] The New York State Court of Appeals, New York's highest court, ruled in *Rivers v Katz*[36] that the civilly committed patient has a right to a hearing to determine his competence to refuse psychotropic medication and, if incompetent, a judicial determination of the psychotropic medication he is to receive. The *Rivers* decision did not deal specifically with the defendant who was involuntarily hospitalized on the basis of incompetency to stand trial. However, the State Office of Mental Health has included this group among those requiring the procedural and legal safeguards mandated by the *Rivers v Katz* decision.

There are situations in which an individual who is not competent to stand trial when off medication may nonetheless refuse medication. In *State v Hayes,*[37] the New Hampshire Supreme Court ruled that defendants should be allowed to appear at trial without medication. The court required that a competent waiver occur regarding the decision to appear at trial without medication. If the individual had been on medication, the court held that the period of time between the defendant's last taking the medication and the trial must be equal to the period between the last medication before the offense and the offense itself. In *Commonwealth v Louraine,*[38] the Massachusetts Supreme Court reversed a conviction of murder on the grounds that by medicating the defendant, who was putting forward a defense of insanity, he was denied the right to present his nonmedicated demeanor to the court.

## AMNESIA

The determination of the competency to stand trial of a defendant who reports that he has amnesia for the events in question raises significant medical and legal questions. The diagnosis of amnesia includes the differential diagnosis of an organic brain syndrome, a conversion reaction, and malingering. Prolonged or unchanging amnesia may prevent the defendant from sharing relevant information and effectively advising his attorney. However, the potential use of amnesia as a ploy to avoid going to trial is great. In most jurisdictions, unless it can be shown that the amnesia is reversible, the courts will direct a trial to take place.

Amnesia is not a defense to a criminal charge and is not an absolute bar to being tried on a charge.[39] In *Wilson v United States*,[40] Wilson was charged with assault and robbery. He suffered a head injury in his ensuing attempt to escape. Although he had obvious brain damage, the court found that sufficient "extrinsic information" was available to the defendant to allow him to overcome his lack of knowledge of the crime. The courts have held that the defendant suffering from a treatable, reversible amnesia should be granted a continuance "to employ such expert assistance, in addition to counsel, as may be required to induce the defendant to remember."[41]

The court's effort to distinguish between temporary and permanent amnesia requires the psychiatrist to function as an expert witness. The discussion of the causes of permanent amnesia and reversible amnesia are discussed by Koson and Robey[42] and Bromberg.[43] In *Morrow v Maryland*,[44] the court stated that "only when a defendant's loss of memory obscures the search for truth should an accused be deemed incompetent to stand trial." As a practical matter, the more serious the charge, the less likely the courts are to find a defendant with permanent amnesia incompetent. Roesch and Golding provide a recent review of the legal and clinical issues involved in amnesia and competency to stand trial.[45]

## THE PSYCHIATRIC REPORT ON THE DEFENDANT'S COMPETENCY TO STAND TRIAL

As with all psychiatric reports, a psychiatrist writing a report on a defendant's competency to stand trial must know to whom the report is being written and who is likely to see the report if the issue goes to a hearing. The report should begin with the identifying information about the defendant, the charges that the defendant faces, and the forensic psychiatric questions that are dealt within the report. The consent to examination, required in some jurisdictions as a specific component of the forensic report, is a required ethical obligation of the psychiatrist to inform the defendant about the purpose of the examination. It is useful to document in the report that this informed consent to examination was obtained. In my view, the next section of the report should contain the conclusions or opinions resulting from the psychiatric examination: the psychiatric diagnosis, if one is present, and the responses to the specific forensic question with a concise account of the reasoning used to arrive at the opinion. The next section provides a description of the nature of the examination including information about interviews (with whom, when, where, how long), as well as the materials reviewed. Next follows the section on the relevant history of the defendant. Depending on the complexity of the data gathered, it may be as simple as one section or it may be several sections long: history of events leading to the current charges; the individual's psychiatric history; and the individual's past and family history. Following a description of the mental status examination and diagnostic impression is a summary paragraph. This summary contains a synopsis of the report and a detailed description of the reasoning used to arrive at conclusions.

The content of the report will vary and the psychiatrist must be discreet while being informative. A well-prepared report allows the courts to make a reasoned decision on how to proceed. In addition, it provides the psychiatrist with a useful framework from which to prepare for testimony, should it be required.


## CONCLUSION

The competence to stand trial evaluation is one of the important interfaces of psychiatry and the law. This consultation calls for a careful psychiatric evaluation of the defendant, after clarification of the question that the referring party is asking. The competence to stand trial evaluation also requires that the psychiatrist have a working understanding of the criminal justice system and the issues involved in the defendant's specific charges. Knowledge of the specifics often requires the psychiatrist to talk with the defendant's attorney. After determining if a mental disorder is present, the psychiatrist considers how any of the impairments resulting from the mental disorder affect the defendant's competence to stand trial; that is, the individual's strengths and weaknesses regarding the specific capacities required to stand trial, given the specific charges, and the specific defenses available are evaluated. In certain cases, observing the attorney–client interaction is essential in order to arrive at an informed opinion on the defendant's competency. The well-written report provides the court with relevant information and is an important framework for the psychiatrist's testimony. Under certain circumstances, there may be weeks or even months between the psychiatrist's writing the report and being called to testify. It behooves the psychiatrist to update the competency evaluation. An opinion on competency to stand trial is based on the defendant's current condition and this condition may have changed considerably between the psychiatrist's writing the report and testifying in court.

The competence to stand trial issue continues to generate legal activity. The courts remain concerned with the application of the legal definition of competence to stand trial to specific cases. The effects of amnesia on competence, the standard of proof, the right to a psychiatric examination and a hearing are just some of the other issues on which the courts continue to hand down findings. In addition, the courts are exploring the incompetent defendant's rights as they affect the defendant's trial demeanor and the right to refuse treatment with neuroleptic medication. As the competence to stand trial interface between psychiatry and the law continues to evolve, psychiatrists must continue to play a crucial role by providing the courts with the information and reasoned opinions that will allow for just and humane decisions.

# REFERENCES


1. Ciccone JR, Barry DJ: Collaboration between psychiatry and the law: A study of 100 referrals to a court clinic. *Bull Am Acad Psychiatry Law* 1977; 4:275–280.
2. Hess JH, Thomas HE: Incompetency to stand trial: Procedures, results and problems. *Am J Psychiatry* 1963; 119:713–720.
3. Halleck SL: *Psychiatry and the Dilemmas of Crime.* New York, Harper & Row, 1967.
4. Scheidemandel PL, Kanco CK: *The Mentally Ill Offender: A Survey of Treatment Programs.* Washington, DC, Joint Information Services, 1969.
5. Group for the Advancement of Psychiatry (GAP): *Misuse of Psychiatry in the Criminal Courts: Competency to Stand Trial.* New York, Group for the Advancement of Psychiatry, 1974, p 887.
6. Walker N: *Crime and Insanity in England, Volume I: The Historical Perspective.* Edinburgh, Scotland, Edinburgh University Press, 1968.
7. *See* Group for the Advancement of Psychiatry (GAP), *supra* note 5, p 889.
8. Ray I: *Treatise on the Medical Jurisprudence of Insanity.* Boston, Charles Little and James Brown, 1838. Cited in Bromberg W: *The Uses of Psychiatry in Law.* Wesport, Conn, Quorum Books, 1976, p 89.
9. *Dusky v United States* 362 U.S. 402 (1960).
10. *Dusky v United States* 271 F.2d 385 (8th Cir. 1959).
11. *Dusky v United States* 295 F.2d 743 (8th Cir. 1961).
12. *See* Group for the Advancement of Psychiatry (GAP), *supra* note 5, p 891.
13. Robey A: Criteria for competency to stand trial: A checklist for psychiatrists. *Am J Psychiatry* 1965; 122:616–666.
14. McGarry L: *Competency to Stand Trial and Mental Illness.* New York, Jacob Aronson, 1974.

15. Menzies RJ, Webster CD, Roesch R, Jensen FA, Eaves D: The fitness interview test: A semi-structured instrument for assessing competency to stand trial, with a proposal for implementation. *Med Law* 1984; 3:151–162.

16. When giving workshops on forensic report writing, including the workshop in Forensic Psychiatry Course: Board Review and Update sponsored by AAPL, it has been my practice to have the participants submit samples of their forensic reports for review and critique by the group. One of the most frequent errors in the submitted reports is equating the presence of a psychotic illness with incompetence to stand trial.

17. Rcich JH, Tookcy L: Disagreements between court and psychiatrist on competency to stand trial. *J Clin Psychiatry* 1986; 47:29–31.

18. Heller MS, Taylor WH, Ehrlich SM, Lester D: Intelligence, psychosis and competency to stand trial. *Bull Am Acad Psychiatry Law* 1981; 9:267–274.

19. *Colorado v Connelly* 305 U.S. 902 (1986).

20. *Washington v Hahn* 726 P.2d 25 (Wash. Sup. Ct. 1986).

21. *New York v Colon* 512 N.Y.S.2d 809 (N.Y. App. Div. 1987).

22. Melton GB, Petrila J, Poythress NG, Slobogin C: *Psychological Evaluations for the Courts: A Handbook for Mental Health Professionals and Lawyers.* New York, Guilford Press, 1987.

23. Weinstein HC: Psychiatry on trial: Clinical and ethical problems in the psychiatric assessment of competency to stand trial, in Wright F, Bahn C, Rieber RW (eds): *Forensic Psychology and Psychiatry.* New York, New York Academy of Sciences, 1980.

24. Ciccone JR, Clements CD: The insanity defense: Asking and answering the ultimate question. *Bull Am Acad Psychiatry Law,* 1987; 15(4):329–338.

25. Ethical guidelines for the practice of forensic psychiatry. *Newsletter Am Acad Psychiatry Law* 1987; 4:16–17.

26. *Pate v Robinson* 383 U.S. 375, 86 (Sup. Ct. 836 1966).

27. *Moore v United States* 464 F.2d 663 (9th Cir. 1972).

28. Roesch R, Golding SL: *Competency to Stand Trial.* Chicago, University of Illinois Press, 1980.

29. *See* McGarry, *supra* note 14, p 55.

30. *Jackson v Indiana* 406 U.S. 715 (1972).

31. Davis DL: Treatment planning for the patient who is incompetent to stand trial. *Hosp Community Psychiatry* 1985; 36:268–271.

32. *State v Murphy* 56 Wash. 2d 761, 355 P.2d 323 (1960).

33. Winick: Psychotropic medications and competency to stand trial. *Am Bar Foundation Res J,* 1979, p 1169.

34. Smith SM: Competence. *Psychiatr Clin North Am* 1983; 6:635–650.

35. *Washington v Lorer* 707 P.2d 1351 (Wash. Ct. App. 1985).

36. *Rivers v Katz* 67 N.Y. 2d 485 (1986).

37. *State v Hayes* 389 A.2d 1379 (1978).

38. *Commonwealth v Louraine* 390 Mass. 28, 453 N.W.2d 437 (1983).

39. *North Carolina v Avery 337 S.E.2d 786 (N.C. Sup. Ct. 1985).*

40. *Wilson v United States 391 F.2d 460 (D.C. Cir. 1968).*

41. *Cornell v Sct 52 Calif.2d 99, 338 P.2d 447 (1959).*

42. Koson D, Robey A: Amnesia and competency to stand trial. *Am J Psychiatry* 1973; 130:588–591.

43. Bromberg W: *The Uses of Psychiatry in the Law: A Clinical View of Forensic Psychiatry.* Wesport, Conn, Quorum Books, 1976.

44. *Morrow v Maryland* 443 A.2d 108 (Md. Ct. App. 1982).

45. Roesch R, Golding SL: Amnesia and competency to stand trial: A review of legal and clinical issues. *Behav Sci Law* 1986; 4:87–97.

# The Use of Psychiatric Evaluations in the Determination of Sentencing

ALAN R. FELTHOUS

Of all the issues in the criminal law that a forensic psychiatrist is likely to address, sentencing is surely one of the most understated. Compared with competency to stand trial and insanity, postconviction sentencing all but goes unnoticed as a phase of the criminal law process that includes psychiatric participation. And yet, psychiatric presentencing evaluations are presumably obtained with some degree of regularity. In the determination of sentencing, legal and clinical aims can complement and confound each other.

Psychiatric evaluations contribute to the sentencing of criminal offenders in two ways: the psychiatric recommendations are considered when treatment is an element of sentencing, and the findings and conclusions from psychiatric assessment are taken into account in determining the severity of punishment.

In addition to retribution, deterence, and incapacitation, rehabilitation or reform is a purpose of the criminal justice system. The mental health system treats mentally disturbed individuals and attempts to effect improvement, remission, or cure by specifically prescribed thera-

**ALAN R. FELTHOUS** • Department of Psychiatry and Behavioral Sciences, University of Texas Medical Branch—Galveston, Galveston, TX 77550.

peutic programs. The rehabilitation of the criminal and the successful treatment of mentally disordered individuals are overlapping aims.

But neither are determination of severity of punishment and therapeutic programming always crisply separate matters. Indeterminate sentencing, for example, is a penal concept in which the rehabilitation of the individual offender is compared with the indeterminate therapy of an individual whose treatment is designed to overcome the disorder or unwanted behavior regardless of how long it takes.

In general, the criminal justice system endeavors to deal with suspected offenders on an equal basis, especially in adjudication of guilt. Everyone is to be protected equally and to be liable equally under the law. There are familiar exceptions, in cases in which the offender is a minor or insane, for example, but generally equal access to legal protections and equal liability to criminal conviction and punishment are principles of fairness. Different crimes are handled differently, but people are not. At least this is the ideal which is presented, as symbolically represented by Astraea—the blindfolded maiden-goddess holding the scales of justice—and vigorously asserted by retributionists.

The mental health system should also provide everyone with equal access to quality treatment, but treatment is specific to mental disorders and not to isolated criminal behaviors. Thus, if the retributive function of the law equalizes, then mental health services individualize, and there is a resulting tension between the push to equalize within the criminal law and the pull to individualize of mental health services.

After a criminal conviction and at the sentencing, the law more openly permits individualized responses, though the notion that the punishment should fit the crime, not the criminal, often prevails at least within sentencing limits. In some situations, for example, in capital sentencing, the law requires some measure of individual assessment.

There are various models for obtaining psychiatric presentencing evaluations. Each model is essentially shaped by specific statutory provisions, or lack thereof, and the availability of appropriate resources. In many situations, the judge simply orders a presentencing investigation by a probation or parole officer. In some cases, a psychiatric presentence evaluation and a report are court ordered as the need presents itself. Several states have statutory provisions for psychiatric presentencing evaluations to be done on convicted felons. In other jurisdictions, whenever the question of mental illness or retardation has already been raised (e.g., competency to stand trial), the issues of treatment and habilitation must be addressed as a matter of law. This latter provision is simply intended to identify individuals who require hospital treatment or placement in a special facility for the retarded.

## INDETERMINATE SENTENCING

In summarizing the evolution of indeterminate sentencing in the United States, Alan Dershowitz identified four periods.[1] During the *Colonial Period*, law enforcement was accomplished by various nonincarcerative methods, including fines and such physical punishments as whipping, the stocks, the pillory, and death. The practice of incarcerating offenders was limited and did not serve the purpose of rehabilitation.

In the *Pre-Civil War Period*, that is, between the Revolutionary War and the Civil War, the use of the death penalty became more restricted, and the purpose of reformation of offenders began to take precedence over retribution or retaliation.

In the *Post-Civil War Period*, crime was regarded as a moral disease for which there was hope for recovery, if the remedy of punishment were prescribed for the needs of the criminal, not for the crime. If criminals were to be reformed, sentences must be individualized or indeterminate with possible early release, once the criminal has recovered. Parole systems and indeterminate sentencing widely replaced fixed sentencing.

According to Dershowitz, in the *Post-World War II Period*, indeterminate sentencing emerged as "the dominant sentencing structure in the United States."[1] The actual time to be served was not established by the sentencing judge, but rather by an administrative body during the course of the offender's sentence. The more humane sentencing practices, the increased emphasis on reform, and the widespread use of indeterminate sentencing developed without much encouragement from psychiatrists.

During the third quarter of the present century, the expanding field of psychiatry exerted progressively more influence on the sentencing process. Several states, including California, Kansas, Maryland, Massachusetts, New Jersey, and North Carolina, enacted statutory provisions for psychiatric presentencing evaluations of convicted felons. Much hope was invested in psychiatry as a discipline to give meaningful, effective, and humane direction to the process of reforming offenders, or at least those offenders with mental disorders. In the shadow of this growing therapeutic positivism, emerged a contrasting skepticism of psychiatry, and some limits were placed on psychiatric authority within the criminal justice system.

## "PRESUMPTIVE" SENTENCING

For years, sentencing was highly individualized. Statutes provided minimum and maximum periods of incarceration, but judges exercised considerable discretion in imposing sentences between the extremes allowed by law.[2] After sentencing, parole authorities applied further discretion in deciding if an inmate was eligible to be released from prison before the expiration of the court-ordered sentence. Especially within the past decade, the discretion allowed for courts and parole agencies has fallen into some disfavor, and indeterminate sentencing has been increasingly replaced by determinant sentencing, wherein prison sentences are more consistent and lacking in individual variations.

Some states, having limited individualized, indeterminate sentencing, have not entirely eliminated discretionary sentencing but rather have restructured this procedure. "Presumptive" sentencing allows for discretionary adjustments by specifying the aggravating or mitigating factors in the sentencing law that would justify a higher or lower sentence. If indeterminate sentencing is restricted further, psychiatric contributions to the sentencing process may also be reduced. However, depending on which aggravating or mitigating factors are enacted into sentencing law, presumptive sentencing could invite greater psychiatric involvement in assisting courts in assessing the severity of the sentence.[2]

## PSYCHIATRIC CONTRIBUTIONS TO SEVERITY OF SENTENCING

It is perhaps more commonly stated that psychiatric evaluations can serve to *mitigate* the severity of sentence[3,4] rather than affect the severity in *either* direction. Mitigation is consistent with the physician's role as a helper who first does no harm to persons who seek his help in time of need. But like other issues to be settled through the adversarial process, mitigation presumes its opposite, nonmitigation, if not enhancement or aggravation. If a psychiatrist can contribute testimony in support of mitigation, he could just as well testify in support of nonmitigated or increased severity.

In practice, the latter procedure seldom happens because treatment recommendations tend to be more consistent with mitigation, psychiatrists do not always explicitly recommend punishment,[5] and punishment decisions are typically made by the judge without as much courtroom controversy as occurs prior to the adjudication of guilt.

Although some psychiatrists assert that psychiatrists should not make specific recommendations for punishment[6] others would allow them to make dispositional comments but only in support of leniency.[7,8] Bartholomew, for example, would permit psychiatrists to recommend imprisonment.[9]

It seems to be a common perception that psychiatric involvement in the sentencing process serves to mitigate the punishment. If recommendations are not followed, they appear useless. But if they are followed, suspicions are expressed that judges either order presentence psychiatric evaluations to confirm their predetermined sentencing option or are too easily persuaded by psychiatric reports.

Campbell, who reviewed studies in various English-speaking countries, including England, Canada, Wales, Scotland, Tasmania, and Australia, noted that the use of presentence psychiatric reports is not frequent; but when they are used, whether reports are "confirmatory or constructive," there is a generally high rate of concurrence between the psychiatric recommendation and the sentence imposed by the court.[4] An especially intriguing observation made by Campbell is that, although courts sometimes disregard psychiatric recommendations for lenient or noncustodial dispositions, they rarely fail to follow a psychiatric recommendation for lengthy custodial disposition or treatment combined with high security.

The American Psychiatric Association's Task Force on Sentencing discourages psychiatrists from making specific recommendations for disposition, "including probation and incarceration."[2] Diagnostic and therapeutic conclusions are more in keeping with the psychiatrist's realm of expertise. Ethically, the psychiatrist is on solid ground if he adheres to the principles of beneficence (seeking to do good) and nonmaleficence (refraining from causing harm). The task force recognized that a psychiatrist should endeavor to protect society, but this obligation is fulfilled by conducting a thorough examination and not withholding information. Although psychiatrists are "severely limited in their capacity to predict violence," they might comment on factors in the person's environment which either increase or decrease the likelihood of violence.[2]

Even if the psychiatrist does not recommend imposition or nonimposition of a specific punishment and even if he does not predict recurrence or nonrecurrence of violent or criminal behaviors, his clinical findings can be used for predictive and punitive purposes, when the court assesses the risks and benefits of various dispositions. Bartholomew was correct in asserting that the psychiatrist's prediction of the future course of any mental illness can be influential in the ultimate sentence, for "the better the prognosis . . . then the more lenient one might expect the sentence to be".[9]

A society-oriented psychiatrist may be tempted to apply a condemning diagnosis even with insufficient findings in order to ensure the maximum sentence. On the other hand, a patient-oriented psychiatrist may avoid using such a diagnosis despite compelling clinical evidence in support of it in order to minimize the likelihood of a severe sentence. Each is allowing a personal moral judgment to compromise clinical integrity. If psychiatrists are to be involved at all, rather than prejudicially protecting society or the individual, the best policy should value clinical integrity foremost.

It is not without reason that James P. Grigson, a Dallas psychiatrist, is regarded as a psychiatric expert who testifies predominantly for the prosecution and in support of severe sentencing for certain offenders. His predictions of dangerousness to satisfy individualizing criteria of the death penalty have been widely criticized. At least, in instances in which the death penalty was concerned, some of his methods were deemed unconstitutional by the United States Supreme Court.

What may not be commonly known is that, according to Doctor Grigson, in over one third of the capital murder defendants he evaluated, he concluded that they did *not* present a continuing threat to society.[10] In what appears to be a token effort, he testified for the defense in several recent capital cases.[10] Regardless of whether he was testifying for the defense or the prosecution, and even without explicitly recommending a disposition, Dr. Grigson has assisted in individualizing and in thus helping the fact finder decide whom the citizens of Texas ought to execute.

Some years ago, upon the request of the defense counsel, Dr. Grigson evaluated a defendant, who was charged with robbery, burglary, and assault to commit murder, to address the defendant's competency to stand trial. Dr. Grigson's final diagnosis was " 'severe sociopathic personality disorder,' not subject to cure or treatment, but not such a 'mental disease or defect' that would constitute a defense to criminal prosecution."[11] The defendant's attorney notified the prosecutor of this diagnosis. At the punishment phase, after the defendant was found guilty of all charges, Dr. Grigson testified according to his diagnostic findings, and the jury then gave the defendant the maximum punishment for each offense.

Attributing this adverse outcome to the psychiatrist's testimony in the punishment phase, the defendant brought action against Dr. Grigson. Among his claims, the defendant complained that he was not informed of the possible consequences of disclosing information to the psychiatrist and how this information could be used in the court. The trial court and the appellate court held that Dr. Grigson had no duty to disclose to the accused the possibility of adverse testimony based on his diagnosis. Thus, before the celebrated Supreme Court cases on the psychiatrist's role in capital sentencing, legal precedent was established, paving the way for psychiatrists, such as Dr. Grigson, to testify so as to enhance punishment without forewarning the defendant of this possibility.

## CAPITAL SENTENCING

Capital sentencing today is perhaps the quintessential example of where the law demands individual appraisal. The punishment must fit the individual offender as well as the capital offense. Psychiatric evaluation is permissible, perhaps, on occasion, even welcomed by the courts, to provide the necessary individualization to support the legitimacy of this severity of punishment. By the same token, the psychiatrist who evaluates a defendant and testifies that the individual is not suitable for execution also supports the legitimacy of the psychiatrist's role in individualizing and in helping to identify who should be executed and who should be spared.

Early in the history of the United States, capital sentencing was accomplished without much consideration given to mitigating or aggravating factors. Once they were adjudicated guilty of a capital offense, most offenders were equally executable under the law. In the 1960s, concern over prejudicial or arbitrary application, resulting in the risk of literally fatal misjudgments, caused much public distrust of capital sentencing laws.

In its 1972 *Furman v Georgia* decision, the United States Supreme Court held that Georgia's capital sentencing law was unconstitutional.[12] Since a case arising in Texas (*Branch v Texas*) was decided together with *Furman,* the capital sentencing law of Texas was struck down by the same decision. Beyond Georgia and Texas, the *Furman* decision essentially ended capital sentencing nationwide over the next four years. In the wake of *Furman,* confusion was generated over whether the previous capital sentencing law in Georgia was unfair and unconstitutional because it was applied inconsistently or because it did not allow sufficiently for mitigating factors.

In 1976, the Supreme Court addressed the matter in its certiorari to the Court of Criminal Appeals of Texas in *Jurek v Texas.*[13] This decision occurred after Texas had enacted a new capital sentencing law that was intended to meet constitutional approval. The new law included three additional questions that must be decided in the affirmative by the jury, after an offender is convicted of a capital offense, before the death penalty can be imposed. Although the law did not use the term *mitigating,* the Supreme Court found these factors sufficiently individualizing to satisfy constitutional requirements.

Incidentally, the Court in *Jurek* also stated its position on the prediction of future dangerousness as an individualizing factor in capital sentencing. In essence, the court stated that attempts at such predictions may not be accurate, but they are nonetheless welcomed in capital sentencing.

In its certiorari to the Supreme Court of Ohio in 1978, the United States Supreme Court clarified the need to individualize in capital sentencing by emphasizing mitigating circumstances that must be taken into account before the death penalty is applied.[14] Not devoid of mitigating factors, the Ohio death penalty statute already considered the following circumstances before the death penalty was imposed:

(1) The victim of the offense induced or facilitated it.
(2) It is unlikely that the offense would have been committed, but for the fact that the offender was under duress, coercion, or strong provocation.
(3) The offense was primarily the product of the offender's psychosis or mental deficiency, though such condition is insufficient to establish the defense of insanity.[15]

The Court held that this was insufficient consideration of mitigating circumstances to permit capital sentencing.[14]

Paradoxically, the inadequate Ohio factors appear more mitigating than the Texas factors, which are aggravating in comparison; yet the aggravating factors set a higher threshold and, therefore, should reasonably spare more offenders from the ultimate punishment. The Court criticized the Ohio capital sentencing law for not allowing the sentencing judge enough opportunity to consider mitigating circumstances in capital cases as required by the Eighth and Fourteenth Amendments. Among other issues, the judge should be permitted to consider as a mitigating factor, "any aspect of a defendant's character or record and any circumstances of the offense that the defendant proffers as a basis for a sentence less than death."[16]

In order to satisfy constitutional requirements, states that have a death penalty in effect today incorporated such factors into their respective capital sentencing laws. Aggravating and mitigating factors, it must be stressed, are opposite sides of the same coin: both are individualizing factors intended to justify severity while at the same time permitting a leniency option.


## THE ROLE OF THE PSYCHIATRIST IN CAPITAL SENTENCING

In the early 1980s, through several decisions, the United States Supreme Court did much to shape the role of the psychiatrist in capital sentencing. In its *Estelle v Smith* decision of 1980, the Court held that if a psychiatrist examines a defendant in pretrial for purposes of capital sentencing, he must warn the defendant that he has a right to remain silent and that any statement he makes can be used against him. Without this two-part caveat, the psychiatrist's testimony cannot be brought into the death-penalty phase without violating the Fifth Amendment:

> An accused who neither initiates a psychiatric evaluation nor attempts to
> introduce any psychiatric evidence may not be compelled to respond to a
> psychiatrist if his statements can be used against him at a capital sentencing
> proceeding. (p 454)[17]

The counsel for the defense should not be excluded from a decision for
the defendant to undergo a precapital sentence psychiatric evaluation to
address the client's future dangerousness. As in *Jurek* five years earlier,[13]
the Court in *Estelle* emphasized the importance of attempting to predict
future dangerousness or criminal conduct within the criminal justice
system and the legitimacy of psychiatric testimony in this endeavor:

> While in no sense disapproving the use of psychiatric testimony bearing on
> the issue of future dangerousness, the holding in *Jurek* was guided by recog-
> nition that the inquiry mandated by Texas law does not require resort to
> medical experts.[18]

More to the point was the Supreme Court's decision in *Barefoot v
Estelle* in 1983. In this case, psychiatrists had provided testimony about
future dangerousness in response to hypothetical questions and without
examining the defendant in a capital murder case. On appeal, the defendant argued that the psychiatric testimony on future dangerousness was
unconstitutional because psychiatrists are not competent to do so. Inaccurate predictors of dangerousness are likely to cause erroneous sentencing in violation of the Eighth and Fourteenth Amendments.[19]

The Court refuted the defendant's argument by asserting the pro-
priety of allowing psychiatrists to testify about a defendant without examining the defendant, to testify about predictions of future dangerousness, and to address hypothetical questions to predict dangerousness.

Even in the face of an amicus curiae brief from the American Psychiatric Association stating the profession's inability to predict future
dangerousness or criminal acts,[20] the Court held that psychiatrists can
make predictions with sufficient accuracy to be of some help to the fact
finder:

> There is no merit to petitioner's argument that psychiatrists, individually or
> as a group, are incompetent to predict with an acceptable degree of reliability
> that a particular criminal will commit other crimes in the future and so
> represent a danger to the community. To accept such argument would call
> into question predictions of future behavior that are constantly made in other
> contexts. Moreover, under the generally applicable rules of evidence cover-
> ing the admission and weight of unprivileged evidence, psychiatric testimony
> predicting dangerousness may be countered not only as erroneous in a par-
> ticular case but also as generally so unreliable that it should be ignored. Nor,
> despite the view of the American Psychiatric Association supporting peti-
> tioner's view, is there any convincing evidence that such testimony is almost

entirely unreliable and that factfinder and the adversary system will not be
competent to uncover, recognize, and take due account of its shortcomings.[21]

On this point the Supreme Court and organized psychiatry are in
sharp disagreement. Although the Court supports psychiatric predictions of violence for purposes of punishment, the American Psychiatric
Association denies that psychiatrists have special expertise in predicting
long-term dangerousness that would grant them a valid role.

Even without the issue of dangerousness, many psychiatrists are
revolted by the knowledge that some of their colleagues assist in identifying whom the state should execute. If physicians, including psychiatrists,
were provided a role in prescribing or administering lethal injections,
the APA might well assert a legal argument against this despite a physician's competence to accomplish this task accurately and efficiently.

If the Court were to doubt psychiatry's ability to contribute to the
grim predictions involved in capital sentencing, it may be forced to question the validity of individualizing predictions of violence made at various steps in the criminal justice system from arrest, indictment, to the
decision of whether to parole an incarcerated inmate. Will the Court
reconsider its charted course of individualizing to provide constitutional
approval for capital sentencing? No, the Court is not expected to re-
trench anytime soon; though the criminal courts could turn to another
discipline that presents some credible evidence of improved predictions
of violence and criminality. If one accepts the APA's position that psychiatrists have no special expertise in predicting future violent or criminal
conduct, not just in the context of capital sentencing, then the question
arises whether or not psychiatrists ought to address long-term security
issues at all. Again, the APA task force recommended against any comment on dispositional issues yet suggested that psychiatrists should be
able to identify factors that would worsen or improve the risks.

Another important aspect of the *Barefoot* decision, was the Court's
explicit approval of hypothetical testimony in capital sentencing proceedings:

> Psychiatric testimony need not be based on personal examination of the
> defendant but may properly be given in response to hypothetical questions.
> Expert testimony, whether in the form of an opinion based on hypothetical
> questions or otherwise, is commonly admitted as evidence where it might
> help the fact finder do its job. Although this case involves the death penalty,
> there is no constitutional barrier to applying the ordinary rules of evidence
> governing the use of expert testimony.[21]

In *Ake v Oklahoma,* the Court held:

> When a defendant has made a preliminary showing that his sanity at the time
> of the offense is likely to be a significant factor at trial, the Constitution

> requires that a State provide access to a psychiatrist's assistance on this issue if
> the defendant cannot otherwise afford one. (p 68)[23]

While protecting the defendant's rights in capital sentencing and promoting a fairer balance in the contest, the *Ake* decision further strengthened the judicial legitimacy of psychiatric testimony in capital sentencing procedures.

> When the state at a capital sentencing proceeding presents psychiatric evidence of the defendant's future dangerousness, the defendant, without a psychiatrist's assistance, cannot offer an expert's opposing view, and thereby loses a significant opportunity to raise in the jurors' minds questions about the state's proof of an aggravating factor. In such a circumstance, where the consequence of error is so great, the relevance of responsive psychiatric testimony so evident, and the State's burden so slim, due process requires access to a psychiatric examination on relevant issues, to a psychiatrist's testimony, *and to assistance in preparation at the sentencing phase* [italics added]. (p 68)[23]

Regardless of what organized psychiatry thinks, the United States Supreme Court believes that psychiatrists have a legitimate role in certain capital sentencing cases provided that the psychiatrist's participation is done in the proper manner.

Capital sentencing law illustrates the fact that psychiatric testimony in the sentencing phase can cut in two directions: to protect the defendant from the death penalty or to establish aggravating factors in support of the death penalty. Although potential consequences are less severe, psychiatric testimony in sentencing is, in general, an equally double-edged sword. An objective evaluator is not predisposed to favor or disfavor the legal interests of a defendant before conducting a psychiatric evaluation. The witness who first and always endeavors to cause no harm to the defendant's legal interests will be biased in favor of the treatment model over the punishment model. This is not an unreasonable orientation for a treater provided his compromise in objectivity is recognizable.

Nonetheless, the evaluator who selectively favors a leniency option also participates by calculated omission in identifying who is not a candidate for leniency. Furthermore, even a pure treatment orientation is not always absolute, and reports of testimony that favor treatment leniency—as we shall see in a later section—in some instances can be viewed by the defendant as harmful to his legal interests.

## STATUTORY PROVISIONS FOR PSYCHIATRIC PRESENTENCING EXAMINATIONS

In most states, psychiatric presentencing examinations are ordered only infrequently at the discretion of the sentencing judge. Sentencing judges make numerically much greater use of presentencing evaluations from probation or parole officers. On entering the state correctional system, the new inmate may undergo an initial diagnostic and classification assessment to ensure that some of his needs are satisfied in prison, but this evaluation has no bearing on sentencing, which by then is already an accomplished fact.

At least six states have long had statutory provisions for psychiatric presentencing examinations: California,[24] Kansas,[25] Massachusetts,[26] Maryland,[27] New Jersey,[27] and North Carolina.[27] Several large metropolitan areas have supported court clinics for the study of adult offenders (e.g., Baltimore, Chicago, Cleveland, Detroit, New York City, Philadelphia, Pittsburgh, and Washington, DC), but our focus here will be on the statewide referral centers.

Does a special diagnostic facility, supported by statute, provide useful diagnostic and therapeutic information on mentally disordered offenders? Is such a facility successful enough in accomplishing therapeutic and rehabilitative goals to be adopted by other states? Or does such a facility consume scarce professional staff and physical resources with little hope for effective follow-through after an inmate is transferred to another facility within the correctional system? Space limits the extent of our inquiry here, but the issue deserves serious consideration because the benefits and risks of such a system could apply to a large number of individuals. Here we will compare some of the similarities and differences of psychiatric presentencing study systems in two states, Kansas and North Carolina.

One of the earliest psychiatric diagnostic centers established pursuant to state penal statute and still functioning today is the Kansas State Reception and Diagnostic Center (KRDC), which opened in Topeka, Kansas, in 1961. The goal then and now is to promote successful *rehabilitation* of male felons.[25]

After a defendant is convicted of a felony, the judge imposes a sentence, and the inmate then undergoes a thorough multidisciplinary evaluation at KRDC. Included in this assessment are the psychiatric evaluation, psychological testing, social history, vocational assessment, and appraisal of religious views. An integrated report presents the inmate's psychiatric diagnosis, treatment needs, and an individualized plan for rehabilitation.

Upon completion, the report is sent to the sentencing judge, who can then modify his original sentence, grant probation, or permit the original sentence to stand. The statute clearly allows the report to be used by the court to modify the original decision in the direction of leniency, not severity. In fact, the court is empowered to reduce the length of minimum sentence below the statutory limit.[28] Findings from this evaluation can lead to community placement.

Thus, the study team is invited to make predictive statements about security needs and to recommend specific dispositions in the direction of leniency for selected felons. A desired effect of addressing both security and rehabilitative needs of individual inmates is to maintain or reduce the state's prison population.[29] Indeed, social concerns about prison population and early release of inmates with insufficient screening are probably much greater today than are concerns over psychiatry's limited ability to predict criminality and anticipate security needs.

Several authors have described the presentence diagnosis study procedure that was established by statute in North Carolina in 1967.[27,29] The statute allows a judge to assign to the study group the responsibility for developing information to be used in sentencing selected offenders, but the judge retains the responsibility for ultimately imposing the final sentence.[30] By means of a comprehensive, multidisciplinary evaluation in a maximum security hospital setting, the judge can make an informed sentencing decision that ideally facilitates more individualized treatment programs. Although sentencing judges do not always formulate specific questions for the study group to address, most questions pertain to the defendant's mental condition, his treatability, and the question of dangerousness. Beyond a consideration of medical and psychiatric needs, the study group also obtains information about the social history and the community's attitude about the offender/and evaluates the offender's educational and vocational training needs. According to Smith, the study group not only addresses diagnosis and treatment but also matters of "prevention, deterrence, punishment, and protection of the community."[27]

Courts follow presentence recommendations in more than 80% of the cases. Aside from strictly treatment issues, the study group recommends probation in a preponderance of the cases. Smith[27] has questioned whether probation recommendations are a proper function of the study group; rather, he suggested, the primary mission ought to be the formulation of treatment plans for felons who will be imprisoned.

Two years after Smith's report, Jones stated that the study team's report to the Court "does not presume to address the Court's prerogative of deterrence or punishment unless germane to the case. That is the province of the courts, not the presentence diagnostic study team."[29] Yet recommendations for probation and active sentence are made regularly. Several studies indicate that recommendations for community-based programs are made in 70% to 80% of the cases. The lower rate of recommendation for probation for KRDC, 30% to 40%[31] in comparison, may be a function of differential selection for the two programs. Available information suggests that the courts make use of the reports from both programs, particularly with regard to the decision of whether to place the offender on probation.[27,29,32]

## PSYCHIATRIC RECOMMENDATIONS AS A CONDITION FOR PROBATION

In contrast to practices in Kansas, North Carolina, and elsewhere, the American Psychiatric Association's Task Force on the Role of Psychiatry in the Sentencing Process recommends that psychiatrists avoid giving specific recommendations for disposition including probation.[2] The clinician's suggestions should be treatment oriented, rather than punishment oriented.

Yet somewhat less directly, the psychiatrist can also affect severity of sentence by addressing the aggravating or mitigating factors. Both individualized capital sentencing and presumptive sentencing for noncapital offenses present such possibilities. Findings from a psychiatric evaluation can affect the decision whether to probate or incarcerate.

As much as one might desire a crisp conceptual dichotomization of punishment and treatment, a measure of external restraint and structure can be therapeutic or countertherapeutic depending on the nature and severity of the offender's mental illness. From the mentally ill offender's subjective experience, he may perceive treatment as punishing (e.g., too restrictive) or punishment as therapeutic (e.g., a welcome withdrawal from alcohol while in jail). Even without making special dispositive recommendations, treatment recommendations alone can affect whether the inmate is placed on probation with required treatment conditions.

The offender may experience the psychiatrist's contribution as either palliative or punitive. Ongoing outpatient treatment may present the best hope for achieving a less symptom-ridden mental state, adaptational success, and a crime-free lifestyle. Treatment conditions may allow the less restrictive option of probation where otherwise incarceration would be the only available disposition. On the other hand, the treatment-resistant offender may regard outpatient treatment as an added imposition that augments the burdensome features of probation.

The United States Court of Appeals, Third Circuit, considered the case of a defendant who, after his conviction of unlawful receipt of a firearm, was sentenced to probation with psychological counseling a specified condition of probation.[33] The defendant was incarcerated and charged with violating his probation when he failed to comply with the outpatient treatment. He appealed claiming that this condition of probation was unconstitutional because it violated his rights of privacy and mentation. He cited case law that supported a mental patient's right to refuse treatment.

The appellate court held that the condition of probation, which required the defendant to submit to psychological counseling, did not violate the defendant's constitutional rights to privacy. Such condition of probation was reasonably related to the purpose of probation, the condition did not lack a factual basis, and the trial judge did not err in determining that incarceration was the only alternative to the probation condition.

The appellate court cited the reasoning of the district court:

> What is required here is not solely consideration of the privacy right of an incarcerated individual to refuse treatment, but rather a balancing of defendant's constitutional rights with society's rights to be protected from further criminal acts by a convicted felon who remains free . . . . In light of defendant's repeated firearms violation and other criminal acts, it is clear that society requires protection from him. This could be accomplished by either incarcerating defendant or rehabilitating him . . . . Psychological counselling could achieve rehabilitation by the less restrictive alternative.[34]

Treatment as a condition of probation can be a powerful tool. The offender who in other situations can refuse treatment without legal consequences can now refuse treatment upon peril of imprisonment. Because the coercive mechanisms of probation have long been preestablished, outpatient treatment as a condition of probation may be more "enforceable" than court-ordered outpatient treatment under a mental health code with such a provision. The psychiatrist who recommends treatment that becomes a condition of probation may be seen as an agent of social control or he may be appreciated for suggesting the least restrictive form of treatment/punishment/management.

## SPECIAL OFFENDER STATUTES

Several special conditions with presumed mental disturbance, acknowledged by various state laws, allow for pretrial psychiatric assessment. If the defendant is adjudicated as belonging to one of these groupings, a corresponding sentence is imposed that incorporates treatment into the disposition. Special offender statutes, which will be mentioned briefly here, include the mentally defective psychopath statutes, sexually disordered offender statutes, and guilty but mentally ill offender statutes.

Although juveniles are not always mentally disordered, because of their youth there is a greater presumption in favor of rehabilitation and individualized predictions. Thus, psychiatrists can also be called on to conduct pretrial assessments of juvenile offenders that will directly affect sentencing.

## DEFECTIVE PSYCHOPATH STATUTES

Of the various states with statutes pertaining to mentally disordered offenders, defective psychopaths, or defective delinquents, Maryland with its celebrated Patuxent Institution is perhaps best known. Codified in 1951,[35] the Defective Delinquent Act of Maryland provided for the establishment of the Patuxent Institution.[36] Pursuant to this statute, offenders convicted of specified offenses could be confined in the Patuxent Institution for an indefinite period.

A study team composed of a medical physician, a psychiatrist, and a psychologist, conducts a comprehensive evaluation and then submits a report of findings and conclusions that includes a statement about whether or not the person is thought to be a defective delinquent. If the clinical findings are affirmative, the offender is brought before the sentencing court. The offender who is adjudicated to be a defective delinquent is then remanded to the Patuxent Institution, and the original sentence is suspended.[36]

Eventually, the Patuxent program encountered constitutional challenges and, consequently, some of its most distinguishing features were relinquished. However, to a degree, the original two-phase sentencing process resembled that of today's psychiatric presentencing statutes. But, in this case, with indeterminate sentencing, one can readily appreciate the tremendous input that clinicians made to sentencing courts, addressing, in effect, both treatment issues and the severity of punishment.

## SEXUAL PSYCHOPATH STATUTES

The term *sexual psychopath* has been applied as a broad quasi-diagnostic category of sexual offenses for which treatment and rehabilitation objectives were given special attention. Diagnosis, offense, treatment, and punishment were all very much interrelated, such that the psychiatric report at once pertained to treatment, rehabilitation, and sentencing.

After 1938, most states enacted "sexual psychopath statutes"[37] that provided for indeterminate sentences and treatment within a hospital or prison.[38] Eventually, the legal procedures for accomplishing indeterminate sentencing were subjected to constitutional challenges, and the vague grouping of "sexual psychopaths" became regarded as conceptually problematic for therapeutic purposes. More recently, many states either amended or repealed their sexual psychopath statutes.

Even in the absence of a specific sexual psychopath statute, defendants who are accused of sexual offenses are one of the more common categories to undergo a psychiatric presentencing evaluation on order of the sentencing judge.[4,5,39,40] In many cases, treatment recommendations and prognosis can conceivably affect the severity of sentencing, even if no dispositional issues beyond treatment are presented in the psychiatric report. Modern technology and therapeutic methods offer more hope for the successful rehabilitation of selected offenders with sexual paraphilias today than was the case when sexual psychopath statutes were the rule. Still, the psychiatrist who conducts a presentence evaluation must bear in mind that mere prognostic statements can have a bearing on the retributive and protective functions of sentencing.

## GUILTY BUT MENTALLY ILL STATUTES

In 1975, Michigan revised its Code of Criminal Procedure to allow the verdict of Guilty But Mentally Ill (GBMI), and since then several states have followed suit. Although some of the other state GBMI verdicts are quite different from that of Michigan, the Michigan law is considered the prototypical model. Not a verdict of acquittal, this option creates another offender category for which psychiatric input can contribute at the sentencing phase. The following facts must be established for a finding of GBMI in Michigan: (1) that the defendant committed the alleged offense; (2) that the defendant was mentally ill at the time of the alleged offense; and (3) that the defendant did not satisfy the criteria for not guilty by reason of an insanity verdict.[41]

In Michigan, prior to imposing a sentence, the trial court may assess available resources for psychiatric treatment, but this is not required.[42] Neither is it a must that the trial court obtain a psychiatric presentencing report from the Center for Forensic Psychiatry. But a psychiatric presentencing evaluation is necessary before sentencing a GBMI offender to probation.[42] In this instance, even if the psychiatric evaluation addresses the treatment issue, it will be used primarily for purposes of disposition.[42]

## JUVENILE OFFENDERS

More than that for adult offenders, rehabilitation is the driving objective, if not the *raison d' être*, of the juvenile justice system. Where the crimes are heinous and other criteria or guidelines are satisfied, juvenile defendants sometimes have a waiver hearing to be tried as an adult. For the youth who is then tried within the adult criminal justice system, the objectives of retribution and incapacitation become more compelling than rehabilitation. As retribution recently became a stronger objective in the adult criminal justice system, this change occurred to a lesser but still significant extent in some juvenile systems.[43] For example, in 1978, New York enacted a law to exclude specified serious offenses from initial juvenile court jurisdiction; however,[44] "reverse waiver" to the family court is provided.[45] A "habitual juvenile offender" law, enacted in Illinois in 1980, allows a juvenile to be tried in a juvenile court, to be given a right to a jury trial, and, if convicted of a third felony, permits the juvenile offender to be consigned to a juvenile facility until 21 years of age.[46]

## SUMMARY

Psychiatric presentence reports can originate in several ways depending on jurisdictional law. According to some state laws, the psychiatrist who evaluates for pretrial purposes, for example, for competency to stand trial, may also be required to submit a separate report that addresses treatment needs. This additional report may or may not be used in sentencing. At his or her discretion, the sentencing judge may request a psychiatric presentencing evaluation and report and may formulate specific questions that are to be addressed. Though such evaluations are not ordered with great frequency by most judges, this is probably the most widespread manner of originating psychiatric presentence reports. Some states have statutory provisions for felons to be sent to a special diagnostic facility before their sentence is finalized.

The diagnostic and therapeutic aims of the psychiatric report are consistent with the psychiatrist's therapeutic role. However, within the context of criminal sentencing, the primary legal concern is appropriate punishment. Then should the psychiatrist address dispositional issues such as severity of sentencing? Or should the psychiatrist address such issues but only when his position favors leniency? The dilemmas of psychiatric input into capital sentencing are to a large extent, though less emotively, generalizable to psychiatric contributions to many types of criminal sentencing. We have attempted to present various ramifications of this issue without providing simple answers. Even if the psychiatrist follows the recommendation of the APA Task Force and does not address disposition, he or she must bear in mind that any effort to protect the public will have security implications, and even clinical conclusions alone can ultimately affect severity of punishment.

The two ideals emphasized here are clinical and legal integrity. If one is to contribute to sentencing, one should be accurate, consistent, and forthright concerning diagnostic and therapeutic conclusions and the limitations of one's conclusions. The ethical psychiatrist will avoid the subterfuge of evaluating a defendant for the stated reason of addressing a pretrial legal issue while also addressing the unstated issue of severity of sentence. The psychiatrist with legal integrity will always be frank with the defendant about the purpose of the examination and the fact that results can serve or hinder the defendant's legal interests. If the psychiatrist could recommend leniency but never severity, perhaps this attempt to cut in only one direction should be mentioned in the report. Even so, any cutting leaves two fractions, not one.

# REFERENCES


1. Dershowitz A: The role of psychiatry in the sentencing process. *Int J Law Psychiatry* 1978; 1:63–78.
2. American Psychiatric Association: Report of the task force on the role of psychiatry in the sentencing process, in *Issues in Forensic Psychiatry*. American Psychiatric Association Press, Inc, pp 185–215, 1984.
3. *First Tentative Draft: Criminal Justice Mental Health Standards*. Washington, DC, American Bar Association, pp 7–353, July, 1983.
4. Campbell, IG: The influence of psychiatric pre-sentence reports. *Int J Law Psychiatry* 1981; 89–106.
5. Bohmer, CER: Mad or bad: The psychiatrist and the sentencing process. *J Psychiatry Law*. 1976; 4, (1):23–48.
6. Scott PD: Psychiatric reports for magistrates courts. *Br J Delinquency* 1953; 4:82,95.
7. Macdonald J: *Psychiatry and the Criminal*, ed 3. Springfield, Ill, Charles C Thomas Publisher, 1976, p 446.
8. Halleck SL: *Psychiatry and the Dilemmas of Crime*. Berkeley, University of California Press, 1971.
9. Bartholomew AA: Some problems of the psychiatrist in relation to sentencing. *Crim Law* 1973; 15: 325,332.
10. Baily B: Dr. Grigson unfazed by *Smith* reversals. *Texas Lawyer*, March 13 1987, p 3.
11. *Clark v Grigson*, 579 S.W. 2d 263,264 (1979).
12. *Furman v Georgia*, 408 U.S. 238 (1972).
13. *Jurek v Texas*, 428 U.S. 262 (1976).
14. *Lockett v Ohio*, 438 U.S. 586 (1978).
15. Ohio Rev. Code Ann. §2929.04(b) (1975).
16. *Lockett*, 438 U.S. at 587.
17. *Estelle v Smith*, 451 U.S. 454 (1980).
18. *Estelle*, 451 U.S. at 473.
19. *Barefoot v Estelle*, 463 U.S. 880 (1983).
20. Brief Amicus Curiae for the American Psychiatric Association to the Supreme Court of the United States, October term, 1987, *Barefoot v Estelle*.

21. *Barefoot,* 77 Ed. 2d at 882.
22. *Ake v Oklahoma,* 470 U.S. 68 (1985).
23. *Ake,* 470 U.S. at 68.
24. Pre- sentence diagnosis for california superior courts. *Correctional Rev,* September–October 1965; pp 16–18.
25. Davis VA Jr, Hedden JM, Miller SR, Witten KE: Comment: The Kansas State reception and diagnostic center: An empirical study. *Kansas Law Rev* 1971; 19:821–845.
26. Mass. Gen. Laws ch. 123, §15e (1970).
27. Smith CE: A review of the presentencing diagnostic study procedure in North Carolina. *NC Cent Law* 1976; 8:17–34.
28. Kan. Sentencing Code §21–4603(3) at 355 (1969).
29. Jones NO: The presentence diagnostic program in North Carolina: Process and problems. *NC Cent Law* 1978; 9(2):133–157.
30. N.C. Gen. Stat., Crim. Proc. Act, ch. 15A, art. 81, §15A–1332 (1977).
31. Personal Communication, Leo (Lee) Taylor, Director, State Reception and Diagnostic Center, June 9 1987.
32. Unpublished Survey of the Judicial and Institutional Use of the State Reception and Diagnostic Center Evaluation, Kansas State Reception and Diagnostic Center, December 31, 1983.
33. *United States v Stine,* 675 F.2d 69 (1982).
34. *United States v Stine,* 521 F. Supp. 808 (E.D. Pa. 1981).
35. Brooks A: *Law, Psychiatry and the Mental Health System.* Boston, Little Brown & Co, 1974, pp 489–522.
36. Md. Ann. Code, art. 31B, 1951.
37. Sadoff RL: Sexually deviated offenders. *Temple Law Q* 1967; 40:305–315.
38. Sadoff RL: The psychiatrist and the rapist: Legal issues, in Rada RT (ed): *Clinical Aspects of the Rapist.* San Francisco, Grune & Stratton, 1978, pp 215–225, 223–224.
39. *See* Smith, *supra* note 27 at 23.
40. Gibbens, Soothill, and Pope: *Medical Remands in the Criminal Court,* Maudsley Monograph, No. 25, p 18, 1977.
41. Public Act 180 of 1975, MCLA 768.36(1).
42. *People v Linzey,* 315 N.W.2d 550 (1982).
43. Hamparian, DM: Control and treatment of juveniles committing violent offenses, in Roth LH (ed): *Clinical Treatment of the Violent Person.* New York, Guilford Press, 1987, pp 156–177, 161,162.
44. N.Y. Fam. C. Act, §§712 753a (1976).
45. N.Y. Penal Law, §30.00(2) (McKinney Supp., 1979).
46. Ill. Ann. Stat. ch. 37, §705–712 (1980).

# 14

# Psychiatric Consultation to a Parole Board


BRUCE HARRY AND NIELS C. BECK


Parole, the early release from a felony prison incarceration to community supervision, is a common part of the criminal justice system's response to crime. By 1981, it was estimated that 243,880 adults, representing 11% of all those under some form of correctional supervision, were on parole in the United States.[1] That same report also noted that "approximately 75% [of all eligible prisoners] are released to parole supervision."

Given the quantitative importance of parole, it is important to understand how such release decisions are made. It seems that parole boards would likely base their decisions in large part on their review of an inmate's antecedent activities with an eye toward predicting how he or she would probably perform on subsequent parole supervision.[2] Thus, parole board members would attempt to decide if the inmate is an acceptable risk for release from prison to the community.

Numerous studies document that parole board members utilize a range of data to assist them in making release decisions. Even though it is outside the scope and space limitations of this chapter to review those investigations in detail, some of these decision variables include: (1) the nature and/or severity of present offense[2-12]; (2) previous juvenile and/or adult criminal record[3-12]; (3) conduct in prison[2-4,6-10]; (4) the offender's attitude/credibility/appearance[2,4,7,9,10]; (5) length of present incarceration[3,5-8,11]; (6) age[2,9-11]; (7) performance on previous com-


BRUCE HARRY AND NIELS C. BECK • Department of Psychiatry, School of Medicine, University of Missouri—Columbia, Columbia, MO 65212.

munity supervision[2,6−8,11,12]; (8) risk of future crime[2,7,10]; (9) risk of future violence[2,7−9]; (10) alcohol and/or drug abuse[6,7−9,12]; (11) release plan (especially regarding residence, job, and family ties)[2,6−10]; (12) supporting recommendations from staff[2,5,9,10]; (13) attitudes and/or morale of others regarding the release[5,6,9]; (14) political and/or publicity implications[8,10]; (15) education[2,7,10,11]; (16) work history[2,4−7,11]; and (17) intellectual and/or mental pathology.[2,6−8,10,11,13]

Additionally, a series of validation studies involving released adult male felony offenders have suggested that at least some of the above factors may predict parole violation or revocation. These outcome variables include: (1) lengthy and/or precocious criminality[2,3,10,14−25]; (2) nature and/or severity of present offense[2,3,10,14−23]; (3) age[2,9−11,18−20,23,25]; (4) previous violations under community supervision[2,11,18,20−23]; (5) alcohol and/or drug abuse[2,10,11,15,17,19,21,27]; (6) institutional conduct[2,3,9,14−16,17,20,23−25]; (7) length of incarceration[3,9,15,16,20,26]; and (8) intellectual and/or mental pathology.[2,3,11,13,15−17,19,20,24,25,27]

It is important to recognize that the different methodologies and the study populations that are listed in the above investigations make it difficult to compare or generalize from them. And, with such a diverse literature, it is not possible to determine further the relative significances of each attribute because many of these offender characteristics are likely to be interdependent.

To illustrate this latter point, the contemporary and widely used Salient Factor Score employed univariate statistical methods to derive nine dichotomized or trichotomized predictive items from 66 variables.[21] These salient factors include: (1) number of prior convictions; (2) number of prior incarcerations; (3) age at first juvenile or criminal commitment; (4) whether the present offense involved automobile theft; (5) prior revocation of probation or parole supervision; (6) history of heroin, cocaine, or barbiturate dependence; (7) educational level; (8) verified employment; and (9) release plan. Each item is simply scored, with the final Salient Factor Index being the algebraic sum of the individual scores. This final score then places the respective offender in one of four categories of parole prognosis ranging from "very good" to "poor." A subsequent analysis of the same data using multivariate techniques reduced the list of items to four: (1) number of prior convictions; (2) whether the present offense involved auto theft; (3) release plan; and (4) previous parole violation.[22] Thus, it appears that several of the better predictor items are interrelated, a point confirmed by two later studies.[11,23]

It seems likely from the above analysis that some mental disorders may, in addition to more criminological characteristics, enter into release decisions and may be associated with subsequent problems on parole.

Unfortunately, there is disagreement on the degree to which psychiatric information is utilized in release decision-making by parole board members. For example, a recent study by Carroll *et al.*,[2] used multivariate analyses to conclude that mental pathology seemed to play a relatively minor role in the release decision, whereas several other observers have concluded that psychiatric opinions and recommendations concerning prison inmates are given considerable weight in parole-release decisions.[28–32] These latter authors have suggested that such input has been used by parole boards to determine whether a candidate has been sufficiently rehabilitated,[28,29] remains dangerous,[30] is likely to recidivate,[31] or appears to have crossed a moral threshold of sorts by having served enough time.[32]

Of interest to us is the relative extent to which a parole board could or would use diagnostic information about mental disorders in its decisions if that information were provided. For example, Wilcox[4] thought that the mental examination should be used to "weed out the feeble-minded, the insane, the sex-pervert, the epileptic, [and] the psychopath." Likewise, the Gluecks[25] felt that 90% of those offenders who continued to have problems after release from prison were those who clearly had "some mental or marked personality abnormality—psychosis, psychopathy, sex perversion, drug addiction, great emotional instability, and the like." Guze[27] concluded that "sociopathy, alcoholism, and drug dependence are the psychiatric disorders characteristically associated with serious crime." Unfortunately, none of those studies looked at whether that information was made available to the release decision-makers or how such information may have been utilized prior to their subjects' respective releases. To our knowledge, only Hare[13] has reported on the outcome of a specific diagnosis—psychopathy—as processed by a parole board. Unfortunately, it is unclear whether that diagnosis was made available to the parole board prior to each subject's release.

Thus, we decided to study the effect of providing a parole board with individual diagnostic information in addition to some traditional criminological data on the members of a group of incarcerated male offenders who were being considered for early release from prison. We were particularly interested in examining the predictive capacity of psychiatric diagnosis versus more traditional variables pertaining to criminological information, and the hypotheses that diagnoses of alcoholism, drug abuse, and antisocial personality disorder would be associated with parole revocation. We also wanted to test the hypothesis that psychosis would be associated with parole revocation, speculating that reality distortion would likely make it particularly difficult for a released offender to understand or adhere to specific release conditions, or both.

## METHODS

All the subjects for this study consisted of adult male offenders who were referred to Bruce Harry by the Missouri State Board of Probation and Parole for preparole psychiatric evaluations during the interval October 1982 through September 1984. Using these dates, we received 207 incarcerated adult male felony offenders into our study population. To our knowledge, Bruce Harry is the only psychiatrist in Missouri who conducts such evaluations on behalf of the board. We assumed, for the purposes of this study, that the men referred for evaluation were likely to be considered as offenders who were at possibly higher risk for problems during postrelease community supervision because of a possible mental disorder. We made this assumption because the board was seeking specific additional information outside that already available to it through traditional correctional channels.

Each evaluation consisted of a thorough review of probation and parole records and a semistructured personal interview. Criminological data were extracted from the official records because it was believed the board used these records as information sources for its decisions. Diagnoses were made according to the *Diagnostic and Statistical Manual of Mental Disorders,* 3rd edition (DSM-III), and Harry reported his results to the board. The board did not seek recommendations from Harry regarding the parolability of any offender, asking rather only for recommendations concerning the appropriate treatment for each man while he remained in prison and on possible community supervision.

## STATISTICAL ANALYSES

Our method of analysis entailed the use of stepwise discriminant function analysis,[33] a multivariate technique that generates an equation which classifies subjects into groups based on combinations of scores on selected predictor variables. Using this method, it is possible to cross-reference predicted group membership with real group membership and arrive at a table that summarizes the predictive accuracy of the generated equation.[34] We used the method described by Pedhazur[35] to code categorical data as dummy variables.

Two discriminant function analyses were performed and, within this context, two criterion variables were developed for use in this study. The first consisted of the decision to grant parole (1 = parole granted; 0 = parole denied). In all, 141 subjects (72.4%) were granted parole and 58 were denied parole. Missing variables excluded eight men from further statistical analysis. The second variable pertained to the 141 men granted release. Of these, we obtained three-year follow-up data on the 117 who were actually released within the time constraints of this investigation. Of this number, 77 (65.8%) did not violate parole whereas 40 did (1 = parole violated; 0 = parole not violated).

## PREDICTOR VARIABLES

### Decision to Release

Based on our review of the literature above, as well as our own clinical experience in working with parole populations, a variety of a priori hypotheses were developed regarding variables that would significantly predict the parole board's decisions to grant parole. The variables included were: (1) whether the present offense was a violent, potentially violent, or nonviolent crime; (2a) the number of previous juvenile detentions; (2b) the number of prior adult criminal arrests; (3) the number of conduct violations per year in prison; (4) the offender's attitude, as determined by whether he pleaded guilty or not guilty to the offense; (5) how many years each man had been in prison; (6) the age of each man on admission to prison; (7) the number of previous probation or parole revocations; (8) each man's total Salient Factor Score (the Missouri Department of Corrections' method for estimating risk of an offender's future criminal conduct; (9) education; (10) employment history; (11) diagnoses of alcohol/drug abuse; and (12) such diagnoses as antisocial personality disorder, psychotic mental disorders, and psychosexual mental disorders. The last two diagnoses were added to our a priori hypotheses because we believed that psychotic inmates would be more likely to behave bizarrely during their incarcerations or during a release hearing, and those having a psychosexual disorder would be more likely denied parole because the Department of Corrections has a special treatment program for sex offenders.

For the purposes of this study, we defined violent crimes as homicide, assault, child abuse, rape, sexual assault, and sodomy; potentially violent crimes were robbery, carrying as concealed or displaying a dangerous weapon, arson, and kidnapping/restraint; nonviolent crimes were drug or alcohol offenses, burglary, theft, bad checks, fraud, forgery, or other property offenses.

We defined psychosis as the presence of any DSM-III diagnosis of schizophrenia, paranoid disorder, schizophreniform disorder, brief reactive psychosis, schizoaffective disorder, or atypical psychosis. We chose these disorders to reflect the DSM-III classification scheme of "schizophrenic disorders," "paranoid disorders," and "psychotic disorders not elsewhere classified."

## Parole Outcome

A priori hypotheses were also developed regarding variables thought to be predictive of parole outcome. These included: (1a) the number of previous juvenile detentions; (1b) the number of prior adult criminal arrests; (2) whether the present crime was violent, potentially violent, or nonviolent; (3) the age of each man on admission to prison; (4) the number of prior revocations of community supervision; (5) a diagnosis of alcoholism/drug abuse; (6) the rate of conduct violations per number of years of incarceration; (7) the number of years each man has been in prison; and (8) the diagnoses of antisocial personality disorder, psychosexual disorder, or psychosis. The reasons for selecting diagnoses numbers (5) and (8) were to validate their use as potential predictors of decision-making and to test the hypotheses that psychosexually disordered or psychotic former inmates were at greater risk of parole revocation. Crime seriousness and psychosis were defined as above.

## RESULTS

### Decision to Release

In this analysis, six predictor variables contributed significantly ($P < .05$) to variance in the criterion (Table I). Together, these variables accounted for approximately 26% of the variance. In order of importance, these predictor variables were: (1) the seriousness of the present offense; (2) how the offender pleaded at the trial; (3) whether the subject had a clinical diagnosis of substance abuse; (4) the number of prior incarcerations; (5) the number of previous revocations of community supervision; and (6) the occupational level.

**Table I.  Discriminant Function Analysis: Decision to Grant Parole**

| Step | Variable | Cumulative variance accounted for | Univariate correlation |
|------|----------|-----------------------------------|------------------------|
| 1 | Crime severity | 0.10 | −0.28 |
| 2 | Trial plea | 0.15 | 0.30 |
| 3 | Substance abuse | 0.19 | −0.16 |
| 4 | Prior incarcerations | 0.21 | 0.14 |
| 5 | Prior revocations | 0.24 | −0.02 |
| 6 | Occupation | 0.25 | 0.07 |

**Table II.  Classification Rate
for Decision to Grant Parole**[a]

|                    | Predicted group |        |
| ------------------ | --------------- | ------ |
| Actual group       | No parole       | Parole |
| No parole (54)     | 22              | 32     |
| Parole (136)       | 16              | 120    |
| Overall correct classification rate = 74.7% | | |

[a]Discriminating variable(s) were missing from 17 cases, thus excluding them from classification.

Based on the use of these variables in the predictive equation, 74.7% of the subjects were classified correctly: 120 men were identified correctly as being granted parole and 22 were classified correctly as being denied parole. Thirty-two who were predicted to be granted release were actually denied, while 16 who were predicted as being denied were actually granted release (Table II).

## Parole Outcome

Three predictor variables contributed significantly to the criterion of parole outcome, together accounting for almost 15% of the variance (Table III). In order of importance, these attributes were: (1) a diagnosis of psychosis; (2) the previous revocations of community supervision; and (3) the rate of conduct violations during the present incarceration. Using these variables in the predictive equation, we were able to classify 69.2% of the cases correctly. This broke down to only 14 men being classified correctly as having their paroles revoked, whereas 67 subjects were found to be identified correctly as having no revocation of their paroles within the study interval. Additionally, 10 subjects were predicted falsely to have no revocation of their paroles, and 26 were classified incorrectly

**Table III.  Discriminant Function Analysis: Parole Outcome**

| Step | Variable              | Cumulative variance accounted for | Univariate correlation |
| ---- | --------------------- | --------------------------------- | ---------------------- |
| 1    | Psychosis             | 0.06                              | 0.26                   |
| 2    | Prior revocations     | 0.11                              | 0.20                   |
| 3    | Conduct violation rate | 0.14                             | 0.16                   |

**Table IV.  Classification Rate
for Parole Outcome**[a]

| | Predicted group | |
| Actual group | No revocation | Revocation |
| --- | --- | --- |
| No revocation (77) | 67 | 10 |
| Revocation (40) | 26 | 14 |
| Overall correct classification rate = 69.2% | | |

[a]Discriminating variable(s) were missing from 6 cases, thus excluding
them from classification.

as parole failures (Table IV). Thus, parole failure was overpredicted by
almost a factor of two, whereas parole success was underpredicted by a
factor of less than one sixth.

## DISCUSSION

Before attempting to place our findings in the context of the literature, it is important to acknowledge that our population was very different from those previously investigated. All prior studies have looked
at samples of prisoners that have not been selected for possible mental
illness. To the contrary, our subjects were referred for psychiatric evaluations prior to their parole-release decision because it was suspected
they might have a mental disorder that put them at a greater risk for
having problems during community supervision.

We examined this highly selected population in an effort to determine the extent to which parole-release decision makers used psychiatric
diagnosis relative to more traditional factors. We also wanted to see if
certain types of psychiatric problems might be associated with greater
risk of parole revocation, again relative to more traditional offender
attributes. We are inclined to believe that our study takes an important,
albeit modest, step toward answering those questions.

We observed that 72.4% of our population was granted parole,
comparing favorably with the nationwide rate of 75% as estimated in
one recent study.[1] In a related report, Reiber[36] found that the rate of
granting parole within Missouri during 1981 was 62%. We have no
reason to think that this rate changed significantly during our study
interval. Thus, our sample of presumably mentally disturbed inmates, in

which only five received a diagnosis of "no mental disorder," were paroled at a rate slightly higher than that of the general inmate population for the state. This suggests that, in general, a reported diagnosis of mental disorder was not a controlling factor in the decision to grant early release from prison. However, it was still possible that certain mental disorders would be considered by the parole board in their release decisions. Thus, we looked at several diagnostic categories that we had reason to believe would influence parole decisions.

In attempting to discern how the hypothesized diagnoses might impact on the decision to release, we first observed that relatively few variables seemed to account for significant proportions of the variance in release decisions and parole outcome. We found that only diagnoses of substance abuse were used by decision makers, whereas all the other decision-related variables were related to attributes of more traditional criminological concern (see Table I). Thus, the board did not appear to use much new information in its decisions, and diagnosis seemed to play a relatively minor role in the decision to release from prison.

Since the board referred these men specifically for psychiatric input, perhaps diagnosis was not what they wanted. It seems likely that the board members in Missouri at the time of this investigation were at least familiar with mental disorders because many had undergraduate or masters degrees in psychology, sociology, and counseling psychology. We suspect that inmates with a diagnosis of substance abuse were more likely denied parole because the board members were already familiar with those disorders being associated with criminality.

We expected antisocial personality disorder to be more common among those who were denied parole compared with those who were granted parole. However, our findings that this diagnosis *per se* did not discriminate between these groups is consistent with Hare's[13] observations that psychopaths are at least as likely to receive parole as are nonpsychopaths. Hare goes on to explain that psychopaths

> may be very skilled in manipulating the justice system, in soliciting community support, and in using facilities and programs that give the appearance of a sincere concern for rehabilitation.

We also think it is important to note that several of the features that did discriminate (e.g., the number of prior incarcerations, the number of previous revocations of community supervision, substance abuse, and occupational status) are recognized as features of antisocial personality disorder in the DSM-III. Thus, certain core attributes may be more predictive of parole denial than the formal diagnosis of psychopathy itself.

The rate of parole revocation was 34.2% for our study population. This compares favorably with the 35% reported for Missouri in 1981,[36] suggesting that presumed mental disorders *per se* did not put our population at greater risk during supervision than the general parole population.

Consequently, we found it somewhat surprising that psychosis was the most powerful predictor of parole revocation. Although this may be the product of our unique population or the board's having already denied release to the most risky offenders, it also suggests it is reasonable for the parole board to be concerned about serious mental illness as a possible risk factor in community supervision. It seems plausible that disorganized or bizarre thoughts, confusion, hallucinations, or delusions would limit a parolee's ability to understand or adhere to specific parole conditions. Likewise, bizarre behavior by psychotic parolees might be more readily interpreted as justification for revocation. We recommend that future investigations attempt to determine whether specific psychotic symptoms or behaviors are more predictive of outcome than simple diagnosis alone.

It is tempting to use our findings to speculate about the impact that treatment might have if it were systematically provided to the mentally-ill ex-offender. But, it must be emphasized that we know nothing about the treatment environment for our parolees, so it is impossible to draw conclusions about its relevance to outcome. We also were not in a position to obtain data about the reasons for parole revocation, although generally this occurs for only the most serious of reasons, such as commission of another crime. This would be an important dimension to a further understanding as to how and why ex-offenders fail during supervision. We believe it demands future investigation.

In closing this chapter, we would like to caution our readers against using the variables identified in this study to make hard-and-fast parole decisions. As mentioned above, our sample was highly preselected and represented only one state. We further point out that our rates of classification were not significantly higher than the base rates for our sample.[34] Although our base rate for allowing parole was 72.4%, our correct classification rate was only 74.7%. Likewise, 65.8% of our released subjects had no problems on parole after approximately three years, yet we could only classify 69.2% of the released subjects correctly. This alone tells us that our predictor variables are not suitable for prediction in an actuarial sense. Rather, we urge that this investigation serve as a stimulus for future research into parole selection and performance on community supervision.

*Acknowledgment*

The authors sincerely thank the Missouri State Board of Probation and Parole of the Missouri Department of Corrections. This study could not have been completed without the generous cooperation and assistance of its staff and members.

# REFERENCES


1. Broder T, Maxwell J, Reiber L, and Valvano V: *Bureau of Justice Statistics Bulletin: Probation and Parole 1982*. NCJ-89874, Bureau of Justice Statistics, U.S. Department of Justice, Washington, DC, September 1983, pp 1–5.
2. Carroll JS, Wiener RL, Coates D, Galegher J, Alibrio JJ: Evaluation, diagnosis, and prediction in parole decision making. *Law Soc Rev* 1982; 17:199–228.
3. Warner SB: Factors determining parole from the Massachusetts Reformatory. *J Crim Law Criminol* 1923; 14:172–207.
4. Wilcox C: *The Parole of Adults from State Penal Institutions in Pennsylvania and in Other Commonwealths*, Ph.D. dissertation. University of Pennsylvania, Philadelphia, 1927. Reprinted by The Report of the Pennsylvania State Parole Commission to the Legislature, Philadelphia, 1927.
5. Pihlblad CT, Kubach T: Factors influencing the decisions of a parole board. *Fed Probation* 1941; 5:31–35.
6. Hawkins KO: *Parole Selection: The American Experience*, Ph.D. dissertation. Cambridge, 1971.
7. Hoffman PB, DeGostin LK: Parole decision-making: Structuring discretion. *Fed Probation* 1974; 38:7–15.
8. Clark R, Rudenstine D: *Prison without Walls: Report on New York Parole*. New York, Praeger Publishers, 1975, pp 52–63.
9. Stanley DT: *Prisoners among Us: The Problems of Parole*. Washington, DC, Brookings Institution, 1976, pp 47–80.
10. O'Leary V, Glaser D: The assessment of risk in parole decision making, in West DJ (ed): *The Future of Parole: Commentaries on Systems in Britain and U.S.A.* London, Duckworth, 1972, pp 135–198.
11. Thies HE, Winfree LT, Griffiths CT: Correlates of the parole-reparole process: An examination of "revolving door" corrections. *Corrective Soc Psychiatry J Behav Technol Methods Ther* 1982; 28:121–130.
12. Gottfredson DM, Ballard KB: Differences in parole decisions associated with decision-makers. *J Res Crime Delinquency* 3:112–119, 1966.
13. Hare RD: Criminal psychopaths, in Yuille JC (ed): *Police Selection and Training: The Role of Psychology*. The Netherlands, Dordrecht, Martinus Nijhoff, in press.
14. Hart H: Predicting parole success. *J Crim Law Criminol* 1923; 14:405–413.
15. Burgess EW: Factors determining success or failure on parole, in Bruce AA, Burgess EW, Harno AJ (eds): *The Workings of the Indeterminate-Sentence Law and the Parole System in Illinois*. Chicago, Committee on the Study of the Workings of the Indeterminate-Sentence Law and of Parole in the State of Illinois, 1928, pp 205–249.
16. Tibbitts C: Success or failure on parole can be predicted: A study of the records of 3,000 youths paroled from the Illinois State Reformatory. *J Crim Law Criminol* 1931; 22:11–50.
17. Ohlin LE: *Selection for Parole*. New York, Russell Sage Foundation, 1951.

18. Metzner R, Weil G: Predicting recidivism: Base-rates for Massachusetts Correctional Institution Concord. *J Crim Law Criminol Police Sci* 1963; 54:307–316.
19. Carney FJ: Predicting recidivism in a medium security correctional institution. *J Crim Law Criminol Police Sci* 1967; 58:338–348.
20. Kassebaum G, Ward D, Wilner D: *Prison Treatment and Parole Survival: An Empirical Assessment.* New York, John Wiley, 1971.
21. Hoffman PB, Beck JL: Parole decision making: A salient factor score. *J Crim Justice* 1974; 2:195–206.
22. Solomon H: Parole outcome: A multidimensional contingency table analysis. *J Res Crime Delinq* 1976; 13:107–126.
23. Brown RC, D'Agistino CA, Craddick RA: Prediction of parole outcome based on discriminant function. *Corrective Soc Psychiatry J Behav Technol Methods Ther* 1978; 24:93–101.
24. Glueck S, Glueck ET: *Five Hundred Criminal Careers.* New York, Knopf, 1930.
25. Glueck S, Glueck ET: *Later Criminal Careers.* New York, The Commonwealth Fund, 1937.
26. Jaman DR, Dickover RM, Bennett LA: Parole outcome as a function of time served. *Br J Criminol* 1972; 12:5–34.
27. Guze SB: *Criminality and Psychiatric Disorders.* New York, Oxford University Press, 1976.
28. Thomas PA: An analysis of parole selection. *Crime Delinquency* 1963; 9:173–179.
29. Kastenmeier RX, Eglit HG: Parole release decision-making: Rehabilitation, expertise, and the demise of mythology. *Am University Law Rev* 1973; 22:477–525.
30. Maguire M, Pinter F, Collis C: Dangerousness and the tariff: The decision-making process in release from life sentences. *Br J Criminol* 1984; 24:250–268.
31. Dawson RO: The decision to grant or deny parole: A study of parole criteria in law and practice. *Washington University Law Q* 1966; 243–303.
32. Hawkins K: Assessing evil: Decision behavior and parole board justice. *Br J Criminol* 1983; 23:101–127.
33. Cooley WW, Lohnes PR: *Multivariate Procedures for the Behavioral Sciences.* New York, John Wiley & Sons, 1962.
34. Huberty CJ: Issues in the use and interpretation of discriminant analyses. *Psychol Bull* 1984; 95:156–171.
35. Pedhazur EJ: *Multiple Regression in Behavioral Research: Explanation and Prediction* ed 2. New York, Holt Rinehart & Winston, Inc, 1982.
36. Reiber L: *Parole in the United States 1980 and 1981.* Washington, DC, Government Printing Office, 1986, pp 4–9.

# V

*Problems in Evaluation*

**15**

# Malingering and the Evaluation of Competency to Stand Trial

NAOMI GOLDSTEIN

## PROLOGUE

The defendant was quite remarkable. He looked perplexed and preoccupied. He informed me that he had been born on Mars and was two million years old. He said he was not under arrest and had never been in jail. "What's jail," he asked, insisting that the long rap sheet was someone else's. He had altogether seven fingers and nine toes. And his horse had five legs.

Exasperated, I finally asked, "Why are you giving me such silly answers?" "Why," he replied with equal exasperation, "are you asking me such silly questions?"

Indeed, why was I? I was uneasy, dissatisfied. In preparation for this man's competency evaluation at the hospital, I had read the charges—a series of robberies—and a referral note, from the court clinic psychiatrists, mentioning his hostile attitude, silly answers, and "failure to make eye contact." I had reviewed the current hospital record, which had accumulated while he was under observation on the Forensic Psychiatry Service at Bellevue. At the start of the first interview, I had introduced myself to him, explained my purpose, and had asked him kindly—I hoped—how things were going. He had responded with a series of nonsense answers and obvious evasions.

---

**NAOMI GOLDSTEIN** • Department of Psychiatry, New York University School of Medicine, New York, NY 10016.

Frustrated, I was fairly certain that the man was malingering. With each additional question, anticipating the quality of his answers, I intentionally pushed him further against the wall, reinforcing my opinion. His only alternative would have been to remain silent or walk out of the room. If I was going to call him a malingerer in my report or use some euphemism, such as voluntary noncooperation, I could anticipate a court hearing to contest the conclusions. I could already hear the lawyer challenging me: "Dr. Goldstein, did you ask him what a lawyer does and what he is charged with? Did he tell you the date? Does he know where he is? Dr. Goldstein, why didn't you ask him those questions? Dr. Goldstein, isn't it true you had made up your mind before you examined him?"

This was the third defendant I had seen that day, and each one had been uncooperative, inappropriate, and each appeared to be malingering. Behaviors were different, charges varied from petit larceny to murder, but each one was maneuvering. Each would require reinterview, checking with additional sources, perhaps psychological testing, and a careful reassessment of any psychiatric findings against the criteria for competency to stand trial.

I had already learned that this defendant presented no special management problems on the hospital ward. He knew his name and was careful about commissary, checking his order in my presence. He had been through the system many times and had been on parole. From my interview with him, I had determined that he was alert and attentive. He had a little sense of humor, was coherent, had some concept of the planets as well as of numbers, and, most important, he understood all my questions, even if he gave silly answers. In informing me that the rap sheet was someone else's, he demonstrated an ability to defend himself against an unpleasant reality. He had studied his prior arrests carefully with me, quite interested. Clearly he could read. I had found no evidence thus far of mental disease or defect—that is, psychosis, mental retardation, or brain damage—that would compromise his competency to stand trial. I also understood that he was very human and had no reason to trust me.

Furthermore, in this context, some of the traditional mental status questions were quite ridiculous and humiliating, for me as well as the defendant, irrelevant to this man's predicament. Maybe he was overly sensitive to deficiencies in his education or intellect. Perhaps, being proud of his intellectual capacities, he found the questions too simple. One psychotic man once said to me sharply, "I've got my faculties," when I queried him about the capital of the United States, the mayor of New York, and the number of nickels in $1.35, all of which he answered easily. I sometimes wonder whether we think these defendants are sheep, ready to follow us over the fence, or, worse, circus animals being put through our hoops.

When I overcame my anger long enough to tackle this defendant's resistance and talked about the silly answers, I told him that I did not want to tell the judge he was faking and that he should think about it. Then, surprisingly, he talked, looking me straight in the eye. "Of course" he knew the charges. The long rap sheet was a testament to his inability to stay out of trouble and to his lack of personal resources. His noncooperation reflected his despair. He wasn't really trying to go to a mental hospital; he just didn't want to go to court, he didn't want to deal with the reality of what one more arrest said about him, and he was in no hurry to plead guilty, to "turn the key" on himself. He was also in no hurry to go back on the streets. He lacked an interested family, education or skills, and had little reason to expect that yet one more incarceration would mean very much in terms of rehabilitation. He talked for quite a while and then said "Gee, how did you get me to say all that? I wasn't going to talk."

Embarrassed by his vulnerability, the defendant was less cooperative and more guarded on reinterview. But I did not use the word "malingering" in my report, which found him competent. He no longer deserved the pejorative connotations of this term since he understood his legal situation and his cooperation was reasonably assured.

## INTRODUCTION

This chapter will address clinical, practical, and philosophical issues in the determination of malingering during the evaluation of competency to stand trial. Although many people believe the competency examination is relatively clearcut, it is fraught with difficulty, not the least of which is the determination that a defendant is malingering. The term *malingering* is defined as the simulation or exaggeration of mental or physical symptoms with the intent to deceive, that is, with the conscious intent to deceive. It is a thorny and fascinating phenomenon known to antiquity as well as to modern times.[1-5] There are theories and stories aplenty; information, however, is scarce.

I have examined thousands of defendants over almost thirty years, for the defense, the prosecution, and most often pursuant to court order, in federal and state systems, and in inpatient and outpatient forensic settings as well as in jails. Simulation and exaggeration of mental and physical symptoms and refusal to cooperate with counsel prior to conviction is relatively frequent, leading to many calls for psychiatric evaluation. These are mostly for competency to stand trial, although some are more specifically for competency to have given a confession, be arraigned, take a plea, or be sentenced. Of course, there are evaluations for mental state at the time of the crime, and for competency to be executed. The malingering is essentially the same for all examinations, only the criteria, ethical and moral issues may differ.

This chapter does not specifically address simulation with respect to the insanity defense or the subsets of competency. However, the psychiatric evaluations may overlap, in actual practice and in the perception of the defendant, who may not distinguish between mental defenses for different purposes. This confusion also applies to those defendants who dissimulate, "faking good" as it is called.[4,6,7] Although fewer in number, dissimulators also cause havoc in the system. It has been suggested that many dissimulators are undetected and that much more attention be given to them.

The term *malingering* in this chapter is used broadly and is meant to include simulation and dissimulation as well as all forms of volitional noncooperation or intentional resistance during criminal proceedings or during the psychiatric evaluation, whether or not there is a specific attempt to feign illness or defect. Judges and lawyers often recognize political positions, purely obstreperous or resistant behaviors for just what they are, but may be compelled, nevertheless, to ascertain whether there is a mental disorder. Fine distinctions of terminology may have little meaning in court. Alternative terms are often used. These include lying, prevaricating (classier than lying), obfuscating, faking bad, exaggerating, feigning, deceiving, goldbricking, shamming, and faking good. Some of these are synonymous; others have different connotations. "Well, Your Honor," I might say during a competency hearing, "He's not really trying to feign an illness," reluctant to pronounce the dirty word, "he's just deliberately not cooperating." "Oh," says the judge, "you mean he's malingering."

Psychiatrists and administrators working with defendants in criminal cases believe the percentage of malingerers to be significant at every level of the system, and in all settings. Higher percentages in certain communities may reflect a contagion factor, greater defendant sophistication, and more experienced psychiatrists. The criminal court clinics in New York City estimate that about 10% of the thousands who are examined for competency may be malingering. Dr. Henry Weinstein, Director of the Forensic Psychiatry Service at Bellevue Hospital in New York, a city hospital, has estimated, for many years, that at least 25% of the admissions to Bellevue from these court clinics and other sources for inpatient competency evaluation are thought to be malingering.* A remarkable number of these defendants are accompanied by referral recommendations for "further observation to rule out malingering" or "volitional components." Data are missing on the number thought to be malingering after hospital evaluation. The final report to the court may be misleading, as the actual term is often avoided or the problem is

---

*These estimates were personally reported to me by psychiatrists and administrators in New York State facilities, and in New York City's forensic facilities, including Bellevue Hospital. It is emphasized again that these are very rough estimates, there being no actual data or even definitions by which some uniform data might be collected.

resolved, sometimes after painstaking work with the defendant, the lawyer, or both.

New York State, where thousands of defendants are examined each year for competency in the court clinics and forensic hospitals, has no formal data. Psychiatrists at the State's forensic treatment facilities, which receive defendants after an incompetency adjudication, estimate that between 5% to 15% of their patients are, in fact, malingerers, who are uncooperative with treatment regimes and fake symptoms.* Many defendants decide to cooperate before or during treatment, thus reducing the numbers in the treatment facilities. Among the defendants who are initially found to be incompetent are many in whom a malingering element was strongly suspected but could not be clearly established, or that might coexist with a major psychiatric disorder. Some of these defendants are returned to court in an attempt to test the question and to press them to cooperate. Hard core malingerers often require disproportionate amounts of care and attention, frequently at the expense of more genuinely disturbed patients, going back and forth to court for years without resolution.

In a recent study of malingering at the Isaac Ray Center in Chicago, the defendants being evaluated for competency and responsibility were given the Minnesota Multiphasic Personality Inventory (MMPI).[8,9] Although a majority of these individuals were not faking according to the MMPI scales, the study found that a significant group (14%–41%) clearly malingered or exaggerated, depending on certain cutoff points in the scoring. These cutoffs may be under- or overinclusive. Other scales give comparable results, clearly suggesting the possibility of a significant degree of exaggeration and faking by defendants in criminal trials. Control studies based on patients acquitted by reason of insanity showed significantly less faking bad and more faking good. Unfortunately, a correlation with clinical assessment was lacking that would have provided a critical element in defining the utility of the MMPI as a tool in the evaluation and in obtaining meaningful data.

## THEORETICAL PROBLEMS IN THE EVALUATION

The evaluation of competency to stand trial raises complex issues that are compounded by the possibility of malingering.

A person is held to be incompetent if, as a result of mental disease or defect, he or she lacks the capacity or ability to understand the proceedings or to cooperate in his or her own defense.[10] Roesch and Golding[11]

---

*See* previous footnote.

described competency as a "construct." In practice, it is ambiguous, and threshold questions must be dealt with case by case. How much mental illness or defect must there be to justify a finding of incompetency? What is required of a defendant in general or in a particular instance? How much of competency is dependant on the chemistry between the lawyer and the client? The leap from clinical observation to forensic opinion is subjective, in spite of attempts to refine decision-making.

Critics have attacked psychiatrists for offering forensic opinions in the criminal setting on the grounds that these are moral, not medical decisions, and that psychiatrists have no expertise in moral issues. Although the American Bar Association[12] has recommended that "mental disease or defect" be excluded from the competency criteria, thirty-seven states presently do require such a finding as a prerequisite for an incompetency determination.[13] Thus, the psychiatrist or psychologist is mandated, by statute and case law in these states, at least, and in most, to do the competency evaluation. This raises a very sensitive question. Can psychiatric diagnosis be made with sufficient precision to satisfy the needs of the court? No one has said that psychiatric diagnosis is easy. Do we really have the skills to weed out malingerers? Szasz,[14] taking an extreme position, has said that there is no such thing as mental illness. Ennis and Litwack[15] and Ziskin,[16] in their extensive writings, have assailed the validity and reliability of psychiatric diagnosis, as well as the credibility of the psychiatrist, particularly in the courtroom.

In his study, "On Being Sane in Insane Places," Rosenhan[17] suggested that psychiatrists can be easily fooled (in the hospital setting) and posed another challenge to psychiatrists' ability to make psychiatric diagnoses. Reasoned response to these attacks,[18] and the vast body of knowledge relevant to psychiatric disorder, do not eliminate the very real problems in practice.

Malingering adds a major dimension of uncertainty to the conundrum, one that must be addressed regularly in competency evaluations. In spite of fortuitous discoveries of malingering and confessions by malingerers of what they have been doing, the diagnosis is extremely difficult at times. We cannot measure emotion or impulse, touch a hallucination, or disprove amnesia. Even extended periods of observation and treatment may not lead to clarification; there is many a defendant with what appears to be a "long malingering illness." In the uncertainty as to whether the defendant is malingering, and often under pressure to make a decision, the psychiatrist is strongly influenced by feelings about the defendant and the nature of the crime, and by his personal philosophy of medicine and justice.

A small sampling of the psychiatric literature on malingering or simulation, as distinguished from hysteria or neurosis, reflects the struggle with the concept. These discussions are permeated with contradictory views that persist and are especially relevant to the problem of malingering in the criminal setting. Two questions seem particularly germane: Is malingering an illness, and should psychiatrists diagnose it?

In 1935, Karl Menninger,[19] exploring the dynamics of self-mutilation, worried about professional antipathy to the malingerer. He noted the psychiatrist's lack of expertise in moral issues and identified malingering as a certain kind of psychopathology, however infuriating and "reprehensible," and hence, a proper area for psychiatric inquiry. He said:

> The malingerer turns his neurotic tendencies to evident profitable account . . . and takes conscious cognizance of this . . . he consciously capitalizes the secondary gain of illness and makes it the predominant motive. (p 508)

To the extent that the neurotic does this, "he is a malingerer." Menninger called attention to "the widespread fallacy that conscious motives can be regarded as explanatory of human behavior" (p 509).

Speaking of the self-mutilators, Menninger said, "Actions speak louder than words, and it is clear that however conscienceless the malingerer appears (or claims) to be, he unconsciously feels guilty and inflicts his own punishment" (p 515). This type of malingerer elicits a punitive as well as sympathetic attitude in others, reinforcing the rewards. Menninger expressed these views again and again,[20] seeming to reflect a psychoanalytic consensus in the mid-20th century on which many psychiatrists were nurtured.

Eissler,[21] a psychoanalyst who explored war neuroses in a 1951 essay, defined malingering conventionally but stated that it was always a disease, "often more severe than a neurotic disorder," and ultimately treatable. Once war neuroses were identified as illness, probably a form of hysteria, they were moved from bad to mad, like criminality itself in those years. The likelihood of inappropriate prosecution or punishment was thus diminished.

In 1963, Menninger again stated his views in "The Vital Balance."[22] Malingering, he said, is an illness, whose very admission by the malingerer is a sign of the illness. Eissler had expressed similar views. The malingerer thinks he has been fooling us but instead he has been fooling himself—truly a catch-22. "No healthy person," Menninger wrote, "would go to such extremes and take such devious and painful routes for minor gains that the invalid status brings to the malingerer" (p 208).

Not every psychiatrist agreed with this thinking. Wertham,[23] in 1949, and Davidson,[24] in 1952, considered malingering in the criminal setting. Though they recognized the complexities of motivation, they concluded that malingerers could be sane in that setting, and that malingering is not in itself a mental disorder. Wertham's discussion highlights the moral implications of the diagnosis. Certainly, malingering to escape the death penalty has been supported by many psychiatrists.

In 1961, Miller[25] explored accident neuroses and seemed to lump the neurotics and the obvious simulators, after ruling out organic pathology. "Whether exaggeration or simulation are conscious or unconscious, their only purpose is to make the observer believe that the disability is greater than it is" (p 993). Recognizing an inability to measure subjective symptomatology, Miller concluded that conscious and unconscious symptoms are a form of feigning. Menninger, also noting the lack of scientific tools to study emotions, had concluded the opposite.

Eissler[21] had said that no one but a psychiatrist should make the diagnosis of malingering. More explosive perhaps was Szasz's view,[26] strongly expressed in a 1956 article in the *Archives of Neurology and Psychiatry,* a journal published by the American Medical Association. Szasz was opposed to the expansion of psychiatric expertise into areas where it did not belong. He considered malingering a moral, not medical, issue. He argued with those psychiatrists who speak of malingering as if it were a diagnosis. Malingering, he wrote, is not a psychiatric diagnosis, "on equal footing with concepts such as conversion hysteria, compulsion neurosis, or schizophrenia" (p 443). Noting that malingering was viewed differently depending on the acceptability of the circumstances, Szasz recommended that we

> suspend our psychiatric tendency to view malingering in terms of "psychopathology" and psychical "mechanisms," and instead, to look upon it from the viewpoint of life as a game. Malingering, then, is the same thing as cheating. (p 433)

In the game, the psychiatrist becomes a moral umpire—not a proper role.

The second edition of the official diagnostic manual published by the American Psychiatric Association in 1968, the DSM–II,[27] mentioned simulation only in the differential diagnosis of hysterical neuroses, conversion type. By 1980, the DSM–III,[28] or its 1987 revision, the DSM–III–R,[29] lists malingering under "Conditions Not Attributable to a Mental Disorder That Are a Focus of Attention or Treatment." According to the DSM–III–R:

> The essential feature of Malingering is intentional production of false or grossly exaggerated physical or psychological symptoms, motivated by external incentives (p 360).

The DSM–III–R distinguishes malingering from factitious disorder "in that the motivation for the symptom production in Malingering is external incentives, whereas in Factitious Disorder there is an absence of external incentives. Evidence of an intrapsychic need to maintain the sick role suggests factitious disorder. Thus, a diagnosis of factitious disorder excludes the diagnosis of malingering . . . . Malingering is differentiated from Conversion and other Somatoform Disorders" by its intentionality. "The person who is malingering is much less likely to present his or her symptoms in the context of emotional conflict, and the presenting symptoms are less likely to be symbolically related to an underlying emotional conflict" (p 360).

In contrast to the 1968 edition, the DSM–III–R recognizes malingering as an entity and clearly identifies it as a nonmedical condition, requiring the psychiatrist to rule out gross psychopathology and to distinguish clearly between external (intentional) and internal (psychogenic) causes so as to make the diagnosis. In effect, the issues our mentors were debating have not been resolved by the careful descriptive classification of the diagnostic manual. The difficulty separating intentional from unintentional motivation in the enormously stressful, highly emotional surroundings of the criminal process, and the symbolic nature of much of the malingering, often defies resolution.

## WHY MALINGER?

Why is there so much malingering, and what are some possible reinforcing internal motivations? It is no simple matter. The most obvious goal of the malingerer is to "beat the rap" or to get a "better deal," perhaps to save his life if facing a death penalty. Ultimately, very few defendants are actually acquitted or have their cases dismissed. But hope remains eternal as alternative defenses are often not available. Data, such as Steadman's review[30] of the New York State experience with incompetent defendants, suggest that few sentences are aborted or shortened, although most cases end in pleas. Defendants charged with serious crimes, such as murder, rape, arson, kidnapping, and robbery, may malinger specifically to establish an insanity defense, to be incompetent to stand trial, to delay or enlist the court's sympathy, or often to raise questions about the validity of a confession. There is very little doubt that lawyers may on occasion subtly encourage some of these practices, even suggesting ways to malinger. Emotionally charged crimes, such as murdering a family member or friend, are particularly difficult for the defendant, as are some sexual offenses. Amnesia, denial, and simulation are common. Many sex offenders deliberately will not talk, sometimes from shame, but often for fear of reprisal by fellow inmates, correctional staff, and the courts.

There are prisoners, bent on escaping, who simulate mental as well as physical symptoms in jail so as to provoke a competency examination and a transfer to a mental hospital. The transfer process itself offers opportunities for escape, as do the less secure facilities to which the prisoner may be taken. Some of these malingerers are successful, often more than once.

The feigning of symptoms to raise the issue of competency may be a stalling device to delay adjudication while the defendant gets himself together mentally (not always unjustified or inappropriate), until perhaps he feels free of drugs or alcohol, or has a chance to think out his strategy. It is certainly more pleasant to wait in a hospital than in a jail. The malingering may delay the proceedings while witnesses are found, bail money is raised, or arrangements are made for a better or more compatible lawyer, or one who is privately retained.

The fear that he is not being represented adequately may lead to all kinds of willful and unpleasant behavior by the defendant to delay the proceedings and manipulate the court. Unfortunately, public defenders or legal aid lawyers in particular are often distrusted and are perceived as part of the system in which they are in collusion with the prosecutor because of their common source of pay, because they whisper together to the judge, because they take coffee together, and because they may press the defendant prematurely to take a plea. Some unsophisticated defendants regard the legal aid lawyer as an "aide," not a lawyer. Lawyers are often hard to reach by telephone and often do not have time for clients, who may be in hard-to-visit places. Frequently, lawyers are not properly prepared and are too rushed to listen to their clients. Thus, the lawyer unintentionally encourages distrust and paranoia.

Most troublesome are real incompatibilities of style and personality between lawyer and client that lead to a breakdown in communications and frequent refusal to cooperate. Most of these stalling defendants ultimately acknowledge their guilt and take a plea, but only when they are ready, when they feel in control, and when they think they are getting a "fair shake."

There is often a pervasive distrust and anticipation of injustice. Cultural and political attitudes as well as past experience may contribute to a deliberate refusal to participate in the system. The depth of this distrust may be difficult for middle-class psychiatrists to understand. However, psychiatrists are part of the system, too, particularly if they work in a government institution, where "you're all paid by the same people anyhow," whether or not this is true:

> For example, a very cooperative, rational defendant in a hospital setting, referred by psychiatrists in the court clinic to rule out malingering, told me he thought the clinic psychiatrists worked for the district attorney and so refused to talk or say anything meaningful to them. His lawyer had not

even told him why he wanted the competency evaluation or who would
do it.

Defendants who have language problems or who are unfamiliar
with the American courtroom or justice system can be very difficult,
frightened, and paranoid. On occasion, they take advantage of the situation, they cooperate poorly, pretend not to understand anything at all,
not even English when, in fact, they may be fluent. It is critical to bring
in a translator if there is any question at all, although even this may not
work:

In another example, a Nigerian charged with attempted manslaughter was
found to have a paranoid psychosis and was considered to be incompetent.
His heavily accented English was almost incomprehensible, and the judge
ordered a translator from the Nigerian Consulate. The defendant refused
to cooperate or consult with her. The case dragged on for years while the
court struggled with this unusual situation, the psychiatrists and lawyer
regularly questioning the defendant's competency, and the defendant rou-
tinely rejecting a favorable plea offer. One day, the defendant was be-
friended by a Nigerian taxi driver who was taking the defendant to court
with his lawyer. With the assistance and reassurance of the new friend, the
defendant quickly pleaded guilty, in English, to a minimum sentence, and
his former paranoid attitude evaporated. We will never know how much of
his resistance was volitional.

Many defendants are concerned that they may give responses during the evaluation that could incriminate them in some way or that could
be used to impugn their credibility. They may refuse to cooperate at all
for evaluation. In spite of appropriate reassurance, in spite of statutory
protections, and in spite of a Supreme Court decision[31] providing protection, defendants are not always wrong about the potential for abuse,
self-incrimination, and distortion of the examination results or report.
Their paranoia is not necessarily pathological.

All malingerers are angry, but there is a coterie of even angrier,
more perverse defendants, not unlike those defendants who want to
take an impossible case to trial, who have a profound need to manipulate
the system, as a child tests and maneuvers a parent. They have need to
retain control and make the government work for the conviction. They
keep company with yet another clutch of malingerers, those who determine with tremendous energy, that they want to do their "time" in a
mental hospital, before or after adjudication being irrelevant. These
defendants find hospitals more comfortable, more protected, less demanding, and preferable even in the absence of significant mental ill-

ness. Conversely, some of the dissimulators are equally deliberate in expressing their preference for a prison over a hospital.

In this setting, it is perhaps impossible to distinguish between internal need and external motivation for malingering. Primary and secondary gains may run parallel, reinforcing each other. Even the healthiest defendant has an instinct toward self-preservation and an intuitive need to control his life, not just to beat the case. The wish to be in a hospital—to be cared for and to deny criminality, and to stay out of prison—may conceivably be experienced consciously and unconsciously for essentially the same reasons. Or a young prisoner may state that he is never going to go to prison where he realistically anticipates being raped or mutilated. Simultaneously, he may have deep-seated expectations of castration for past fantasized indiscretions or have terrifying latent homosexual wishes. Guilt for the crime may not be accessible, nor may there be any feeling either for the victim, society, or the defendant's own family. However, real tears may flow for the defendant himself, not just for a loss of self-esteem, but for the defendant's perception of himself as victim. Consider the possible conflicts of a man who deliberately will not deal with the drunken murder of his common-law wife, described as his "best friend." From discussion, it appears that he may be avoiding guilt over deep anger toward his mother, intolerable feelings of separation from the wife, and mourning, not just for the wife, but for the idealized image of himself. Although he has a prison record, he never saw himself as a violent criminal, a bad person. Is denial of criminality and refusal to cooperate by a relatively new offender, perhaps a former judge or a lawyer, even after conviction, a reflection of badness, or a desperate defense, a last stand against a devastating loss of self-esteem and a collapse of the ego?

Perhaps we are the crazy ones when we identify as malingerers individuals with histories of hospitalization, who are known to be infantile, dependent, impulsive, and self-destructive, perhaps borderline personalities, but who are currently competent and clearly faking. They malinger with impunity, while telling us that they have serious emotional problems for which they need treatment. They plead to be sent to a hospital as incompetent and then proceed to confirm their problems almost spitefully.

## CASE HISTORY

Mark, a 28-year-old white male, was charged with reckless endangerment. While under police observation, he allegedly burglarized a car, stealing credit cards. He immediately jumped into his own car, which later proved to be stolen, smashed into a police car and led a high-speed chase down a major avenue, causing more damage and terror. He punched the police officer who apprehended him. A vial of crack was found in the car.

A former heroin addict and alcoholic, Mark had a ninth grade education, supposedly played in a rock band, and reported several voluntary hospitalizations for depression and suicide gestures, possibly related to substance abuse or to one of his many arrests. Immediately after the new arrest, Mark claimed to be depressed and suicidal and was hospitalized for brief observation before being returned to the local jail's mental observation unit. Simultaneously, an independent team of psychiatrists found him incompetent to stand trial. One examining psychiatrist made a diagnosis of paranoid schizophrenia, the other, atypical psychosis.

The court confirmed the finding of incompetency, and Mark was sent to a state forensic facility for treatment. He claimed to hear voices that tortured him and maintained that people, including his lawyers, were plotting against him. The backs of his arms were covered with old scars from self-inflicted lacerations, and his abdomen was criss-crossed with laparotomy scars. X-ray examination revealed multiple foreign bodies in his abdomen. He was treated with antipsychotic medication, and his impulsivity was discussed with him. His hospital course was described as stormy and chaotic, marked by attempts to "cut up" or threats to "hang-up." He was considered to be too unstable to be returned to court as competent. As court orders were being obtained to retain him further in the treatment facility, Mark announced that he was competent and ready to go back to court. He was then returned to the local jail, considered fit to proceed.

On the morning before Mark was to go back to court for a competency hearing, he reported he had swallowed a pen. He claimed voices had ordered him to do it. He was immediately hospitalized as he appeared to be in pain. An X ray confirmed his claim, and a pen was removed surgically. At this point, I was asked to evaluate Mark for suicidal potential and to recommend a treatment plan. He immediately asked for substantial amounts of Valium, claiming he had been given the drug at the state forensic hospital (he had not). He asked to be sent to a forensic hospital again. He said he was hearing voices saying, "happy birthday" or "to kill myself."

Mark denied knowing any details of his case, although he eventually told me that it had to do with a car, and all he remembered was waking up in the police station. He expressed no interest in the case and alleged that everyone, including his lawyer, was plotting against him, though he claimed not to know who represented him. There was no overt evidence of psychosis, no evidence that he was hallucinating. Finally, after some additional evasive answers, I confronted Mark gingerly. He confessed frankly that he was afraid of "blowing up" in court. Subsequently he was again found to be incompetent. Months later, after a finding of competency, he pled guilty and was sentenced. Before he was sent to prison he swallowed yet another pen.

There is always a group of suspected malingerers (as well as certain recidivists) for whom the gain could only be to remain institutionalized indefinitely—a reflection of the immaturity, dependency, helplessness, and need for structure that is characteristic of many defendants. Psychiatrists, and the court also, may find inadequacy to this extent quite inconceivable. Such defendants delay adjudication way beyond the possible sentence they might have to serve (or get themselves rapidly rearrested). This form of malingering may again raise the specter of factitious illness, intentional behavior motivated by unconscious forces, almost impossible by definition in this setting as external incentives are so overwhelming.

Dissimulation is usually associated with a denial of mental illness or retardation and a wish not to be identified as "crazy," or dumb, labels that increase the defendant's or prisoner's vulnerability.[32] Defendants who have a potential valid mental defense may be resistant to the defense, which, in turn, may raise issues as to competency. Defendants who are sensitive to the stigma of mental illness, and who are concerned they will be forced to take medication in a hospital, frequently express a not always unjustified wish to serve the anticipated sentence in a prison rather than in a psychiatric facility.

Guilt, real or imagined, conscious or not, may play a major role in the refusal to use illness to "get off easy." The defendant may express an expectation and anticipation of punishment and may be deliberately passive in defending his case. This is of particular concern if the defendant has suicidal wishes or is facing the death penalty. Some sophisticated defendants fear they may be institutionalized almost indefinitely if they are acquitted by reason of insanity. By contrast, a prison sentence is finite, a known quantity. Dissimulators may not cooperate, may claim amnesia, or may refuse to speak to the psychiatrist in an attempt to hide mental illness.

## WHO MALINGERS?

I do not know who is likely to malinger in this setting, but no one social or economic class, no single criminal, intellectual, or ethnic group, or type of psychiatric patient has a corner on the market. Certainly, it is more evident among persons with serious charges and those who are sociopathic. There are healthy malingerers, those with severe personality disorders, and psychotic malingerers, all of whom share no common psychological finding other than their malingering.[33] There are malingerers with limited intelligence, who are so impaired, unimaginative, and scared that they are unable to reason in their own interest.

Successful malingerers may be more intelligent, more sociopathic and opportunistic; they may have more energy, determination, and more coexisting pathology, all of which confuses the psychiatrist. Many malingerers have a capacity to enlist the psychiatrist's empathy and guilt, often reaction against the rage generated in the professional by ethical and moral conflict, the crime itself, and the hostility of the malingerer. Thus, the psychiatrist is placed on the defensive.

Less successful malingerers usually have less determination and capacity, and are more likely to experience guilt, consciously or without awareness, that sabotages the malingering attempt. Eissler[21] suggests that some of these feeble attempts should not even be catalogued as malingering; but whatever the label, it is costly to the entire system.

## PATTERNS OF MALINGERING IN THE CRIMINAL SETTING

Defendants have an intuitive understanding of how to malinger, though they often are quite well versed in the criteria for competency or insanity, studying assiduously in the law library. Hence, they may make an attempt to simulate mental disease or defect or both, or may take a more literal approach to the competency standard by trying to establish either a lack of knowledge or understanding of the charges or proceedings, or an inability to cooperate. They may even volunteer that they cannot cooperate! There is no end to human ingenuity.

The psychiatrist evaluating defendants in all forensic settings for competency and possibly insanity may be faced with a plethora of challenging and unpleasant behaviors, which must be explored, sorted out, checked against other data, and often treated. Defendants who attempt to simulate mental illness or retardation, claim all kinds of bizarre symptoms and feign stupidity or both. They will lie, refuse to answer, and give silly or approximate answers. They may be facetious, teasing, paranoid, evasive, irrelevant, and may perseverate. They may be openly hostile, vicious, and threatening. They may act out sexually toward other inmates and staff. Fire setting is not uncommon. Families report false or exaggerated history. Outside therapists, often with no knowledge of the crime, are asked to provide letters stating how ill the defendant is.

Defendants may refuse to leave their rooms or cells, spending weeks in bed, often demanding medication and then refusing it. Their personal hygiene may be neglected. They can remain mute for months, or scream, shout, and bang their heads against the walls. They may claim paralysis, amnesia, and loss of speech from head injury. Some defendants are far more primitive; they throw urine and feces about. One very angry borderline defendant carried dried stool in his pocket for appropriate moments.

Not at all uncommon are prolonged hunger strikes, extraordinary, atypical seizures, and remarkable dystonic reactions (although the defendant may not be taking antipsychotic medication), and claims of auditory and visual hallucinations. Defendants may cut and burn themselves ferociously, oozing with rage. They may whip out razor blades from their mouths or cigarette packs right in front of the judge. They scratch themselves delicately with toothpaste tubes or playing cards, tie sheets around their necks, or make serious destructive gestures by swallowing bedsprings, poison, pens, pencils, eating utensils, and razor blades (carefully wrapped). Such defendants, some of whom are impulse ridden or borderline personalities, risk their lives to manipulate the system; hoping to enlist the court's sympathy; hoping to delay the proceedings; hoping to go to a hospital. Just hoping.

We do not know why defendants choose certain styles or patterns of malingering but undoubtedly the choice reflects experience, specific intent, sophistication, availability, and probably most important, preexisting mental illness or psychological determinants including personality structure and organic changes. It is easy to malinger hallucinations if at some earlier date the defendant has actually experienced them. However, the general lack of knowledge about mental illness results in a peculiar hodgepodge of symptomatology. Most defendants have not read psychiatric textbooks, although the many mental hospitals and jails in which these defendants have dwelled are unwitting training grounds for malingering. Defendants coach one another in what to say and do and borrow symptoms freely from each other. Sometimes psychiatrists are the best teachers of all. "You look very depressed Mr. Jones. Have you thought about hurting yourself? What do the voices say to you?" What better clues could there be for a ready student? Malingerers are most suggestible, the hysterics are not alone. Certain favored patterns of malingering do emerge from the wide range of symptoms.

Claims of total or partial amnesia for personal history and the crime are perhaps the commonest of symptoms after arrest, particularly if the charge is serious, emotionally loaded, if there is a history of substance abuse or even the slightest suggestion of head injury.[34–36] Recent data suggest the frequency is high, as much as 40%–70% of the persons charged with murder. Some of this activity is feigned, a research finding which supports our clinical impression, as amnesias develop conveniently after confessions are given, and memories are recovered during interview or in time for trial. However, amnesia may be claimed long after adjudication, some of which is still thought to be feigned.

Hallucinations seem to have a magical connotation of illness and are said to be the most common feigned complaint in forensic hospitals.[37] The defendant reports that the voices call him names, tell him he is bad, or command him to kill himself. Sometimes he hears his late "grandmother's" voice at night (not *per se* a fake symptom and almost common in jail). The malingering defendant requests medication for the voices in the mistaken belief that taking medication will make him appear sick and incompetent in the eyes of the court.

Mutism,[38] with no other psychopathology, may be maintained for many months. If not altogether mute, the defendant may speak no more than absolutely necessary and participate minimally in activities. Unfortunately, many genuinely paranoid or depressed patients who are not competent do the same thing, leaving very little record of behavior, of interpersonal relations, or of the ability to communicate reasonably. Or the malingerer, usually with real borderline pathology, may be loud, disruptive, agitated, abusive, and out of control, at least in the psychiatrists' or nurses' presence. Such people seem unable to concentrate or sustain an interview, but they can when they want to, and when the interviewer sets limits.

Feigning intellectual retardation is more difficult than it looks but is frequently attempted. Why not try? The tragedy is that genuinely retarded individuals may feign a pseudocompetency, mouthing words they have learned from more capable peers so as to hide their limitations, which are often missed.

The malingerer may simply be hostile and evasive, may make the examiner repeat every question, and may take a long time to answer, thinking out each response. Such negativism may be associated with depression, which is frequent and real, although not to the depth claimed. Complaints of depression are often associated with suicide threats and gestures, complaints of command hallucinations, and sometimes with pleas to be given more time for treatment and to get collected. Such defendants may burst into tears when attempts are made to discuss the charges, or they may refuse to be interviewed, preferring "to leave it up to God."

Posttraumatic stress disorder is easy to feign, complete with flashbacks. Most of the complaints, if not all, are self-reported. My impression is that there is less of this form of malingering for competency purposes now than in the 1970s, during and after the Vietnam war. Many of the malingerers had never been to Vietnam.

Imposters, to be distinguished from patients with fugue states, multiple personality, or psychosis, deny the charges, the possibility of such charges, and insist that they really are someone else. They raise tough, perplexing questions about their capacity to test reality and defend themselves. Some of these defendants have conned the public so effectively for so long, about their assumed identities and credentials, that they seem to believe themselves. They may not be considered psychotic, but the denial appears to take on psychotic dimensions in its intensity. Multiple personalities may be malingered as well, but this simulation is generally clumsy, and usually not accepted by the court.

Two more complex patterns can be identified. One cluster of malingerers presents a syndrome I call "a little bit of this, and a little bit of that," not unlike grandmother's cooking. The multiplicity of the symptoms reflects the malingerer's concept of mental illness, with little resemblance to any known disorder. In this presentation, there are signs of intellectual limitation, perhaps a few auditory hallucinations, sudden remarkable visual experiences of little green men marching across the office wall, and many "can't remember" or "don't know" replies. The defendant may turn his back to the examiner; he may be stoney faced, tearful, and hesitant in response. He may look preoccupied and leap up suddenly to the invisible or inaudible call. This syndrome may be hard to maintain, so the same inmate may spend hours just lying on his bed, very withdrawn and uncommunicative.

Another well-known behavior cluster is called the Ganser Syndrome,[3,23,39] identified in the DSM–III[28] as a Factitious Disorder with Psychological Symptoms, and in the DSM–III–R[29] as a Dissociative Disorder Not Otherwise Specified. The DSM–III–R description includes giving approximate answers (*Vorbeireden* in the original German), in association with other symptoms, such as amnesia, disorientation, preoccupation, perceptual disturbances, fugue, and conversion symptoms. These symptoms allegedly persist even when the examiner or other staff are not looking; but sometimes they do not. Contrary to some descriptions, we have not found any pattern of intellectual impairment in these patients.

Reflecting the uncertainties of this diagnosis, a description of Ganser-like behavior remains under Factitious Disorders in the DSM–III–R, although it is not identified there by name. Some psychiatrists believe this syndrome is a psychosis, others have identified it as organic in origin or a severe neurosis with hysterical features, and still others have identified it as a form of malingering. Ganser described it in a prison setting and did not consider it voluntary. Unfortunately, the term is often used incorrectly as synonymous with all malingering. In my opinion it is a special pattern of malingering, perhaps unconsciously structured, that may be seen in the presence of psychosis or personality disorder, or in the absence of major psychopathology.

The Ganser syndrome is most often combined with some of the behavior described in the first major cluster, the hodgepodge of symptoms. Perhaps these clusters reflect the same confusion about mental illness and cannot be distinguished from each other. Research on malingering has demonstrated that approximate answers, very common in our experience, are a reflection of a pull toward the normal or appropriate response by someone who wants to appear abnormal, but who is afraid to exaggerate too much, who cannot quite go all the way. Other symptoms in this syndrome do not require much imagination, are relatively easy to feign and to maintain, even when the defendant believes he is not being watched. Internal determinants may be operative parallel to the more obvious gains.

## A GUIDE TO THE PERPLEXED: CLUES TO MALINGERING

Although experience has provided some guides to the determination of malingering in the criminal setting, psychiatrists must have a high index of suspicion in every evaluation. The incentive to malinger is great, and defendants are resourceful and desperate:

1. The psychiatrist should be familiar with the charges against the defendant, and, if possible, should find out what is happening with the case and what he is facing. Be ahead of the defendant, and if something does not feel right, follow up. A phone call may reveal that the forgetful, feeble, little old lady in your office, who is speaking gibberish, has just vigorously and rationally declined an unsatisfactory plea offer, and is stalling for time, hoping for better.

2. Be suspicious of scattered clinical pictures inconsistent with known diagnostic entities. Be leary of isolated symptoms. They may be valid, but usually do not support a finding of incompetency by themselves.

3. Listen and watch for contradictions in the defendant's responses and presentation. Body language may be revealing.

4. Check for prior findings of incompetency in earlier cases or successful use of a psychiatric defense. History repeats itself, not always for valid reasons. Successful malingerers build up records that serve them well from crime to crime.

5. Be wary of self-serving defendants who exaggerate symptomatology or insist on talking about it, often to the exclusion of anything else. True schizophrenics, for example, are rarely proud of their illness, the possible secondary gain having little meaning in the criminal setting, unless they are maneuvering to go to a hospital rather than face charges. Hysterics and malingerers may exhibit "la belle indifférence."

6. Watch for discrepancies between behavior in your office and behavior on the ward, at home, or in jail. An exacerbation of symptomatology, when the defendant thinks he is under observation or during interview, cannot always be attributed to the stress of the interview, as is often suggested. Check with family members who sometimes report behavior that suggests the defendant is dissembling; sometimes unsympathetic to the defendant, they report normal behavior or substance abuse. Check with all staff, including correction officers. Occasionally

fellow prisoners give valuable unsolicited clues. Does the defendant socialize, stand on line for his tray, and eat appropriately? Does he play games, make phone calls, and read the newspaper? Mentally ill persons may or may not participate in all kinds of activities, but some malingerers are often afraid to reveal themselves. Less committed malingerers are careless. What does the defendant do in the waiting room or late at night when he thinks no one is looking? For example:

A defendant who controlled a major "numbers" racket had at least "eleven fingers" and could not add five and five on interview. He was certain that George Washington was still president. He had been withdrawn on the ward for many months, remaining day after day quietly in his bed in the hospital. He was found on the phone one night by a shocked nurses aide, intensely negotiating a six-figure transaction.

A defendant who was guarded, bizarre, paranoid, and withdrawn during interview was found immediately afterward by the examiner articulately teaching another inmate how to use a set of weights, touchingly concerned for his safety.

Raul, charged with serious medicare fraud, did not sit down publicly in prison as well as during psychiatric examination, alleging, among other delusions, that electronic signals were being transmitted through his anus to his hair, which he had cropped closely to cut the emissions. He ate dead birds in the prison yard and garbage, while the professionals argued about him for two years. By night, unknown to the psychiatric evaluators, he had prepared the most sophisticated papers on behalf of his own competency hearing and made numerous appropriate phone calls. He had a prior history of using psychiatric grounds to evade prosecution on serious frauds as well as the draft.
Once again the ploy worked. The court deferred the charges and arranged for civil committment. Shortly after hospitalization, the psychiatrist at the state facility called the probation officer to ask why Raul was there, as he could detect no psychopathology. Was it now a case of faking good? He discharged the happy patient whose miraculous recovery was confirmed by subsequent contact, when he appeared well dressed, well groomed, and appropriate.
Members of the prison staff were convinced that the bird-eater had been faking, but no one was asked for his or her observations/or raw data for making a diagnosis. Somehow Raul had engaged everyone involved with the case sympathetically, including the psychiatrists; everyone, that is, except the prosecutor, who was livid, and the caretakers, who knew better.

7. When malingering is suspected it is critical to get records, contact other sources and be alert to discrepancies between this material and the defendant's version.

8. Be skeptical about psychiatric symptoms in sociopathic persons, or in persons with long criminal records, when there are codefendants, and when an ordinary crime required careful planning.

9. Be suspicious of defendants who avoid you, are hostile or negative, make you work, ask you to repeat questions, do not know or remember anything, or take their time answering while looking ever so preoccupied and perplexed. Most likely they are weighing every little word and taking your measure while they are at it.

10. Be careful when there is no prior history of mental dysfunction, although this is not diagnostic of malingering. Anticipating the use of a psychiatric defense, some malingerers establish a psychiatric record even before committing the crime.

11. Investigate carefully a diagnosis of atypical psychosis. It is a catchall for inconsistent or unusual symptoms that may suggest malingering.

12. Be patient and persistent; extend the interview or the period of observation. With fatigue or boredom, the defendant may "blow his cover" as did the "numbers" operator:

A relatively sophisticated man bludgeoned his wife to death with an iron. There was was no history of mental illness. In the months after arrest, he feigned stupidity and amnesia. He was born in the forensic unit, had never had another home, did not know how many fingers he had, and so on, and he spoke very little to anyone. There was no meaningful discussion of any issue, much less the charges. As the days went by, he spoke less, until most of his responses during the interview were "I don't know" or he remained silent, looking withdrawn and depressed. There was nothing further he could malinger. One day a Yiddish-speaking prisoner arrived on the ward. A movie was shown in English, and the "silent" patient, watching the movie, translated carefully for the new arrival. He was eventually found competent.

A middle-aged man had been found competent and was sentenced for a series of robberies in one jurisdiction. Simultaneously, he was charged with murder in the course of a similar robbery in another jurisdiction and was found incompetent for trial. He asserted that he was Joseph Kennedy's grandson and that he had killed the President. He always gave a fictitious name on interview and reported numerous other delusions. He carried a diagnosis of paranoid schizophrenia. It is noteworthy that he always came to interview in response to his correct name and that he picked up the right commissary, certainly good reality testing. After four years of going back and fourth between psychiatrists, courts, and hospitals, this man finally gave up the charade, "bored" he said, with "playing poker with the same bunch of loonies" year after year in the forensic hospital. He was ready to go to prison.

13. Be alert to your own feelings of rage and hostility, the "itchy toe" as experienced psychiatrists have called it. You may be dealing with a possible malingerer. Your hostility may engender more resentment in the malingerer, and more resistance.

## THE CLINICAL EVALUATION WITH SPECIAL REFERENCE TO MALINGERING

When it is time to do the formal interview for competency evaluation, the psychiatrist should fetch the defendant from the waiting room or ward. Watch the defendant carefully; do not let this opportunity slip, as amazing things happen may happen along the way. There is no substitute for personal observation outside the office, which will stand up well if your conclusions are contested.

In doing the clinical evaluation, it is a good practice to do a general psychiatric evaluation, in addition to asking questions about the charges and legal proceedings. A checklist of legal issues addresses the real concerns of the evaluation, but may reveal little about significant pathology that might interfere with the ability to cooperate, and yields little information about possible malingering. The psychiatrist is not out to "catch" the defendant, as one man accused me, but first to enlist the defendant's cooperation. Starting the interview with hard legal questions or with overly personal questions may encourage resistance before a relationship is established.

We can all tell stories of uncooperative, lying, and bewildered defendants who turn out to be the wrong person. As you start, identify the defendant and introduce yourself; explain the authority by virtue of which you are there, and the purpose and lack of confidentiality of the examination. Was the defendant told about the examination? Explain why you are taking notes. Following this, or even before explanations, I like to ask the defendant how he is feeling or doing, as you might ask a patient. The defendant may have waited for weeks for this moment, or may be tired after sitting since 5 A.M. in the court pen. This possibility needs some recognition. Anxiety and hostility need to be diffused, if at all possible, or the defendant may join the ranks of the malingerers if he has not already.

Take a cue from the initial responses and follow this before going on to the more formal questions. Even if time is short, try to take a history. Some defendants resist this procedure as irrelevant, but if malingering must be ruled out, the psychiatrist needs every scrap of information.

Discrepancies should be discussed firmly and fairly with the defendant, and the quality of response and cooperation noted. Let the defendant explain things his way. Let him save face too, and give him space before confronting him. He may lie in his defense or even his history as long as he is addressing the issues appropriately. The answers may be satisfactory for the purposes of competency and may be quite informative. Truth of the defense is in the court's domain. The psychiatric interview may be the first opportunity the defendant has to talk about his case in a quiet place. Misunderstandings may be cleared up, particularly if the lawyer is called in. One defendant, when told he would have to go to a psychiatric hospital if he kept up the faking, finally after a year's delay, said "Why didn't someone tell me?" The case went forward.

Confrontation may not work, and some malingerers will continue to deny everything or refuse to speak. Most defendants know something about the charges even if they say they do not. The defendant may not know all the details, and, if charged with a rape or child molestation, may not want to know anything, and will claim something silly, like loitering. Defendants may not want to articulate the charges, for fear of saying it wrong or as if just knowing the charge will suggest guilt. Very often such defendants get nasty, refuse to listen to a reading of the charges, or walk out. Some defendants, even while they claim not to know the charge, will quickly add, "but I didn't do it," or, "it's a case of mistaken identity."

If a defendant is not responsive, try another tack. Use open-ended questions to get the defendant talking, structuring it as needed. Find out what he wants to talk about; what he is worried about; what he likes and what he misses—television, sports, work, hobbies, even his mother's cooking; what about the noise in jail? All the while, try to capture the quality of the defendants thinking and the level of intellectual functioning. You may be able to do all this, in the course of taking the history, using the traditional mental status or forensic questions. But malingerers often refuse to answer or offer silly and irrelevant answers that need further exploration and other approaches.

Certain aspects of the general examination deserve special attention in the criminal setting:

The *history* itself may easily be exaggerated or manufactured as well as denied.[40] Although not always necessary in a routine competency examination, it is helpful to obtain as much ancillary information as possible when malingering is suspected. Defendants are not always devious; sometimes they are just embarrassed by the truth. History, psychological testing, or other data should be consistent with alternative diagnoses, otherwise faking should be suspected. Malingerers often refuse to give information that allows corroboration and often claim they have no family or knowledge of where relatives can be located.

*Failure to make eye contact* and *blunted* or *flat affect* are frequently described signs of schizophrenia. If I were malingering and trying to keep a secret, I would start there, along with silence. It is a natural response. Long pauses, in which the defendant looks perplexed and thoughtful, are not necessarily signs of depression or autistic preoccupation. The defendant may be weighing the impact of every word. It is toe to toe, eyeball to eyeball, in this situation in which so much hangs in the balance. If you interview the defendant long enough, try to kid around a little, put the pen down, just talk. You might even get a nice appropriate laugh, a sure sign of good affect. Watch the defendant's response to other people.

*Mutism*[38] is a frustrating symptom, but does not reflect mental illness unless there are other signs. Catatonic patients may be rigid, bizarre, agitated, ominous. Deaf persons may be mute, but they will try to communicate. The interview may have to be written or signed. Psychogenic mutism may sometimes be relieved by amytal interview or hypnosis, but feigned mutism usually persists. The malingerer does not want to communicate.

*Depression* is a very common finding in the criminal setting. Distinctions between major depression, or reactive and situational depressions, are difficult enough, at times, but are complicated by the ease with which they are feigned. How long should a defendant be given for treatment before being pushed to trial, particularly, if there does not appear to be an immediate risk of a *serious* suicide attempt, and general functioning is adequate? For whom were the tears? How suicidal is a defendant who asks for dental care and refuses antidepressant medication because he is afraid the medication may cause a blood pressure elevation? Manipulative hunger strikes must be distinguished from the anorexia of serious depression, and may need to be confronted by a threat of forced feeding. It is very easy to sneak a snack.

*Loose associations and word salad* are easily simulated but are difficult to maintain. The malingerer lacks any schizophrenic subtlety. The schizophrenic patient with a thought disorder is not suddenly clear after the interview.

*Perseveration,* or what appears to be perseveration, is not unusual. There are interviews during which the defendant answers, "I don't know" or "I can't remember" to every question. More difficult is an irrelevant, repetitious response to every question, such as "two weeks." Is there an organic or psychotic illness, or is the defendant just being careful not to give any meaningful answer?

Although much is known about *hallucinations,*[24,41] they still cannot be verified. The finding of competency or incompetency should never depend on this symptom alone. Hallucinations are probably not an all-or-nothing phenomenon but exist on a continuum.[42] At times, the hallucinations expressed by defendants seem to be quite primitive, bringing a lost object closer, helping to deny reality, sometimes supplying a missing superego. Absurdities should alert the examiner as should convenient hallucinations, such as a report that a voice instructed the defendant to burglarize an apartment. Although not diagnostic and nonspecific, there are differences in hallucinatory patterns in different disorders, and in the way that genuinely disturbed persons respond to them. Careful questioning about hallucinations may reveal they are longstanding and do not bother the defendant; he just throws them out to see if the examiner will bite. For purposes of the competency examination, the critical question is whether these reported hallucinations appear to interfere with concentration and attention, and not just during the examination.

*Delusions*[22] do not just develop overnight, particularly organized delusions, which may take weeks to develop. They are easy to fake. When did the delusions start in relation to the arrest? How diffuse or distracting are they? When delusional ideas are expressed, whether or not they are feigned, the competency decision should not rest on the existence of delusional thinking, but on the possible impact of these delusions on the defendant's cooperation and judgment about his case. Paranoid thinking is common, and sometimes much embroidered, particularly about the charges and the court. Paranoia is a difficult issue, frequently making cooperation with a lawyer impossible and leading to repeated changes of lawyer and persistent refusal to cooperate. Such defendants, who are frequently very withdrawn, hostile, guarded, and who talk to no one, may or may not be malingering. But they are often found incompetent for lack of any other documentation establishing competency.

*Disorientation* is easy to simulate if the examination is limited to a formal series of questions. Some defendants really do not know the date and may not care. A few may be genuinely confused. But what happens when they are shown a calender or are asked other questions that might reveal their sense of the seasons or of holidays? Genuine disorientation for person is rare in this population, and there usually are other signs of impairment. A malingerer asked to find his name on a list may painstakingly choose the one next to it, or may write it backward. The defendant may say he does not know the name or kind of institution he is in; but does he use the facility appropriately? Does he relate correctly to correction officers, and if there are doctors and nurses, does he ask for medication or make medical complaints?

Little is known about types of *amnesia* in the forensic setting,[34–38] and there seems to be little agreement, in general, except following head injury. Even here, patterns are not as consistent and diagnostic as formerly thought. Psychogenic and feigned amnesia may look similar and are hard to differentiate. Studies suggest that claims of amnesia in homicide are more frequent among individuals who show higher levels of hysteria and hypochondriasis on psychological testing. Conversely, testing may show sociopathic trends suggesting the possibility that the amnesia is not genuine. Alcoholic blackouts, other intoxications, sometimes psychoses and fugue states may produce genuine loss of memory, as may acute agitation, repression, and suppression, but there is *no* agreement on patterns of memory loss. It has been suggested that the only valid amnesias are those with organic etiology. The malingerer often describes a global amnesia for his life or a total, hazy or patchy amnesia for the event. Selective and global amnesias should be suspect.

In trying to assess the validity of an amnesia, take a careful history of when memory loss starts and stops, exactly what the defendant does remember, and what other factors existed such as substance abuse or head injury, that might impair memory. Malingerers may exaggerate the history, and the loss may seem conveniently selective and self-serving. Fugue states are rare as are the amnesias of multiple personality, although sophisticated sociopathic persons may try to make these claims. The amnesia may or may not be relieved by hypnosis or amytal interviews.[43–45] On occasion, memory may be restored if the amnesia is psychogenic. Often a malingerer will either refuse amytal or hypnosis or will continue to malinger even while under their relaxing influence. Conversely, these techniques may be face-saving devices for purposes of confession in the absence of a twilight state.

The presence of an amnesia does not in itself preclude a fair trial, the essential purpose of the competency evaluation. The courts have generally supported findings of competency in the presence of amnesia for various legal and policy reasons. The defendant usually does not know that he can be found competent and go to trial without remembering, and it is advisable to tell him so.

A claim of *memory loss,* that is, *a loss of memory function,* is another approach to malingering. Elderly defendants may exaggerate the normal forgetfulness of old age, or claim senility. Substance abusers may claim brain damage. When defendants claim that they do not know and cannot learn or are forgetful, some psychiatrists try to force the issue by providing needed information, such as the functions of a lawyer, or a jury, and then asking the defendant to repeat these answers later on. Teaching can be reassuring, but the demand to regurgitate the answers to these critical questions, on the spot, as a test of memory, can be quite threatening to some defendants and may lead to more negativism. Less threatening, perhaps more traditional ways of evaluating short-term memory should be tried, including psychological testing, although this may evoke the same resistance. Depressed and anxious patients may have difficulty learning and remembering; the malingerer does not want to learn:

A young drug dealer claimed memory troubles. He drove across the George Washington bridge every day in the same car to the same address, but claimed he knew neither the make of his car, the name of the bridge, the streets he traversed, nor the address of his destination. The capacity to remember was critical to his competency, whereas inability to remember was being asserted in his defense. He readily acknowledged, proudly in fact, that he was a very safe driver, never got lost, never got a ticket, and never had an accident. All this with "bad" memory!

A businessman had a confirmed history of concussion five years before perjuring himself during a friend's trial. Charged with perjury, he alleged incompetency because of short-term memory trouble due to the head injury, also his defense, in that he might have made a misstatement because he could not remember what he said. Although he was somewhat imprecise during the interview, detailed minutes of the meetings of a business association over which he presided certainly did not support his claim. An inspection of relevant grand jury minutes revealed the precision with which he testified. At one point, while being examined under pressure before the grand jury, this man stopped suddenly and said, "Excuse me, but I think I gave you a wrong answer two questions ago," and he corrected the answer. He eventually decided to plead guilty and arranged to "cooperate" with the government. It was then necessary to prove that he was competent, that, in fact, there was no memory impairment.

*Intellectual function* may vary a little, but it is relatively stable in the absence of brain injury, dementia, severe depression, acute psychosis, or delirium. Therefore, if during a previous competency examination the defendant gave adequate answers, he still has the same *capacity* to know or comprehend, no matter how much he now obfuscates. Defendants do not always understand this, but if the psychiatrist accepts as valid the data in a prior record or intelligence test, he may use this information to assist him in coming to his own conclusions. This step reinforces the need to obtain other records and competency reports, if possible, as well as current and past intelligence scores.

*Head injury and seizures* sometimes associated with amnesia, feigned or not, may be used to assert an insanity defense. More often, the history will be used to generate a competency examination. If a head injury is suspected and may be legally significant, neurological and psychological workups are indicated and a confirmatory history should be obtained. Seizures are often self-reported, are easily but not well feigned, and should be observed carefully. Often they are reported by persons who do not know how to evaluate seizurelike activity, and every odd movement or fall is then documented as a seizure. Often these claims become the focus of expensive workups and many delays. There should be some historical and clinical validity to a claim, and it must have some bearing on the competency issue. Seizures themselves may be irrelevant to competency, although not necessarily to the matter of responsibility:

> Tony was the major perpetrator of a much publicized multimillion dollar armed robbery during which he swindled his partners, secretly stashing some of the loot in Swiss banks. After his arrest, he claimed head injury, amnesia, and seizures, and was found incompetent to stand trial. Two years of additional psychiatric, psychologic, and neurologic observation and testing did not support his claims, and malingering was suspected. A defense psychiatrist maintained that Tony was brain damaged from earlier head injury and that he was schizophrenic and incompetent. When asked, at that point, to examine Tony for the court, I requested the hospital records, which were not previously obtained, of the alleged head injuries. I was shocked. So much had been made of so little. Tony had been in three minor automobile accidents, leading to brief visits to a hospital emergency room (perhaps for purposes of civil suit), with no evidence of head injury and no referral. There was no organic basis for the amnesia, which seemed feigned during interview, nor the seizures, which were all described as atypical or probably feigned by professional staff. The court found him competent and disallowed psychiatric testimony at trial.

## PSYCHOLOGICAL ASSESSMENT AND OTHER AIDS

*Psychological evaluation* is a valuable adjunct in assessing a defendant's intellectual capacity, personality, and other mental functions. There is considerable discussion as to whether psychological tests can be faked. Many tests, such as the MMPI, have faking scales, which are useful although not foolproof.[45—49] Unfortunately the MMPI has limited utility with defendants who have poor reading skills, no patience, or marginal intelligence, and whose examinations are often conducted under miserable conditions. Extremely high scores on faking scales may be indicators of severe pathology as well as faking. If the cut-off score is lowered on the faking scales, a number of genuinely disturbed persons may be caught in the faking net. There is a substantial percentage of persons whose faking bad scores on the MMPI cannot be validated clinically.

Feigning on intelligence tests may produce erratic and inconsistent scores, such as easy questions failed, hard ones answered. The malingerer may respond on these tests in the same manner as on the psychiatric examination, giving chaotic, bizarre, or exaggerated responses. It is difficult to simulate the subtleties of schizophrenic thought on a Rorschach,[50,51] or organic impairment on a Bender–Gestalt.[52] Yet, under experimental conditions, experienced reviewers have been unable to detect malingering when the test data suggest diffuse disturbance. Some malingerers give minimal and avoidant responses with little interaction on the testing, as they may have done during a psychiatric interview. This is one way of dissimulating or hiding pathology, by minimizing exposure, but avoidance can also reflect the negativism and evasiveness of the simulator. Schizophrenic and paranoid patients are not the only ones with a paucity of thought when confronted with the unknowns of the test situation.

Psychologists recommend the use of a battery of tests in trying to establish malingering, thereby vastly increasing reliability.[33,37] Despite their limitations, testing provides a different format and a different kind of professional to whom the defendant does not know how to respond. Testing may expose malingering while uncovering dynamics and real pathology. If a psychologist is unavailable, the psychiatrist may be able to do some testing himself.

There are other more modest tools that may be helpful in assessing the real capacities of a suspected malingerer, particularly, if psychological testing cannot be done. These should not be neglected. Does the defendant know how to read? Does he borrow the correction officer's newspaper? Does he have a driver's license, and does he actually drive? This requires a certain minimal level of intelligence, possibly literacy and concentration for a written test. Even though this ability is not necessarily reflective of the defendant's current capacity, it does help to establish a prior level, because driving requires attentiveness, alertness, and memory.

Does the defendant who claims to have no family or not to know his lawyer make phone calls to these people? One defendant who denied knowing or having a lawyer called him immediately to complain about involuntary medication. Check visiting lists if possible.

The ability to play board games, cards, chess, and checkers, demonstrates certain intellectual functions. Most games require an ability to understand rules and concepts, however simple, planning, concentration, attention and memory, simple arithmetic, as well as some ability to relate appropriately to others. This information can be particularly convincing if the psychiatrist has seen the defendant play the game or has discussed the rules with him, and if the quality of participation can be confirmed. An ability to play Monopoly does not inform us if the defendant knows the charges or can cooperate, but it does provide some information relevant to competency. It is remarkable how little information is available about some defendants, but each scrap helps.

*Polygraphy*[53] is a tool that may be used to establish credibility for defense purposes, perhaps to test feigning of amnesia. But one can lie even on this instrument, and, ultimately, there is some subjectivity in administering the test and interpreting the results. I prefer to rely on my own evaluation, as there is so little known about the use of polygraphy in the determination of competency.

## TREATING, CONCLUDING, AND REPORTING

If a suspected malingerer has what may be a treatable illness, he should be treated appropriately with medication, milieu therapy, and counseling, while being observed carefully for response. A treatment attempt may be instructive and may satisfy the psychiatrist's need to address possible pathology, quelling the fear of missed or neglected pathology. Malingerers often refuse antipsychotic medication because it makes them uncomfortable.

We tend to give more serious offenders who may be malingering the benefit of the doubt by calling them incompetent and referring them to the next level of the system for further observation and treatment. At some point, the buck must stop. Eventually, most of these defendants are returned to court to deal with the charges. Then, the cycle may start all over. With court dates approaching, the defendant starts to look bad. Is the defendant actually receiving recommended medication or is he refusing it? Has he decompensated again under the stress of reality, or did he get cold feet, once again resorting to a simulated illness?

When writing in a chart, preparing a report on a suspected malingerer, or testifying, the question always arises: Should the psychiatrist use the term *malingering*? Probably the term is best reserved for those defendants who are the healthiest, who are clearly out to "beat the rap" by conjuring up nonexistent pathology, or whose intentional refusal to cooperate is the most obvious. These defendants presumably are aware of the voluntary origins of their symptoms. Regardless of their internal motivation, such defendants are judged to have a reasonable ability to control or contain themselves.

The standard in court for the physician is the "medical opinion," "professional opinion," or a "reasonable degree of medical certainty."[54,55] Although these standards have been interpreted to mean "more likely than not" or at least 51% certain, they have defied precise definition and allow considerable uncertainty. The psychiatrist does not have to establish malingering or competency with absolute certainty, nor does the psychiatric opinion have to reach or match the threshold for the judicial determination of competency, which may be the same or higher. The forensic psychiatrist must offer an opinion with which he is comfortable, as when advising a patient about a diagnosis or treatment, and which is meaningful and useful to the court.

The psychiatrist should never offer a diagnosis of malingering based on intuition, but must be able to offer data that support this finding and be prepared to discuss diagnoses relevant to competency that have been ruled out. It is most important, when testifying about malingering, to be flexible and to acknowledge some of the limitations of psychiatric diagnosis. In spite of the large body of psychiatric knowledge, its application is admittedly difficult. The identification of any coexistent diagnoses is appropriate if malingering is found. I might report that the defendant has a personality disorder or mental illness, or some major conflict, but is competent, for example, and "can cooperate if he choses to." I am not shy about identifying malingering—it is so outrageous at times—but I tend to avoid the actual use of the word in the final report, mindful of the pejorative connotations. My early training still clings.

## CONCLUSION

I am alarmed when I hear psychiatrists say that we have no business diagnosing malingering or that we are ethically committed to doing no harm. Szasz[14] said that malingering involves a moral judgment, and I do not disagree, particularly in the criminal setting. There is little doubt about the dual allegiances of the forensic psychiatrist, and the tension between these commitments that are greatly exacerbated when treatment is involved. Beyond this, however, our conclusions differ. The American Medical Association, in its code of ethics,[56] has said that physicians shall respect the law. To that extent, if we refuse to recognize malingering in the criminal setting, we may be undermining the administration of justice. A failure to identify malingering, perhaps because of our own prejudice against prison over hospital, certainly when it is clear, is peculiarly harmful, causing chaos in the psychiatric as well as in the judicial systems. while encouraging dysfunction, immaturity, and regression in the defendant. I have always thought that psychiatry's task was to help people cope with reality and to help them act responsibly. This may even include helping a prisoner to cope with the death penalty. Psychiatrists have a heavy responsibility to assist society within their capabilities, to protect the credibility of psychiatry, and to identify and protect appropriately the genuinely impaired defendant.

The amount of malingering, not just transient moments of resistance in the initial phases of the judicial process, is significant. Malingering may start before or at the moment of arrest, or often immediately after a critical confession. Most malingerers drop the pose along the way, leaving a hard core of defendants, frequently facing serious charges, who require enormous amounts of time and energy to bring to trial. The psychiatrist must identify malingering in this setting; he cannot avoid it. Although the diagnosis should be made by exclusion, it is not that clean, and coexisting pathology must be identified and treated.

It is evident that, in theory, the diagnosis of malingering is controversial, and that, in actual practice, it can be most difficult. There is ample, sane, reason to malinger in the criminal setting. Simultaneously, it must be assumed that powerful underlying protective forces, perhaps dependancy, conflict, and rage, are operative in the psyche of all defendants, reinforcing any external motivation to malinger. The persistence of feigning may be related to the intensity of more primitive needs or defenses, as opposed to feelings of guilt, which may generate dissimulation. After clearing away gross pathology, distinctions between external and internal etiologic factors, as directed by the diagnostic manual, may be virtually impossible. The motivation to malinger never really fits an "either-or" paradigm but a "both." Henderson and Batchelor[57], crediting Kretschmer, summarized this fact:

> The criteria "conscious or unconscious" will not serve to distinguish simulation from hysteria, for not all the motives of the healthy mind are conscious, and not all hysterical ones are unconscious. There are all gradations between hysteria and simulation. (p 155)

However, forensic psychiatrists must try to assess, as in the insanity defense, how much awareness and control the defendant does have, and to distinguish between that which is determinate, and that which is a product of free will.

The courts generally need black-and-white answers, competent or not competent. Thus, the psychiatrist cannot usually come to gray conclusions, even if he is only 51% certain. Explanations and recommendations for further observation also must usually come to an end. The court may be unable to respond to the many psychiatric uncertainties that arise, and to psychological interpretation that is so critical to the understanding of some malingerers. These subtleties fall in the realm of the psychiatrist or therapist who may use them to advantage in working with malingerers, and in helping them cope more effectively with their situations. We are physicians, not just detectives, and the malingerers, no matter how venal their crimes and behavior, are human beings under stress. Incompetency and malingering cannot be treated *per se*, but real problems and the underlying anxieties that lead to malingering and dysfunction deserve attention.

Collecting information that is needed to detect malingering in the competency examination, and for the competency examination itself, can be arduous. Often, it entails lengthy interviews and observation. It demands imagination and energy, and even an ability to empathize while not condoning behavior. Mental-status questions and legal checklists are inadequate when dealing with a person who would rather swallow a razor blade than deal with truth. There really is life beyond "the last five presidents of the United States," or "what's the tallest building?" The psychiatrist needs to broaden the inquiry when questioning suspected malingerers, trying always to estimate the *capacity* or *ability* to comprehend, reason, remember, and cooperate in the legal setting. A specific question, for example, "what does a lawyer do?," may elicit the needed answer, but the malingerer's capacity to frustrate standard technique is limitless. Structured approaches and formal lists of questions give the malingerer an open sesame to play his game.

Lastly, there is the problem of dissimulation, which should be "referred for further observation" because it is too complex an issue for justice to be done in this chapter. Concern about dissimulation is expressed relatively infrequently as compared with simulation. Faking good raises a different set of thresholds for the psychiatrist who may worry that a disturbed or defective defendant will be denied justice or treatment, or even may lose his life. Most troublesome is the individual who confesses to a crime he has not committed. At issue, often, is the defendant's sense of autonomy and self, and perhaps his right to punish himself. Dissimulation demands that psychiatrists ask where pride and personality stop and illness begins. The psychiatrist is really challenged by a defendant of questionable mental state who says, in effect, "I'll take my chances in court. I don't need or want you. It's my life." The countertransference problems may be even greater than in simulation.

I look forward to further study of the challenges posed by malingering. Research is needed in the criminal setting to clarify every aspect of this complex, bizarre, frustrating, and sometimes quite adaptive behavior. Certainly, we need a better understanding of the stresses on defendants, of the psychopathology that lends itself to simulation, and of the subjective elements that enter into psychiatric decisions in these particular circumstances.

When one has had enough of faking, of endless testing, and of manipulation of the system through psychiatry and when one's anger becomes palpable, it is time to take a coffee break or, perhaps, a vacation.


*Acknowledgments*

I want to express my appreciation to Judith Groch for her skilled assistance in editing this manuscript, to my family for its loving support, and to all those defendants and co-workers who have taught me so much.

## REFERENCES

1. Gorman WF: Defining malingering. *J Forensic Sci* 1982; 27:401–407.
2. Resnick PJ: The detection of malingered mental illness. *Behav Sci Law* 1984; 2:21–38.
3. MacDonald JM: *Psychiatry and the Criminal,* ed 3. Springfield, Ill, Charles C Thomas Publisher, 1976.
4. Ray IR: *A Treatise on the Medical Jurisprudence of Insanity.* Boston, Charles Little and James Brown, 1838.
5. Schwartz DW: The problem of the malingering defendant, in Rosner R (ed): *Critical Issues in American Psychiatry and the Law,* vol 2. New York, Plenum Press, 1985.
6. Quen JM: *Johann Ludwig Casper—On Dissembling and the Insane.* The Newsletter of the American Academy of Psychiatry and the Law, vol 11, no 1, Baltimore, April 1986.
7. Quen JM: *The Simulation of Sanity: Thomas Erskine, Bernard L. Diamond, and the Marcus Kidnapping Case.* The Newsletter of the American Academy of Psychiatry and the Law, vol 11, no 3, Baltimore, December 1986.
8. Wasyliw OE, Grossman L, Cavanaugh JL, Haywood T: The detection of Malingering in Forensic Groups: MMPI validity scales. *J Pers Assess* 1988; 52(2).
9. Grossman L, Wasyliw OE: A psychometric study of stereotypes: Assessment of malingering in a criminal forensic group. *J Pers Assess* 1988; 52(3).
10. Curran WJ, McGarry AL, Shah SA: *Forensic Psychiatry and Psychology: Perspectives and Standards for Interdisciplinary Practice.* Philadelphia, Davis, 1986.
11. Roesch R, Golding SL: *Competency to Stand Trial.* Chicago, University of Illinois Press, 1980.
12. American Bar Association: *Proposed Criminal Justice Mental Health Standards.* Chicago, American Bar Association, 1984.
13. Brakel SB, Parry J, Weiner, BA: *The Mentally Disabled and the Law,* ed 3. Chicago, American Bar Foundation, 1985.
14. Szasz TS: *The Myth of Mental Illness.* New York, Harper & Row, 1961.
15. Ennis BJ, Litwack TR: Psychiatry and the presumption of expertise: Flipping coins in the courtroom. *Calif Law Rev* 1974; 62(1):693–752.
16. Ziskin J: *Coping with Psychiatric and Psychological Testimony,* vol I. Venice, Calif, Law and Psychology Press, 1980.
17. Rosenhan D. On being sane in insane places. *Science* 1973; 179:250–258.
18. Spitzer RL: More on pseudoscience in science and the case for psychiatric diagnosis. *Arch Gen Psychiatry* 1976; 33:459–470.
19. Menninger KA: Psychology of a certain type of malingering. *Arch Neurol Psychiatry* 1935; 33:507–515.
20. Menninger KA: *Man against Himself.* New York, Harcourt, 1938.
21. Eissler KR: Malingering, in Wilbur GB, Muensterberger W (eds): *Psychoanalysis and Culture.* New York, International Universities Press, Inc, 1951.
22. Menninger KA: *The Vital Balance.* New York, Viking Press, 1963.
23. Wertham F: *The Show of Violence.* New York, Doubleday, 1949.
24. Davidson HA: *Forensic Psychiatry,* ed 2. New York, Ronald Press, 1952.
25. Miller H: Accident neurosis. *Br Med J* 1961; 1:992–998.
26. Szasz TS: Malingering: Diagnosis of social condemnation. *Arch Neurol Psychiatry* 1956; 76:432–443.
27. American Psychiatric Association: *Diagnostic and Statistical Manual of Mental Disorders,* ed 2, DSM–II. Washington, DC, American Psychiatric Association, 1968.
28. American Psychiatric Association: *Diagnostic and Statistical Manual of Mental Disorders* ed 3, DSM–III. Washington, DC, American Psychiatric Association, 1980.

29. American Psychiatric Association: *Diagnostic and Statistical Manual of Mental Disorders* ed 3, rev, DSM–III–R. Washington, DC, American Psychiatric Association, 1987.
30. Steadman H: *Beating a Rap? Defendants Found Incompetent to Stand Trial.* Chicago, University of Chicago Press, 1979.
31. *Estelle v Smith*, 451 U.S. 454 (1981).
32. Halleck S: The criminal's problem with psychiatry, in Allen RC, *et al.* (eds): *Readings in Law and Psychiatry.* Baltimore, Johns Hopkins University Press, 1975, pp 51–54.
33. Bash IY, Alpert M: The determination of malingering. *Ann NY Acad Sci* 1980; 347:86–89.
34. Schachter DL: Amnesia and crime: How much do we really know. *Am Psychol* 1986; 41(3):286–295.
35. Kopelman MD: Crime and amnesia: A review. *Behav Sci Law* 1987; 5:323–342.
36. Parwatikar SD, Holcomb WR, Menninger II KA: The detection of malingered amnesia in accused murderers. *Bull Am Acad Psychiatry Law* 1985; 13:1 97–103.
37. Bash IY: *Malingering A Study Designed to Differentiate between Schizophrenic Offender and Malingerers,* PhD dissertation. Department of Psychology, New York University, New York, NY 1978.
38. Daniel AE, Resnick PJ: Mutism, malingering, and competency to stand trial. *Bull Am Acad Psychiatry Law;* 15:301–308.
39. Arieti S, Bemporad JR: Rare, unclassified and collective psychiatric syndromes, in Arieti S, Brody EB (eds): *The American Handbook of Psychiatry,* vol 3. New York, Basic Books, 1974.
40. Kerns LL: Falsifications in the psychiatric history: A differential diagnosis. *Psychiatry* 1986; 49:13–17.
41. Goodwin DW, Alderson P, Rosenthal R: Clinical significance of hallucinations in psychiatric disorders. *Arch Gen Psychiatry* 1971; 24:76–80.
42. Strauss JS: Hallucinations and delusion as points on continua function. *Arch Gen Psychiatry* 1969; 21:581–586.
43. Orne MT: The use and misuse of hypnosis in court, in Rosner R (ed): *Critical Issues in American Psychiatry and the Law,* vol 2. New York, Plenum Press, 1985, pp 211–245.
44. Redlich FC, Ravitz LJ, Dession GH: Narcoanalysis and truth. *Am J Psychiatry* 1951; 107:586–593.
45. Herman M: Amytal and the Detection of Deception, in Rosner R (ed): *Critical Issues in American Psychiatry and the Law,* vol 2. New York, Plenum Press 1985, pp 187–194.
46. Graham JR: *The MMPI: A Practical Guide.* New York, Oxford University Press, 1977.
47. Grow R, McVaugh W, Eno TD: Faking and the MMPI. *J Clin Psychol* 1980; 36:910–917.
48. Gough HG: Simulated pattern on the Minnesota Multiphasic Personality Inventory. *J Abnorm Soc Psychol* 1947; 42:215–222.
49. Beaber RJ, Marston A, Michelli J, *et al.:* A brief test for measuring malingering in schizophrenic individuals. *Am J Psychiatry* 1985; 142:1478–1481.
50. Exner Jr. JE: *The Rorschach: A Comprehensive System,* vol 2. New York, John Wiley, 1978.
51. Albert S, Fox HM, Kahn MW: Faking psychosis on the Rorschach: Can expert judges detect malingering? *Am J Pers Assess* 1980; 44:115–119.
52. Bruhn AR, Reed MR: Simulation of brain damage on the Bender-Gestalt Test by college subjects. *J Personality Assessment* 1975; 39:244–255.
53. Abrams S: Polygraphy. in Imwinkelried EJ (ed): *Scientific and Expert Evidence,* ed 2. New York, Practicing Law Institute, 1981.
54. Diamond BL: Reasonable medical certainty, diagnostic thresholds and definitions of mental illness in the legal context. *Bull Am Acad Psychiatry Law* 1985; 13:121–128.

55. Rappeport JR: Reasonable medical certainty. *Bull Am Acad Psychiatry Law* 1985; 13:5–15.
56. American Psychiatric Association. *The Principles of Medical Ethics, with Annotations Especially Applicable to Psychiatry.* Washington, DC, American Psychiatric Association, 1986.
57. Henderson D, Batchelor IR: *Henderson and Gillespie's Textbook of Psychiatry.* London, Oxford University Press, 1962.

**16**

# Clinical Neuropsychology
## Application in Criminal, Civil, and Family Court Matters

RICHARD SCHUSTER

Neuropsychology is a growing subspecialty. As sophistication in neuropsychological assessment has increased, applications for neuropsychology have expanded as well. Neurology and rehabilitation medicine have discovered the applicability of clinical neuropsychology. Forensic psychiatry and psychology have also begun to recognize its effectiveness. This chapter first briefly highlights the basic theory and rationale of neuropsychology. The interface of neuropsychology with the law is then examined by specific cases concerning civil, criminal, and family court matters. The aim is to demonstrate how clinical neuropsychology can illuminate issues meaningful to the mental health forensic investigation. In conjunction with a forensic mental health examination, a clinical neuropsychological assessment can often clarify areas that in the past were obscure.

## THE RATIONALE OF CLINICAL NEUROPSYCHOLOGY

Neuropsychology is akin to behavioral neurology.[1] Behavioral neurology focuses on signs, symptoms, and syndromes indicative of neurologic pathology. Behavioral aberration suggests an area and etiology

**RICHARD SCHUSTER** • Comprehensive Rehabilitation Consultants, 310 Madison Avenue, Suite 618, New York, NY 10017; Department of Psychology, Derner Institute, Adelphi University, New York, NY 11530.

of nervous system dysfunction. Clinical neuropsychology works on similar assumptions. Extensive neuropsychological research highlights areas of the brain that tend to be associated with specific behavioral manifestations. In addition, patterns of test variability and behavioral change are also associated with disease processes and/or lesions. For instance, improving or deteriorating conditions show different behavioral patterns; right and left hemispheric dysfunction produce different behavioral aberrations (i.e., language versus nonlanguage); posterior versus anterior lesions tend to produce distinct symptom clusters (i.e., motor executive versus sensory). In addition to simple motor and sensory functions, higher cognitive processes also tend to be associated with different locales of the brain. The work of Luria,[2] highlighting primary (areas which receive and send impulses), secondary (areas in which information is processed), and tertiary (overlapping areas of complex mental processing), is often helpful in this regard. Simply put, language tends to lateralize (or be located) in the left hemisphere while spatial skills tend to lateralize to the right hemisphere. Executive functions (i.e., motor, organizing, planning, etc.) are frequently located anteriorly, while sensory constructional skills are more often located posteriorly (i.e., in the back). Likewise, different lesions foster different symptomatologies. For instance, traumatic head injury frequently results in two main areas of deficit, not only at the point of impact, but frequently on the opposite contralateral side to the impact as well. Disease processes, such as multiple sclerosis, will frequently result in inconsistent motor and sensory findings incongruent with structural organic damage. The neuropsychologist is aware of where skills/functions/abilities tend to be localized in the brain and the course of neurologic disease. Additionally, the neuropsychologist recognizes the idiosyncratic interactions between these two factors. Such a background provides the foundation for neuropsychological investigation. The neuropsychologist also utilizes a sophisticated assessment procedure to investigate neurobehavioral aberration. Such instruments provide a qualitative and quantitative evaluation of brain behaviors often more exact and sensitive than that possible by a clinical examination. In addition, deficits not evident on standard laboratory procedures (such as a CAT scan or EEG) can be reflected in neuropsychological tests. The focus on functional neurobehavioral components in a standardized fashion can provide empirically based information otherwise not available. This conclusion has been repeatedly borne out in research. A wide range of studies indicate that the rate of accuracy for neuropsychological assessments compared favorably to other neurodiagnostic techniques. At times neuropsychological investigations can be more sensitive to deficits than neurologic tools or procedures. Neuropsychological evaluations have thus been firmly established as reliable and valid.[3]

The rationale underlying much of clinical neuropsychology begins with the concept of deficit measurement. An estimate is made of premorbid (i.e., before the injury/disease) capacities; deviations from this level are then noted. Ideally, the patient serves as his own control, such as preinjury test scores or comparisons of motor or sensory responses from each side of the body. Marked deviation from expected patterns of performance is a deficit requiring explanation. Obviously, the deficit can be reflective of any number of factors (i.e., motivational, characterological, psychiatric, medical, orthopedic, neurobehavioral, etc.). If the pattern of deficit is congruent with neurobehavioral syndromes and other variables are deemed by investigation to be insignificant (i.e., the patient is motivated, without significant psychiatric disorder, not orthopedically impaired, etc.), an inference can be made that the deficit is related to neuropsychological limitations. If there are contaminating variables, then these must be investigated further to "tease out" their importance and their contribution to the symptom picture.

Clinical neuropsychological investigations rely on three main methods of examination. The first is highlighted by the Halstead Reitan Neuropsychological Battery.[4] This battery relies on quantitative analysis of deficit measurement. The battery entails a wide variety of assignments that measure motor, sensory, language, tactual, and higher cognitive processes, with cutoff scores based on empirical research to separate the brain impaired from normal populations. (A cutoff score is the optimal score that differentiates these two groups.) The second method of investigaton is highlighted by the extensive work of A. R. Luria. Luria believed that clinical intuition and qualitative evaluation of behavior were the best ways to evaluate the neurologically impaired. His approach emphasizes a qualitative assessment of performance in terms of assessing neurobehavioral deficit, recently incorporated into a standardized neuropsychological battery.[5] The third method centers on a "pathognomonic sign approach." These signs are behaviors that occur almost exclusively in brain-injured groups; a deficit here is strongly indicative of the organically impaired. For instance, a sensory suppression (i.e., no experience of sensation on one side of the body when both sides are touched simultaneously) or a visual field cut (i.e., a loss of one portion of the visual field), are strong indicators of neurologic dysfunction.

Although many neuropsychologists feel comfortable with a standardized neuropsychological investigation, a large number of neuropsychologists apply a more varied approach, selecting a battery geared to the needs of the patient and/or referring physician.[6-8] This flexible battery often consists of a core battery (such as intelligence test, motor test, educational tests, drawing tasks, and personality tests) augmented by specific neuropsychological tests (frequently from standardized batteries) to focus on assessing neuropsychological status relevant to the referral question. Although standardized batteries certainly can be administered in forensic areas, and are at times suggested,[9] they lack the flexibility, adaptability, and specificity needed to answer most questions posed by the court. At the very least, they will frequently need to be augmented by other neuropsychological procedures to provide quantifiable findings necessary to clarify forensic issues and thus may be inordinately time-consuming.

## FORENSIC ASSESSMENT BATTERIES

Given the multitude of questions the forensic mental health expert must address, there is no single procedure geared to answer all forensic issues. Rather, the forensic mental health expert must utilize a variety of techniques and instruments to answer questions posed by the court. A neuropsychological assessment is no exception. Each case demands the development of a battery geared to address the pertinent issues, sensitive to the needs of the court. Consequently, when a neuropsychological examination is suggested, the clarity of the referral question is important. The neuropsychological assessment should be viewed as one part of the mental health forensic investigation, with information incorporated into the total picture to provide an explanation of relevant variables.

## APPLICATIONS OF CLINICAL NEUROPSYCHOLOGY TO FAMILY COURT MATTERS

In family court, the mental health expert is most often involved in the dispositional phase. The Judge has great latitude regarding dispositional alternatives, and the mental health expert is frequently asked for recommendations in this regard. In other matters, the mental health recommendation is central to the court's finding. Custody matters and termination proceedings are two such circumstances. Neuropsychological investigations can be helpful in both dispositional and fact-finding phases. For instance, many of the adolescents before a family court are learning disabled. Investigation of their neuropsychological system and associated learning handicap are often helpful in developing appropriate dispositional alternatives. The following cases, however, were chosen to illustrate the effectiveness of neuropsychological assessment in predispositional studies. In each case neuropsychological assessment was essential in uncovering areas of deficit obscured by standard interview/mental status techniques, providing valuable data to the judge aiding the decision-making process.

## CASE 1

Ms. M. is a 39-year-old woman before the court on a custody visitation dispute. She and her husband are currently estranged, the two children residing with her husband. He alleges that his wife has a severe drinking problem, has been drinking excessively for years, and has failed to take care of the children adequately due to her alcoholic patterns. The children, age 10 and 12, have opted to live with their father, describing their mother as so drunk at times that she is unable to provide parental supervision. Ms. M. asserts that she does not have a drinking problem, that Mr. M. has influenced the children against her, and that the children only wish to live with their father because he is more lenient and permissive in his parental role. She adamantly insists that the issue of alcoholism is a "red herring" and that the best interests of the children would be satisfied if they were returned to her care. After a review of the background data, an interview of family members, and an interview of Mrs. M., she was referred for neuropsychological evaluation.

Clinically, she impressed as a nervous woman not manifesting signs of marked psychiatric dysfunction, such as psychosis. She was pleasant, cooperative, and task involved, obviously interested in doing her best and making a positive impression. There were no indications of current alcohol intoxification when evaluated. Previous family interviews had elicited statements that her drinking at times was excessive (poor work performance, inconsistency in visits, etc.). When interviewed, she provided explanations for these "mishaps," consistently minimizing drinking as a contributor to poor functioning. In order to investigate her disclaimers of alcohol abuse, she was administered a neuropsychological battery geared to assess the neuropsychological deficits typically associated with alcoholism. Statements had been made that she had been drinking heavily for the past 15 years, excessively for the past 10; consequently, there was already a suggestion of chronic long-term alcohol abuse.

Research with alcoholics reveals patterns of neuropsychological deficit most evident in relatively intact language skills (often obscuring intellectual deterioration), with poor nonverbal problem-solving abilities (for instance, rapidly putting blocks together to replicate a pattern), deflated tactual/spatial capacities (for example, rapidly placing forms in a form board, when being blindfolded and remembering their location), and slowed visual-motor learning (i.e., writing corresponding symbols under numbers as quickly as possible). These deficits are noted in relatively intact functioning on the verbal part of the intelligence test, with deflated score on nonverbal functioning, particularly on those tasks that demand new learning or problem-solving ability. Such tests as Block Design and Digit Symbol (replicating designs with blocks and coding symbols to numbers, respectively) are thus often impaired when compared to more intact functioning on tasks highlighting "crystallized" skills (i.e., heavily learned and entrenched), such as vocabulary and general fund of basic knowledge, all subtests from the Wechsler Adult Intelligence Scale—Revised (WAIS-R), a standardized intelligence test. Tasks from the Halstead-Reitan Neuropsychological Test Battery, one of the most researched batteries in neuropsychology, demonstrate typical patterns of deficit. The Category Test (an assignment relying on nonverbal problem-solving abilities) and some components of the Tactual Performance Test (placing forms in a form board as rapidly as possible, blindfolded, with dominant, nondominant, and both hands and then drawing the design board from memory), involving tactual/spatial speed, problem solving, and incidental memory are often impaired as well. Likewise, Trailmaking B (connecting alternate numbers and letters in sequence as rapidly as possible), stressing visual motor speed, concentration, and set flexibility, is frequently impaired. Consequently, Ms. M. was administered a battery that not only focused on personality issues, but was also geared to assess neuropsychological deficits most likely to emerge with alcoholics.

The protocol showed a pattern of expected alcoholic deficits, with significant deficiencies noted in those areas as delineated in the research arising from chronic alcoholic abuse. The findings not only suggested cognitive and neuropsychological limitations in Ms. M.'s basic adaptive functioning, but additionally corroborated family statements. They further suggested that she was a chronic alcoholic, who had been drinking heavily for many years (to the point of developing neuropsychological deficits), and who was still unwilling to accept the extent of her drinking difficulties. The neuropsychological battery was congruent with statements of other family members and collateral sources indicating that this woman had a severe drinking problem, required alcohol rehabilitation, and was not the preferred parental figure because of her drinking difficulties.

## CASE 2

A 45-year-old woman, Mrs. S., was referred for assessment in connection with a neglect proceeding. She was blind, with significant right frontal lobe damage, the result of an automobile accident while intoxicated several years previously. She had a history of explosiveness, and was arrested for assault on several occasions. Mrs. S. also had children from a relationship prior to her accident but had not maintained contact with them. Several years post-injury, she married a man who had had extensive psychiatric hospitalizations, who was diagnosed as schizophrenic, and had a child from this union. History indicates the couple had frequent violent altercations. During one such episode, their child fell or was thrown down a flight

of stairs, sustaining severe head injuries and requiring extensive hospitalization and rehabilitation. After a family court hearing, the child was
subsequently removed and placed in foster care, still requiring a good deal
of therapeutic and special services. At the time of the present assessment,
the question of extension of placement or return of the child was before
the court. The child had made a good adjustment to foster care; Special
Services for Children feared that return would be detrimental to the
child's best interest. At the time of the examination, Mrs. S. had been seen
by a neurologist and psychiatrist retained by her attorney. The neurologist
found no significant neurological limitation or impaired ability to function
as a parent, and this impression was confirmed by the psychiatrist. Although visits had been inconsistent and there were still reports of violent
arguments between Mr. and Mrs. S., neither examiner felt that Mrs. S.
showed significant impairment that would interfere with the child's return. In this context, Mrs. S. was referred for evaluation to the Family
Court Mental Health Clinic and was seen by a staff psychiatrist and a
neuropsychologist. She was verbal and able to provide a basic chronological case summary, and showed no marked psychiatric disorder. Although
her history suggested significant characterological problems, Mrs. S. had
been involved in a neighborhood mental health center (from which she
received a positive report), and believed that she and her husband were
now capable of having their child returned. She asserted that she had no
difficulties functioning (aside from her blindness), and that she and her
husband were capable parental figures. A neuropsychological assessment
was administered to investigate the intactness of her neuropsychological
system with implications concerning parenting abilities.

Because Mrs. S. was blind, a select neuropsychological battery was
required. The battery consisted of assignments that would not be affected
by her blindness. This entailed the WAIS-R Verbal IQ, the Tactual Performance Test (normally this assignment is executed blindfolded), the
Rhythm Test (identifying rhythms as the same or different), the Wepman
Auditory Discrimination Test (identifying similar sounding words as the
same or different), the Finger Tapping Test (tapping a telegraph key as
rapidly as possible, with one's hand resting on the key platform), and the
Single and Double Tactile Simultaneous Stimulation (i.e., lightly touching
either hand, cheek, both hands, both cheeks, or hand/cheek on opposite
sides of the body). If impaired, even this truncated battery should reveal in
Mrs. S. neuropsychological deficits impeding functioning and deficiencies
obscured by her good verbal presentation. Results indicated marked neurologic dysfunction, congruent with the history and area of lesion, indicative of significant limitations in her neuropsychological system. As her
deficits were most prominently right frontal in nature, fostering relatively
intact verbal skills (particularly in light of her blindness, which obscured
testing spatial/perceptual deficits), her clinical presentation seemed more
"intact" than was in fact the case. Impaired planning, strategy formation,
and poor impulse control were evident in the manner she executed the
neuropsychological assessments. Even episodic social judgment (as noted

on responses to the social comprehension questions of the intelligence test) was evident. Although verbal intelligence tested in the average range, her performance nevertheless suggested problems with judgment and impulse control (such as shouting fire in a movie theater), congruent with neurobehavioral deficits of frontal lobe dysfunction. These findings, in light of her history of explosive behavior, her chronic problems in interpersonal relations, and her limited judgment, painted a picture of an individual whose premorbid personality characteristics and current neuropsychological deficits augured poorly for her ability to be an adequate parental figure in the foreseeable future. The neuropsychological assessment augmented historical data suggesting that if a young child was returned to her care, inconsistent detrimental parenting would be likely. Evaluation of her spouse revealed significant parenting deficiencies as well. Return at this juncture thus seemed premature; recommendations were made for continued services in the community. The judge concurred, keeping the child in foster care with recommendations to improve Mr. and Mrs. S.'s parenting skills and augment the parent–child bond.

## NEUROPSYCHOLOGICAL APPLICATIONS IN CRIMINAL PROCEEDINGS

The interplay of brain dysfunction and behavior can be of importance in numerous aspects of criminal proceedings. The importance of clarifying neurobehavioral aspects of functioning can arise from the moment of arrest to sentencing and dispositional guidelines. Obviously, cognitive and neuropsychological capacities are of extreme importance in terms of competency to stand trial. However, neuropsychological deficiencies can be of relevance in other less obvious areas. The more objective and empirical manner in which neuropsychological tests arrive at conclusions can be helpful in examining ambiguous and/or "unexplainable" behaviors. The case examples that follow were chosen with this in mind.

### CASE 4

John, a 17-year-old adolescent, was accused of murdering a young child while babysitting. Although charges were not brought for over a year (despite a Bureau of Child Welfare investigation), finally, at the insistence of the baby's parents, John was accused of murder and arrested. At the time of arrest, John made statements that "seemed" to implicate him as being responsible for the child's death.

John had always been in special classes for the language impaired. Although he was of overall average intellectual capacity, his history revealed that his language skills were significantly deflated in receptive and expressive areas (i.e., his ability to understand and speak language), both being markedly below chronological age. He consistently received diagnoses from the Committee on the Handicapped of minimal brain dysfunction and developmental expressive and receptive language disorders. His attorney had severe doubts that John understood the *Miranda* warnings at the time of his arrest and requested an investigation in this regard.

John's investigation entailed a review of his records (including school reports, school evaluations, police reports, and MHC summaries), a parent conference, a detailed interview with him, and a neuropsychological assessment. He was administered a battery not only to examine broad cognitive and personality functioning, but also to assess language and academic skills specifically as they relate to the question posed by his attorney. Congruent with past findings, there was a significant differential between verbal and nonverbal skills. John's Performance (nonverbal) IQ was in the low average/average range; his language skills were in the mild retarded range. His Full Scale IQ was on borderline level. His academic skills were extremely poor, below third grade, and below the first percentile for individuals his age. He was able to read only an occasional simple word. When given a test relying on receptive language skills (Token Test, following simple commands with different colored tokens, i.e., "put the red circle on the green square"), he was constantly confused, falling within the range for individuals with known aphasic (i.e., organically related language dysfunction) disorders. The aphasia screening test (Reitan-Indiana) revealed pervasive language problems, including naming deficits, spelling handicaps, expressive limitations, articulation problems, and right-left disorientation. For example, when asked to read a simple phrase, "place left hand to right ear", John said "please lift, leave hand off right ear." His motor sensory survey indicated anomalies indicative of left-hemisphere dysfunction: his dominant right hand showing reduced motor speed as compared to his nondominant left hand and right-sided tactile skills (i.e., touch sensation) additionally limited on a task of single and double simultaneous stimulation (i.e., the left hemisphere "controlling" right-sided motor/sensory capacities). Assignments testing both expressive and receptive vocabulary revealed marked deficits as well, congruent with his verbal intelligence. The protocol was indicative of significant left-hemisphere dysfunction (i.e., the hemisphere associated primarily with language), highlighting neuropsychological deficits as the prime impediment to impaired language/educational ability. Because John is illiterate and the *Miranda* warnings require at least a fifth-grade reading level,[10] giving him the *Miranda* warnings to read would in no way enhance his understanding. When the *Miranda* warnings were recited to him by the examiner, John was asked if he understood what was said. Although he nodded affirmatively, when asked to explain what each meant, he was markedly confused, even with concretization he found it difficult to grasp what was required. Finally, after much explanation, he grasped the essence of the *Miranda* warnings, but only after considerable time, effort, and alternate examples were supplied by the examiner. It was concluded that, because of pervasive language and educational impairments, John would not have adequately understand the *Miranda* warnings when arrested, even if he nodded affirmatively. After this report was presented, the charge was reduced, and John was given probation.

## CASE 4

Kenny, who is 23 years old, was accused of sodomizing his step-mother's 7-year-old daughter. At the time of his arrest, Kenny made a videotaped statement that he had sexually abused this child. His attorney, when discussing the case with his client, suspected that Kenny had been coerced or unduly influenced to make the videotaped confession. This was Kenny's only arrest. There were indications that the police had told him that, if he made the confession, he could go home, and that they were only interested in "helping him." After a background investigation and a viewing of his videotaped confession, Kenny was seen for neuropsychological assessment. Prior to the assessment, he had been seen by a forensic psychiatrist who had referred Kenny for testing; the psychiatrist subsequently integrated the evaluation into a comprehensic forensic report.

Review of records revealed that Kenny had a history of placement after he was abandoned by his family. There were indications he was a hyperactive child with additional learning problems. He was in special classes for children with learning difficulties. He had a history of impulsivity and poor judgment, and was often described as a follower. He corroborated statements made to his attorney that the police told him, if he just answered a few questions, he would be released and referred for outpatient care. He added that, when he made his confession to the assistant district attorney, he believed this man to be a "therapist." He was confused and bewildered, uncertain as to what to do, looking to the police and believing what they told him was true. He added: "I was pressured and rushed, I had no time to think, I just wanted to get back home." Given this set of circumstances, the neuropsychological assessment was especially geared to evaluate Kenny's judgment and higher executive functions, including his capacity to plan, assess situations, and develop independent strategies. Susceptibility to subordinate himself to authority, especially in novel or unstructured circumstances, also needed to be examined. Neuropsychological investigation revealed overall cognitive functioning in the borderline range (outperformed by 94% of his peers). He performed poorest on tasks highlighting social judgment/comprehension, social sequencing (i.e., rearranging cards to tell a story), and visual-motor learning (i.e., rapidly coding symbols to digits). Congruent with his history of learning difficulties, his academic skills were barely third grade. The battery consistently highlighted left frontal dysfunction. Skills sensitive to right-hemispheric dysfunction, particularly posterior (i.e., in the back part of the brain), were best preserved (i.e., simple copying tasks, tasks of visual memory, assignments relying on sensory skills, etc.). Manual dexterity though showed anomalies suggestive of left frontal dysfunction with his dominant right hand consistently outperformed by his nondominant left hand. Of particular note was the extreme problem he had on a task relying on new learning strategy and conceptualization. His performance on this task was essentially random on the more demanding subtests, and he was unable to develop a strategy or devise the principle. Projective testing suggested an immature adjustment, an inability to assess highly complex social situations, perservative features, and a tendency to look to others for direction and advice. The protocol strongly indicated that when Kenny is unable to develop independent strategies and plans, he consistently looks to others for such input, particularly in new, complex, or threatening social situations. As noted, this was Kenny's only arrest. The examiner concluded that, in such a stressful and novel situation, Kenny's neuropsychological/personality deficits, especially frontal lobe dysfunction, which impairs executive behaviors (i.e., planning, initiating, and formulating actions), would make him particularly susceptible to authority figures. It was felt that he could be easily influenced in situations such as that presented when arrested, charged with a crime, and (according to Kenny) assured that if he made a confession all would be well. His capacity to assess the ramifications of his actions would be undermined by his inability to process novel information and independently develop an alternate response. Presentation of the forensic evaluations resulted in the district attorney's allowing Kenny to plea to the minimum offense.

## NEUROPSYCHOLOGICAL APPLICATIONS TO CIVIL MATTERS

Neuropsychological testing is often initiated in civil cases involving postconcussion syndrome.[11] This syndrome is frequently not readily manifest in obvious neurologic findings, thus requiring neuropsychological assessment to delineate areas of deficit. Consequently, when a client complains of typical postconcussion symptoms (changes of personality, depression, emotional lability, fatigue, irritability, etc.), without clear neurologic findings, a neuropsychological assessment can clarify the extent and severity of the symptom picture. It can also help differentiate between the psychiatric and neurologic reaction to trauma, a distinction that will have ramification concerning outcome, intervention, and vocational rehabilitation. Obviously, where brain insult is an issue, the need for neuropsychological investigation is immediately suggested. The next case was selected to emphasize the effectiveness of a clinical neuropsychological examination to discover missed deficits despite extensive rehabilitation. Although deficits were not readily identifiable clinically, they had significant repercussions vocationally and personally, and were a prime factor in terms of assessing eventual damages.

## CASE 5

Jim is a 22-year-old man, who was injured at age 19, and is currently involved in personal-injury litigation. At the time of the injury, Jim was attending college; he was an A student, whose functioning throughout high school had also always been superior. Pre-injury educational testing had revealed his functioning consistently in the top 2% of the population. He performed excellently on the college boards (SATs) with scores on both English and Mathematics in the 700s. Achievement test scores were all in the 98th and 99th percentiles. An IQ test that was given upon entrance to a private school in first grade revealed Jim's functioning to be within the very superior range (IQ 148). His accident had resulted in an orthopedic injury, which, after extensive rehabilitation, now only impeded left-handed manual dexterity mildly in terms of basic adaptive abilities. Although a head injury was initially suspected, neuropsychological deficit was never investigated throughout 2 years of rehabilitation. Mental status examinations consistently described him as unimpaired. Eventually, Jim returned to college and, although requiring an extra year to complete his college education, he eventually did so. Although his grades fell from essentially an A average to Bs and Cs, he nevertheless proceeded to find employment in a hospital. He had always planned to be a doctor but had performed so poorly on the Med Boards that he decided to work first in a hospital on a semiprofessional level, not attempting medical school at this juncture. The neuropsychological investigation was precipitated by his failure to work effectively in the hospital even in a semiprofessional capacity. After six months, he was fired with complaints from his employer that he was unable to meet levels of productivity.

After review of background information (including medical records and prior educational reports), discussion with his family, and an interview with the client, a neuropsychological/vocational evaluation was administered. The battery included intelligence testing, academic survey, constructional tasks (i.e., drawing and copying assignments), memory tests, motor/sensory survey, and complex tests of neuropsychological intactness stressing higher integrative capacities and efficiency. Standard vocational tests (clerical aptitude test, test of spatial mechanical abilities) and projective techniques were also administered. The results indicated pervasive neuropsychological deficit. Overall cognitive functioning had fallen from well within the very superior range to the high average range with a 30-point discrepancy between verbal and nonverbal skills (i.e., verbal skills now in the superior range, nonverbal skills in the low average/average range). Although Jim's word recognition was in the superior range, his reading efficiency was barely competitive for incoming college students, well below expectations for a young man with excellent verbal abilities planning to enter medical school. His arithmetic skills were only average for individuals his age. His performance on neuropsychological tests consistently revealed deficits on these skills associated with right-hemispheric dysfunction. Even rather simple drawing and copying tasks were done poorly. Assignments relying on visual scanning (i.e., rapidly and accurately scanning visual material) showed impairment. His ability to plan, devise new principles, and develop alternate strategies was in the impaired range, despite excellent verbal capacities. His performance on routine vocational aptitude tests centered around the low average range as well. It was clear that Jim had suffered neurologic damage. There were also indications of neurobehavioral deficits. Paradoxically, the history, interview, and testing revealed that he seemed more placid and "laissez-faire" than previously, despite obvious deficits, an observation congruent with neurobehavioral changes associated with right frontal damage. These results suggested the need for a complete neurologic evaluation. A subsequent CAT-scan revealed right-hemisphere atrophy. The neuropsychological report provided a strong basis to predict significant vocational losses unsuspected prior to the investigation. As he was right-hand dominant, left orthopedic impairments would not have significantly impeded his ability to function in many vocational areas. However, his significant neuropsychological deficits undermined his ability to function in advanced training, limiting his options markedly. Investigation indicated a reduction in future earning capacity and suggested a possible need for cognitive retraining and additional vocational exploration, all areas of damages that, prior to the neuropsychological investigation, were never even considered. Jim's excellent verbal skills, very superior premorbid intelligence, and left-hand orthopedic impairment had effectively occluded the extent of his neuropsychological deficit. As is often the case with right-hemisphere dysfunction, this "silent" area of the brain is frequently "missed" clinically until neuropsychological investigation reveals impairment.

## CONCLUSION

Clinical neuropsychology can be an effective adjunct to the forensic mental health investigation. Neuropsychological examination often provides a more objective and quantifiable evaluation of neurobehavioral dysfunctions than that gleaned through clinical interview, standard psychological testing, or standard neurologic examination. It is hoped that this chapter demonstrates the potential uses of clinical neuropsychology in areas not typically associated with its effectiveness. As stressed, the neuropsychological assessment is one part of an overall forensic approach, geared to provide useful information to clarify the forensic picture. Its effectiveness in highlighting neurobehavioral components is noted, particularly in areas in which clinical interviews alone are insufficient to amplify symptomatology.

## REFERENCES

1. Rourke BP, Brown G: Clinical neuropsychology and behavioral neurology: Similarities and differences, in Filskov SB, Boll T (eds): *Handbook of Clinical Neuropsychology*, vol II. New York, John Wiley & Sons, 1986, pp 3–18.

2. Luria AR: *The Working Brain: An Introduction to Neuropsychology.* New York, Basic Books, Inc, 1973.
3. Crockett D, Clark C, Klonoff H: Introduction—an overview of neuropsychology, in Filskov SB, Boll T (eds): *Handbook of Clinical Neuropsychology,* vol I. New York, John Wiley & Sons, Inc, 1981, pp 1–37.
4. Reitan RM, Wolfson D: *The Halstead-Reitan Neuropsychological Test Battery.* Tucson, Ariz Neuropsychology Press, 1985.
5. Golden CJ, Moses JA, *et al.: Clinical Neuropsychology: Interface with Neurologic and Psychiatric disorders.* New York, Grune & Stratton, Inc, 1983.
6. Goodglass H: The flexible battery in neuropsychological assessment, in Incagnoli T, Goldstein G, Golden C (eds): *Clinical Application of Neuropsychological Test Batteries. New York, Plenum Press, 1986, pp 121–134.*
7. *Lezak M: Neuropsychological Assessment.* New York, Oxford University Press, 1976.
8. Hartlage L, Telzrow C: *Neuropsychological Assessment and Intervention with Children and Adolescents.* Sarasota, Fla, Professional Resources Exchange, 1986.
9. Golden CJ: Forensic neuropsychology: Introduction and Overview, in Golden C, Strider M (eds): *Forensic Neuropsychology.* New York, Plenum Press, 1986, pp 1–47.
10. McMahon EA: Forensic issues in clinical neuropsychology, in Golden CJ, Vicente PJ (eds): *Foundations of Clinical Neuropsychology.* New York, Plenum Press, 1983, pp 401–427.
11. McMahon EA, Satz P: Clinical neuropsychology: Some forensic applications, in Filskoz SB, Boll T (eds): *Handbook of Clinical Neuropsychology,* vol I. New York, John Wiley & Sons, Inc, 1981, pp 686–701.

# 17

# Special Considerations in the Evaluation of Alleged Sex Offenders



## J. M. W. BRADFORD



## INTRODUCTION

There are various indications that sexual offenders demand intensive and urgent study. In the lay press, such recent reports as the allegations of sexual abuse at the Manhattan Beach preschool in California have alerted North American citizens to the very serious problem that exists. A national poll by the *Los Angeles Times* (1985) showed that between 10.9 and 17.6 million American men have sexually abused a child. It also showed that 27% of females and 16% of males were victims of a sexual assault.[1] In Canada, the federal ministries of Justice and National Health and Welfare and the Attorney General of Canada established, in 1980, a committee on Sexual Offences Against Children and Youths. Commonly known as the Badgley Committee, it reported, in 1984, that one in two females and one in three males were victims of unwanted sexual acts on the basis of a Gallup survey. These acts included the whole spectrum of sexual activity from minor fondling to a sexually aggressive act such as rape.[2] According to the study, 4 out of 100 young females are raped and 2 out of 100 are subjected to unwanted anal penetration.



**J.M.W. BRADFORD** • Department of Psychiatry, Faculty of Health Sciences, University of Ottawa, Ottawa, Ontario, Canada; Forensic Psychiatry and the Sexual Behaviors Clinic, Royal Ottawa Hospital, Ottawa, Ontario, Canada K1Z 7K4.

Sixty percent of these children are reported as having been threatened or physically coerced. At least a quarter of the perpetrators were a family member or an adult in a position of trust in relation to the children. In only about one sixth of the cases was the perpetrator a stranger. Forty percent of all sexually motivated homicides are perpetrated against children. Virtually all the perpetrators are males, with only 1% being female.

When studies look at the number of victims per offender, some startling findings have been reported. Abel *et al.* (1981) have reported that frotteurs and exhibitionists have the highest numbers of victims per offender, with 528.8 for frotteurs and 199.5 for exhibitionists. In the same study, homosexual pedophiles had an average of 31 victims, whereas heterosexual pedophiles had 62 victims.[3] The pedophiles were found to have approximately 10 times as many victims as the rapists. In a later study, Abel *et al.* (1985) found that 411 paraphiliacs admitted to 238,711 attempted sex acts and completed 218,900 on 138,137 victims.[4] Most significantly, they showed that there was a high degree of crossover between the various paraphilias. Fifty percent of pedophiles were rapists, 29% were exhibitionists, 13% were voyeurs, 5% were sadists, 3% masochists, 8% frotteurs, and, in addition to these, other paraphilias were present. A similar crossover occurred in the men who primarily presented as rapists. This study had elaborate safeguards to protect confidentiality. In a similar study, Bradford *et al.* (1987), without employing the same safeguards with regard to confidentiality and using a proportional index of multiple deviations, found that a very similar pattern of crossover exists between the various paraphiliac groups.[5] In this particular study, 443 adult males, who presented the Sexual Behaviours Clinic of the Royal Ottawa Hospital, were studied in relation to admitted sexually deviant behaviors. Out of the primary paraphilias, significant crossover occurred. For example, exhibitionists admitted to a proportional index of .200 for heterosexual pedophilia. This means that 20% of the exhibitionists have also engaged in heterosexual pedophilia. Further, 20% admit to heterosexual hebephilia, 10% to homosexual pedophilia, 8% to homosexual hebephilia, 11% have engaged in transvestism, 51% in voyeurism, 21% in scatologia (or telephone lewdness), 30% in frotteurism, 13% have attempted rape, and 6% have raped. What is more shocking is that these results were obtained from a pretrial forensic psychiatric population without the same confidentiality safeguards that Abel and his coworkers had. This type of disclosure must be considered an underestimate of the true levels as it could have severe negative consequences if considered on an individual basis. What is of the utmost clinical relevance is the multidimensional nature of the paraphilias and the importance of taking this into account in the clinical assessment of the paraphilias. One cannot assume that if a patient presents with exhibitionism, he has no tendency toward pedophilia or that he is not a sexually aggressive or "rape prone" male. It also clearly emphasizes the need for special expertise in assessing the sexual offender and supports the need for a specialized evaluation of all sexual offenders, using sex hormones, sexual questionnaires, and penile tumescence testing in order to make a diagnosis. Simply relying on a clinical interview and mental status examination is insufficient and unreliable.

## THE ROLE OF SEX HORMONES

Testosterone (T) is the hormone that is essential for the maintenance of male sexual behavior. The testes are the principal organs in the male for T synthesis and are responsible for 95% of the body's total T production. If there is an androgen deficit, a decline in sexual behavior occurs. The rate of decline is variable but it is usual for ejaculation to be affected first, then erections, and lastly copulatory behavior.[6] Surgical castration has been widely used to treat sexual offenders as a result of this effect.[7–9] The effect of castration is the reduction of available androgen, specifically T but also dihydrotestosterone (DHT). T is converted to DHT in various target organs. Both T and DHT have an effect at the androgen receptors. It is the sensitivity of the androgen receptors in the central nervous system, provided there is sufficient T above a specific individually determined threshold, that determines male sexual behavior patterns.

### The Role of Testosterone in Sexual Aggression

The relationship of T to aggressive sexual behavior in man has also been extensively researched since 1971. Various studies have shown positive correlations between plasma T levels and sexual aggression as measured by questionnaires on aggression.[10–20] In a recent study of 146 sexual offenders, a highly significant correlation was found between plasma T and a highly violent group of sexual offenders when compared to less violent sexual offenders. The classification of "no" ($n=23$), "low" ($n=101$), and "high" ($n=22$) violence groups was on the basis of manifested violent behavior rather than on the use of questionnaires on aggression. In the "high" violence group, there was additional physical injury caused by the perpetrator other than the sexual act itself. Sexually motivated homicide and attempted homicide and sadistic rape and child molesting formed the "high" violence group. The "no" violence group was mostly nonviolent pedophiles and some exhibitionists. Further, the "high" violence group had a mean plasma T level that was at the upper limit of the normal range (mean = 29.6 nmol/L, SD = 5.84). The normal range is 10 to 30 nmol/L with a sensitivity of 0.3 nmol/L and a coefficient of variation of 10%. The normal range is standardized on the mean and 2 standard deviations from the mean. This differed at statistically significant levels from the "no" violence (mean = 23.8 nmol/L, SD = 6.11) and the "low" violence groups (mean = 22.8 nmol/L, SD = 7.05). The three groups were studied, using analysis of variance (ANOVA) and analysis of covariance (ANCOVA) procedures, and using the Neuman-Keuls multiple comparison technique (ANOVA $f = 9.42$, $P = .0001$). When controlled for age, the plasma T of the "high" violence group remained statistically significant when compared to the "low" and the "no" violence groups (ANCOVA $f = 7.08$, $P = .001$). Plasma T levels may therefore be a factor associated with helping to identify a high-risk sexual offender, if the levels are greater than 30 nmol/L and, particularly, if the plasma T is above 35 nmol/L. If the levels are low and vary, and high levels of luteinizing hormone (LH) and follicle stimulating hormone (FSH) are present, this could be indicative of Klinefelter's syndrome or a mosaic of Klinefelter's syndrome. Klinefelter's syndrome and other sex chromosome abnormalities have been described in the literature, and, in my clinical experience, I have found them to be associated with a wide range of paraphilias.[21–30] There are also potential risks for treatment with replacement T, if the person is not carefully assessed for the presence of paraphilia prior to starting treatment.

Plasma T levels can also be an indication of hypersexuality that has treatment implications. If the plasma T levels are above normal range or in the upper limits of the normal and are accompanied by a high sex drive and high levels of deviant sexual fantasy, the treatment of choice would be antiandrogen treatment. This could either be the use of medroxyprogesterone acetate (MPA) or cyproterone acetate (CPA). CPA is not currently available in the United States. The actual schedules of treatment and management are outlined below. In broad terms, hypogonadism is associated with hyposexual behavior and clearly this is desirable in a patient with a paraphilia. There is also considerable research on sex-hormone-dependent brain differentiation that has been well described by Dorner.[31] This factor is likely to play an increasingly important clinical role in evaluating the paraphilias, as androgen-dependent brain differentiation permanently establishes the central nervous system response to androgen- and estrogen-specific sexual behavior. In the future, this factor is also likely to have an important role in the evaluation of the paraphilias, particularly in the evaluation of pedophilia, where there are significant differences in recidivism rates between heterosexual and homosexual pedophiles.

## THE SEXUAL AROUSAL PATTERNS

Clinical experience in the evaluation of sexual offenders has shown that the self-reports of deviant sexual behavior in this population are clearly unreliable. Sexual offenders tend to minimize the nature of their activities or deny them completely, particularly when these activities are bizarre and socially unacceptable. This would include sexual sadism in which the importance of identifying the problem cannot be overemphasized. It has to be accepted, therefore, that sexual offenders will conceal the true nature of their deviant sexual arousal patterns which, in turn, dictates the degree and nature of their deviant sexual behavior. Over the past decade, the psychophysiological assessment of the sexual arousal patterns has become an important diagnostic tool in the evaluation and treatment of sexual offenders. The psychophysiological assessment of sexual arousal patterns was developed by Freund in the mid-sixties.[32–34] Since then many studies have shown that the sexual arousal patterns of almost all the paraphilias can be identified by this method. Rapists, child molesters, sadists and responses to treatment have all been quantified and distinguished.[35–39] Although there is ample evidence of the clinical relevance of these assessments, using either a Barlow gauge or a mercury-in-rubber or indium and gallium strain gauge, there are still questions about the reliability and validity, particularly in cases in which the person denies any paraphiliac or sexually aggressive tendency. Although these are important clinical tools, their use in a medicolegal context has to be subject to a considerable element of caution. They are not to be used to decide the guilt or innocence of a person but can be used as part of treatment planning in a predispositional assessment.

The actual clinical technique involves measuring the change in penile circumference of the sexual offender in response to various stimuli. The stimulus material varies from one laboratory setting to another. A typical assessment would involve a series of 35-mm color slides depicting nude males and females of various ages. Closeups of genital areas would also be included. This part of the evaluation would be used to judge the age and sexual erotic preference of the offender. A series of audiotape depictions of various sexual acts then follows. The audiotape depictions are typically 120 seconds in length, and include sexual aggression, sadism, scenarios of rape, mutually consenting heterosexual sexual activity, and nonsexual assault. In the case of pedophilia, there are scenarios of both homosexual and heterosexual pedophilic acts, including acts depicting both nonphysical and physical coercion, sexual sadism, and incest. The response to the deviant stimuli is compared to the response to adult mutually consenting heterosexual sex. A number of laboratories have started to use videotaped stimuli. These explicit stimuli involve both visual and audio modalities and usually elicit higher levels of sexual arousal.

There are many elements of variability that make it difficult to compare the results of one assessment to another. The stimuli vary in content, presentation, and degree of explicitness. The internal validity of the procedure has been brought into question by the observations that males have a degree of voluntary control over their erections.[40,41] The external validity has been questioned because of poor correlations between the self-report measures of sexual arousal and the penile tumescence responses.[42,43] In addition, there is a degree of satiation that occurs if the stimuli are used recurrently in the same subject. This means there are potential differences between naïve subjects and subjects recurrently exposed to this type of measure. In my own laboratory, a recent analysis has shown that incest should be seen as a special category in assessment. Incest perpetrators do not consistently present as pedophiles when their sexual arousal responses are analyzed even in "admitter" perpetrators of incest. This finding has enormous implications for the assessment of alleged incest perpetrators who are "nonadmitters." If they complete an assessment and are found to be nonpedophilic, the conclusion has implications for treatment and prognosis but cannot, under any circumstances, be construed that they did not commit any incestuous act.

There are also measurement issues that have to be considered. The penis is a soft, expansile organ that can shrink as well as expand in response to a sexual stimulus. This potential means that establishing the outer limits of the percentage of full erection scales can be difficult. Some studies have found a test–retest reliability for a basal penile circumference correlation of $r = .94$, and for 100% of full erection, the correlation was $r = .75$.[44] It has been concluded that simple peak amplitude measures are just as accurate as the percentage of full erection measures. There is also the minimum erectile response that can be considered as a valid response. Even the most accurate equipment has a 2% to 3% of full erection margin of error. In millimeter measurements, this means an error of at least 1mm of circumference change can occur in the equipment. Responses less than 5% of full erection are unreliable and inconclusive and should mostly be ignored. Responses of 10% of full erection and above are most reliable and should be considered for clinical interpretation.

Therefore, in spite of the extensive research that clearly shows that penile tumescence responses have the capacity to discriminate rapists and pedophiles from normals, the validity and interpretation of the results of the procedure remain controversial.

## SEXUAL QUESTIONNAIRES

Sexual questionnaires assist in the assessment of sexual offenders in a number of ways. First, they ease the acquisition of information based on the clinical interview of the individual and ensure that all important areas are covered. Second, questionnaires are a less threatening forum for acquiring detailed sexual information than a face-to-face interview even with the most skilled interviewer. In the Sexual Behaviors Clinic of the Royal Ottawa Hospital, a standardized package of questionnaires is used. We have found that the Derogatis Sexual Functioning Inventory (DSFI) is a very useful investigatory tool. It is a multidimensional test that evaluates the current sexual functioning of the individual.[45] It covers 10 essential areas of sexual functioning; specifically, information, experience, drive, attitudes, symptoms (of psychopathology), affects, gender role definition, fantasy, body image, and sexual satisfaction. In addition, there is a global summary score, the Sexual Functioning Index (SFI), and an overall self-report measure of the individuals' subjective judgment of their sexual functioning, the Global Sexual Satisfaction Index (GSSI). The scales that are the most clinically useful in the assessment of the paraphilias are information, experience, drive, and fantasy. Masters and Johnson reported that sexual dysfunction was frequently related to a lack of accurate sexual information.[46] The same is true, to a lesser degree, for the paraphilias, where inadequate sexual knowledge leads to sexual dysfunction difficulties, reduces sexual experience, and hampers the establishment of mature sexual relationships. This, in turn, aggravates the paraphiliac tendency. The measure of sexual experience is important as it provides information with regard to the social skill functioning of the patient. The lack of adequate heterosexual social skills is an important deficiency in the paraphilias and particularly in pedophilia. The drive measure that is taken in conjunction with the sexual fantasy scale assists in the diagnosis of hypersexuality, which has important treatment implications.

Other useful questionnaires are the Bradford Sexual History Inventory, which quantifies a number of different paraphiliac activities, and also a pedophile cognition scale developed by Gene Abel and his associates, which quantifies the degree of pedophilic cognitive distortions present. Questionnaires that evaluate the heterosexual social skill capacity of the individual should also be considered.

## TREATMENT AND MANAGEMENT PLANNING

If as a result of the assessment there is evidence of anomalous sexual preference, or evidence of "rape proneness," or sadism, or if one of the paraphilias is present, a management plan linked with a treatment program is the next step.

The management plan would have to consider the legal status of the individual and the degree of potential dangerousness necessitating inpatient as opposed to outpatient treatment of the individual. (In my experience, 90% of patients are manageable as outpatients.) An often misunderstood facet of the management plan is the motivation of the individual for treatment. Certain individuals with a paraphilia are dismissed by psychiatrists as "unmotivated and therefore untreatable." This is a complex issue but one which has to be considered in the management plan. The legal status of the individual can be used as a motivating force. The prospect of probation with a condition of psychiatric treatment can be a strong motivating force in the face of incarceration as an alternate possibility. Further, the person could be severely traumatized as result of marital and family difficulties with the disclosure of his deviant behavior. Dealing with these issues ahead of any specific treatment program for the paraphilias can be crucial in obtaining cooperation and adequate levels of motivation. This is accomplished by educating the family and other support systems as to the nature of the paraphilias and the prospects for treatment.

The aim of treatment is to assist the patient in reducing his deviant sexual arousal. The treatment choices are either an antiandrogen treatment program or a behavioral treatment program. The treatment depends on the person's informed consent and also the clinical aspects of the case. If there is evidence of serious sexual aggression or sadism, this would be a strong indication for an antiandrogen approach. If there is evidence of hypersexuality (i.e., high levels of plasma testosterone and a high sexual drive), this would be an indication for sex drive reduction using antiandrogens. The presence of anomalous sexual preference without the above clinical features can be treated by antiandrogens, or a behavioral treatment approach, or a combined treatment program with the antiandrogen being used initially to suppress the deviant sexual behavior and to avoid any further conflict with the law, and the behavioral treatment program providing self-control strategies, including relapse prevention measures. Antiandrogen and hormonal treatment approaches include the use of cyproterone acetate (CPA), a very powerful and specific antiandrogen which is not available in the United States, and medroxyprogesterone acetate (MPA), a progestational agent with antigonadotropic properties that has had a fairly wide exposure in different treatment programs in the United States.

## Antiandrogens and Hormonal Agents

The antiandrogen and hormonal treatment of sexual offenders is a pharmacological method of reducing the sexual drive and, consequently, affecting the sexual behavior of sexual offenders. It has always been assumed that the direction of the sexual drive was unaffected, although recent work with CPA shows differential effects on sexual arousal patterns with a reduction of pedophilic sexual arousal but less effect on the sexual arousal to adult mutually consenting heterosexual intercourse.[47] Hormonal agents, starting initially with estrogens, have also been used for sexual drive reduction.[48–50] The hormonal agent that has received the most attention in the treatment of sexual offenders in North America is MPA. A number of studies have shown its efficacy in the treatment of sexual offenders.[51–57]

MPA has a mechanism of action principally through the induction of testosterone-A-reductase in the liver, which accelerates the metabolism of T. The plasma production rate of T is reduced through increased clearance.[58] The levels of T are also reduced by the antigonadotropic effect. It also possible that MPA has a degree of activity on the androgen receptors.

CPA has antiandrogenic, antigonadotropic, and progestational effects.[59] Its principal mode of action as a true antiandrogen is on the androgen receptors. CPA blocks the intracellular T uptake, the intracellular metabolism of the androgens, as well as the receptor binding.[60] CPA appears to have a main effect on receptors that have a high affinity for dihydrotestosterone (DHT).

CPA has a number of therapeutic indications other than the treatment of sexual deviation, including treatment of prostatic carcinoma. It has also been used for the treatment of hirsutism, alopecia, and associated acne and seborrhea, and in the treatment of idiopathic precocious puberty.

CPA has some undesirable side effects,[61] including fatigue, seen temporarily early on in treatment, decreased spermatogenesis and the possibility of an increase in abnormal sperms, temporary and, very occasionally, protracted episodes of depression, and a risk of some degree of feminization through the development of gynecomastia. Some weight gain can also occur if diet and exercise are neglected. The side effects are, to a large degree, dose dependent and reversible. The manifestation of the undesirable side effects have a temporal sequence that can be considered in treatment planning.[62] The effects on sexual behavior are the desired treatment effects and comprise a reduction in all aspects of sexual behavior, including paraphiliac behavior and deviant sexual fantasy.

Some other theoretical risks of CPA treatment are the possibility of liver dysfunction as small rises in serum bilirubin have been found in the first 6 weeks of treatment.[63,64] Further animal research has shown adrenal suppression can occur, and parallel findings are reported in children treated for precocious puberty. The evidence for any similar findings in adults is equivocal. Feminization depends on the relative levels of plasma androgens and estrogens. With CPA, it has been my experience that the plasma T levels can be allowed to rise to the normal range without any recurrence of the paraphiliac behavior. This strategy decreases the likelihood of feminization taking place.

Many patients who are treated with CPA report a feeling of calm that appears to be specifically related to a reduction of anxiety and irritability.[65] This diminishment in irritability appears to be part of the general reduction in psychopathological symptoms that is found during treatment with CPA.

There are important effects on sexual behavior that are the rationale for its use in the treatment of the paraphilias. These include a reduction in sexual interest and sexual drive and also a reduction of sexually deviant fantasy and behavior.

The first clinical studies of CPA were published in Germany. Laschet and Laschet (1971) reported on over 100 men who were treated with CPA, half of whom were sexual offenders. The duration of treatment varied from 6 months to over 4 years. The effects of the treatment were reversible in about 6 weeks. The paraphilias that were treated were pedophilia, sexual aggression including lust murder, incest, and exhibitionists, the largest group. In about 5% of the cases, there was a complete elimination of all deviant behavior even after treatment with CPA was terminated.[66] Undesirable side effects included fatigue, transient depression, weight gain, and some episodes of gynecomastia. No specific effect against sexual aggression was reported. The effect of CPA on hypersexuality was emphasized. Since this initial study, a number of other studies have been reported which generally support these findings.[67–73]

CPA has an important role to play in the treatment of sexual offenders, because well-documented studies indicate that it can substantially reduce recidivism rates and that it appears to have an effect on sexually driven aggression.

### Behavioral Treatments

The specific behavioral treatment programs that are used to eliminate deviant sexual arousal and interest in deviant sexual behavior are masturbatory satiation and conditioning and covert sensitization. Masturbatory satiation and conditioning, a treatment program developed by Marshall, requires the offender to repeat his deviant sexual fantasy in the postorgasmic period, during which it is very difficult or even impossible to experience further sexual arousal accompanied by an act of masturbation. This technique rapidly satiates the individual to the deviant stimuli that caused his deviant sexual arousal previously. As this technique is also accompanied by conditioning to nondeviant sexual stimuli and the development of sexual arousal to nondeviant stimuli, it provides a further safeguard against a relapse back to previous deviant sexual behavior.[74,75]

The other treatment approach that is used to disrupt the behavioral antecedents to paraphiliac behavior is covert sensitization. In this treatment program, the offender sets up scenarios that link the deviant behavior with the negative consequences and aversive consequences of the behavior. The treatment also sensitizes the offender to the sequences early in the behavioral chain that lead to a paraphiliac act. Although covert sensitization gives greater awareness and control to the individual, it may not necessarily eliminate the deviant sexual arousal.[76]

The development of adequate adult heterosexual social skills is crucial to the treatment of sex offenders because some offenders have adequate arousal to adults but do not have the social skills to be successful in developing mature sexual relationships. This fact is particularly true in the case of pedophiles, but it is also an important component of a wide range of paraphiliac behavior that possibly can be rectified by heterosexual social skills training. There is a similar need for assertive training with these offenders.

Another component in the multidimensional treatment program that is needed to treat sexual offenders, is sexual education, which is of particular importance in the low functioning group of offenders.

In summary, the assessment and treatment of sexual offenders are demanding but also rewarding clinical activities. With regard to clinical research, they are areas that are in a state of infancy while occupying, nevertheless, a high profile in our present society.

## REFERENCES

1. Timnick L: 22% in Survey Were Child Abuse Victims. *Los Angeles Times*, August 25, 1985, p 1.

2. Report of the Committee on Sexual Offences against Children and Youths: *Sexual Offences Against Children in Canada: Summary*: Ministry of Supply and Services, Ottawa, 1984, pp 1–2.

3. Abel GG, Becker JV, Murphy WD, *et al.*: Identifying dangerous child molesters, in Stuart R (ed): *Violent Behavior: Social Learning Approaches to Prediction; Management and Treatment.* New York, Brunner/Mazel, Inc 1981.

4. Abel GG, Mittelman M, Becker JV: Sexual offenders: Results of assessment and recommendations for treatment, in Ben-Aron MH, Hucker SJ, Webster CD (eds.): *Clinical Criminology: Current Concepts.* Toronto, M&M Graphics, 1985.

5. Bradford JMW, Boulet J, Pawlak A: The paraphilias: A multiplicity of deviant behaviours. *Can J Psychiatry* (accepted for publication).

6. Bancroft J: *Human Sexuality and Its Problems.* Edinburgh, Churchill Livingstone, 1983.

7. Le Maire L: Danish experiences regarding the castration of sexual offenders. *J Crim Law Criminol Police Sci* 1956; 47:295–310.

8. Ortmann J: The treatment of sexual offenders, castration and antihormone therapy. *Int J Law Psychiatry* 1980; 3:443–451.

9. Heim N, Hursch CJ: Castration for sexual offenders: Treatment or punishment? A review and critique of recent European literature. *Arch Sex Behav* 1979; 8:281–304.

10. Bradford JMW: Research on sex offenders, in Sadoff RL (ed): *The Psychiatric Clinics of North America.* Philadelphia, W.B. Saunders Co, 1983, pp 715–733.

11. Bradford JMW, McLean D: Sexual offenders, violence and testosterone: A clinical study. *Can J Psychiatry* 1984; 29:335–343.

12. Persky H, Smith KD, Basu GK: Relation of psychologic measures of aggression and hostility to testosterone production in man. *Psychosom Med* 1971; 33:265–277.

13. Kreuz LE, Rose RM: Assessment of aggressive behavior and plasma testosterone in a young criminal population. *Psychosom Med* 1972; 34:321–332.

14. Meyer-Bahlburg HFL, Nat R, Boon DA, *et al.*: Aggressiveness and testosterone measures in man. *Psychosom Med* 1974; 36:269–274.

15. Ehrenkranz J, Bliss E, Sheard MH: Plasma testosterone: Correlation with aggressive behavior and social dominance in man. *Psychosom Med* 1974; 36:469–475.

16. Brown WA, Davis GH: Serum testosterone and irritability in man. *Psychosom Med* 1975; 37:87.

17. Rada RT, Laws DR, Kellner R: Plasma testosterone levels in the rapist. *Psychosom Med* 1976; 38:257–268.

18. Monti PM, Brown WA, Corriveau DD: Testosterone and components of aggressive and sexual behavior in man. *Am J Psychiatry* 1977; 134(6):692–694.

19. Olweus D, Mattsson A, Schalling D, *et al.*: Testosterone, aggression, physical and personality dimensions in normal adolescent males. *Psychosom Med* 1980; 42:253–269.

20. Scaramella TJ, Brown WA: Serum testosterone and aggressiveness in hockey players. *Psychosom Med* 1978; 40:262–265.

21. Nielsen J: Gender role identity and sexual behaviour in persons with sex chromosome abberations. *Dan Med Bull* 1972; 17:269–275.

22. Hunter H: A controlled study of the psychopathology and physical measurements of Klinefelter's syndrome. *Br J Psychiatry* 1969; 115:443–448.

23. Schroder J, De La Chapelle A, Hakola P, *et al.*: The frequency of XYY and XXY men among criminal offenders. *Acta Psychiatr Scand* 1981; 63:272–276.

24. Money J, Annecello C, Van Orman B, *et al.*: Cytogenetics, hormones and behavior disability: Comparison of XYY and XXY syndromes. *Clin Genet* 1974; 6:370–382.

25. Baker P, Telfer MA, Richardson CE, *et al.*: Chromosome errors in men with antisocial behavior. *JAMA* 1970; 214(5):869–878.

26. Nielsen J: Criminality among patients with Klinefelter's syndrome and the XYY syndrome. *Br J Psychiatry* 1970; 117:365–369.

27. Wakeling A: Comparison study of psychiatric patients with Klinefelter's syndrome and hypogonadism. *Psychol Med* 1972; 2:139–154.

28. Crowley JT: Klinefelter's syndrome and abnormal behavior: A case report. *Int J Neuropsychiatry* 1964; 5:359–363.

29. Pasqualine RQ, Vidal G, Bur GE: Psychopathology of Klinefelter's syndrome: Review of 31 cases. *Lancet* 1957; 2:164–167.

30. Beumont PJV, Bancroft JHJ, Beardwood CJ, *et al.*: Behavioral changes after treatment with testosterone: Case report. *Psychol Med* 1972; 2:70–72.

31. Dorner G: Sex-hormone-dependent brain differentiation and reproduction, in Money J, Musaph H (eds): *Handbook of Sexology II, Genetics, Hormones and Behavior.* New York, Elsevier North Holland, Inc, 1978.

32. Freund K: Diagnosing heterosexual pedophilia by means of a test for sexual interest. *Behav Res Ther* 1965; 3:229–234.

33. Freund K: Diagnosing homo- or heterosexuality and erotic age-preference by means of a psychophysiological test. *Behav Res Ther* 1967; 5:209–228.

34. Freund K: Erotic preference in pedophilia. *Behav Res Ther* 1967; 5:339–348.

35. Abel GG, Blanchard EB, Barlow DM: Measurement of sexual arousal in several paraphilias: The effects of stimulus modality, instructional set and stimulus content on the objective. *Behav Res Ther* 1981; 19:25–33.

36. Abel GG, Blanchard EB, Becker JV, *et al.*: Differentiating sexual aggressives with penile measures. *Crim Just Behav* 1978; 5:315–332.

37. Barbaree HE, Marshall WL, Lanthier RD: Deviant arousal in rapists. *Behav Res Ther* 1979; 17:252–259.

38. Abel GG, Barlow DH, Blanchard EB, *et al.*: The components of rapists' sexual arousal. *Arch Gen Psychiatry* 1977; 34:895–903.

39. Stuart RB (ed.): *Violent Behavior: Social Learning Approaches to Prediction, Management and Treatment.* New York, Brunner/Mazel Inc, 1981.

40. Laws DR, Rubin HB: Instructional control of an autonomic response. *J Appl Behav Anal* 1969; 2:93–99.

41. Freund K, Chan S, Coulthard R: Phallometric diagnosis with "nonadmitters." *Behav Res Ther* 1979; 17:451–457.

42. Farkas GM, Evans IM, Sine LF, *et al.*: Reliability and validity of the mercury-in-rubber strain gauge measure of penile circumference. *Behav Ther* 1979; 10:555–561.

43. Wincze JP, Venditti E, Barlow D, *et al.*: The effects of a subject monitoring task in the physiological measure of genital response to erotic stimulation. *Arch Sex Behav* 1980; 9:533–545.

44. Farkas GM, Evans IM, Sine LF *et al.*: Reliability and validity of the mercury-in-rubber strain gauge measure of penile circumference. *Behav Ther* 1979; 10:557.

45. Derogatis LR: Psychological assessment of psychosexual functioning, in Meyer JK (ed): *The Psychiatric Clinics of North America.* Philadelphia, W.B. Saunders Company, 1980.

46. Masters WH, Johnson VE: *Human Sexual Inadequacy.* Boston, Little, Brown & Co, 1970.

47. Bradford JMW, Pawlak A: Sadistic homosexual pedophilia: Treatment with cyproterone acetate a single case study. *Can J Psychiatry* 1987; 32:22–31.

48. Foote RM: Diethylstilbestrol in the management of psychopathological states in males. *J Nerv Ment Dis* 1944; 99:928–935.

49. Golla FL, Hodge SR: Hormone treatment of sexual offenders. *Lancet* 1949; 1:1006–1007.

50. Whittaker LH: Oestragens and psychosexual disorders. *Med J Aust* 1959; 2:547–549.
51. Heller CG, Laidlaw WM, Harvey HT, *et al.*: Effects of progestational compounds on the reproductive processes of the human male. *Ann NY Acad Sci 1958; 71:649–655.*
52. *Money J: Use of androgen depleting hormone in the treatment of male sex offenders. J Sex Res* 1970; 6:165–172.
53. Money JM, Wiedeking C, Walker PA, *et al.*: Combined antiandrogen and counselling program for treatment of 46, XY and 47, XYY sex offenders, in Sachar E (ed): *Hormones, Behavior and Psychopathology.* New York, Raven Press, 1976, pp 105–120.
54. Wiedeking C, Money J, Walker PA: Follow up 11 XYY males with impulsive and/or sex-offending behavior. *Psychol Med* 1979; 9:287–292.
55. Walker PA, Meyer WJ: Medroxyprogesterone acetate treatment for paraphiliac sex offenders, in Hays JR, Roberts TK, Solway KS (eds): *Violence and the Violent Individual.* New York, S.P. Medical and Scientific Books, 1981, pp 353–373.
56. Gagne P: Treatment of sex offenders with medroxyprogesterone acetate. *Am J Psychiatry* 1981; 138:644–646.
57. Berlin FS, Meinecke CF: Treatment of sex offenders with antiandrogenic medication: Conceptualization, review of treatment modalities, and preliminary findings. *Am J Psychiatry* 1981; 138:601–607.
58. Southren AL, Gordon GG, Vittek J, *et al.*: Effect of progestagens on androgen metabolism, in Martini L, Motta M (eds): *Androgens and Antiandrogens.* New York, Raven Press, 1977, pp 263–279.
59. Liang T, Tymoczko JL, Chan KMB, *et al.*: Androgen action: Receptors and rapid responses, in Martini L, Motta M (eds): *Androgens and Antiandrogens.* New York, Raven Press, 1977, pp 77–89.
60. Mainwaring IP: Modes of action of antiandrogens: A survey, in Martini L, Motta M (eds): *Androgens and antiandrogens.* New York, Raven Press, 1977, pp 151–161.
61. Chapman MG: Side effects of antiandrogen therapy, in Jeffcoate SL (ed): *Androgens and Anti-androgen Therapy.* New York, John Wiley & Sons, 1982, pp 169–178.
62. Laschet U, Laschet L: Antiandrogens in the treatment of sexual deviations of men. *J Steroid Biochem* 1975; 6:821–826.
63. Neumann F: Pharmacology and potential use of cyproterone acetate. *Horm Metab Res* 1977; 9:1–13.
64. Cremonocini C, Vignati E, Libroia A: Treatment of hirsutism and acne in woman with two combinations of cyproterone acetate and ethinylestradiol. *Acta Eur Fertil* 1976; 7:299–314.
65. Bradford JMW, Pawlak A: Double-blind placebo crossover study of cyproterone acetate in the treatment of sexual deviation. *Can J Psychiatry* (accepted for publication).
66. Laschet U, Laschet L: Psychopharmacotherapy of sex offenders with cyproterone acetate. *Pharmakopsychatr Neuropsychopharmakol* 1971; 4:99–104.
67. Ott F, Hoffet H: The influence of antiandrogens on libido, potency and testicular function. *Schweiz Med Wochenschr* 1968; 98:1812–1815.
68. Mothes C, Lehnert J, Samimi F, *et al.*: Schering Symposium uber Sexual Deviationen und ihre medikamentose Behandlung. *Life Sci Monog* 1971; 2:65.
69. Cooper AJ, Ismail AA, Phanjoo AL, *et al.*: Antiandrogen (cyproterone acetate) therapy in deviant hypersexuality. *Br J Psychiatry* 1972; 120:59–63.
70. Bancroft J, Tennent G, Loucas K, *et al.*: The control of deviant sexual behaviour by drugs: 1.Behavioral changes following oestrogens and anti-androgens. *Br J Psychiatry* 1974; 125:310–315.
71. Murray MAF, Bancroft JHJ, Anderson DC, *et al.*: Endocrine changes in male sexual deviants after treatment with antiandrogens, oestrogens or tranquilizers. *J Endocrinol* 1975; 67:179–188.

72. Davies TD: Cyproterone acetate for male hypersexuality. *J Int Med Res* 1974; 2:159–163.
73. Cooper AJ: A placebo controlled study of the antiandrogen cyproterone acetate in deviant hypersexuality. *Compr Psychiatry* 1981; 22:458–464.
74. Marshall WL: The modification of sexual fantasies: A combined treatment approach to the reduction of deviant sexual behavior. *Behav Res Ther* 1973; 11:557–564.
75. Marshall WL, Barbaree HL: The reduction of deviant arousal: Satiation treatment for sexual aggressors. *Crim Just Behav* 1978; 5:294–303.
76. Abel GG, Blanchard EB, Becker JV: An integrated treatment program for rapists, in Rada R (ed): *Clinical Aspects of the Rapists.* New York, Grune & Stratton Inc, 1977, pp 161–214.

# 18

# Psychiatrists and the Media

## IRWIN N. PERR

Dealing with the media is one of the more ticklish, sensitive activities of the psychiatrist who, as a result, may be put into a difficult position in which conflicting interests are many. On the one hand is the dominating professional ethic of the right to privacy and confidentiality; a right that has both ethical and legal roots. Many states have adopted privilege statutes that protect privacy of communication, in recognition of the demand made by the medical profession for such protection not only for their patients but also for their professional practices. On the other hand, a number of motivations for recourse to the media exist. Some of these are external to the psychiatrist, whereas some are internal.

A major external influence is the desire of the media to promulgate information about newsworthy items, particularly when the individual patient involved is a public figure or when the events in which the population at large has a legitimate interest are public or notorious.

The goal of the media person may be multifold. Superficially, the search for news and information is socially approved and useful. Public anxiety may be allayed by appropriate information, or, at the very least, awareness of a problem may create a means by which it can be managed.

Some situations revolve around a problem greater than the individual. For example, information about acquired immune deficiency syndrome (AIDS) was required to assess the extent of the current threat and to develop modes of management, control, prevention, and treat-



**IRWIN N. PERR** • Department of Psychiatry, Robert Wood Johnson Medical School, University of Medicine and Dentistry of New Jersey, Piscataway, NJ 08854; Rutgers Law School—Newark, Newark, NJ 07102.

ment. The media have the responsibility of clarifying the social significance of what is occurring and to keep the public up-to-date in further developments. Information *per se* does not necessarily lessen fear; the facts may be such that information may increase public anxiety. Nonetheless, in the long run, accuracy is usually the best policy.

Some media people can exaggerate fears and promulgate erroneous or promotional information. In such cases, the public may be harmed by such media abuse, and the welfare of the community may be affected. This is especially a concern when health in the community, safety in the community, and faith in the system are involved.

Some media people are not motivated by altruistic, unselfish, social betterment goals or by devotion to the ideals of their profession. Bylines and scoops are too highly valued; fame and reimbursement march hand in hand. The search for status and recognition by their peers and by the general public can remain a dominant force in their use of communication modalities.

Similarly, the informant, the one who possesses special knowledge, may be seduced by the same prospects. For example, the psychiatrist may face a conflict in deciding what is appropriate for a public thirsting for knowledge yet, at times, unsophisticated either about issues or people. Providing information may be harmful to the cause of the patient. It is clear that such an issue is delicate. Who is to decide? And what information should be provided?

With regard to media-sensitive patients numerous issues can be raised. The status of the patient may be important in a number of circumstances. If the patient is a criminal defendant, the public may wish for disclosure, even premature disclosure, when a competency to stand trial is involved in an insanity defense. Similarly, psychiatric input is relevant to disposition, affecting a variety of outcomes from capital punishment to probation.

If the person is a prominent public figure, the quest for details by media people may be unrelenting. Frequently, attorneys play the media in the hope that, in addition to giving vent to their own narcissistic exhibitionism, somehow public opinion will be aroused to the extent that it can ultimately affect the legal process. Psychiatrists should avoid such a practice.

Psychiatrists have an obligation not only to protect the privacy of individual patients but also of patients as a group. Violations of privacy, therefore, must be clearly acknowledged and explained in terms of why something is being done, particularly in making anything public in a fashion that is considered acceptable and not opportunistic.

The role of the psychiatrist and his or her attendant obligations may vary according to the circumstances. For example, a person who has been a patient may become involved in a notorious event that may or may not be criminal. Ordinarily, the psychiatrist should not go public either with or without consent. At times, the patient, or family, or the attorney for the patient may request that certain information be made public. If consent issues are satisfied and the information is deemed appropriate by the professional person, a certain amount of information may be released. Depending on the delicacy of the situation, a prepared statement may be helpful in controlling the information made available. Personally, I feel that every statement should be truthful and not misleading—a combination of art and honesty.

A second role of the psychiatrist is that of examiner in determining the disposition of a person who is being seen after the trouble has arisen. If the person is seen on his or her own behalf, the responsibility of controlling any communication should be determined according to the wishes of the person, if suitable, or a responsible relative, particularly if the psychiatrist is involved in a treatment capacity. If the psychiatrist is also involved in an evaluative capacity on behalf of the person, the responsibility of communication may fall to the attorney to whom the psychiatrist is obligated in recognition of the work–product protection. Ordinarily, the psychiatrist need not say anything, though an awkward situation may arise when the attorney publicly ascribes, in a self-serving fashion, statements to the psychiatrist that do not reflect the reality of the situation as the psychiatrist sees it.

A third situation may occur when the psychiatrist is involved on behalf of another party, as, for example, the prosecutor in a criminal case or the defendant in a personal injury case. Although there is no responsibility to the person being examined (if the person understands that matters are not confidential), the other professional person must be aware of the possible public perception of abuse of the psychiatrist's role.

Certainly, while legal matters are pending and before final resolution, there would seem to be little rationale in going public. After the legal process has been completed, the circumstances may be different, especially when the subject matter has become public knowledge by virtue of its use at trial. Because legal settlements outside the courtroom may not provide for any type of waiver of information, ethical problems may arise, particularly with patients or when treatment was done on behalf of the person examined.

Other situations may arise during which psychiatrists may be enticed by the media to offer opinions in cases in which the psychiatrists have had no contact with the patients or persons, either on their behalf or on behalf of their antagonists. In a criminal case, it may be the event that requires the psychiatrist to provide an expert opinion as to the nature of the perpetrator. This procedure may occur before the identity of the perpetrator is known. In another instance in which the perpetrator is a notorious or public figure who is known, it is because of that notoriety that the psychiatrist may be asked to discuss motivation or to provide a psychological explanation.

The use of the word *media* may vary with reference to two types of situations. The first deals with the psychiatrist's cooperation with a media person, who is involved in radio, television, or the press. The second refers to the psychiatrist as the media person. For example, a psychiatrist who has access to special knowledge may use that knowledge to write a book or article dealing with the event. Consequently, the psychiatrist may be a direct beneficiary either in terms of monetary benefit or in terms of recognition and publicity.

In any event, the safest course of action for a psychiatrist to take is to decline to make any statement. Statements that are made when one is attempting to justify an action or which are defensive in nature are likely to backfire.

In this chapter, I shall attempt to discuss some of these issues, giving examples of past significant situations. I am further reminded of two old adages that may have some applicability. One is that it is better to be silent and be thought a fool than to open one's mouth and remove all doubt. The second, which is similar in meaning, is the proverb, "A closed mouth gathers no feet."

## ATTITUDES TOWARD THE MEDIA

How one behaves toward the media may be determined by one's attitude. If one is unduly suspicious, fearful, or hostile, then one is likely to communicate poorly and to reflect adversely on the profession.

My own attitude is that the media are neither my friends nor my enemies; that media people are trying to do a job; that, as a group, they are of above average intelligence; and that they are appreciative of cooperation and are appropriately understanding when it is not obtained. Nonetheless, the goals of the parties (media people and psychiatrists) do not coincide. The psychiatrist may find himself or herself as spokesperson for a profession (actually, that is always the case), and therefore he or she cannot abrogate that responsibility.

The search for "experts" is a never-ending one for the media. The more dramatic the offering, the better. I recall being on an hour-long television show dealing with psychiatry for a metropolitan New York station. A law school colleague and I were invited to share a 15-minute slot on the evolution of commitment laws. The only 15-minute segment given to an individual on the program was to a psychiatrist, who extolled the virtues of megavitamins for schizophrenia. At the time, I was Vice-President of the American Psychiatric Association. I asked the master of ceremonies not to introduce me in that capacity, when I learned of the other participants of the program, because I did not want the name of the association mentioned in conjunction with a program that I felt delivered misleading and incorrect information.

The same situation may arise when one speaks by telephone to a reporter who is preparing an article on a subject. By the time the article is written, others may have been interviewed and quoted. Although it may prove uncomfortable for one to be placed in juxtaposition to others who are considered unacceptable, this is one of the realities of participation. Generally, it is better to take advantage of the opportunity to contribute to public information and hope that one has been quoted correctly. The power of communication lies with the media; therefore, humility by an examiner, when one is confronted with superior communicative influence, is a cardinal virtue.

Nowadays each exotic crime becomes the subject of a short-lived journalistic scrutiny of extreme intensity of the motivation of the perpetrator. People are especially intrigued by multiple killers or by those persons whose position and power seem incongruous to their purported criminality—like clergymen, politicians, and the rich.

When Patty Hearst was arrested, numerous "psychologizers" analyzed her and explained her behavior in various terms. Some offered to help the defense. An attorney acquaintance of mine, who had been associated with a professional organization dealing with evidentiary matters, tried to sell an aritcle to a major periodical on why Ms. Hearst should have been innocent based on his analysis of her psychological state. He had no professional background for such an endeavor, and, fortunately, his article was not published. But even if he had published, one would question his giving opinions on a matter about which he had little contact—professionally, educationally, or through personal experience.

I, for one, find ridiculous the public statements of defense attorneys, before, during, and after trials, that justify positions and attempt to explain a point of view. I also find ridiculous "top-of-the-head" and "half-way" psychologizing, in which an individual makes sweeping unfounded generalizations that may or may not be applicable to the individual case. This skepticism is especially applicable to evolving psychiatric concepts, such as posttraumatic stress disorder, the premenstrual tension syndrome, and pathological gambling.

Another public relations debacle is the use of "profiles" in the popular media. Frequently, as I read them, the statements given merit bear little credence and are generally an embarrassment to the profession. It is all too easy to accuse old paranoids or young psychopaths of everything.

Any discussion dealing with the media should make reference to the behavior of so many psychiatrists in 1964 (about 5%), who offered opinions as to the mental stability of one of the presidential candidates. The American Psychiatric Association, amid much embarrassment, was forced to disavow the "study" or "expression of professional opinion" as unsound and unmerited.

Psychiatrists must be careful not to mix their own political ideologies with slander by psychiatric innuendo. To the extent that psychiatrists make silly public statements, the future credibility and utility of other psychiatrists are affected. Psychiatrists must be most circumspect in offering opinions about people that they have not examined (and, of course, because of professional obligations about those that they have).

Nonetheless, guidelines cannot be made explicitly clear. Numerous psychohistories, which have been accepted as part of our literature, are not usually written contemporaneous to the events discussed and are not reflective of the acute passions and manipulations of the concurrent analysis. Some have unique purposes, such as the speculative study of Adolf Hitler by Walter Langer prepared for our policymakers during World War II. Sigmund Freud wrote about Moses and Leonardo da Vinci; Erik H. Erikson about Gandhi and Luther; Meyer A. Zeligs about Alger Hiss and Whittaker Chambers; John E. Mack about Lawrence of Arabia; and a number of writers about Richard Nixon. I think that it is now generally acceptable for a writer to attempt to use a psychodynamic approach in conveying a rationale for the behavior of the subject described. Such attempts can be both informative and fun, if one accepts their limitations. (Perhaps psychohistories should carry a warning from the surgeon general, as is done with certain other products in which reliability has not been shown but which are marketable otherwise.) One may even ponder the expertise of various writers and opinion-givers about the psychodynamics of nonexistent creations in fiction, of which my favorite is Sherlock Holmes who, ultimately, was treated fictionally by Sigmund Freud.

Probably the greatest explosion of editorial imaginativeness in recent years occurred in New York in the infamous Son of Sam case.[1] Many speculations were offered by "experts," none of which contributed to the immediate apprehension of the perpetrator. One wonders if any public purpose is served by such professional involvement. The general statements made may even have some applicability, but they tend to overemphasize the danger inherent in the behavior of mental patients at large and thus do a disservice to all peoples with such problems. One should recognize that very few notorious murderers or other criminals have a history of mental illness which has involved prior diagnosis and treatment.


## OTHER MEDICAL PROFESSIONALS—FORENSIC PATHOLOGY

In addition to psychiatrists, very significant medical-scientific input into legal proceedings is derived from forensic pathologists, whether they are associated with a medical examiner's or a coroner's office.

Noguchi, formerly the Los Angeles County Medical Examiner, has been highly critical of the role of the media.[2] He has stated that:

> The medical examiner, by the very nature of his profession, attracts the interest of news people. News media persons seek items of news value. The more sensational the story, the greater the news value and the greater the sale of newspapers and the larger the broadcast audience, which all translates into more money for the news media corporations. As one reporter explained to me, their criteria of newsworthy material involve 3 D's: death, disaster, and dirt.

The most prominent newspaper articles dealing with forensic pathology have occurred in large cities where the impact of the media is greatest. Los Angeles and New York, in particular, have been subject to medical investigation and criticism in this area. There are two primary reasons to account for such scrutiny. First, the medical examiner's (or coroner's) office is a public entity that is supported by taxes and represents an administrative empire (with budgets, staff, and facilities, like any other institution). It is subject to criticism on both professional and administrative grounds. The pathologist may become involved in the prominent news stories of the day, and the adequacy of his professional work may be the subject of inquiry, as it was in the assassination of President Kennedy. Second, the medical examiner's office is usually an appointive one, subject to oversight by elected officials (or politicians, depending on how one wishes to express it). Thus, the medical examiner may be in a more vulnerable position than the coroner, who is an elected official with a set term of office. As Noguchi states, forensic pathology in this country "is the only medical specialty which is almost exclusively practiced in the government sector."

These observations do not refer in a particular manner to psychiatrists who are involved in criminal cases. In general, psychiatrists are not allowed to communicate to the media before a trial and rarely do so afterward. They have no obligation to the public or the media and are not responsible to a public agency and are therefore not expected to be responsive to the media. Certain public psychiatric institutions do considerable forensic work, but there is no tradition of discussing this with the media, either before or after a prominent case. Thus, they simply do not have the same problem confronting medical examiners.

Each party in a psychiatric criminal case has access to its own experts and, therefore, in most jurisdictions, the work of the public psychiatric institution is not crucial. This is not so in forensic pathology, where the public agency is often the only one with the broad technology needed.

## THE HINCKLEY AND THE M'NAGHTEN CASES

I have previously reviewed[3,4] some of the media activities in the John W. Hinckley, Jr., and the Daniel M'Naghten cases. (Note that I use the spelling "M'Naghten" contained in the *Psychiatric Glossary,* 5th edition; other references use different spellings.)

Moran's book on M'Naghten (which he spells "McNaughtan") reviews the furor involved in that famous insanity defense trial and provides examples of media involvement in what was, in England, the eminent issue of the day.

He[5] states that:

> The *Times* [London] expressed its concern that the physicians had invaded the traditional province of the judiciary. "The judge in his treatment of the madmen yields to the decision of the physician, and the physician in his treatment becomes the judge."

The *Standard,* another London newspaper, went beyond this, arguing that the "mad doctors" were permitted "to dictate the law" and that the court had given too much credence to their "crude" and "absurd" pronouncements. The court examiner wondered how much the medical practitioners could be certain about the state of M'Naghten's mind, since none of them had examined him prior to the assassination. All the evidence derived from the prisoner was obtained "after his life depended on his being judged insane." The newspaper concluded that when the mad doctors gave testimony, they were "under the delusion that they . . . were reasoning."

The *Times* of London[6] on March 6, 1843 published a letter in which it was said:

> Sir,
>
> If the result of McNaughton's trial satisfies the end of justice, by proving the moral irresponsibility of the murderer, it undoubtedly leaves the security of Her Majesty's subjects from similar murderous attacks in a very unsatisfactory state. . . . again it appears that one of his illusions was that he had been attacked by paragraphs in The Times and the Glasgow Herald; it is quite as probable that McNaughton should have carried out his revenge on his fancied prosecutors, and exercised his "homicidal monomania" by waiting at the

office of your journal, Sir, and shooting the first man who came out of the door, as that he should have taken the life of Mr. Drummond.

One word on the affected sentimentality of the day. A perusal of the second day's proceedings in the Central Criminal Court would almost persuade us to give our sympathy to the murderer, and not to the murdered. No words applicable to such a deed of horror are used, though our forcible Anglo-Saxon idiom supplies them in abundance. The prisoner is "unfortunate"—"is in an unhappy situation, and all must regret the fate of the victim." Such is the dainty language in vogue which tends to foster the false morality of the morbid humanitarians of the day.

Justus

The *Times* also published these verses[7] which were attributed by Moran to Thomas Campbell:

On a Late Acquittal
Ye people of England exult and be glad
For ye're now at the will of the merciless mad
Why say ye that but three authoritites reign
Crown, Commons and Lords?—You omit the insane.
They're a privileged class whom no statute controls,
And their murderous charter exists in their souls.
Do they wish to spill blood—they have only to play
A few pranks—get asylum'd a month and a day
Then heigh! to escape from the mad doctor's keys
And to pistol and stab whosoever they please.

Now the dog has a human-like wit in creation
He resembles most nearly our own generation
Then if madmen for murder escape with impunity
Why deny a poor dog the same noble immunity
So if a dog or man bite you beware being nettled
For crime is no crime—when the mind is unsettled.

Reacting to the jury's findings, Queen Victoria wrote, "The law may be perfect, but how is it that wherever a case for its application arises, it proves to be of no avail?" (p 21). She also said, in a statement of perhaps delightful ambiguity, that she "did not believe that anyone could be insane who wanted to kill a Conservative Prime Minister"[8] (p 44). The Lord Chancellor lamented that M'Naghten had "escaped with impunity." He also noted that the circumstances had created a deep feeling in the public mind that "there was some deficit in the law with reference to this subject"[4] (p 874).

Political figures in the United State reacted in similar fashion after the Hinckley trial. Treasury Secretary Donald Regan was quoted as saying, "Frankly I'm outraged." Senator Strom Thurmond stated:

It is deeply troubling to me when the criminal justice system exonerates a defendant who obviously planned and knew exactly what he was doing.

> There must be an end to the doctrine that allows so many persons to commit
> crimes of violence, to use confusing procedures to their own advantage, and
> then to have the door opened for them to return to the society they
> victimized.

Russell Baker, the prominent *New York Times* columnist, wrote: "For an exercise in legal absurdity it would be hard to improve on the trial of John W. Hinckley, Jr." He ridiculed both the testimony of the psychiatrists and the decision of the jury, the former for not agreeing and the jury for agreeing. He did not question the nuances of the insanity defense but doubted the capacity of the jury to decide such issues. In a later personal correspondence to me, Baker indicated that his article, which was published after the verdict, had been written just before the verdict and that he had anticipated a finding of guilty. He felt that his main point, confused by the jury decision, was that the determination of sanity should not be left to a jury of laymen.

Previously, I myself had published in the *New York Times* a letter[9] dealing with the Baker column.

Tom Wicker, also a feature writer in the *New York Times,* discussed his concern about witnesses who contradicted each other and described psychiatrists as the biggest "losers" in the whole affair. He also felt that the public deserved assurance that Hinckley would not be ruled "sane" in a few months or a few years and then be turned loose—shades of the M'Naghten era.

Daniel Robinson, who was identified as a psychologist in his article in the *Wall Street Journal,* attacked psychologists and psychiatrists for their "wanton" theories and their "self-congratulatory" opinions, their poor predictive powers concerning future events, and their lack of expertise. He further proposed that expert opinions resulting in the release of those defendants previously committed on the basis of a finding of not guilty by reason of insanity be a basis for civil or even criminal liability, apparently as a safety measure for future adverse behaviors by those defendants so released. That procedure certainly would take care of the fear of a release; for, if such were the policy, who would be so foolish as to participate in the process?

These are just a few comments by media people and political figures with regard to the two most famous forensic psychiatric cases in the last two centuries.


## THE MEDIA AND THE DEAD

The ethical issues involving the media in the case of prominent living persons are many. Many eminent people receive psychiatric care and some are hospitalized. One can readily think of the entertainment and sports personalities who were institutionalized for alcohol and drug abuse as well as for the gamut of other psychiatric disorders. Usually mental health professionals are careful in not releasing information or in releasing only sufficient information that will cover the public relations needs of the patient when the fact of treatment has become known.

A different problem may arise when the person involved is a prominent public figure with a defined responsibility to the community. For example, the lesson of a disabled Woodrow Wilson is one that has not provided an easy answer, though there is now a system to declare a president of the United States unfit for office either on a temporary or permanent basis—a mechanism that thus far has never been used. This precaution resulted from the uncertainty after President Dwight D. Eisenhower had a minor stroke during his tenure.

James Forrestal, Secretary of Defense, became psychotic and died by suicide while he was hospitalized. The potential for a psychotic general to do damage, like the fictional General Jack D. Ripper in "Dr. Strangelove," remains a threat. And the problems of Senator Thomas F. Eagleton in 1972 reflected another crucial public and media issue when initially the fact of several of his psychiatric hospitalizations was withheld. The news was "leaked" or released to the media by unknown sources, and Senator Eagleton was forced to resign as a Vice-Presidential candidate on the George S. McGovern ticket, with much damage to the Democratic candidacy. Certainly, such cases raise a moral dilemma in terms of deciding the point where the public's right to know—if there is one—exceeds the individual's right to privacy.

Even as the living have a right to privacy, another concern is a consideration of the right to privacy of the dead. Do the dead have a right to privacy in terms of protecting their reputation or in terms of protecting the sensitivities of the surviving family? To this day, for example, the public has not been informed about the physical condition of John F. Kennedy. After his assassination, the results of his autopsy have been released only in part, though it seems to be common knowledge (or, at least, it is so believed) that he had Addison's disease and required delicate endocrinologic maintenance.

The physicians for Franklin D. Roosevelt and Winston Churchill wrote about the medical conditions of their famous patients after their deaths. The allegation has frequently been made that Franklin Roosevelt had ultimately become severely handicapped prior to his death. The physicians were criticized for violating the privacy of their patients, and yet the rightness or wrongness of making public such information is still problematic.

One of the few significant examinations dealing with this subject is

Robitscher's article, "Public Life and Private Information,"[10] published twenty years ago. Inasmuch as "public personages often manipulate the content of information released about their health during their lifetime," Robitscher felt that physicians should have the right after their patients' deaths to "reveal information clarifying and supplementing lifetime reports without violating the general rule of confidentiality." These issues are not easy. Lord Moran, who wrote about Churchill, was criticized by *Lancet,* which expressed the opinion that confidentiality owed to the living is doubly owed to the dead. Also, the British Medical Association asserted its view that the death of the patient did not terminate the obligation to secrecy. McIntyre's book, *White House Physician,* about Franklin Roosevelt was preceded many years ago by Keen's report on President Cleveland's secret operations.

Robitscher felt that such situations merit or justify an exception to the rule that a patient's health is a private rather than a public matter and that there should be an opportunity after death to set the record straight.

The issue of public personages continues to be difficult. When a Southern governor became psychotic and was hospitalized at a state hospital, confidentiality was not of much value. But then the question of the right of the public to accuracy of information became an issue, particularly since the continued functioning of the state government was at stake.

Whatever the obligations of the physician, the media do play a very valuable role in protecting the public. Fortunately, the attitude of public personages seems to be changing. In recent years, the wives of a president and of a presidential candidate have offered to the public information about their problems with alcohol and prescription drug abuse; so did a midwestern governor. How far this should extend is not clear. Certainly, a sexual disorder or an eating disorder does not necessarily affect a person's ability to govern.

The primary issue seems to be focused directly at the problem of the psychosis in an important public personage who is in a position of authority. A psychosis, such as schizophrenia, bipolar disorder, or paranoia, can blatantly affect the functional capacity of the individual, and drug and alcohol abuses are indeed legitimate concerns. On the other hand, if only behaviors are concerned, what about the media's current preoccupation with the sexual activities of public figures? And what about organic brain changes that are even more insidious, where the evidences of impaired functioning are not so blatant? The issue of brain organicity has periodically arisen during our history. Similarly, a deteriorating physical condition may also affect the physical capacity of a person to govern or be associated with a concurrent mental impairment to carry out the duties of that position. These types of allegations have been made retrospectively in the cases of Franklin D. Roosevelt and, I understand, Winston Churchill—two of the heroic figures of the twentieth century.

## PROFESSIONAL ATTITUDES

The concept of confidentiality and privacy cannot be discussed in depth here, as I have reviewed these same aspects of ethical and legal practice previously.[11] Generally, neither ethical principles nor legal rules apply with specificity to the issues that have been raised. The British Medical Association has made some effort to deal with these issues (see below), but their rules are not very clear.

The code of Hippocrates has a general statement dealing with privacy, but it, too, does not deal with the complex issues that we have examined. For example, the Hippocratic Oath states that "whatever in connection, with my profession or not in connection with it, I may see or hear in the lives of men which ought not to be spoken abroad, I will not divulge as reckoning that all should be kept secret." Hippocrates predated television, the daily newspapers, and the mass book market.

In its 1981 Statement of Principles the American Psychiatric Association provided a summary of medical ethics applicable to psychiatry[12]:

> Section 2.
> 2. The psychiatrist should diligently guard against exploiting information furnished by the patient and should not use the unique position of power afforded him/her by the psychotherapeutic situation to influence the patient in anyway not directly relevant to treatment goals. . . .
> Section 4. A physician shall safeguard patient confidences within the constraints of the law.
> 1. Psychiatric records . . . must be protected with extreme care. . . .
> 2. A psychiatrist may release confidential information only with the authorization of the patient or under proper legal compulsion. . . .
> 3. Clinical or other materials used in teaching and writing must be adequately disguised in order to preserve the anonymity of the individuals involved. . . .
> 11. It is ethical to present a patient or former patient to a public gathering or to the news media only if that patient is fully informed of enduring loss of confidentiality, is competent, and consents in writing without coercion. . . .
> Section 7. A physician shall recognize a responsibility to participate in activities contributing to an improved community. . . .
> 2. Psychiatrists may interpret and share with the public their expertise in the various psychosocial issues that may affect mental health and illness. . . .
> 3. On occasion psychiatrists are asked for an opinion about an indi-

> vidual who is in the light of public attention, or who has disclosed informa-
> tion about himself/herself through public media. It is unethical for a psychia-
> trist to offer a professional opinion unless he/she has conducted an
> examination or has been granted proper authorization for such a state-
> ment.

Interpretation of these guidelines is not easy. Generally, the stipulations apply to "patients," and, therefore, those not seen in a patient capacity would logically not seem to be included in the principles. On many occasions, people are examined for third parties, and legally the right of privacy is generally that of the third party. Thus, an examination performed for a lawyer usually is included under the lawyer–client privilege. This right is not absolute, however. When a psychiatrist examines a person for an antagonistic party, such as a prosecutor or district attorney, one can scarcely claim a doctor–patient relationship (the person should, of course, be informed of such a status before the examination).

In notorious cases in which suppression of identity is not possible, psychiatrists cannot meet the standards of Section 4, paragraph 3, dealing with the stipulation that anonymity be maintained.

Although the issues of death or significant public policy (the right of the public to know) are not referred to in the body of the guidelines, many professionals, of course, interpret the guidelines as extending to such situations unless clear authorization is given by law; others do not.

In criminal cases, the data or the patient material often has already been submitted to a court or has been the subject of testimony and is thus a matter of public record. Can the psychiatrist augment or supplement the information made public? The answer is not clear, although one ethics committee decision dealing with a specific case indicated that this was not permissible.

Section 7, paragraph 3, indicates that a psychiatrist may not offer an opinion about someone that the psychiatrist has not examined. This apparently was in response to the 1964 national election episode alluded to above. Yet, if taken literally, this would preclude any psychohistorical review, and even Sigmund Freud (and numerous others) would be guilty of unethical behavior. I do not believe that this specific aspect has been clearly addressed. Is the situation any different when the person, like Woodrow Wilson, is a prominent public figure who is dead, or when the person, like Adolf Hitler, is still alive at the time of the review, or is even still living, like Richard M. Nixon? And what are the standards when the person is a notorious criminal? Where does that leave the psychohistorian?

In 1980, the British Medical Association in a section of the *Handbook of Medical Ethics* stated[13]:

8. The Doctor and the Media

8.1. Increasing public interest in health matters has brought doctors more and more into contact with the media. It is therefore essential that doctors should be aware of the ethics involved with the media.

8.2. Those doctors able to comment authoritatively on medical subjects should be prepared to do so in order that the public may be informed. Those doctors able to help the public with information should regard talking to the media as an extension of their medical practice.

8.3. A doctor has the responsibility to ensure that when a subject under discussion is controversial within the medical profession, the producer or editor of a programme is made aware of the fact.

8.4. It is unacceptable for a doctor publicly to discuss his own ability in a particular field in such a way as to imply that his methods are superior to those of other doctors.

In its section on confidentiality, the British Medical Association stated:

1.6. A doctor must preserve secrecy on all he knows. There are five exceptions to this principle:

1. The patient gives consent
2. When it is undesirable on medical grounds to seek a patient's consent
3. The doctor's overriding duty to society
4. For purposes of medical research
5. The information required by due legal process

1.7. A doctor must be able to justify his decision to disclose information.

The Canadian Medical Association in its code states[14]:

An Ethical Physician

11. Will recognize his responsibility to give generally held opinions of the profession when interpeting scientific knowledge to the public and in presenting any personal opinion which is contrary to the generally held opinion of the profession, he will indicate he is doing so, and will avoid any attempt to enhance his own reputation.

Apparently many countries have ethical codes dealing with confidentiality, usually in a proscriptive form derived from or similar to the Hippocratic Oath. Of necessity, these guidelines cannot anticipate all the issues that arise in a changing world, resulting in the numerous ambiguities and conflicts that have been discussed.

## CONCLUSIONS

The role that a psychiatrist should play in relation to the media remains uncertain. I have attempted to discuss some of the dilemmas confronting the psychiatrist in this regard.

The psychiatrist must consider two aspects of media relationships: (1) his or her relationship as a psychiatrist to media people, such as television, radio, or newspaper personnel or writers dealing with psychiatric issues, whether for articles or books, and (2) the relationship the psychiatrist has as a media person for the same media or as an independent author.

In both capacities, the psychiatrist cannot avoid the fact that he or she acts as a spokesperson for the profession, and, therefore, the profession has a legitimate interest in the conduct of the psychiatrist. In recent years, the profession, through its organized representatives, has been keenly aware of the public relations benefit to be derived from reasonable participation in the media. Other motives for participation by the individual psychiatrist may be for monetary gain or to satisfy a need for recognition. Narcissistic motivations are not necessarily bad and are quite legitimate, for what is important is not the motivation but the performance. Between narcissism and exploitation, the line is indeed murky.

All too frequently, broad public issues are involved, particularly the conflict between the patient's right to privacy and the public's need and right to know. Psychiatrists are often split on this dispute, which may be categorized as the battle between the strict constructionists and the loose constructionists. The strict constructionists adhere rigorously to a code of not providing information about individual patients or in not proffering information or thoughts about parties that they have not examined.

Compounding this overall conflict of principles is the dilemma that arises when the person is not a patient, or when the right to privacy as covered by privilege laws is no longer present in certain public matters. Forensic psychiatrists seeing a patient or person on his or her behalf have one relationship with the patient or the patient's representative, usually a lawyer. When such patient services as therapy are provided, one set of ethical principles is involved. When the services are strictly for a third party, such as an employer, opposing attorneys, or government agencies, another more ambiguous set of principles is involved.

Forensic psychiatrists have felt free to write about cases in which they did not participate in the patient's behalf, typically when they were employed (literally) by adverse parties. My own feeling is that that should be a legitimate activity. If the person is a patient, then permission for such an activity would seem to be required. Where a psychiatrist plays more than one role, the situation becomes unclear or ambiguous, and the profession would seem to endorse the right to privacy over other principles.

Certainly no psychiatrist can be criticized for being a strict constructionist. On the other hand, much is to be said for loose constructionism that requires a greater degree of discretion and judgment. Strict constructionism is a simple code; loose constructionism is more difficult. In notorious cases (especially cases of great public interest), the guidelines are not clear, and numerous issues arise, some of which have been presented here.

Psychiatrists must also consider their obligation to education, both professional and lay, and their possible obligation to the recording of accurate history. This latter issue is no better exemplified by the M'Naghtens and the Hinckleys, the Kennedys and the Roosevelts, the Hitlers, the Nixons, and the Wilsons. Did Lincoln have Marfan's syndrome? Did King George III have a bipolar disease that possibly could have influenced the initiation of the American Revolution? How many dictators were or are paranoids? If analysis of the role of the dead is important in understanding the present, how important is understanding the living, where history is in the making and can be affected by the acts of the living generation?

I do not pretend to have the answers and recognize that legitimate disagreements exist within the profession. It is hoped that continued discussion in the light of the changing times will result in a more agreeable consensus than is the case today.

# REFERENCES


1. Perr IN: Psychiatry, the law, and the media—the Son of Sam debacle. *Leg Aspects Med Pract* 1977; 5:23–25, November, psychiatric ed.
2. Noguchi TT: Conflicts and challenges for the medical examiner. *J Forensic Sci* 1987; 32:829–835.
3. Perr IN: The Hinckley case, the media, and the insanity defense. *J Forensic Sci* 1983; 28:815–822.
4. Perr IN: The insanity defense: A tale of two cities. *Am J Psychiatry* 1983; 140:873–874.
5. Moran R: *Knowing Right from Wrong: The Insanity Defense of Daniel McNaughtan.* New York, The Free Press, 1981, p 20.
6. Ormond R: The McNaughton case and its predecessors, in West DJ, Walk A: *His Trial and Aftermath.* Ashford, Kent, England, Gaskell Books, 1977, p 8.
7. *See* Ormond, note 6 above, p 9; and Moran, note 5 above, p 19.
8. Glueck S: *Law and Psychiatry: Cold War or Entente Cordiale?* Baltimore, Johns Hopkins University Press, 1962.
9. Perr IN: Hinckley verdict proves the system works. *New York Times,* July 1, 1982.
10. Robitscher JD: Public life and private information. *JAMA* 1967; 202:96–98.
11. Perr IN: Privilege, confidentiality, and patient privacy: Status 1980. *J Forensic Sci* 1981; 26:109–115.
12. American Psychiatric Association: *The Principles of Medical Ethics.*
13. British Medical Association: *The Handbook of Medical Ethics.* London, 1980, pp 45–46.
14. *See* British Medical Association, note 13 above, p 73.

# Index